MORE PRAISE FOR *AN ORAL HISTORY OF THE PALESTINIAN NAKBA*

'Moving and acutely observed, this timely and necessary anthology is an indispensable addition for all readers concerned with the Israeli colonisation of Palestine.'

Ronit Lentin, author of *Thinking Palestine*

'Reveals the full magnificence of Palestinian responses to Israel's systematic post-1948 programme of memoricide. Abdo and Masalha are here establishing a new interdisciplinary field, Nakba Studies, in which Palestinians become subjects and agents in their own history.'

John Docker, University of Western Australia

'A landmark intervention, this cross-disciplinary book provides innovative analytical frameworks for studying the persistent erasure of Palestine. This insightful and comprehensive work proposes alternative ways of knowing and telling, rearticulating the Nakba as an ongoing process of dispossession.'

Ella Shohat, NYU, and author of *On the Arab-Jew, Palestine, and Other Displacements*

An Oral History of the Palestinian Nakba

Edited by Nahla Abdo
and Nur Masalha

ZED

An Oral History of the Palestinian Nakba was first published in 2018
by Zed Books Ltd, The Foundry, 17 Oval Way, London SE11 5RR, UK.

www.zedbooks.net

Typeset in Adobe Garammond Pro by seagulls.net
Cover design by Andrew Brash

A catalogue record for this book is available from the British Library

ISBN 978-1-78699-349-6 hb
ISBN 978-1-78699-350-2 pb
ISBN 978-1-78699-351-9 pdf
ISBN 978-1-78699-352-6 epub
ISBN 978-1-78699-353-3 mobi

Contents

Acknowledgments

At the outset, the editors would like to extend a special thanks to Dr Rosemary Sayigh for her central role in initiating this project. Thank you Rosemary for your inspiring scholarship and your unwavering commitment to keeping Palestinian memory alive. Our greatest thanks go to ordinary Palestinian women and men, victims of the Nakba/genocide whose voices, oral histories, narratives and memories and indomitable spirit made this work possible and without whom this project would not have seen the light. Our thanks also go the anonymous reviewers of this collection and to the editors at Zed Books for their generosity, patience and practical advice. Finally, and most importantly, our thanks go to all the authors/contributors whose extraordinary insights and passions enabled this collective project to come to fruition.

Introduction

NAHLA ABDO AND NUR MASALHA

Oral history challenges the artificiality of the academic separation of the disciplines or, in Sherna Gluck's words, "the academic division of knowledge" (Gluck 1991: 3).

This collective work uses oral history, personal memories, narratives and interviews to study, analyse and represent the Palestinian Nakba/genocide, before, during and after the establishment of the Israeli settler-colonial state in 1948. The multiplicity of disciplines and approaches presented in this book cover the complexity, and poignancy, of the Palestinian Nakba, reproducing in the process its historical and lived implications in a new light. Almost all authors in this volume attest to the resilience of the Nakba as experience and memory and its rootedness in the existential life of Palestinians. This rootedness defies all Israeli and international efforts at silencing the Nakba for the past seventy years. All authors in this book see the Nakba as a process and not as an event. Still, the memories and narratives of the specific calamities and horror inflicted on the Palestinians during the months of the establishment of the state of Israel have carved and continue to carve a deep space in the memory of those who lived it and the generations that followed.

Part I theorizes the Nakba and oral history from two different, yet complementary perspectives. Nur Masalha provides a conceptual, analytical and critical framework for Palestinian oral history and memories of the Nakba. His chapter explores the role of individual, social and collective memories in shaping individual and national identity in Palestine. Applying social memory theory and cross-disciplinary and decolonizing methodologies to the knowledge–power nexus in Palestine, the chapter challenges settler-colonial histories and critiques the manipulation of collective memory by hegemonic elites and top-down nationalist approaches.

1

Nahla Abdo theorizes the Nakba as genocide. She critiques existing feminist approaches to the marginalized, and specifically the colonized, insisting on the need to apply historically and culturally specific concepts to our methodologies. She contributes to the development of anti-colonial feminist analysis suitable for understanding indigenousness and the settler-colonial state. Land and genocide, this chapter contends, need to be placed at the centre of feminist analysis of the marginalized, colonized indigenous analysis.

Part II analyses the close relationship between what women knew and experienced during the Nakba, and focuses on the intimate relation and direct impact this knowledge has on indigenous bodies.

Diana Allan's chapter explores the interweavings of affect and intellect in interviews recorded with Palestinian elders in Lebanon for the Nakba Archive. She examines the role that sensory and embodied experience play in recollection and in the narration of oral histories, and the forms of knowledge carried in embodied gestures, tone and the senses. Rather than viewing the sensuous simply as narrative embellishment, Allan considers what might be gained from re-centring the body as the locus of historical study, allowing for more diverse and non-coercive forms of remembering and knowledge creation.

Lena Jayyusi addresses the themes and idioms of Palestinian memory narratives of the Nakba, exploring the sites and features of affect, connectedness and resistance, both then and now. In this chapter special attention is placed on how the Palestinian population was struggling to hold on, if not to place, then at least to communal space, to vicinity as a lived affective and phenomenal field.

Part III archives the Nakba through Palestinian refugee women's voices. These voices cover various areas, including Shu'fat refugee camp in the West Bank, refugees in Jordan and refugees in Lebanon. Rosemary Sayigh establishes the centrality of oral transmission of family and community histories that enabled and continues to enable the Palestinian people to assert their existence in the face of Zionist settler-colonial and international silencing.

Laura Khoury analyses the process of self-reflexive awareness that women undergo when they narrate the Nakba, contributing to the movement of writing history from below. Based on collective memories of elderly Palestinian women refugees in Shu'fat refugee camp, Khoury offers an indigenous feminist reading of the memorization of the Nakba by Palestinian women as they transmit some of the past, both consciously and subconsciously, to the present, creating continuity and transcending the present. Under scrutiny here, Khoury asserts, is what was not disrupted: something "old" that transformed into something "new"; new in its effect or its use, new in terms of formulating new activism and situating it in the present.

Faiha Abdel-Hadi's chapter presents Palestinian women's narrations of their displacement during 1948. The chapter focuses on the challenges these women faced and the agency and resistance they presented against such challenges. Women's testimonies uncover the vital role they played in the political, social and economic life in Palestine and the diaspora.

Part IV documents Nakba stories and memories, based on specific cases of cities and villages in 1948 Palestine. Chapters in this part use a multiplicity of methods, including oral history, interviews, personal memories and Zionist archives.

Himmat Zubi adds to this collection the perspective of Haifa (urban) Palestinian memories of the Nakba. She utilizes oral history testimonies to bring to life Haifa women's daily experiences as they re-live the Nakba. Zubi establishes the importance of Palestinian city life and the role that urban Palestinians played before and during the Nakba, and examines the ongoing consequences of the Nakba for Haifa residents.

Amina Qablawi Nasrallah uses personal memory to draw on the experience of her grandmother and narrates the tale of her family and community during and after the Nakba. Particularly poignant in Qablawi's chapter is the murder of her father by Zionist settlers in her own village, Saffouryeh. Hisham Zreik uses oral history of fellow men and women and records their experiences during and after the Nakba. The author used this oral history research in his documentary film "The Sons of Eilaboun" (2007).

Safa Abu-Rabi'a presents voices of Naqab Bedouin women from the 1948 generation and their daughters, and highlights their collective resistance to ongoing displacement, reflecting on how women re-tell Naqab history and reclaim their terrain. Through oral and spatial practices, these stories establish a territorial identity and sense of belonging to the place among their children, and educate them to be owners of the land across the seventy-year gap.

Part V documents Nakba narratives from the Gaza Strip and the *shatat* (refugeeism/exile).

Using personal memory and some interviews, Mona Al-Farra reflects on the Nakba, providing a vivid picture of the events. She uses her own experience during the devastating 2014 Israeli war on Gaza as a backdrop for highlighting the continuous Nakba in Gaza. The author reflects on her late mother's experiences and memory of the Nakba and Palestinian women's resistance.

Malaka Mohammad surveys some of the oral history projects in Gaza, centring on the work of the Oral History Centre in Gaza and on the youth projects of the Tamer Institute for Community Education.

Chandni Desai's chapter outlines how the Israeli/Zionist settler-colonial project engaged in the systematic erasure of the material culture of Palestine, with a specific focus on toponymicide. She argues that Palestinian cultural producers (past and present) disrupt and reconfigure Zionist toponomy and national settler-colonial mythologies of land and belonging, by producing counter-hegemonic and anti-colonial narratives of the *al-Nakba* and its afterlife through "resistance culture" (*thaqafat al-muqawama*).

PART I
Theorizing the Nakba and oral history

1
Decolonizing methodology, reclaiming memory: Palestinian oral histories and memories of the Nakba

NUR MASALHA

> No need to hear your voice when I can talk about you better than you
> can speak about yourself ... Only tell me about your pain. I want to
> know your story. And then I will tell it back to you in a new way ...
> Re-writing you I write myself anew. I am still author, authority. I am still
> colonizer the speaking subject and you are now at the center of my talk.
> (Hooks 1990: 241–243)

2017 is a year of "fateful anniversaries" for the Palestinians: (a) it is the cente-
nary of the Balfour Declaration, when an imperialist power, Britain, denied the
indigenous people of Palestine the right to self-determination and nurtured a
European settler-colonialist movement; (b) it is seventy years since the Nakba,
which began in late 1947, when the majority of Palestinians were driven out
from their homeland; (c) it is fifty years since the military occupation of the
remainder of Palestine in 1967. Of the three events, the Nakba was the worst
catastrophe that ever befell the Palestinians. The ethnic cleansing of Palestine
(Masalha 1992, 1997, 2012; Pappe 2006) and the traumatic rupture of 1948 are
central to both the Palestinian society of today and Palestinian history and
collective identity.

Erasing Palestine and appropriating its material and cultural heritage has
been fundamental to Zionist colonial practices before, during and since the

Nakba. In 1948 the Israeli state appropriated for itself immovable Palestinian material assets and personal possessions including schools, rich private libraries, books, pictures, private papers, historical documents and manuscripts, furniture, churches, mosques, shrines, historic public buildings, archaeological sites and artefacts, urban residential quarters, transport infrastructure, seaports and airports, police stations, prisons and railways (Khalidi 1992; Masalha 2012). The appropriation of Palestinian records, documentation and cultural heritage by the Israeli state has made it possible for Israeli historians ("old and new") to claim that there is no Arab *documentation* on 1948 of the sort historians must rely on (Morris 1994: 42–43).

Conventionally history has been written by the powerful, the conqueror, the colonizer; the discipline of history has long been a tool of dominant elites used to reinforce hegemonic narratives and existing power relations. Clearly there is a need for articulating new counter-hegemonic narratives and devising new liberationist and decolonization strategies in Palestine. The disciplines of history and memory should be a site of hope, liberation and decolonization. To write more truthfully about the Palestinian Nakba is not merely to practise professional historiography, it is also a profoundly moral act of liberation and a struggle for truth, justice, equality, return (both mental and physical return) and a better future.

In recent decades two distinct historiographical approaches concerning the birth of the Palestinian refugee problem have evolved. Recent debates on 1948 tell us something about the historian's method, power and the meaning of the "historical document" (Pappe 2004). Methodologically, many historians have displayed a bias towards archival sources; Israeli revisionist historians, in particular, believe they are both ideologically and empirically impartial (Masalha 2007: 286), and that the only reliable sources for the reconstruction of the 1948 war are in the Israel Defence Forces (IDF) archives and official documents. This bias towards high politics and "archives" has contributed to silencing the Palestinian past. The silencing of the Nakba by mainstream historians in Israel and the West follows the pattern given by Michel-Rolph Trouillot in *Silencing the Past: Power and the Production of History*:

Silences enter the process of historical production at four crucial moments: the moment of fact creation (the making of sources); the moment of fact assembly (the making of archives); the moment of fact retrieval (the making of narratives); and the moment of retrospective significance (the making of history ...). (Trouillot 1995: 26)

Not surprisingly, Israeli historians (old and new) have long emphasized and indeed privileged Israeli state papers and official documents and downgraded the voices of the indigenous people of Palestine. By contrast, in recent decades Palestinian oral histories have attempted to redress the imbalance of the modern historiography, by developing methodologies for understanding the contexts, objectives, power and meanings of documents. Oral histories are not just about facts and evidence but also ways of exploring subtle narratives and voices of the people who are silenced in state papers and official documents. Indeed, oral histories revolutionized our "historical knowledge" methodologies by appreciating the "shadows" and by bringing to light hidden, suppressed or marginalized narratives. Oral histories have, in fact, brought together academics, historians, filmmakers, artists, archivists and librarians, novelists, indigenous activists, museum professionals and community-based arts practitioners. As producers of knowledge and meaning, oral histories have become a major catalyst for new creative practices and interpretations in history-related fields and on the construction of alternative histories and the recovery of memories of lost practices.

Furthermore, the ideological context and limits of the Israeli state and archival documents are very clear. Israeli archives can tell us very little about the narratives of the Palestinian victims of the Nakba or the experience of millions of Palestinian refugees. Also, those of us who have used Israeli archival sources know that there are many files of the Israeli army from 1948 which are still closed and not accessible to the historian or the public. But what are the overall historiographical implications of the debate on 1948? The first point concerns the military historiography of 1948, which tends to dominate Israeli and Western historiographies. The clashes taking place in Palestine during the late Mandatory period have been treated as part of an overall war between the Arab and Israeli armies. Such a paradigm calls for the expertise of military historians (Pappe 2004: 185–186). Military historians tend to concentrate on the balance of power and military strategy and tactics. They see actions and people as part of the theatre of war, where events and actions are judged on a moral basis very different from that applicable in a non-combatant situation.

Therefore, conventional writing on the historiography of 1948 is inherently biased and tends to favour military history and the victorious Israeli army. Ilan

Pappe and Nur Masalha have long argued that the events of 1948 should be examined within the paradigm of "transfer", ethnic cleansing and erasure rather than as part of elite military history, written by the victorious conqueror. Unlike the 1937 Peel partition proposal, the UN partition plan of November 1947 did envisage some form of bi-nationalism for Palestine-Israel; the UN certainly did not envisage an exclusive (ethnically cleansed) Jewish state in 1948. This means that the expulsion of Palestinians in 1948 by the Israeli army was part of the *domestic* policies implemented by an Israeli regime vis-à-vis the indigenous citizens of Palestine. The decisive factors in 1948 were ethnic ideology, colonial-settlement policy and demographic strategy, rather than military plans or considerations (Pappe 2004: 186; Masalha 1992, 1997). In *Expulsion of the Palestinians* (1992), I show that the concept of "transfer" was from the start an integral part of Zionism and that much of the "ethnic cleansing" of the Nakba was not related to the battles taking place between regular armies waging war.

This chapter explores ways of experiencing and remembering the Nakba, with emphasis on oral accounts and within the context of the powerful oral cultures of Palestine. It concentrates on Palestinian oral histories and narratives of memory. With the history, rights and needs of the Palestinian refugees being excluded from recent Middle East peace-making efforts and with the failure of both the Israeli state and the international community to acknowledge the Nakba, "1948" as an "ethnic cleansing" continues to underpin the Palestine–Israel conflict. The chapter argues that to write more truthfully about the Nakba is not just to practise a professional historiography; it is also a moral imperative of acknowledgement and redemption. The refugees' struggle to publicize the truth about the Nakba is a vital way of protecting their rights and keeping the hope for peace with justice alive. Other key themes emphasized here are: (a) oral history projects are a major means of reconstructing the history of the Palestinian refugees and internally displaced Palestinians as seen from the perspective of the primary subjects; (b) as is the case with other marginalized groups, Palestinian oral testimony projects are a vital tool for recovering and preserving the voices of the Palestinian peasants (*fallaheen*) who for centuries (and until 1948) constituted the overwhelming majority of the inhabitants of Palestine.

Today, accounts from indigenous memory of the traumatic events of 1948 are central to Palestinian society and its collective struggle. By Palestinian society I mean *all* its three main constituencies: Palestinians inside Israel, Palestinians in the occupied territories and the refugee communities. The Nakba remains a key site of Palestinian collective consciousness and the single most important event that connects *all* Palestinians to a specific point in time. The collective memory of the Nakba unites *all* three Palestinians constituencies deeply and emotionally – three constituencies separated by geography and expedient politics; by fragmentation and the colonial boundaries imposed by the Israeli state; by differences derived from different legal and political conditions in Palestine-Israel and host countries.

With no independent state or state papers, and with the difficulties of establishing or maintaining "public archives" in exile or in Palestine under Israeli occupation, Palestinian and Arab intellectuals continued to produce Nakba memoirs and "archive" the catastrophe in books and articles. As early as 1949 Constantine Zurayk published *The Meaning of the Nakba* (1956), which was translated into English. This was followed by Palestinian historian and native of Jerusalem 'Arif Al-'Arif, who published six volumes in Arabic in the period 1958–1960, entitled *Al-Nakba: The Catastrophe of Jerusalem and the Lost Paradise*. Also in the late 1950s and early 1960s Palestinian historian Walid Khalidi published three pioneering articles on the circumstances surrounding the Nakba (Khalidi 1959a, 1959b, 1961). However, with the exception of these three articles, based on written documentation, and an important article by Irish journalist Erskine Childers (1961) in *The Spectator* (London), entitled "The Other Exodus", in fact little was published in English about the Nakba during the first two decades following 1948. In 1972 Palestinian author Mustafa Dabbagh began publishing in Arabic his eleven-volume work, entitled *Our Country: Palestine*, describing all the villages of Palestine during the British Mandate (Dabbagh 1972–1986). However, with the exception of a few sympathetic books in English on the Palestinian question – books whose emphasis was on the loss of land and property in 1948 and on legal and political issues – these recorded some Palestinian elite voices but never brought out ordinary people's voices. This almost total silencing of Palestinian people's voices and the Palestinian Nakba, which was associated with defeat and shame, went largely unchallenged until the 1970s.

In December 1963 Walid Khalidi went on to co-found (and since then has served as Secretary General) of the Institute for Palestine Studies (IPS), established in Beirut as an independent research and publishing centre focusing on the Palestinian problem and the Arab–Palestine conflict. Under his guidance the IPS produced a long list of publications in both Arabic and English and several important translations of Hebrew documents, texts and books into Arabic. In 1984, the IPS published *Before Their Diaspora: A Photographic History of the Palestinians, 1876–1948*, by Walid Khalidi. However, Khalidi will always be best known for his encyclopaedic work on the Palestinian villages occupied and depopulated by Israel in 1948, *All That Remains* (1992). This work of monumental collective memory includes several hundred photographs and has clearly benefited from the contribution of Palestinian oral historians.

However, in view of the fact that Israel continues to loot and destroy Palestinian archives, and in the absence of a rich source of contemporary Palestinian documentary records, oral accounts and interviews with Palestinian (internal and external) refugees are a valuable and indeed essential source for constructing a more comprehensible narrative of the experience of ordinary Palestinian refugees and internally displaced Palestinians across the Green Line.

TYPOLOGY OF PALESTINIAN ORAL HISTORIES AND MEMORIES OF THE NAKBA

Conventionally memory has been understood in terms of *individual* versus *collective* memory. Individual memories are often studied by psychologists, neurologists and oral historians, while collective memory is studied by sociologists and cultural theorists. However, this binary (individual versus collective) fails to account for a whole range of *particular* memories. By adopting a pluralistic approach to memories and by combining this approach with a knowledge–power analysis (Foucault 1972, 1980) and with a "history from-below" approach (Guha 1997; Guha and Spivak 1988; Prakash 1994), it should be possible to distinguish between top-down elite "collective memory" and people's "shared memories". Oral history "from below" and shared memories are central to historical writing, shared values and the construction of (group) multi-layered, multi-cultural identity.

All histories are forms of representation of the "past" and "present". Representations of the Nakba can be categorized as follows: speaking of the actual experiences of the Nakba; speaking about the Nakba; and speaking for and on behalf of the victims of the Nakba. These multiple representations of the Nakba should be kept in mind. Furthermore, broadly speaking, four distinct types of Palestinian oral histories and memories of the Nakba have emerged since 1948. These forms of representation have also contributed to the emergence of the new sub-discipline of Nakba Studies. These forms of representations are:

a) *Personal experiences and individual memory accounts of 1948*: These oral accounts of 1948 centre on the "Nakba Generation" and those refugees who experienced the 1948 Nakba first-hand through actual expulsion, dislocation, loss, personal trauma and/or exile.

b) *Collective memory of the Nakba*: This nationally constructed macro memory of 1948 is often elite framed and ideologically constructed as a top-down, collective memory.

c) *Shared memories of the Nakba*: These group memories of 1948 are often framed "from below" and focus on ordinary Palestinians or marginalized groups of refugees.

d) *Trauma and cultural memories of the Nakba*. The traumatic experiences of the Nakba have had a profound impact on the lives of Palestinians over seven decades and across three generations. Cultural memories of the Nakba are often produced by the second and third generation. They include poetry, popular songs, folklore, refugee camp embroidery, *dabke* (Palestinian folk dance), fiction, films, landscape paintings, traditional storytelling practices and the literature of exile. These diverse and rich forms of oral testimony and archiving memory began in the late 1950s, with examples found in Ghassan Kanafani's novels (Kanafani 1998, 2000; Kanafani et al. 2004), Mahmoud Darwish's poetry (2000, 2003) and Ismail Shamout's paintings. These forms of oral memory paved the way for the emergence of Palestinian academic works on oral histories of the Nakba in the 1970s and 1980s.

RETHINKING PALESTINIAN COLLECTIVE AND SOCIAL MEMORIES

The seminal and highly influential work of Maurice Halbwachs (1980) on the formation of "collective memory" focused on the construction of socially and politically framed memory and collective identity. Collective memory has also increasingly become a major interdisciplinary area of investigation in several academic fields. Today the production of collective memory is widely recognized as critical in shaping the way in which people not only learn about and view the past but also construct and enrich their collective identity and human experiences in the present.

However, Halbwachs himself – a student of Emile Durkheim, who had reformulated sociological positivism as a foundation of social research – like other positivist scholars of his age, conflated "history" with "the past" and sharply contrasted "history"' with "collective memory". The poverty of modern positivism derives from its simplistic, reductionist, objectifying thinking. Reality is always complex, multi-layered and multi-dimensional and the human (individual and collective) agency is central to disentangling this complexity. Scientifically driven positivist historians tend to eliminate the human agency and objectify and totalize "historical knowledge". Furthermore, positivist historians tend to confuse "history" with the "past" and conceptualize history as an accurate "knowledge of the past", and memory as "knowledge from the past". This modern positivism has been widely criticized by a range of modern humanist theorists for failing to account for human agency and the living and inner nature of the historical experience. Following this humanist tradition, this chapter argues that the human agency is central to the production of historical knowledge.

In his seminal work on conscious temporality and "sense of being", *Time and Being (Sein und Zeit)*, Martin Heidegger ([1927] 2010) argued that the abstract concept of "time" is meaningless. Heidegger emphasized the "sense" and "experience"' of "being" over other interpretations of conscious existence and argued that specific and concrete ideas form the foundation of our perceptions; working from abstractions or pure theories leads to confusion and obfuscation. Heidegger also advanced the thesis that ontologically the notion of the "past" is only one dimension of a whole phenomenon which we call "time", and this encompasses the past, present and future. In effect, the Heideggerian methodology encompassed (and linked) the past, present and future and argued that time is only meaningful as it is experienced by human beings. Working from the *specific* and *concrete* human experiences of time, Heidegger advanced the idea that time (Greek: Khronos) cannot just be understood quantitatively or chronologically. Meaningful time (Greek: Khairos) has to be experienced concretely and qualitatively. If the "sense of time" is experienced qualitatively and in particular situations by human beings, then understanding and archiving the particular 'memories' and concrete human experiences of the past become central to narrating and historicizing. In the particular case of the Palestinian refugees, a true understanding of their trauma and concrete experiences of displacement and exile can only begin by allowing them to speak for themselves, by recovering their own voices and recording their own stories.

Moreover, rather than applying abstract strategies or a one-dimensional methodology to explaining the history and shared memories of the Nakba, I suggest a multiple approach with special reference to (a) speaking of the experiences of the Nakba and history from within; (b) history from below and recovering the voices of the subaltern, marginalized and refugees; and (c) speaking in solidarity with the victim of the Nakba. This multifaceted approach offers liberating strategies and decolonizing methodologies for the practice of narrating and frees history from the straitjacket of objectivity and abstraction. Furthermore, history from below would also mean that the primary object of historicizing and historical knowledge are to give us insight into the historical phenomena and human experiences of people in the past and in the present, including their thoughts, feelings and desires. Knowledge production and empowerment have always been intertwined (Foucault 1972, 1980) and the production of historical knowledge on Palestine and the Palestinians has always been driven by underlying causes and a mix of material, political and epistemological considerations. Moreover, historians live in the present and their knowledge production affects the future. However, although the primary object of history is narrating and explaining the past, historians are also influenced by social and political considerations in the present. I argue here that being/becoming historical narratives and knowledge production on Palestine and the Palestinians can only work within a pluralistic ontological framework by including human experiences, memories and remembering. Historians work like any other human agents. They produce historical knowledge and meanings about the past in the present and this historical knowledge helps shape the future.

It is the recovery of the experiences of the Nakba and production of indigenous knowledge on Palestine which link the history and memories of the Nakba to the wider discipline of oral/aural history. Consequently, rather than treating Halbwachs' socially framed memory within a positivist framework, this chapter argues for a multifaceted approach to representation of "memory" (including individual memories, collective memory, group memories and fictionalized resistance memory) and for treating Halbwachs' socially framed "collective memory" as only one way of seeing memory. Consequently other types of memories such as oral narratives should be conceptualized ontologically differently and epistemologically contextually. By contextualizing, I mean that historians cannot just proceed from pure theories of history, memory or oral narratives, but need to particularize their methodology and show how in practice a particular methodology can be relevant and effective within a particular context.

PALESTINIAN COLLECTIVE VERSUS SHARED MEMORIES OF THE NAKBA

The politics of collective memory can imprison minds and enslave people; but history can also be liberating and empowering. The cynical manipulation of collective memory by powerful and hegemonic elites is often top-down, silencing and exploitative. But collective memory can also be liberating and empowering for oppressed, indigenous and marginalized groups.

In the Zionist and Israeli settler-colonial collective memory and mega-narrative, Palestine was a semi-deserted "land without a people for a people without a land"; a *terra virgina* (virgin territory) of hard soil or swamps only made fertile, productive and "blooming" by the genius and hard labour of the European Zionist settlers. European hegemonic movements and settler-colonial ideologies such as political Zionism have always tried to impose their own mega-narrative and memories on the colonized and indigenous. In response in occupied and colonized Palestine – as throughout much of the Third World – shared cultural and indigenous memory projects have played an important role in decolonization, cultural resistance, counter-hegemonic discourses, decolonization processes, liberation and nation-building processes and as a vehicle for victims of colonialism and historical injustice and violence to articulate their experience of suffering.

Narratives of learning and shared memory have also been part of grassroots democratic initiatives to empower people and bring to life marginalized and counter-narratives that have been suppressed, either by hegemonic discourses or the unwillingness on the part of repressive regimes to acknowledge the past.

The approach adopted here recognizes that social and cultural shared memory has always been more than simply recollecting or recording of 'the past': recollection and "re-membering" serve to create, sustain and nurture collective identity. Individual and group memory should not be treated as dichotomous or constituting oppositional binaries. For both individuals and groups (which can be any group related to tribe, band, ethnicity, gender, class) to "remember" is to learn and form social norms and habits, while incorporating significant memories and experiences of the past in a meaningful way. No experience has shaped Palestinian attitudes and lives since 1948 more than the traumatic events of the 1948 Nakba and the devastating loss of hearth, home and land.

In the case of the indigenous inhabitants of Palestine, the Nakba – the exodus of the Palestinians and the dismemberment of historic Palestine – has been a key site of collective memory and history that connects *all* Palestinians to the most traumatic event in Palestinian history. In addition to the terrible suffering inflicted upon the Palestinian people in the process of the establishment of the State of Israel, few of the hundreds of once-thriving communities remained. Not only they have been erased from the Palestinian landscape, but their very names have been removed from contemporary Israeli maps.

Although Palestinian national identity took root long before the 1948 Nakba, indigenous Palestinian memory accounts of the post-Nakba period – responding to the new reality of Palestinian dispersal and the fragmentation of Palestinian society – played a major positive role in the recovery and reconstruction of Palestinian national identity and the emergence of the Palestine Liberation Organization (PLO) in the 1960s; in recent decades, in particular, there has been an intense and complex relationship between the 1948 Nakba and the preservation, articulation and sustaining of Palestinian national and cultural identity.

Today, with millions of Palestinians still living under Israeli occupation or in exile, the Nakba remains at the heart of indigenous collective memory, national identity and the struggle for self-determination. Also to the millions of dispersed Palestinians living in exile and the *shatat*, the pre-1948 villages and towns were home, and continue to be poignantly powerful symbols of their personal, national collective identity.

One of the key themes for consideration here is Palestinian cultural memory and the recovery and reconstruction of Palestinian cultural identity in the post-Nakba period; there was always an intense relationship between the 1948 Nakba and the formation of Palestinian national identity, especially from the late 1950s onwards.

While the multi-layered Palestinian national identity existed long before the 1948 Nakba, the collective consciousness of the Nakba played a major role in the reconstruction of Palestinian national and cultural identities and the re-emergence of popular Palestinian nationalism in the 1960s. More crucially, it was the (historically marginalized) Palestinian refugees themselves who played a central role in preserving Palestinian national identity and in setting up the PLO and the guerrilla movements in the 1960s.

In the absence of a Palestinian state, which would have been expected to devote material and cultural resources to collective memory projects, archives and museums, Palestinian refugee communities in Palestine and elsewhere in the Middle East have actively promoted collective memorialization projects as a form of cultural resistance. Since 1948 Palestinian refugees from individual villages marked "their" Nakba, or the anniversary of the date of the fall of their village.

In the post-1948 period Palestinians maintained the multiple meaning of their Arabic names and the multi-layered Palestinian identity deeply rooted in the land and embedded in ancient sites and place names (toponyms).

At the same time, however, in the post-1948 period new naming traditions and new resistance strategies emerged among the different communities of Palestinians reflecting the various fates suffered by the indigenous population of Palestine. The depopulated and destroyed villages and towns were often kept alive by passing place names down through generations of Palestinian family members. Even inside Israel, those internally displaced refugees regrouped in different localities to create new definitions of kinship structures. Post-Nakba conditions of displacement and dispersal gave rise to circumstances in which a person from the destroyed village of Ruways, for instance, would be given the surname Ruwaysi – someone from Ruways – instead of the customary clan eponym. Village solidarity stood in place of the absent village and dispersed clan members. The name of the original village also replaced the name of the *hamula* (clan), and the relationship among persons who belonged to the same original village became similar to *hamula* solidarity. The *hamula* did not disappear or weaken, but some of its basic functions were transferred to the wider kinship structure and social solidarity based on the original (destroyed) village. For those Palestinians forced into exile outside Palestine, one convention was to name children for the lost but not forgotten site.

FROM MEMORY TO ORAL HISTORY: ORAL ACCOUNTS, PEOPLE'S VOICES AND LIVING PRACTICES

The developments in recent decades in the academic discipline of oral/aural history and individual memories has revolutionized historical writing and the recovering of the past by bringing to light hidden, suppressed or marginalized narratives and voices – marginalized in official documents of state archives. Oral history captures a variety of individual testimonies, people's lives and living practices. Oral/aural narrative projects have, in fact, brought together academics, archivists and librarians, oral historians, museum professionals, community-based arts practitioners and community-oriented activists. As producers of meaning, oral history projects have become a major catalyst for creative practices and interpretations in history-related fields and for the construction of alternative histories and memories of lost practices. Oral/aural narrative projects, like written documentation and archival material, are never free from factual error and have to be treated critically.

State-supervised archival collections and official documents can be restricted and access to them can be limited to powerful elites or favoured social groups and thus the control of access can reinforce hegemonic ideological discourses. The same state-controlled archives and official collections are often based on (individual and collective) memory; and they can distort, misinform, omit, restrict or even fabricate evidence.

Individual memories are also generally selective and fallible; egos distort and contradictions sometimes go unresolved. However, problems of critical evaluation are not markedly different from those inherent in the use of archival documents, letters, diaries and other primary sources. The scholar must test the evidence in an oral history memoir for internal consistency and, whenever possible, by corroboration from other sources, often including the oral history memoirs of others on the same topic (Starr 1984).

From the 1970s onwards, local historical research and oral history studies began to be considered in a highly positive light by the academy (Allen and Montell 1981), partly following work by scholars such as Luisa Passerini who studied the social history of the Turin working class under Italian fascism (Humphries 2009: 78; Passerini 1998). Since then, and especially in the last four decades, there has been a proliferation of oral history archiving memory projects throughout the world, which promote the collection, preservation and use of recorded memories of the past and people's voices.

In the UK, the BBC has developed an archive of World War II memories, based on oral histories and written by the public and ordinary people, and BBC Memoryshare, which is described as "a living archive of memory from 1900 to the present day ... the majority of content on Memoryshare is created by Memoryshare contributors, who are members of the public".[1] Ordinary people can contribute memories, research events and link to context material relating to any date back to 1 January 1900. As for the WW2 People's War archive, the BBC asked the public to contribute their memories of World War II to a website between June 2003 and January 2006. This "people's memory archive" has collected 47,000 stories and 15,000 images – stories not just about air raids, military operations and the armed forces, but also about the concentration camps in Europe created by the Nazis, the roles of women, peaceful resistance and occupation, civilian internment and critical conscientious objectors.

ORAL HISTORIES AND MEMORIES OF THE NAKBA AND HOLOCAUST: DEIR YASSIN AND YAD VA-SHEM

Israeli oral history as a producer of meaning and testimony in the museum and gallery has been of great importance in the recollection and collective memorization and memorialization of the Holocaust. The Israeli state memorial at Yad va-Shem, the Holocaust Martyrs' and Heroes' Remembrance institution, is predominantly based on oral history and millions of pages of testimony. Yad va-Shem itself is situated on the lands of Deir Yassin, as is the city of Jerusalem western (Jewish) cemetery (Davis 2003: 25). The irony of Yad va-Shem and Deir Yassin is breathtaking; any Israelis and foreign visitors to Yad va-Shem go to DeirYassin, and during dedication ceremonies at Yad va-Shem no one ever looks to the north and remembers Deir Yassin (McGowan 1998: 6–7).

Founded and managed by the Israeli state, Yad va-Shem is completely silent about the atrocities of Deir Yassin, and contains a contain amount of anti-Palestinian propaganda. In essence, Yad va-Shem represents official Israeli "collective memory" for forgetfulness. Together with genuine oral history of the Holocaust, Yad va-Shem was established in 1953, five years after Deir Yassin, by a Knesset act and located in West Jerusalem. According to its website, Yad va-Shem is a vast, sprawling complex of tree-studded walkways leading to museums, exhibits, archives, monuments, sculptures and memorials. It has been entrusted with documenting the history of the Jewish people during the Holocaust period, preserving the memory and story of each of the 6 million victims, and imparting the legacy of the Holocaust to generations to come through its archives, library, school, museums and recognition of the "Righteous Among the Nations". The archive collection of Yad va-Shem comprises 62 million pages of documents, nearly 267,500 photographs along with thousands of films and videotaped testimonies of survivors. The Hall of Names is a "tribute to the victims by remembering them not as anonymous numbers but as individual human beings". The "Pages of Testimony" are symbolic gravestones, which record names and biographical data of millions of martyrs, as submitted by family members and friends. To date Yad va-Shem has computerized 3.2 million names of Holocaust victims, compiled from approximately 2 million pages of testimony and various other lists. The collections of Yad va-Shem include tens of thousands of digitalized testimonies.

However, in contrast to the Israeli national memorial at Yad va-Shem and other Holocaust museums (including the Berlin Holocaust Museum and the US Holocaust Memorial Museum), there is no Nakba museum, no Nakba Hall of Names, no Central Database of Nakba Victims' Names, no tombstones or monuments for the hundreds of Palestinian villages ethnically cleansed and destroyed in 1948. The hundreds of Palestinian villages and towns destroyed in 1948 are still forced out of Israeli public awareness, away from the signposts of memory. What is also chilling is the fact that the Deir Yassin massacre of 9 April 1948 took place within sight of the place which became the Holocaust museum in Jerusalem; only a mile from where Jewish martyrs are memorialized lie the Palestinian martyrs of Deir Yassin whose graves are unknown and unmarked (McGowan 1998: 6–7).

For Palestinians inside and outside Israel Deir Yassin has remained a potent symbol of collective memory and cultural resistance. But in Israel the ghosts of Deir Yassin, Lubieh, Kafr Bir'im and the hundreds of villages destroyed in 1948 are rendered completely invisible:

> The villages that no longer exist were forced out of [Israeli] public awareness, away from the signposts of memory. They received new names – of Jewish settlements – but traces [of their past] were left behind, like the *sabr* [cactus] bushes or the stones from fences or bricks from the demolished houses. (McGowan 1998: 6–7)

There are some important recent developments with major implications for the study of Palestinian historical consciousness and Nakba memory. The rise of the new global media and the internet, in particular, has strengthened the role of Palestinian oral/aural histories and personal narratives in shaping Palestinian historical consciousness. In the last decade the internet, in particular, has become one of the most important sites of archiving Palestinian oral histories and personal narratives. Since its creation, the Archive has recorded over 650 video interviews with first-generation refugees in Lebanon about their recollections of 1948. This project was conceived as a collaborative grassroots initiative in which the refugees themselves were encouraged to participate in the process of representing this historical period. The project, which consists of about 1,000 hours of video testimony with refugees from more than 135 villages in pre-1948 Palestine, has its work centred on the twelve official UNRWA (United Nations Relief and Works Agency for Palestine Refugees in the Near East) camps in Lebanon. But it has also conducted interviews within unregistered refugee "gatherings", and with middle class and elite Palestinians living in urban centres in Lebanon. Six duplicate sets of the interviews have been produced, along with a detailed database and search engine.[2]

PALESTINIAN ORAL/AURAL HISTORIES "FROM BELOW" AND ARCHIVING PEOPLE'S VOICES

In order to understand and appreciate the richness of Palestinian oral/aural histories and social and cultural memories, rather than imposing settler-colonial narratives on the indigenous people of Palestine, a range of voices and multiple narratives of competing memories, the archaeology of a people criss-crossed with individual experiences – including narratives of suffering (*mua'ana*), survival (*baqa'a*) and *sumud* (steadfastness), of courage and resistance born out of anger and revolt against oppression – must be allowed to flourish and be nurtured further. This section suggests that the "history from below" approach, with its emphasis on "speaking of experiences" and the multiplicity of popular memories and people's voices rather than high politics, decision makers or top-down approaches, can challenge hegemonic discourses or colonial method-ologies based on Israeli- or Western-dominated archival sources.

Ilan Pappe makes an important point which centres on the difference between macro- and micro-histories of 1948. The Israeli "new historiography" of 1948 has remained largely macro-historical. This is partly due to the nature of the Israeli archival material. In general, Israeli archival sources give us a sketchy picture of 1948. This means that a detailed description of what happened in the case of each Palestinian village and town remains largely elusive. Often a docu-ment produced in 1948 by an Israeli army officer refers briefly to the occupation of a Palestinian village, or to the "purification" of another. Pappe points out that Palestinian oral histories can produce historically accurate accounts of 1948, showing that the same events in 1948 appear in a detailed and graphic form in accounts of memory, often as a tale of expulsion, and sometimes even massacre. Israeli historians who reject Palestinian oral history may conclude there was no massacre until the precise documentary sources assure them otherwise. Avishai Margalit (2003), Alessandro Portelli (1994, 1997, 2006) and others generalize about "memory" and argue that it should be treated like fiction or as *knowledge from the past*, not *knowledge of the past*. This approach echoes positivist thinking, contrasts "history" with "memory" and tends to conflate "history" with the "past". Although "'collective memory' is not necessarily *knowledge of the past*" (quoted in Fierke 2008: 34), oral testimonies – like archival records – are forms of representation of the past. Of course, oral histories may tell us less about events in the past and more about the significance of the events in the present. But written documents are also often the result of a processing of oral testimonies (Pappe 2004: 186). Therefore Palestinian refugee memory accounts could be as authentic as the documented ones. But also the narrative of individual villages and towns in Palestine can *only* be constructed with the help of Palestinian oral testimonies. Consequently, oral testimony is a crucial methodology for pursuing further research on the Nakba. Although oral testimonies are not a totalizing substitute for archival material, they can supply crucial material for filling gaps and be cross-referenced with archival sources and documentary evidence.

Oral testimony, like written documentation, is never free from factual error and has to be treated critically. Morris (2004: 4) argues that written documents (and Israeli archives) distort far less than interviews with Palestinian refugees. But archival documentations are often based on memory; they can distort, misinform, omit or even fabricate evidence (Humphries 2009: 79–80). Louis Starr notes that memory is "fallible, ego distorts and contradictions sometimes go unresolved". Nevertheless:

> Problems of evaluation are not markedly different from those inherent in the use of letters, diaries, and other primary sources … the scholar must test the evidence in an oral history memoir for internal consistency and, whenever possible, by corroboration from other sources, often including the oral history memoirs of others on the same topic. (Starr 1984: 4–5)

Palestinian oral culture is a significant framework not only for the construction of an alternative, counter-hegemonic history of the Nakba and memories of the lost historic Palestine but also for an ongoing indigenous life, living Palestinian practices and a sustained human ecology and liberation. In contrast with the hegemonic Israeli heritage-style industry of an exclusively biblical archaeology, with its obsession with assembling archaeological fragments – scattered remnants of masonry, tables, bones, tombs – and officially approved historical and archaeological theme parks of dead monuments and artefacts destined for museums, in recent decades Palestinians have devoted much attention to the "enormously rich sedimentations of village history and oral traditions" as a reminder of the continuity of native life and living practices (Said 2004: 49; Masalha 2008).

As Linda Tuhiwai Smith (1999) has effectively demonstrated, decolonizing methodologies are central to both settler-colonial studies and indigenous studies. In the context of both Zionist (power/archival knowledge) epistemology and indigenous rural and peasant Palestinian society, Palestinian oral/ aural histories are a particularly useful decolonizing methodology; throughout much of the twentieth century the majority of the Palestinians lived in villages and were *fallaheen*; in 1944 66% of the Palestinian population was agrarian with a literacy rate, when last officially estimated, of only 15% (Esber 2003: 22). Their experiences in the fields, in their villages and in exile are largely absent from history-writing and much recent historiography (Issa 2005). Moreover, the Nakba itself, and the political instability and repression faced by the dispersed Palestinian communities since 1948, have also impeded Palestinian research and studies (Khalidi 1997: 89, 98).

As is the case with other subaltern groups, Palestinian oral testimony is a vital tool for recovering the voice of the subaltern: peasants, the urban poor, women, refugee camp dwellers and Bedouin tribes. An important feature of the Palestinian oral testimony of the Nakba from the inception has been its popular basis with the direct participation of displaced community (Gluck 2008: 69). Since the mid-1980s this grassroots effort has shown an awareness of the importance of recording the events of the Nakba from the perspective of those previously marginalized in Palestinian elite and male-centred narratives. Although gender (both female and male) imagery and symbols have always been prevalent in Palestinian nationalist discourses (Khalili 2007: 22–23), the Palestinian National Charter of 1964 (revised in 1968) and the Palestinian Declaration of Independence of 1988 had both imagined the Palestinian nation as a male body and masculinized political agency (Massad 2005).

FROM MEMORY TO HISTORY: PERSONAL EXPERIENCES, ORAL HISTORIES AND MEMORIES OF THE NAKBA

Palestinian oral histories of the Nakba should not be conflated with the Israeli "new historiography" of 1948. However, Palestinian oral histories of the Nakba both preceded and were incentivized by the emergence of Israeli revisionist historiography in the mid-to-late 1980s. Yet not until the 1970s did scholarly Palestinian oral history begin to offer a picture of events in the eyes of the refugees. It should be pointed out, though, that these new oral narrative perspectives based extensively on interviews with and testimonies of the refugees began in the early 1970s – before the opening of the Israeli governmental and institutional archives in the late 1970s and at least a decade before the emergence of the Israeli "new historiography" in the mid-to-late 1980s.

In the 1960s and early 1970s the Palestinian collective nationalist resistance discourse about history, as articulated by the PLO, was dominant, effectively eclipsing personal narratives of individual refugees. Typically, this "heroic" nationalist memory was designed to paint an ideal type of history and suppress the darker side of Palestinian history, including accounts of internal infighting and stories about many Palestinian collaborators with Zionism. From the early 1970s, however, the *Journal for Palestine Studies*, *Shuun Filastiniyah*, the Centre for Palestine Studies, the Palestinian Research Centre and *Arab Studies Quarterly* began to publish pioneering articles and books based on individual oral evidence, personal narrative and interviews with ordinary refugees to tell the history of Palestine before and during the Nakba. This included works by Elias Shoufani (1972), Nafiz Nazzal (1974a), Fawzi Qawuqji (1975), Rega-e Busailah (1981), Elias Sanbar (1984), Walid Khalidi (1984) and 'Ajaj Nuwayhid (1993). In 1978 the Institute for Palestine Studies in Beirut published Nafiz Nazzal's, *The Palestinian Exodus from Galilee 1948* (1978), based on his doctoral dissertation (1974b), which brought to academic attention important oral accounts of Galilee dispossession as recalled by refugees exiled in Lebanon.

Ironically, Israeli historian Benny Morris (1987: 2), who claims to distrust Palestinian oral evidence on 1948, cited Nazzal's work repeatedly and extensively (as well as Shoufani's) in *The Birth of the Palestinian Refugee Problem, 1947–1949* (Morris 1987). Despite his anti-Palestinian polemics, Morris found Nazzal's oral evidence research extremely useful in reconstructing several of the Israeli massacres of Palestinians in 1948.

The 1970s and 1980s were two of the most creative and inventive decades in Palestinian history and popular memory. In the 1970s Rosemary Sayigh, an anthropologist based in Lebanon, pioneered a whole new discipline of narrating the subaltern. She began to record and translate conversations with and individual testimonies of Palestinian refugees in the mid-1970s and she made them into a number of articles in *Journal of Palestine Studies* (1977a, 1977b) and her book *Palestinians: From Peasants to Revolutionaries* (1979). Both Sayigh and Nazzal extensively interviewed refugees in Lebanon and drew to academic attention oral accounts, based on personal experiences, of Galilee dispossession as recalled by refugees themselves, thus pioneering new perspectives on the Nakba. However, in the 1970s neither Sayigh – who pioneered working with women in the camps – nor Nazzal theorized oral accounts in their work; later Sayigh recalled: "In my approach to oral history I was simply doing it, using large chunks of what people told me. I didn't have any idea of what oral history was or about its potential for liberation struggles" (R. Sayigh 1997).

However, this potential for Palestinian liberation and women's struggles in the seminal works of Sayigh and Nazzal encouraged other oral accounts projects at Birzeit University, initially proposed in 1979 by Sharif Kanaana (1992) and Kamal Abdel Fattah (cited in Jawad 2007). In 1985 the Birzeit University's Documentation Centre launched a series of monographs on the villages destroyed in 1948. Since 1993 this work has been overseen by Saleh Abdel Jawad (2007: 59–127; also Gluck 2008: 69).

As time went on, Sayigh, working with the General Union of Palestinian Women and with women in the camps, became more systematic and more "theoretical".

Until the 1970s Palestinian collective memory of the Nakba was largely divorced from the broader political contexts and class structures which inform and shape them. However, in the last three decades there has been an explosion of contextualized oral history scholarship and popular memory studies in Palestine. Many original works and collections relevant to Palestinian popular memories, women's liberation struggles, narrative histories and gendered memory have been produced.[3] Today Sayigh, and other oral historians working with Palestinian refugees, advocate a fresh examination of Palestinian history from an oral history perspective. They have been working in a field in which there are already dominant male and elite narratives which rely on official documentation and archival material. This "history from below" approach and popular memories rather than high politics or top-down approaches has both powerfully challenged and enriched the written historiography of Palestine.

Moreover, since the late 1990s there has been a remarkable proliferation of Palestinian films, memoirs and archival websites, online archives, oral history projects and several cultural museums and centres across Palestine, all created in the aftermath of the fiftieth anniversary of the Nakba. In conjunction with this, several films have since been released, including Edward Said's *In Search of Palestine*, Muhammad Bakri's *1948*, Simone Bitton's film about the poet Mahmoud Darwish, *Et la terre comme la langue*, and Maryse Gargour's *La Terre Parle Arabe*, with which I have been personally and closely involved.

In her book, *What it Means to be Palestinian: Stories of Palestinian Peoplehood*, Palestinian scholar Dina Matar points out that her work on Palestinian popular memory aims to complement, rather than subvert, the top-down approaches prevalent in most modern histories of Palestine and adds to burgeoning oral history and popular memory research on the Palestinian people pioneered by the seminal works of Rosemary Sayigh and Nafiz Nazzal. Sayigh's highly original contribution to the field of oral testimony has made it possible for the victims, the subaltern, the marginalized and women to challenge Zionist hegemonic and Palestinian elite narratives. In 2002 the editors of a special oral history edition of the Beirut-based *Al-Jana* (the Harvest, Arab Resource Centre for the Popular Arts) pointed out that individual initiatives were being undertaken even before the 1980s,[4] when more projects began to develop with institutional support, especially from NGOs.

From the late 1980s onwards, with the decline of the Palestinian elite discourses, there has been another development in Palestinian historiography, pointing towards a different discourse and a "history from below" approach. This new approach pointed to "people's past as a source of authenticity". This approach was given a major boost in the 1990s with the publication of Ted Swedenburg's seminal work on the great Palestinian rebellion of 1936–1939: *Memories of Revolt: The 1936–1939 Rebellion and the Palestinian National Past* (1995). Earlier in 1990 Swedenburg commented on the internal silencing of the Palestinian past and popular memory by both the Palestinian traditional and PLO leaderships:

[The] PLO, which funded numerous projects in Lebanon during the seventies and early eighties, never supported a study of the [1936–1939 revolt] based on the testimony of the refugees living in Lebanon. Maybe the resistance movement was hesitant to allow any details about the internal struggle of the thirties to be brought to light because bad feelings persisted in the diaspora community. (Swedenburg 1990: 152–153; also Swedenburg 1991)

The powerful oral/aural culture of Palestine survived into the post-Nakba period. In the immediate post-catastrophe period the Arab tradition of storytelling in the form of *al-hakawati* (the storyteller) was deployed as a way of countering Zionist memoricide and toponymicide – the erasure of the material culture of Palestine and Palestinian cultural memory. *Al-hakawati* is part of a long popular oral tradition in Arab cultures. While both Israeli official and revisionist historiographies have long emphasized Israeli state papers and official documents rather than the people's voices behind the documents, oral and people's history is often richer and goes much deeper than the official records. Furthermore, in recent decades, Palestinian oral histories – which are partly inspired by the popular *al-hakawati* tradition and partly by the oral and cultural traditions of Islam – has attempted to redress the imbalance of the modern historiography and the hegemonic Zionist narrative by developing methodologies for understanding the contexts, objects and meanings of documents, facts and evidence, and generally for exploring the history and voices of the people behind hegemonic Israeli state papers and Zionist official records.

Yet in *Palestinian Women: Narrative Histories and Gendered* memory, Palestinian scholar Fatma Kassem (2011) shows that in Palestinian oral and verbal traditions (as opposed to male-written official and religious traditions) the storytellers are often women – women who live beneath the official version – who often challenge and sometimes undermine official and patriarchal narratives. Popular storytelling was deployed in the post-1948 period by the Palestinian refugee and internally displaced communities as an "emergency science" and a liberating experience. Individual accounts of struggle and revolt (*thawra*), displacement and exodus, survival and heroism served as a buffer against national disappearance. Narrative histories, memory and oral accounts have become a key genre of Palestinian historiography – a genre guarding against the "disappearance from history" of the Palestinian people (Sanbar 2001; Masalha 2012).

In recent decades there has been attention to the idea of "history from below" – from the ground up – thus giving more space to the voices and perspectives of the refugees, rather than of policy makers, and also incorporating extensive oral testimony and interviews with the first generation of the Nakba. The vitality and significance of Palestinian oral history "from below" in the reconstruction of the past is central to understanding the Nakba. The most horrific aspects of the Nakba – the dozens of massacres that accompanied the ethnic cleansing of the Nakba, as well as a detailed description of what ethnic cleansing was from the point of view of the one ethnically cleansed – can only be recovered when such a historiographical approach is applied (Pappe 2004, 2006).

Taken as a whole, Palestinian oral accounts and refugee recollections give a good idea of reality. However in the case of the Palestinian Nakba, oral accounts are not merely one choice of methodology. Rather its use can represent a decision as to whether to record any history at all (Esber 2003). Oral accounts are the major means of reconstructing the history of the Palestinian refugees and internally displaced Palestinians as seen from the perspective of primary subjects.

PALESTINIAN WOMEN'S VOICES AND REFUGEE CAMP STORIES

From the early 1980s onwards, and for nearly three decades, Rosemary Sayigh, in particular, has been working with Palestinian women in the refugee camps of Lebanon on oral history projects. In *Voices: Palestinian Women Narrate Displacement* (2005),[5] a digital book with an introduction by Sayigh, you can hear the voices of Palestinian women telling their stories of the loss of home through displacement, refugeedom, deportation, imprisonment, Israeli shelling and siege of refugee camps in Lebanon in 1982 and total transformation of their environment.

The voices of Palestinian women and Palestinian oral accounts from survivors of destroyed villages in the Galilee provided the Lebanese novelist and brilliant narrator Elias Khoury (born in 1948) with material for his 1998 novel *Bab al-Shams* (Gate of the Sun), which was also turned into a film in 2004. Khoury was highly critical of the traditional male-dominated Palestinian leadership and its role in silencing the Nakba. In the late 1969s Khoury had joined the Fatah, the largest resistance organization within the PLO, and he subsequently worked as a researcher at the Palestine Research Centre in Beirut. Khoury's *Gate of the Sun* (translated from Arabic in 2006), an epic retelling of the life of Palestinian refugees in Lebanon since the Nakba, later made into a film, subtly addresses the ideas of memory, truth and storytelling. Khoury had the initial idea of turning stories he heard in refugee camps in Beirut into a memorial narrative in the 1970s, when he worked for the Palestine Research Centre. He spent much of the 1980s gathering thousands of stories before writing *Gate of the Sun*. The story of love and survival is told by Khaleel, a doctor at a hospital in Shatila refugee camp in Beirut. It involves a dying Palestinian fighter called Yunis and his wife Naheeleh, an internal Palestinian refugee inside Israel, in

Galilee, whose relationship forms during secret visits across the Lebanese–Israeli border to a cave renamed "Bab al-Shams". The cave is a house, a village and a country, and the only bit of Palestinian territory that has been liberated. The relationship produces a secret nation: a family of seven children who have borne four more Yunises by the end of the book. For Khoury:

> Yunis, of course, is a hero. He used to go to Galilee, he used to cross the borders ... but in the end we discover that he was nothing, that Naheeleh was this whole story; her relationship with the children, and how she actually defended life. In the refugee camps I met hundreds of women like Naheeleh. Then it's no more a metaphor. It's very realistic. (Khoury 1998, 2006)

Khoury was a close friend of Mahmoud Darwish, the Palestinian national poet, and had worked very closely with Darwish in the PLO organ Shuun Filastiniyya. Both Darwish and Khoury were very critical of Palestinian elite- and male-dominated narratives and, in *Memory for Forgetfulness* (1987) and his other poems, Darwish (1987) attacked the record of the PLO leadership during the Lebanese period (1970–1982) – including the construction of a "state within a state" in Palestinian refugee camps in Lebanon – and of the Arab leaders during the Israeli invasion of Lebanon for their indifference to the Israeli shelling of Palestinian refugee camps and the suffering of people in Beirut in August 1982. Both Darwish and Khoury challenge Arab indifference and the silencing of the events surrounding the Nakba in Palestinian elite- and male-dominated narratives.

However, Palestinian women continue to be excluded, even within the subaltern narrative and even the relatively more democratic New Global Media. Fatima Kassem (2011), Rema Hammami (2003), Isabelle Humphries and Laleh Khalili (Humphries 2009: 90–91; Humphries and Khalili 2007; Khalili 2005) have all shown that gender narratives and women's voices, and their contribution to collective Nakba memory and Palestinian historical consciousness, are doubly marginalized within the generally marginalized Palestinian refugee story. Often women's memories are silenced because they complicate Palestinian nationalist narratives, an issue that Palestinian subaltern studies have failed to address adequately (Humphries 2009: 90–91). Despite interviews with women, men are the main protagonists in Michel Khleifi's *Ma'loul* [sic] *Celebrates Its Destruction* and Rachel Leah Jones' *500 Dunam* [sic] *on the Moon* (Humphries

2009: 90–91). Clearly, more accounts of memory and oral history research are still needed on the events surrounding the Nakba and the post-trauma period as experienced and remembered not just by particular subaltern groups but by the whole non-elite majority of Palestinian society.

In recent decades, Palestinian filmmakers have produced a number of films and documentaries which have documented and examined the oral histories and the memories of the last decades. A number of recent edited collections and books authored by Palestinians also explore the complex narratives of the last seven decades. Documentary films, in particular, have explored concepts of 1948 Palestine, home and exile, identity and its relationship to individual and memories, and exilic cinema and its characteristics, cinematic use of narrative devices and storytelling and the struggle between two opposing narratives: the hegemonic (Zionist) narrative which tries to displace, replace and suppress the narrative of the indigenous people of Palestine. Of course, as Palestinian film-maker Omar al-Qattan (2007: 191) points out, "There is no single Palestinian memory" of the Nakba; "rather, there are many tangled memories". Yet understanding the links between the apparently tangled and fragmented memories of 1948 is central to appreciating the significance of the Palestinian experiences of the traumatic events and to comprehending the inner meanings of the Nakba.

RE-MEMBERING AS A REUNITING STRATEGY

The *dismemberment* of Palestine – a country which had existed for thousands of years – in 1948, the destruction of its ancient cities and villages and the shattering defeat of the Nakba, also resulted in the destruction of the urban notables and the old social, political, cultural and national elites of Palestine; the ethnic cleansing of Palestine effectively emptied the urban hinterlands of the educated and cultural elites of the country. The Palestinian leadership, consisting mainly of urban notables, led by the Arab Higher Committee, the central political organ of the Palestinians in mandatory Palestine, and headed by the conservative leader Haj Amin al-Husseini, the Mufti of Jerusalem, had been totally discredited in the post-Nakba period (Achcar 2010; Y. Sayigh 1997: 665).

As Palestinian sociologist Jamil Hilal pointed out, from the Nakba and until the mid-1960s there was no Palestinian national elite. This vacuum was largely filled by local leaders, *mukhtars* or tribal leaders (Hilal 2002: 29–32). Despite this fragmentation and dispersal, in the decade after 1948 Palestinian "marginality" (to use Bell Hooks' term) became "a site of resistance" (1990). From "below", popular and refugee-led resistance and "Palestianism was a natural response to *al-nakba*, but it was the experience of social and political marginality that effectively transformed it from 'a popular grass-roots patriotism' into a proto-nationalism in the decade after 1948" (Y. Sayigh 1997: 46).

In the 1950s the absence of independent Palestinian leadership and representation was much in evidence: from the Nakba and until the establishment of the PLO in the 1960s Palestinians were in effect without formal political representation; they were also without a single territorially based cultural elite.

To compound things further, on anniversaries of the Nakba and on Israel's Independence Day (15 May), the Israeli state actively encouraged the so-called "Israeli Arabs" to celebrate the Zionist settler-colonization of Palestine and the destruction of historic Palestine; this strategy scored some successes in the first two decades of the state (Cohen 2010). In Jordan a key priority of the Hashemite regime (which controlled the West Bank and ruled many Palestinians) was to keep the Palestinian refugee camps and Palestinians in the West Bank under close surveillance and prevent Nakba commemoration (Sayigh 1979: 111). Although Israel's strategy of control, erasure of memory and Nakba denial, through the combination of military rule, repression, fear, segmentation and patronage, looked fairly effective in the 1950s, today it looks as though Israel's efforts at encouraging the Palestinian citizens to embrace the Zionist ideological discourse of 1948 have largely ended in failure (Cohen 2010).

Today Palestinians commemorate the Nakba through *Ihya'a Dhikra al-Nakba*, with its emphasis on collective togetherness, recovery and reconstitution, while the English term "re-membering" emphasizes group "membership" and re-uniting people. From the 1960s onwards, recovery and *re-membering*, re-linking and re-uniting the fragmented, exiled and colonized Palestinians through a range of cultural and artistic media and through collective, individual and shared memories of the pre-Nakba and post-Nakba periods, as embodied in fiction, novels, paintings and resistance poetry, was central to consolidating contemporary Palestinian identity. The trauma of the Nakba affected Palestinian national identity and memories in two contradictory ways. On the one hand the Nakba led to the destruction of much of Palestinian society and the dispersal and fragmentation of the Palestinian people. But, from the encounter with and rejection of neighbouring Arab states, the Nakba also led to the crystallization, re-membering and collectivization of a distinct and resistant Palestinian identity (Litvak 2009: 103–111). While the formation of Palestinian *national* identity had taken root long before 1948, there is no doubt that the Nakba was a key event in the consolidation and reconstruction of a strong, clearly defined and vital contemporary Palestinian identity (Sayigh 1977a, 1977b).

INDIGENOUS MEMORIES AND THE CREATION OF A PALESTINE MEMORYSHARE PROJECT

The production and archiving of Palestinian social history and cultural memories, the documenting of the uprooting of the indigenous people of Palestine and the archiving of refugee voices, experiences and stories about places from their past – that appear in films, recent oral history collections, autobiographies, novels, poetry collections, paintings and memorial books, electronic encyclopaedias, digital archives and refugee camp embroidery projects – focus on both the symbolic and the emotional connections of Palestinians to the land and homeland, and to their former homes and villages (Al-Qalqili 2004). This rich production of oral memory is also the "documentary evidence" that proves their existence and legal right to the land of their ancestors.

These shared memories, with their affirmative narratives about the land, testify to the intimate and intense experience of everyday life on the land – the names of the valleys, hills, tombs and shrines, streets, beaches, springs and water wells, cultivated fields and vineyards – and the importance of all kinds of trees and other natural elements in visual memories of the past (Masalha 2005, 2012; Sa'di and Abu-Lughod 2007). In addition, hand-drawn maps marking the places of importance to the villagers, personal documents, personal memories and oral accounts all intertwine to create a larger picture and a collective narrative of life before the Nakba.

The heritage of the country and memory accounts of historic Palestine testify to the cultural richness and social multiculturalism of the country and the beauty of the countryside, mountains and valleys, religious shrines and historic sites. Memory accounts of Palestine before 1948 reflect the fertility of the land, the beauty of the landscape, the richness and diversity of culture and of village and city lives. One of the most famous Palestinian sites is the Dome of the Rock (Masjid Qubbat As-Sakhrah), located in the centre of a greater Muslim shrine, known as the Haram al-Sharif (Noble Sanctuary) in the Old City of Jerusalem. Completed in 691 AD by the Muslim Umayyad Caliph Abdel Malik, the building is the oldest Islamic shrine in the world and also one of the most beautiful and instantly recognizable buildings.

People's history projects are an essential tool for recovering the voice of the subaltern and ordinary people: peasants, the urban poor, refugee camp dwellers, Bedouin tribes, but also women. In Palestinian oral histories, gendered memory and verbal traditions (as opposed to male-written official and religious traditions) the storytellers are often refugee camp women.

Inspired by the BBC Memoryshare project, this work recommends the creation of a similar digital Memoryshare project in Palestine. This project would encourage ordinary people and people from all walks of life to share, record and upload pre- and post-Nakba stories and memory accounts – old photos, documents, Sharia court records, drawings, maps, recorded voices or videos, or material evidence. This people's history archiving project can serve as an anchor that connects communities in Palestine and the diaspora. It will be assisted and run by a team of volunteers and archivists based at several universities and cultural and community centres in Palestine.

In recent years we have seen a considerable expansion of Nakba studies internationally and some of the international programmes have developed oral history projects and archival collections. Several Palestinian digital film and newspaper collections and online archives have also been developed by Palestinian refugee networks and communities based in the diaspora. Two examples of these excellent web-based archives are:

- the Palestine Poster Project Archive which displays more than 4,500 Palestine-related posters from the late nineteenth century to the present;
- and the Nakba Archive: a video archive of oral histories of the Nakba, the creation of the Palestinian refugee diaspora displaced during the 1948 Nakba.

However, the ongoing dispossession of the Palestinian people, their ongoing plight and trauma, have brought me to the conclusion that there is a need to nurture and establish an interdisciplinary subfield to be called Nakba Studies. This subfield would bring in historians, both literary and theorist, and scholars of trauma studies. It would continue documentation and expression of the embattled popular and cultural memories of Palestine as a liberating scholarly and ethical imperative.

NOTES

1 http://www.bbc.co.uk/dna/memoryshare/about.
2 http://nakba-archive.org/?page_id=954.
3 See Al-Azhari (1996), Yahya (1998), Shoufani (2001), Sa'di (2002), Al-Qalqili (2004), Humphries (2004, 2009), (Issa 2005), Gluck (1994, 2008), Sayigh (2007a, 2007b, 2011), Matar (2011), Humphries and Khalili (2007), Sa'di and Abu-Lughod (2007), Kassem (2011), Masalha (2005, 2008, 2012), Manna' (2016).
4 http://al-jana.org/programs-activities/active-memory/.
5 al-Mashriq, http://almashriq.hiof.no/palestine/300/301/voices/index.html.

REFERENCES

Achcar, G. (2010) *The Arabs and the Holocaust: The Arab-Israeli War of Narratives*. London: Saqi Books.

Abdel Jawad, S. (2007) "Zionist Massacres: The Creation of the Palestinian Refugee Problem in the 1948 War", in E. Benvenisti, C. Gans and S. Hanafi (eds.), *Israel and the Palestinian Refugees*. Berlin: Springer.

Abu Sitta, S. (1998) *The Palestinian Nakba 1948: The Register of Depopulated Localities in Palestine*. London: Palestinian Return Centre.

Abu Sitta, S. (2010) *The Atlas of Palestine 1917–1966*. London: Palestine Land Society.

Al-'Arif, A. (1958–1960) *Al-Nakba: Nakbat Bayt al-Maqdis Wal-Firdaws al-Mafqud, 1947–1952* [The Catastrophe: The Catastrophe of Jerusalem and the Lost Paradise, 1947–52], 6 Vols. Beirut and Sidon, Lebanon: Al-Maktaba al-'Asriyya [in Arabic].

Al-Azhari, A. (1996) "Memories of Saffuriyeh ref"ugees with Israeli IDs", *Palestine-Israel: Journal of Politics, Economics and Culture* (originally published in Hebrew in *Ma'ariv* daily, 15 October 1995, translated by Yael Lotan), 3(1).

Allen, B. and W.L. Montell (1981) *From Memory to History: Using Oral Sources in Local Historical Research*. Nashville: American Association for State and Local History.

Al-Qalqili, 'A.F. (2004) *Al-Ard fi Thakirat al-Filastiniyyun: I'timadan 'ala al-Tarikh al-Sha-fawi fi Mukhayyam Jenin* [The Land in Palestinian Memory: Based on Oral Histories in the Jenin Refugee Camp]. Ramallah, Palestine: Shaml-Palestinian Diaspora and Refugee Centre [in Arabic].

Al-Qattan, O. (2007) "The Secret Visitations of Memory", in A.H. Sa'di and L. Abu-Lughod (eds.), *Nakba: Palestine, 1948, and the Claims of Memory*. New York: Columbia University Press.

Ankori, G. (2006) *Palestinian Art*. London: Reaction Books.

Busailah, R. (1981) "The Fall of Lydda, 1948: Impressions and Reminiscences", *Arab Studies Quarterly* 3(2): 123–151.

Childers, E.B. (1961) "The Other Exodus", *The Spectator* (London), 11 May, http://archive.spectator.co.uk/article/12th-may-1961/8/the-other-exodus.

Cohen, Hillel (2010) *Good Arabs: The Israeli Security Agencies and the Israeli Arabs, 1948–1967*. Berkeley, CA: University of California Press.

Dabbagh, M.M. (1972–1986) *Biladuna Filastin* [Our Country, Palestine]. Beirut and al-Khalil: The Research Centre and Matbuʻat Rabitat al-Jamiʻyyin fi-Muhafazat al-Khalil [in Arabic].

Darwish, M. (1987) Memory *for Forgetfulness* [Arabic: *Dhakirah li-al-Nisyan*]. Berkeley: University of California Press.

Darwish, M. (2000) *The Adam of Two Edens.* Syracuse, NY: Syracuse University Press & Jusoor.

Darwish, M. (2003) *Unfortunately, It Was Paradise: Selected Poems.* Translations by M. Akash, C. Forché and others. Berkeley: California University Press.

Davis, R. (2007) "Mapping the Past, Re-creating the Homeland: Memories of Village Places in pre-1948 Palestine", in A.H. Saʻdi and L. Abu-Lughod (eds.), *Nakba: Palestine, 1948, and the Claims of Memory.* New York: Columbia University Press.

Davis, U. (2003) *Apartheid Israel: The Possibilities for Struggle Within.* London and New York: Zed Books.

Esber, R. (2003) "War and Displacement in Mandate Palestine, 29 November 1947 to 15 May 1948". PhD dissertation, SOAS, University of London.

Fierke, K.M (2008) "Memory and Violence in Israel/Palestine", *Human Rights & Human Welfare* 8: 33-42.

Foucault, M. (1972) *The Archaeology of Knowledge.* New York: Harper and Row.

Foucault, M. (1980) *Power/Knowledge.* New York: Pantheon.

Gluck, S.B. (1994) *An American Feminist in Palestine: The Intifada Years.* Philadelphia, PA: Temple University Press.

Gluck, S.B. (2008) "Oral History and *al-Nakbah*", *Oral History Review* 35(1): 68–80.

Guha, R., ed. (1997) *A Subaltern Studies Reader, 1986–1995.* Minneapolis: University of Minnesota Press.

Guha, R. and G.C. Spivak, eds. (1988) *Selected Subaltern Studies.* New York: Oxford University Press.

Halbwachs, M. (1980) *Collective Memory.* New York: Harper and Row.

Hammami, R. (2003) "Gender, *Nakbe* and Nation: Palestinian Women's Presence and Absence in the Narration of 1948 Memories", in R. Robin and B. Strath (eds.), *Homelands: Poetic Power and the Politics of Space.* Brussels: P.I.E. Peter Land.

Heidegger, M. (2010) *Being and Time.* New York: State University of New York Press.

Hilal, J. (2002) *Takween al-Nukhba al-Filastiniyya Mundhu Nushu al-Haraka al-Wataniyya al-Filastiniyya ila ma baʻda Qiyam al-Sulta al-Wataniyya al-Filastiniyya* [The Making of the Palestinian Elite from the Eemergnce of the Palestinian National Movement until after the Establishment of the Palestinian National Authority]. Ramallah: Muwatin [in Arabic].

Hooks, B. (1990) "Marginality as a Site of Resistance", in R. Ferguson et al. (eds.), *Out There: Marginalisation and Contemporary Cultures.* Cambridge, MA: MIT.

Humphries, I. (2004) "Palestinian Internal Refugees in the Galilee: From the Struggle to Survive to the New Narrative of Return (1948–2005)", *Holy Land Studies: A Multidisciplinary Journal* 3(2): 213-231.

Humphries, I. (2009) "Displaced Voices: The Politics of Memory amongst Palestinian Internal Refugees in the Galilee (1991–2009)". PhD diss., St Mary's University College and University of Surrey, England.

Humphries, I. and L. Khalili (2007) "Gender of Nakba Memory", in A.H. Sa'di and L. Abu-Lughod (eds.), *Nakba: Palestine, 1948, and the Claims of Memory*. New York: Columbia University Press.

Issa, M. (2005) "The Nakba, Oral History and the Palestinian Peasantry: The Case of Lubya", in N. Masalha (ed.), *Catastrophe Remembered*. London: Zed Books.

Jawad, S.A. (2007) "Zionist Massacres: The Creation of the Palestinian Refugee Problem in the 1948 War", in E. Benvenisti, C. Gans and S. Hanafi (eds.), *Israel and the Palestinian Refugees*. Berlin: Springer.

Kanaana, S. (1992) *Still on Vacation: The Eviction of the Palestinians in 1948*. Jerusalem: Jeruaslem International Centre for Palestinian Studies.

Kanafani, G. (1998) *Men in the Sun and Other Palestinian Stories*, translated by H. Kilpatrick. Boulder, CO: Lynne Rienner.

Kanafani, G. (2000) *Palestine's Children: Returning to Haifa & Other Stories*, translated by B. Harlow and K.E. Riley. Boulder, CO: Lynne Rienner.

Kanafani, G., with R. Allen, M. Jayyusi and J. Reed (2004) *All That's Left to You*. Northampton, MA: Interlink World Fiction.

Kassem, F. (2011) *Palestinian Women: Narrative Histories and Gendered Memory*. London: Zed Books.

Khalidi, R. (1997) *Palestinian Identity: The Construction of Modern National Consciousness*. New York: Columbia University Press.

Khalidi, W. (1959a) "Why Did the Palestinians Leave?", *Middle East Forum* 24: 21–24. Reprinted as (2005) "Why Did the Palestinians Leave Revisited", *Journal of Palestine Studies* 34(2): 42–54.

Khalidi, W. (1959b) "The Fall of Haifa", *Middle East Forum* 35: 22–32.

Khalidi, W. (1961) "Plan Dalet: The Zionist Master Plan for the Conquest of Palestine", *Middle East Forum* 37(9): 22–28.

Khalidi, W. (1984) *Before Their Diaspora: A Photographic History of the Palestinians, 1876–1948*. Beirut: Institute for Palestine Studies.

Khalidi, W. (1988) "Plan Dalet Revisited: Master Plan for the Conquest of Palestine", *Journal of Palestinian Studies* 18(1): 3–37.

Khalidi, W. (1992) *All That Remains: The Palestinian Villages Occupied and Depopulated by Israel in 1948*. Washington, DC: Institute for Palestine Studies.

Khalili, L. (2005) *Places of Memory and Mourning: Palestinian Commemoration in the Refugee Camps of Lebanon'*, *Comparative Studies of South Asia, Africa and the Middle East* 25(1): 30–45.

Khalili, L. (2007) *Heroes and Martyrs of Palestine: The Politics of National Commemoration*. Cambridge: Cambridge University Press.

Khoury, E. (1998) *Bab al-Shams*. Beirut: Dar al-Adab [in Arabic].

Khoury, E. (2006) *Gate of the Sun*. Brooklyn, NY: Archipelago Books.

Khoury, E. (2008) "For Israelis, an Anniversary. For Palestinians, a Nakba", *The New York Times*, 18 May, http://www.nytimes.com/2008/05/18/opinion/18khoury.html.

Litvak, M. (2009) "Constructing a National Past: The Palestinian Case", in M. Litvak (ed.), *Palestinian Collective Memory and National Identity*. London and New York: Palgrave Macmillan.

Manna', 'A. (2016) *Nakba and Survival: The Story of Palestinians Who Remained in Haifa and the Galilee, 1948–1956*. Beirut and Ramallah: Institute for Palestine Studies [in Arabic].

Mannes-Abbott, G. (2005) "Elias Khoury: Myth and Memory in the Middle East", *The Independent*, 18 November, http://www.independent.co.uk/arts-entertainment/books/features/elias-khoury-myth-and-memory-in-the-middle-east-515728.html.

Margalit, A. (2003) *The Ethics of Memory*. Cambridge, MA: Harvard University Press.

Masalha, N. (1992) *Expulsion of the Palestinians: The Concept of "Transfer" in Zionist Political Thought, 1882–1948*. Washington, DC: Institute for Palestine Studies.

Masalha, N. (1997) *A Land Without a People*. London: Faber and Faber.

Masalha, N., ed. (2005) *Catastrophe Remembered: Palestine-Israel and the Internal Refugee –Essays in Memory of Edward W. Said*. London: Zed Books.

Masalha, N. (2007) *The Bible and Zionism: Invented Traditions, Archaeology and Post-Colonialism in Palestine-Israel*. London: Zed Books.

Masalha, N. (2008) "Remembering the Palestinian Nakba: Commemoration, Oral History and Narratives of Memory", *Holy Land Studies: A Multidisciplinary Journal* 7(2): 123–156.

Masalha, N. (2012) *The Palestine Nakba: Decolonising History, Narrating the Subaltern, Reclaiming Memory*. London: Zed Books.

Massad, J. (2005) "Conceiving the Masculine: Gender and Palestinian Nationalism", *Middle East Journal* 49(3): 467–483.

Massad, J. (2008) "Resisting the Nakba", *Al-Ahram Weekly On-line* (15–21 May), No. 897, http://weekly.ahram.org.eg/2008/897/op8.htm.

Matar, D. (2011) *What it Means to be Palestinian: Stories of Palestinian Peoplehood*. London: I.B. Tauris.

McGowan, D. (1998) "Deir Yassin Remembered", in D. McGowan and M.H. Ellis (eds.), *Remembering Deir Yassin: The Future of Israel and Palestine*. New York: Olive Branch Press.

Morris, B. (1987) *The Birth of the Palestinian Refugees Problem, 1947–1949*. Cambridge: Cambridge University Press.

Morris, B. (1994) *1948 and After: Israel and the Palestinians*, revised and expanded ed. Oxford: Clarendon Press.

Morris, B. (2004) *The Birth of the Palestinian Refugee Problem Revisited*. Cambridge: Cambridge University Press.

Nazzal, N. (1974a) "The Zionist Occupation of Western Galilee, 1948", *Journal of Palestine Studies* 3(3): 58–76.

Nazzal, N. (1974b) "The Flight of the Palestinian Arabs from the Galilee: A Historical Analysis". PhD diss., Georgetown University, Washington, DC.

Nazzal, N. (1978) *The Palestinian Exodus from Galilee*. Beirut: Institute of Palestine Studies.

Nora, P., ed. (1996) *Realms of Memory: Conflicts and Divisions*, Vol. I. New York: Columbia University Press.

Nora, P., ed. (1997) *Realms of Memory: Traditions*, Vol. II. New York: Columbia University Press.

Nora, P., ed. (1998) *Realms of Memory: Symbols*, Vol. III. New York: Columbia University Press.

Nuwayhid, 'A. (1993) *Mudhakkirat 'Ajaj Nuwayhid: Sittuna 'Aman ma' al-Qafila al-'Arabiyya* [The Memoirs of 'Ajaj Nuwayhid: Sixty Years with the Arab Caravan], edited by Bayan Nuwayhid al-Hout. Beirut: Dar al-Istiqlal lil-Dirasat wal-Nashr [in Arabic].

Pappe, I. (2004) "Historical Truth, Modern Historiography and Ethical Obligations: The Challenge of the Tantura Case", *Holy Land Studies: A Multidisciplinary Journal* 3(2): 171–194.

Pappe, I. (2006) *The Ethnic Cleansing of Palestine*. Oxford: Oneworld Publications.

Passerini, L. (1998) "Work Ideology and Consensus under Italian Fascism", in R. Perks and A. Thomsen (eds.), *The Oral History Reader*. London: Routledge.

Portelli, A. (1994) "The Peculiarities of Oral History", *History Workshop Journal* 12: 96–107.

Portelli, A. (1997) *The Battle of Valle Giulia: Oral History and the Art of Dialogue*. Madison: The University of Wisconsin Press.

Portelli, A. (2006) "What Makes Oral History Different", in R. Perks and A. Thomson (eds.), *The Oral History Reader*, 2nd ed. London: Routledge.

Prakash, G. (1994) "Subaltern Studies as Postcolonial Criticism", *The American Historical Review* 99(5): 1475–1490.

Qawuqji, F. (1975) *Filastin fi Mudhakkirat al-Qawuqji, 1936–1948* [Palestine in the Qawuqji Memoirs, 1936–1948], edited by K. Qasmiyya. Beirut: Markiz al-Abhath [in Arabic].

Said, E.W. (2004) *Freud and the Non-European*. London: Verso, in association with the Freud Museum.

Sa'di, A. (2002) "Catastrophe, Memory and Identity: Al-Nakbah as a Component of Palestinian Identity", *Israel Studies* 7(2): 175–198.

Sa'di, A.H. and L. Abu-Lughod, eds. (2007) *Nakba: Palestine, 1948, and the Claims of Memory*. New York: Columbia University Press.

Sanbar, E. (1984) *Palestine 1948: L'Expulsion*. Paris: Revue d'études palestiniennes.

Sanbar, E. (2001) "Out of Place, Out of Time", *Mediterranean Historical Review* 16(1): 87–94.

Sayigh, R. (1977a) "The Palestinian Identity Among Camp Residents", *Journal of Palestinian Studias* 6(3): 3–22.

Sayigh, R. (1977b) "Sources of Palestinian Nationalism: A Study of a Palestinian Camp in Lebanon", *Journal of Palestinian Studies* 6(4): 17–40.

Sayigh, R. (1979; 1981) *Palestinians: From Peasants to Revolutionaries*. London: Zed Books.

Sayigh, R. (1994) *Too Many Enemies: The Palestinian Experience in Lebanon*. London: Zed Books.

Sayigh, R. (1997) Interview by T. van Teeffelen, *The Jerusalem Times*, 10 October, http://www.palestine-family.net/index.php?nav=3-83&cid=90&did=671.

Sayigh, R. (2007a) "Women Nakba's Stories", in A.H. Sa'di and L. Abu-Lughod (eds.), *Nakba: Palestine, 1948, and the Claims of Memory*. New York: Columbia University Press.

Sayigh, R. (2007b) "Product and Producer of Palestinian History: Stereotypes of 'Self' in Camp Women's Life Stories", *Journal of Middle East Women's Studies* 3(1) 86–105.

Sayigh, R. (2011) "Palestinian Camp Refugee Identifications: A New Look at the 'Local' and National", in A. Knudsen and S. Hanafi (eds.), *Palestinian Refugees: Identity, Space and Place in the Levant*. London and New York: Routledge.

Sayigh, Y. (1997) *Armed Struggle and the Search for State: The Palestinian National Movement, 1949–1993*. Oxford: Clarendon Press.

Shatzky, J. and M. Taub, eds. (1994) *Contemporary Jewish-American Novelists: A Bio-Critical Sourcebook*. Westport, CT and London: Greenwood Press.

Shoufani, E. (1972) "The Fall of a Village", *Journal of Palestine Studies* 1(4): 108–121.

Shoufani, E. (2001) "Testimonies from Tantura", *Journal of Palestine Studies* 30(3): 5–19.

Smith, L.T. (1999) *Decolonizing Methodologies: Research and Indigenous Peoples*. London: Zed Books.

Starr, L. (1984) "Oral History", in D.K. Dunaway and W.K. Baum (eds.), *Oral History: An Interdisciplinary Anthology*. Tennessee: American Association for State and Local History.

Swedenburg, T. (1990) "The Palestinian Peasant as National Signifier", *Anthropological Quarterly* 63(1): 18–30.

Swedenburg, T. (1991) "Popular Memory and the Palestinian National Past", in J. O'Brien and W. Roseberry (eds.), *Golden Ages, Dark Ages: Imagining the Past in Anthropology and History*. Berkeley and Los Angeles: University of California Press.

Swedenburg, T. (1995) *Memories of Revolt: The 1936–1939 Rebellion and the Palestinian National Past*. Minneapolis: University of Minnesota Press.

Trouillot, M.-R. (1995) *Silencing the Past: Power and the Production of History*. Boston, MA: Beacon Press.

Yahya, 'A. (1998) *Palestinian Refugees 1948–1998: Oral History*. Ramallah, Palestine: Palestinian Institute for Cultural Exchange [in Arabic].

Zurayk, C. (1949, 1956) *Ma'na al-Nakba* [The Meaning of the Catastrophe]. Beirut: Khayat [in Arabic].

2
Feminism, indigenousness and settler colonialism: oral history, memory and the Nakba

NAHLA ABDO

This chapter contributes to a feminist analysis of indigenousness and settler colonialism through an application of the method of oral history to Palestinian women's (and men's) voices during the Nakba, or the genocide, as the Nakba will be defined here. The chapter begins with a critical examination of existing progressive feminist approaches, pointing to their contributions and examining their problematics. Using the method of oral history, this chapter highlights Palestinian experiences under British colonialism and Zionist settler colonialism, suggesting, in the process, the need to re-examine our concepts by historicizing them to fit the specific context within which they operate.

At the centre of this chapter lies the voices of Palestinian women (and some men) narrating their loss of lives, homes and homeland under the terror and brutality of the British colonial and Israeli settler-colonial regimes. These voices and lived experiences establish the ground for an alternative feminist theorization, one that places land and genocide at the centre of its analysis. The chapter then concludes by advocating an anti-colonial feminism as the feminist methodology appropriate for analysing, understanding and acting on the context of indigenousness and settler colonialism.

EXISTING PROGRESSIVE FEMINISMS: A CRITIQUE

Feminists of all strands realize the crucial role women have had and continue to play in making their socio-economic, political and cultural history. The gendering of human history through feminist critique of official history has made a substantial contribution to reinstating women in their/our proper place in history. The development of feminism from its 1960s- and 1970s-era theory based on the concept of patriarchy and of men as the main oppressors into one that articulates and analyses the interlocking of the forces of class and race has contributed tremendously to our understanding of women "Others".

In 1983, Angela Davis published her seminal book *Women, Race and Class* in which she demonstrated the interlocking of these forces and their effects on Black women; simultaneously, a feminist debate on the integration of the forces of class and race had developed in Britain. The idea of the interlocking of the forces of violence against and oppression of women was later developed by Kimberlé Crenshaw in the notion of "intersectionality" (Crenshaw 1989, 2016; Matsuda et al. 1993). Since the 1990s, this concept, which came to reinforce already existing feminist approaches concerning the interconnectedness of the forces of gender, race, class, sexuality and so on, has become both a trend and a mantra among most progressive feminists and has been adopted by the UN Gender Unit (Yuval-Davis 2006). The inclusive approach of intersectionality provided a wider analytical framework for theorizing women and gender and has been used in various research methodologies, including oral history. In this context, intersectionality succeeded in exposing the power dynamics that exist between the researcher and the researched, the interviewer and the interviewee, contributing in the process to a highlighting of the difference between elite history and people's history, between history from above and history from below.

Intersectionality as method has contributed to the moralizing of the research process, especially in the forms of interviews and oral history. More importantly, through its emphasis on researchers' positionality and political ideology (Sangster 1994, 2012) and its stress on the roles played by class, racial and other conditions of privilege (Armitage and Gluck 1998; Fleischmann 1996), it was able to remove from sociological and historical research the veil of neutrality and the Weberian notion of "objectivity". This methodology enabled the removal of emphasis from the "ideal type" or official history, replacing it with one based on women's – indeed, people's – materiality and lived experience. In other words, feminism not only reinstated women into history, but it also changed the way history is read and recorded; the centrality of women for oral history, as this chapter and this volume will show, is vital.

FEMINISM: HISTORICAL AND CULTURAL SPECIFICITY

Still, as with all our concepts, the force of intersectionality as method is historically and culturally specific. This conceptual framework, which recognizes the different experiences of women Others, has in fact been widely concerned with Black women and women of colour in general. In considering intersectionality to be historically and culturally specific, and the fact that such specificity demands the recognition of specific experiences and refuses overgeneralizations, two questions are posed here. First, is feminist intersectionality theory capable of properly and sufficiently understanding the experiences of all Others? Second, is intersectionality as a research method (say, of oral history) capable of resolving existing feminist debate on the insider–outsider question? It is to these issues we now turn.

The Other in intersectionality appears to be largely bounded within the settler-immigrant context of the capitalist West, especially that of the United States; the category includes poor women, Black women, women of colour and others. While at a surface level this Other seems general and the theory appears to be universal in applicability, the fact remains that intersectionality fails to include indigenous people (especially indigenous women); nor does it account for the historically specific forces of their marginalization or oppression, namely the settler-colonial state. Later in this chapter we will provide a detailed analysis for theorizing or framing indigeneity and the settler-colonial state; first, we deal with the feminist dilemma of doing research with the Other. Against intersectionality, which presumes a generalized or universal epistemology, Black feminist theory as advocated by Amoah Jewel (2013), among others, argues for the need for the specificity of the marginalized and their experiential life as well as the experience of the researcher. Jewel contends that without experiencing Black women's lived reality, an outsider is incapable of adequately representing Black women's lives. Considering the oppression and marginalization of Black Americans as unique, Jewel (2013: 89) asserts that "Feminist theory is made of women's narratives that are based on women's experiences and that such experiences are *only lived by the women who underwent them*" (emphasis added). While having some merits, this position is quite problematic, as will be seen in the following section.

DOING ORAL HISTORY AMONG THE MARGINALIZED: BETWEEN THE ABSTRACT AND UNIVERSAL AND THE UNIQUE AND ESSENTIALIST

The feminist debate about who can do research on the Other, while an old one, remains problematic, especially within the two most recent feminist developments, namely intersectionality and Black feminist thought. Whereas the former advocates a universal theory or conceptual framework, the latter emphasizes specificity as uniqueness or even as essentialism. Jewel's contention that only Black women can understand the experiences of Black women – and by extension that only women understand women, only the poor understand the poor, and so on – is problematic on several levels. History has shown us that some of the best analyses of patriarchy have been conducted by men (for example, Engels' work on *The Origin of the Family, Private Property and the State*); similarly, the best work on class has been done by Marx in general, and especially in *Capital*. Moreover, ascribing uniqueness or essentialized qualities to any marginalized group is a rather dangerous act. In her response to Susan Armitage along the same lines, Sherna Berger Gluck noted: "I would put considerably more faith in the ability of some of my male colleagues in oral history to apply what we have often referred to as feminist principles than I would some women who are more bound by race, class, gender and sexual orientation" (Armitage and Berger Gluck 1998: 5).

Essentialism is also problematic at the level of shared experiences and solidarity. Prioritizing one form of oppression over another, such as Afro-American experiences over other marginalized experiences, is quite limiting; it restricts the important role of comparability and solidarity under conditions of capitalist imperialism. History provides ample examples of solidarity among women of various cultures and specific instances of oppression, as the Palestinian case demonstrates. My *Captive Revolution* (Abdo 2014) provides a study of the importance of shared experiences within women's struggles, especially among women political detainees; in that book, I compared the struggles of Palestinian women political detainees in Israeli prisons to those of women in other countries and continents during the 1960s. As such, these comparisons enable us to see the shared experiences of women from different cultures and who have different histories.

This brings us to another danger: essentializing victimization and resistance as characteristics of certain marginalized groups. Positioning women in such particularity blinds us to recognizing the possibilities and importance of solidarity these women potentially generate with other women or groups of people, even without prior connection. In my conversations with Palestinian women ex-political detainees, they were very clear on the one hand about who they considered to be "insiders" that support and stand in solidarity with them, and on the other hand who they deemed to be "outsiders", the enemy in their struggle. Women proudly relayed their experiential knowledge of the close solidarity they received while in detention from various other women, including European, North African and North American ones. They knew who practically and actually stood in solidarity with them and their struggle and who among Western (and Israeli) feminists were antagonistic, oppressive and colonialist (Abdo 2014). The women even named foreign (Arab and Western) women who joined their struggle against Israeli occupation and settler colonialism and who were consequently detained by the Israelis.

The critique of the essentialist Black feminist, however, does not invalidate this approach altogether. Jewel's demand that researchers possess a close knowledge and immersion in the culturally and historically specific conditions of the marginalized is important. One needs to remember that not all groups of marginalized women possess the same degree of comfort with an "outsider" such as a researcher. One such "outsider", Ellen Fleishman, in her interviews with Palestinian women found that they "were very wary of the very notion of 'interviews', and that interviews intimidate these women" (Fleishmann 1996: 358). The specific history of this example is that interviews with and questioning of Palestinian women under occupation by "outsiders" has usually involved the occupying forces: that is, the police, security personnel or soldiers – a frightening experience for the occupied. There is no doubt here that an "insider" who experienced occupation might realize the existence of such fear and act accordingly.

My oral history research, based on lengthy conversations with Palestinian women fighters (Abdo 2014), pointed to the importance of language and even of the vernacular as a potential challenge to the outsider-researcher. Language expresses cultural experiences and is grounded in people's material life conditions, and as such requires knowledge of that cultural specificity. For example, some of the women in our conversations together found it difficult to share with the group certain specifics of their sexual harassment in prison, although almost all women prisoners experienced one form or another of such harassment. Some women were unable to name – at least publicly – certain verbal sexual abuses they had experienced, notably being labelled with the socially taboo curse term *sharmouta* (whore, bitch), a word used by Israeli prison officials against the women (on which see Abdo 2014: 160). The courage exhibited by other women participants made it easier for those women to name the act of violence for what it was.

Finally, familiarity with local cultural expressions (e.g. literature, poetry, popular songs, and so on) is also a valuable asset in doing research with the "Other". In my experience, I found familiarity with Palestinian resistance culture – for example, *adab al-muqawama* (resistance literature) and *adab al-sujoun* (prison literature) – to be very useful not only for comprehending women fighters' general status within Palestinian society, but also for appreciating the depth of their expressions and feelings. As I have argued elsewhere, there were few woman who did not recite a poem or a verse or who did not make reference to a particular piece of resistance literature as integral to their political consciousness and their willingness to make sacrifices for the cause (e.g. Abdo 2014: 100, 105, 109–110). In other words, neither an insider (i.e. a member of the class, gender or race) nor an outsider who is equipped only with a general theory of intersectionality can provide a sufficient understanding of all marginalized groups.

Another problematic in the universalist methodology of intersectionality concerns the absence of cultural and historical specificity in its founding concepts. This absence corresponds to the exclusion of the concept of the state as a primary ingredient for a theoretical framework capable of understanding the political economy within which the forms of violence are identified and operate. Intersectionality, which suggests that the forces of violence against women (e.g. gender, class and race) are universal, does not help us understand indigenous women in the context of settler colonialism. Yet, as we shall see later, these forces of violence in a different historical stage, under a different form of state – say, the settler-colonial state – express different relations and take different forms. For example, the existing context of the state in which feminists can speak about concepts like public–private or gender differentiation, as well as the existing highly developed concept of class differentiation, are not applicable to settler colonialism or to understanding the life conditions of indigenous people. Hence the need for a different conceptual framework capable of understanding indigenousness and settler colonialism. An analysis of the lived experiences of indigenous women, as the following argues, necessitates a different feminist approach: one close to the experiences of the indigenous and cognizant of the violence of the settler-colonial regime and which acts with and on behalf of its victims. A feminism with such characteristics, in addition to being able to reach and represent the voices and experiences of indigenous women, can also provide a solution to the feminist debate on representation and the Other.

FEMINIST ANALYSIS OF INDIGENEITY AND SETTLER COLONIALISM

The above critique of the feminist debate on doing research with the Other will be re-examined in the following by focusing on Palestinian women in pre- and post-Nakba Palestine. Highlighted in the process will be the historical and cultural specificity of the settler-colonial state, its role in shaping gender relations, and its impact on women. This analysis will be largely based on raw oral history material (videotapes) of Palestinian refugees gathered through the project *Palestine Remembered*.[1] I will discuss the historically and culturally specific notions of gender and class before and during British and Zionist settler colonialism. The main force of violence faced by indigenous Palestinians, I argue, is the settler-colonial state and not necessarily gender or class. It is this state that decomposes prior social forms and relations and recombines them into settler relations of gender and class. As such, the settler-colonial state must be logically prior to units of analysis such as gender or class. Indigenous peoples who fell under the wrath of the settler-colonial state experienced a totally different history and processes of change and violence than that experienced by marginalized settlers or immigrants. While economically the settler-colonial state – for example, British colonialism and the Zionist settler movement (1920–1948) – engendered many changes in the Palestinian peasant economy as the latter was transformed into a capitalist one, it is the political – and in fact, the existential – ideology of settler colonialism which made the greatest impact.

Unlike capitalism, which is characterized by inclusion and exploitation (e.g. of immigrants, Blacks and people of colour), settler colonialism is a form of capitalism that is primarily genocidal. It targets the physical existence of indigenous people; its ideology is based on wiping out the very physicality or bodies of the indigenous, grabbing and controlling their land, and erasing their culture and history. An epistemology of indigeneity, therefore, will be based on conceptualizing gender and class in their pre-capitalist (peasant) context. It will also be centred on the ontological existence of a group and not on individuals, as in the case of intersectional theory. One distinguishing feature of a feminist indigenous framework will be the latter's focus on genocide and the notions of loss, absences, and erasure of the material and cultural existence of the indigenous.

GENDER AND CLASS AMONG INDIGENOUS PALESTINIANS UP TO THE NAKBA

Until 1948, Palestine had an overwhelmingly agrarian social structure, the vast majority of Palestinians being peasants, producing and reproducing themselves on the land. Both women and men partook in cultivation, planting, cropping and harvesting along with other forms of husbandry, caring for and raising cattle, pigeons, chickens and so on and using them in food production. Until 1948, the division of labour was more sex-based than gender-based: women assumed an equally important role in the production and reproduction processes of the household. In addition, there was very little if any real division between the private and the public spheres. The peasant household was an extension of the field, of the agricultural land, the place for the cattle, the vegetables and trees, the crops and plants. The term *dar* (home) used by the peasants did not express the nuclear home or house that we are familiar with, but rather was used for the space of the *hamula* (the extended family); this was also women's space of work and socialization and of social, political and economic decision-making for the extended family or the village. In pre-conquest Palestine, the *hamula* might occupy a whole village or more than one village.

Upon listening to the voices of many women (and some men) recorded by the *Palestine Remembered* project, I realized the impressive volume of productive work done by women. For example, in one case in the village of Birya (Safad district), Fatima al-Sayyed, a refugee living in Syria, said: "some of the young women would take the figs [fresh and dried] and sell them in the Jewish corner … the road to there is hilly – no busses or cars, we would walk or use donkeys. I used to help my mother in making yogurt, *labneh* [strained yogurt], cheese and honey". In responding to a question concerning schooling, she said:

There were no schools in our village. My father sent me to Ein al-Zatoun [another village] for one day only, one day! My mother complained, telling him, "I am alone and cannot do everything by myself: working outside, inside, caring for the cows, the sheep, the chicken and the grape field". They pulled me out of school after only one day – how sad I became.

When asked about what she played with as a child, she responded: "I never had the time to play; I worked on the land with my father and helped my mother".

> Speaking about healthcare in the village, she said that Amneh, a female villager, used to *tshatteb* [make a cut on the leg or shoulder of the sick person], then burn and wrap the cut. They also used *kasat hawa* [cupping] and herbs, like mint, sage and camomile. The younger girls walked to the well – a long walk from our house – and would fill pots with water, or took the clothes and washed them there. My grandmother was the *daya* [midwife] of most women in the village.

When asked about how the older women entertained themselves, she said: "After they separate the wheat grains, they would take the canes [long wheat straws], colour them, weave them together, and make *atbaq* [straw plates of all sizes for use at home]". As such, even leisure time could have a component of what we might see as work.

Ratiba Abu-Fannah from Kufur Qari' (Haifa district), a refugee from Jordan, had something similar to say:

> We used to bring the water from the well in clay pots. Each one of us would have one pot on her head and two on the donkey. We would take our clothes and wash them there … we also used to make our oven [*taboun*] using fire and clay topped with manure until ready, then bake the bread in it; we planted and harvested using the sickle. One woman would separate the corn, and another, standing with a large *quffah* [a straw bucket] gathered it, and when the *quffah* was full, the men would place it on the donkey or on carts for sale. I used to sew clothes; I swear by God, some nights I slept on the sewing machine out of exhaustion, especially during Ramadan. We also made *khawabi* [clay storage jars] for storing wheat and olive oil. We would go to the wheat mill to grind the wheat and bring the flour. In our house we had cows and sheep; we used to milk the cows and make *labneh* and cheese. I used to collect the eggs from the chicken and sell some of them. We also had pigeons which I took care of and fed.

The testimony of Aisha Khalil from Deir Tarif (al-Ramla district), a refugee in Jordan, corroborated the above experiences of peasant women's work:

In my village there were three or four *dayas*, and they were midwives for all of the women. Every day we used to carry the clay jars, walk to the well and bring water back. At the age of five or six, I started working on our land ... we would spend the whole day working – watering the land by carrying water from the well. We would take turns with the other villagers, using the same well. I used to go fetch *hatab* [wooden logs] for the *taboun* and its fire and fetch the water; we girls would go and pick *fool* [fava beans]. No, no, women never rested or stayed at home ... we would work every hour of the day. I remember how women used to give birth in the field, while working. At the age of six, I used to water the field, one tree after another. My older sister and I would spend the whole day in the field, picking corn, sesame and all ... No sitting at home ... every day we went to the field and returned home with them [the men in the family]. Our life was work ... no rest ... always at work to feed the family ... those in the *dar* worked on cleaning wheat, sesame, barley, hummus, lentils ... we would clean the sesame, let it dry, then clean it and sell it in Ramla [a nearby city].

These oral histories demonstrate a non-capitalist definition of the concept of work as opposed to the form of labour under capitalism, and challenge the distinction between the public and private spheres. Most importantly, they show the strong relationship between land and indigenous women's lives.[2] The work experiences of indigenous peasant women as presented above challenges the gender division of labour in the capitalist context. It also challenges Orientalist feminist perspectives on Muslim/Arab/Palestinian women in which they are cast as "traditional" and silent recipients of their patriarchy (Abu-Lughod 2002).[3] These voices demonstrate that males and females were largely sovereign in their own domains, and male power, while not absent, was not "patriarchal" in the way it is now. "Patriarchy", in other words, is more a result of imperial settler colonialism, which intensified post-Nakba, than being something primordial. A feminist analysis of the colonized, as the following shows, must be cognizant not only of the colonial violence and its direct and indirect effects on women, but also of the latter's experiential reality as agents of change and resistance. Palestinian women's work under colonialism was not confined to the economic sphere of production and reproduction, but also ventured into the political sphere as agents of change and anti-colonial resistance.

WOMEN'S AGENCY AND RESISTANCE

Between 1920 and 1948, a process referred to by Marx as "so-called" primitive accumulation, one defined by Rosa Luxemburg as "imperialism", began to encroach on Palestinian lives. The British, in an effort to pay for the maintenance of their colonial administration, began to impose high taxes on the peasants' lands and property. They also introduced the Land Registry Ordinance in 1920, which aimed at parcelling the otherwise collectively possessed/owned lands for the purpose of taxing them. The inability to pay cash for the tax, as most peasants used a barter system and not money, led to imprisonments and the impoverishment of peasants – estimated in 1930 at 30% – and the confiscation of their land (see Nadan 2007). This process was further exacerbated by the British policies of "opening up" Palestine to the European (Jewish) settlers, policies aimed at establishing a Jewish entity in Palestine. This meant further land confiscation and then transfer to the Zionist settlers.

The violence of settler colonialism in Palestine was met by an equally fierce resistance, especially on the part of its direct victims, the *fallaheen* (peasants). The 1936–1939 revolution, which included a six-month general strike, epitomized this resistance. As the guerrilla war was waged against the British and the Zionist colonial project, violence perpetrated by both the British and the Zionists was inflicted on the indigenous Palestinians; many men were executed, killed, tortured, and imprisoned while women suffered the loss of their loved ones and, in many cases, the destruction of their homes and the ruin of the fruits of their work.

Reflecting on this period, Najiyyeh Ahmad, from Indoor (Nazareth district) and now a refugee in Jordan, had the following to say: "The British were putting a lot of pressure on us; they refused our men the right to sell or export their oranges … you would see the older men sitting and crying". She added that,

> In 1936 after six martyrs from our village fell – I don't know who would inform the *Ingleez* [British] about the *thuwwar* [revolutionaries] in our village … the soldiers surrounded our village, invaded our homes and messed them up; they spilled the oil, mixed the flour with lentils and other grains, and dumped everything on the floor. They killed four men, including my uncle.

Similarly, Said Zubi from Sirin (Beisan district), a refugee in Jordan, whose village was wiped out by the Zionists, reported the following:

Our village revolted in 1936. The British imposed excessive taxation on us; they never accepted produce [in return for taxes], only cash, and we didn't have it. The revolutionaries in Sirin were in the mountains. Most men in the village were trained in using arms. Sheikh Nayef Zubi, a leader in the 1936 revolution, trained all the young men in the village. The British starved us during the revolution ... but we were steadfast and continued with the revolution. The revolutionaries used to hide their weapons in a hole inside the cow barn. My mother snatched a rifle from a lone British soldier and hid it.

The memory of Palestinian women peasants helping and protecting the revolutionaries from the British by hiding their weapons or hiding them in the house and feeding them is a recurrent narrative among many of the stories of the indigenous refugees.

Here is Shahira Sadeq from Deir al-Qadi (Akka district), a refugee in Jordan:

We never wore veils; we wore *mandil* [a traditional Palestinian headdress] decorated with *oya* [needlework]⁴ ... all the women of the village would go out to the main roads and spray the stone roads with water [to prevent dust]. My family helped the *thuwwar*; they cared for them and fed them. One day, the British gathered the *shabab* [young men], brought the *mukhtar* [village elder], and asked him to name them all. He started by saying, "This is ibn N [the son of N], *abu* X [the father of X] ... he named them all, including the *shab* [a young man] whom he didn't know, but who was one of the *thuwwar*. One of the villagers was an informer and told about the *thuwwar*. They used to raid the homes, break the doors, ruin the *mooneh* [food saved from one season to the next], and wreak chaos in the homes. The women in the village knew the *thuwwar*, they cared for them, would cook for them and send them food.

Fatima al-Sayyed, mentioned above, speaks highly of her neighbour's wife, Nathmeh al-Arnous,

who used to wear a cloth belt to hide weapons and would deliver them to her husband ... these were heroes. The British came to the village and demolished four houses ... when he [Nathmeh] was followed by the

British, as I was back from fetching water, I saw him entering my Aunt's house ... she protected and hid him.

Said Zubi succinctly described British and Zionist settler colonialism in Palestine, saying: "The British committed many crimes against us; they intended to erase our identity as Palestinians while at the same time aiding the Zionists against us. We were poor, and the rifle was very expensive ... many villagers sold all they had to buy a rifle and fight them".

The crushing of the Palestinian revolution in 1939 and the start of World War II led to the increased militarization of the Zionist settler movement and intensified violence against indigenous Palestinians, a process which led to the establishment of the state of Israel and to the Palestinian Nakba (catastrophe), which I define as genocide. Genocide, which represents the utmost form of violence afflicting the indigenous people, must be at the core of our feminist analysis.

THE NAKBA THROUGH INDIGENOUS PALESTINIAN VOICES

Before theorizing the Nakba as genocide, we shall refer to the voices of Palestinian women (and men) expressing the violence of the Zionist settler-colonial forces – violence which targeted their physical and bodily existence in addition to their cultural and historical being. In Sirin, where most of the village males were involved in anti-colonial resistance in the 1930s and throughout the 1940s, Said Zubi testified:

The Zionists forced the village women to leave in 1947, and led them by force towards Jordan ... Until May 1948, the men kept infiltrating their village during the *hasad* [harvest season] to bring wheat to their families. But they would be attacked by the Zionists, forcing them to flee under fire. In May 1948, after they occupied Nazareth, the Zionists destroyed Sirin, turning it into rubble. They bombed Sirin and all the villages around Beisan. How hard we fought them, but [Said Zubi was crying at this point], we were defeated!

Aisha Khalil recalls:

Before we *tahajjarna* [were forced to leave], *ahel* [families/villagers] of Deir Tarif each owned a rifle. Each day, one *hamula* member would spend the night out, protecting *athyal al-balad* [the outskirts of the village] … until the Jews surrounded us and we became very frightened. In the meantime, we were hearing news about the massacre in Ramla, where they killed people in the Mosque, and we became very scared. The whole village also heard about the massacre of Deir Yassin [where 249 women, men, and children were massacred by the Zionist Irgun] and the news about butchering pregnant women. Our family, like others in the village, said that we didn't want this to happen to us. The *shabab* in our village would go to the *Abbasiyya* district and partake in the resistance. One day a plane dropped bombs at the outskirts of my village. I was fetching water at the *Ain* [well] when I heard the bombs; I ran back home with the empty *jarra* [water jar] and saw two villagers and told them: "Let's leave before they kill us all".

Heavy Zionist shelling of Palestinian villages and towns from late 1947 and throughout 1948 and the terrorizing of the Palestinians was frequently recounted by those interviewed. Suad and Mary Andrawus from Tiberias, who both said they had a good relationship with their Jewish neighbours before "those who came from outside [i.e. Zionist settlers]" arrived, tell horrifying stories about how the Arabs in Tiberias were treated by the British and explaining how the real terror that forced them to leave the city was from those "Jews who came from outside". Mary said:

My younger brother was with the *thuwwar* until the end … one day, a British soldier knocked our door with the butt of his gun. My mother opened the door, and she told him in English that he could come in and search the house. He wanted to go up into the *siddeh* [an attic used for storage], my mother went and brought him a ladder and told him to climb … he realized there was nothing there and left. The British terrified our neighbourhood. One day a man who was afraid of their raids carried his baby on his arm and tried to leave his house … when the soldier saw him, he shot and killed both of them.

Speaking of her own encounter, Mary recalled: "One day my brother saw the soldiers coming; he rushed to the house and said, 'They are here', and he asked me to hide the Sten [a British sub-machine gun]. I didn't know we had weapons … I took the Sten, broke it into three parts … and hid it there … that day ended peacefully." Urban middle-class women like Mary and Suad remember the terrifying attacks of the Zionists which led them, and others, to leave Tiberias:

> The *thuwwar* defended the city until May 1948, when the Jews – not our neighbours, but those who came from outside – surrounded Tiberias on three sides. The city was shelled day and night; you could see the women, children, and the old running from house to house seeking shelter … a state of utter terror … this is how we left.

This is also how Najiyyeh Ahmad, her family and members of the village "left". Referring to the Zionists, she said: "They shelled us with their artillery. They would fire on us early in the morning while we were still asleep. Some of the villagers who were protecting us were martyred … this is how we left. We left under fire and shells."

The Palestinian Nakba/genocide was not an event or a moment, but rather a process which began before 1948 and which has continued from 1948 until the present. Further uprootedness, massacres, bombardments, destruction of homes and erasure of whole villages accompanied the Palestinians even during and after their *tahjeer* (forced expulsion) from their homes and villages. The terror of Zionist settler colonialism haunted the refugees until many had fled the country. This and the following voices and testimonies present a clear indication of the historically specific nature of the Palestinian Nakba: a step-by-step yet continuous genocide.

Initially, the movement of those who left was out of the home but not out of the Palestinian homeland, and each village and town had its own story of the process of forced displacement. Importantly, these expellees never thought they were leaving their homes for ever, let alone leaving their homeland altogether. Forced to leave their homes, most villagers took refuge among family and friends in nearby villages; they stayed there until those villages and cities were also attacked and they were all forced out of the land of Palestine. In other words, the path of almost all Palestinians was not a straight one to the outcome that the Israelis had planned for them: a total displacement from the whole of Palestine; again, leaving the homeland had not been the intention of the Palestinians. Instead, a temporary departure was what they imagined, hence the rush of most expellees and the terrorized, leaving their homes open, running barefoot and in their nightwear, leaving behind all of their personal belongings.

Ibrahim Saleh from al-Shajarah (Tiberias district), a refugee in Syria, described what happened in his village:

Ten days before May 1948, after hearing about the massacres in the neighbouring villages of Lubieh, Deir Yassin, Arab al-Safih, Ain al-Yassin and Ain al-Zaitoun, we sent the women and children, those who could walk, to Nazareth and Reineh, where we had friends and relatives. They took nothing with them … all properties and belongings were left in the homes. On May 1948, at three a.m., a large number of Zionists [the Hagana] raided the village. They used artillery and not tanks, as in the case of Lubieh, because our village was hilly. My father took his rifle, and I and my cousin ran out. They surrounded al-Shajarah from all sides, and started shelling … 28 martyrs fell. We thought it would be a matter of seven or eight days and then the attack would stop. We left for Kufur Kanna [a village near Nazareth] and stayed there for three months. During this period, the *hasad* [harvest] began; we used to infiltrate al-Shajarah to harvest the wheat and bring it to our families.

Ibrahim continued:

One night, while in Kufur Kanna, we were shocked to see women and children from Saffourieh passing through the village and heading towards Shafa-Amr, which was already occupied. It turned out their village [Saffourieh] was bombed by planes, and they escaped under the heavy bombardment. The next day they surrounded Nazareth with tanks. I took my mother out of Kufur Kanna and walked to Arraba [a village in the upper Galilee]; my father, who was injured, stayed in Kufur Kanna. We stayed in Arraba for ten days. While walking through the corn fields I saw many corpses. The next day in Kufur Kanna, the Jews surrounded the village and searched it for infiltrators. I was rescued by the village *mukhtar* who identified me as a member of the village. That night my mother and I left Kufur Kanna and reached al-Bieineh; I left my mother there and ran to Arraba, found a room and then brought my mother back with me. After one week the Jews occupied Sakhnin and continued on to Arraba … it is only then that we left Palestine for Bint Jbeil [in southern Lebanon].

This narrative, which turned into a pattern, was corroborated by many others, including Abu Raed from Beisan, Huda Hanna, Shahira Sadeq and Najiyye Ahmad.

Fidda Issa from Breij (Jerusalem district) related the tale of her village:

> They were hailing bombs on us. The bombs fell on people's sheep and between the houses. I am so sad for the *fallaheen*! We, the women and children, ran for our lives, while the men stayed in Breij, fighting. When we arrived in Zakariyya, we found its villagers running ahead of us ... all of us were tired and exhausted ... The people of Surif who were resisting the Jews also ended up *shardeen* [running with no end in sight]. We went crazy and couldn't see anything in front of us. We stayed in the open for a long time... *Wallahi* [I swear by God] no one knew where her husband or family were.

A similar story was told by Mary and Suad:

> Fear for our lives led us to leave Safad. The Arab quarter in Tiberias was attacked, day and night. They used bombs and artillery; we were terrified ... we did not want to leave our home, but in the absence of our mother and father who had already died and my younger brother who was with the resistance, the two of us ran for safety to my aunt's house. After a few days, I went to my house to bring some stuff only to find our house full of bullets. We left for Rameh, carrying with us only a few clothes and the key to the house ... One night in Rameh there was shelling, and the whole village left their homes and took shelter, some in the church and others in the mosque. After this, the people of Safad started to arrive in Rameh under heavy rain and with their feet covered in mud.

Fatima al-Sayyed, from the village of Birya, again:

> It never occurred to us that we would leave Birya, but *shoo bti'emal el-ain quddam al-makhraz* [what can the eye do when faced by the needle – an expression of powerlessness]? Birya was on the hill; we saw the bombs falling on Safad. They killed 25 people and I know each one of them by name. They came against us with tanks. Most of the Hagana were

Hagganat [female members of the Hagana]. We ran; those who had flour carried some on their heads, and many were hungry. It was harvest time. I had to sell my bracelet in order to buy olive oil. People would come to us, begging for flour to eat. I wish we could have harvested more wheat … It was left for the Jews. My father left Birya barefoot and came to Safad crying. We left on 15 May; I carried both my six-month-old baby and two-year-old. My mother-in-law was killed by one of the shells, and my brother-in-law was shot and killed by them. We left Safad with nothing, nothing whatsoever.

Fatima, although she had been smiling throughout the interview, started crying when asked about how her family left Birya: "We were forced to leave our homes, our belongings [crying and wiping her tears] what can I tell you? I am pained, my heart is bleeding." Without any hesitation, almost all of the Palestinian women and men interviewed insisted that if they had known that they would never be returning to their homes, land and homeland, they would never have left and would have preferred to die there rather than become refugees.

Palestinian victims of the genocide also stated what they want, need and hope for. Shahira Sadeq: "If they refuse to give us our 1967 lands, surely they would not give us our 1948 lands? I wish we could return. I just want to see my home, our land." Najiyyeh Ahmad: "Wallahi, Ain Ndoor is my life, my mother, grandfather and father. We will stay in a cave, but let us return. We constantly sit with our children and tell them, 'If you don't return, your children will'." Aisha Khalil, who ended up in Ramalla, visited her village after the 1967 occupation and recalled: "All the houses were destroyed; the Jews did not leave a stone untouched. I cried for more than a whole week. I used to cry and say: 'Allah Akbar [God is Great] and with His help, our rights will be regained'."

Similar hopes and wishes were voiced by almost all those interviewed. The evidence in all of the oral stories of the Palestinians recorded by the *Palestine Remembered* project is that despite the passage of time, their memory of identity, belonging and history has never faded away. While historically specific, the Nakba, the Zionist settler-colonial project – Israeli terror – against the Palestinians was and remains a clear form of genocide. This is true both empirically, as demonstrated above in the voices and experiences of the Palestinians, as well as theoretically and conceptually, as will be shown shortly.

LAND AND GENOCIDE: THE ESSENCE FOR INDIGENOUSNESS AND SETTLER COLONIALISM

Land

Land for indigenous peoples is not simply a commodity, a piece of real estate, as so often is the case with settlers and immigrants; rather, for indigenous women (and men), it serves as the primary material source of life. It is also the major constituent of natives' sense of community and peoplehood and the space where social organization happens, as well as their source of pride, honour and integrity as a nation or collectivity. The loss of land for indigenous Palestinians meant the loss of their lives as they had experienced them; it was and is the loss of their very history and existential being. More than any other identity (say gender, class, etc.), land constitutes the distinctive identity and belonging for the indigenous women (and men), the victims of settler colonialism. Therefore land, its meaning for the indigenous people and the implication of its loss to the settler-colonial states, must occupy a central place in any feminist theory. After all, the loss of land for these people means the loss of their identity as a people, as the victims of settler-colonial violence. It follows that a proper analysis of the "marginalized" – in this case, indigenous women – is not attainable unless special consideration is given to this force – land – in the lives of the indigenous and the meaning of its loss under settler colonialism.

Nakba as Genocide

For the last decade or so, the discourse on the Palestinian ordeal of Israeli atrocities between 1947 and 1948 has largely been discussed in the context of the Nakba. This term, when used in Arabic, indicates a major loss, the death of not only loved ones but also the death or end of life for the *mankoub*, the individual or the group upon which a Nakba has befallen. However, local and international academics engaged in the discourse on the Nakba have rarely, if ever, attempted to theorize the Nakba as a form of genocide. Studies on genocide have largely been centred around the *Shoah* (Holocaust), the Nazi atrocities against the Jews, and rightly so. Yet even the first Western genocide against the aboriginal/native peoples in North America has not been able to engender any significant attention until very recently (see Churchill 1998).

Determining whether or not Israel has been responsible for appropriating the term genocide, rendering it applicable only to Jews, is not the point of this discussion. Nor does this specific chapter deal with how or why Israel and the United

States have been ignoring and silencing any discussion of the Nakba (on these issues, see Rosemary Sayigh's chapter in this volume; and Finkelstein 2015). What is important is that more scholars, including Israeli and Jewish ones, have begun using terms that signify something close to the meaning of the term genocide in order to describe the Nakba. For example, the terms "ethnic cleansing" introduced by Ilan Pappé (2006) or "incremental genocide" used by, among others, Ilan Pappé (2015a), Martin Shaw (2010), and Philip Weiss (2017) have become part of the discourse on the Nakba. In fact, the term genocide itself has been used by international law professor Francis Boyle (2013) in referring to the Nakba. This is in addition to the recently growing body of literature describing Israel as a settler-colonial apartheid state (Pappé 2015b; Davis 1987; Abdo 2011, 2014).

Central in most studies on the genocidal processes of the Nakba has been the question of "erasure" as the primary marker of settler-colonial Israel; thus the concept "toponymicide", used to describe the erasure of place names in Palestine and their replacement with Hebrew (Jewish) names; "cultural genocide", used in reference to the erasure of about 500 Palestinian villages and towns; "memoricide", used of the erasure of the Palestinian identity from Israeli (Jewish) memory; and "politicide", referring to the erasure of Palestinian identity as a political collectivity (see Masalha 2012: 1, 4, 10; Abdo 2014: 78). Combined, these policies and acts of erasure conducted by the Zionist settler-colonial project during and immediately after the Nakba constitute a major part of the definition of a genocide; while accepting the concept of "incremental genocide", I consider the Nakba itself to be an act of genocide. The concept of genocide was introduced in 1944 by Raphael Lemkin and adopted in 1948 through the UN Convention on the Prevention and Punishment of the Crime of Genocide:

> More often [the term genocide] refers to a coordinated plan aimed at destruction of the essential foundations of the life of national groups so that these groups wither and die like plants that have suffered a blight. The end may be accomplished by the forced disintegration of political and social institutions, of the culture of the people, of their language, their national feelings and their religion. It may be accomplished by wiping out all bases of personal security, liberty, health and dignity ... Genocide is directed against a national group as an entity and the attack on individuals is only secondary to the annihilation of the national group to which they belong. (Lemkin 1945)

Lemkin's definition of genocide as an act "directed against a national group as an entity and the attack on individuals is only secondary to the annihilation of the national group to which they belong" aptly describes the Palestinian Nakba and removes any ambiguity concerning it being an actual genocide.

The Zionist genocide in Palestine, reflected in the experiences of loss and erasure, has affected about 80% of the pre-Nakba Palestinians, forcing them off their land and out of their homes and homeland, turning them into refugees. Not unlike the experiences of other indigenous groups that faced the wrath of settler colonialism, understanding Palestinian women's experiences must account for these two forces: the absence of land and genocide.

CONCLUSION: TOWARDS AN ANTI-COLONIAL FEMINISM OF INDIGENEITY

As indigenous Palestinians have testified, land constituted their way of life. It was and continues to be remembered by the uprooted – the uprooted-cum-refugees – as the source of their economic, social and cultural identity. Despite the passing of over seven decades in their *shatat* (dispersed existence), refugee women (and men) continue to reproduce their homes, land and homeland through their vivid memories. This memorialization of the indigenous Palestinian life experiences constitutes the basis of any theorization or framing of their history.

Consequently, feminist theorization of indigenousness in general, including Palestinian indigenousness, needs to historicize its conceptual bases, adopting historically and culturally specific concepts suitable to the time, history and context within which women are located. This means refraining from the imposition of concepts developed within the capitalist system onto pre-capitalist economies. It also means that gender, race and class must not be dealt with as independent and universal categories or concepts, but rather as historically and culturally specific forces moulded within a specific political economy, in this case the settler-colonial state. As such, feminist theorization of indigeneity would become centred on the interlock between indigenous women (and men) with the land; it would be entrusted with analysing the dynamics between women and land. Moreover, situating feminist analysis of the violence against the natives within the context of land furnishes the grounds for a more holistic theory, one that goes beyond the individual into the group/nation, recognizing, in the process, their existence as a cultural and historical collectivity.

Centring indigenousness as a collectivity and realizing women's (and men's) connection with the land enables us also to recognize the meaning and effect of the loss on the souls that inhabited it. The loss of land in this case constitutes the utmost violence inflicted on indigenous peoples as a group. This loss establishes the erasure of their very existence as an economic, cultural and national group. It also establishes the elimination of the body, the social fabric and the history of the indigenous. A feminism which fails to account for all such losses also fails to properly capture the actual experiences of indigenous women in general, including those of the Palestinians.

At this point I would like to say that recent feminist contributions by Lena Jayyusi and Diana Allan have made an important feminist breakthrough in discussing the relationship between epistemology and ontology based on women's memories and stories of the Palestinian genocide. Using interdisciplinary approaches, these authors employ powerful concepts such as "valency" and "affect" to describe the implications of the Nakba/genocide for women's bodies, enriching, in the process, feminist understanding of such severe losses or genocide (see both chapters in this volume).

Finally, feminist conceptualization and contextualization of indigeneity and settler colonialism expands feminist research methods, and especially oral history, by focusing on questions such as how the very existence of a whole collectivity – or part thereof – along with its economic, cultural and geographical identity, gets wiped off of the map. How do women remember land and genocide? How do they recount or remember their experiences of death, loss, absence and so on? With such questions asked, feminist analysis will be able to surpass its purely academic state and move into the practical realm of acknowledging the plight of indigeneity. This recognition would be an important message to the state and the world, asking for recognition of its role in land theft and genocide and, implicitly, would demand that the right of the indigenous to their lands and homeland be respected. In the Palestinian context such a vital message would remind the world as well as the settler-colonial states, including Israel, of the just right of the Palestinians to return; it would remind them of the needs, wants, hopes and dreams of Palestinian refugees/expellees.

In other words, using anticolonial feminist methodology can turn feminism from its existing purely academic endeavours into an active call for the right of indigenous peoples; it would transform the discipline of feminism into an anti-colonial voice of action. With such a message, feminist oral history of indigenousness would become entrusted with not only reinstating women into their own history, but also reinstating the history of indigeneity itself, that of both women and men. Within the context of the Middle East in general and the Palestinians more specifically, an anti-colonial feminist methodology would become a means to counteract both Israel's continuing settler-colonial policies and its denial of the very existence of Palestinians. Used as a compass for feminism, anti-colonial analysis would serve as the true voices of women (and men) from below. Such a position, I conclude, can contribute to solving existing feminist debate on who can research whom or the debate between a generalized theory and the unique/essentialist one.

NOTES

1   See http://www.palestineremembered.com/OralHistory/Interviews-Listing/Story1151. html.

2   The question of whether there was a class difference between peasants, for example between the peasant and the big landlord or landowner, is clearly to be answered in the affirmative. However, and throughout British colonialism, considering that most Palestinian landlords were absentee, this meant very little to the peasants, who in most cases recognized the landowners not directly but indirectly as crop-sharers. Peasants recognized the land which they have been living on and off for hundreds of years as being their own possession. The division among Palestinian women in terms of work and education was rural–urban. It is important to note that many villages never had a school under British colonialism. Children, mostly boys, would travel by foot to a nearby village or town for basic elementary schooling (grades 1–4), whereas most cities had some schools, primarily but not solely built by Christian missionaries. This point was clarified by Mary from Tiberias, who attended elementary school in her city and went to the teachers' college in Jerusalem. Mary also named several other upper-middle class urban women from Nazareth, Yafa and Jerusalem who attended the collage at the same time.

3   The oral narratives also contradict male Palestinian impressions of women as *hadar* (stay-at-home women with no presence in the public sphere), as some men interviewed in the same refugee camp suggested. It is important to remember that all interviewers in the *Palestine Remembered* project were males, who, when interviewing the men, hardly asked them about women's work.

4   During the late 1960s and early 1970s I, along with many other young women in Nazareth, used to don this kind of headdress as a national marker.

REFERENCES

Abdo, N. (2011) *Women in Israel: Race, Gender and Citizenship*. London: Zed Books.

Abdo, N. (2014) *Captive Revolution: Palestinian Women's Anti-Colonial Struggle within the Israeli Prison System*. London: Pluto.

Abu-Lughod, L. (2002) "Do Muslim Women Need Saving? Reflections on Cultural Relativism and its Others", *American Anthropologist* 104(3): 783–790.

Armitage, S. and S.B. Gluck (1998) "Reflections on Women's Oral History: An Exchange", *Journal of Women Studies* 19(3): 1–11.

Boyle, F. (2013) "The Palestinian Genocide", A testimony before the Kuala Lumpur War Crimes Tribunal, 21–24 August.

Churchill, W. (1998) *A Little Matter of Genocide*. San Francisco: City Lights.

Crenshaw, K. (1989) "Demarginalizing the Intersection of Race and Sex: A Black Feminist Critique", *University of Chicago Legal Forum* 140: 139–167.

Crenshaw, K. (2016) "The Urgency of Intersectionality", http://www.ted.com/talks/kimberle_crenshaw_the_urgency_of_intersectionality.

Davis, A. (1981) *Women, Race and Class*. Toronto: Vintage.

Davis, U. (1987) *Israel, an Apartheid State*. London: Zed Books, The Holocaust Industry.

Finkelstein, N. (2015) *The Holocaust Industry: Reflections on the Exploitation of Jewish Suffering*. London: Verso.

Fleishmann, E.L. (1996) "Crossing the Boundaries of History: Exploring Oral History in Researching Palestinian Women in the Mandate Period", *Women's History Review* 5(3): 531–571.

Jewel, A. (2013) "Narrative: The Road to Black Feminist Theory", *Berkeley Journal of Gender, Law and Justice* 12(1): Article 5.

Lemkin, R. (1945) "Genocide – A Modern Crime", http://www.preventgenocide.org/lemkin/freeworld1945.htm.

Masalha, N. (2012) *Palestine Nakba: Decolonizing History, Narrating the Subaltern, Reclaiming Memory*. London: Zed Books.

Matsuda, M.J., C.R. Lawrence, R. Delgado and K.W. Crenshaw (1993) *Words that Wound: Critical Race Theory, Assaultive Speech and the First Amendment*. Boulder, CO: Westview.

Nadan, A. (2007) "The Palestinian Peasant Economy under the Mandate: A Story of Colonial Bungling", *Middle East Journal* 61(4): 734–736.

Pappé, I. (2006) *The Ethnic Cleansing of Palestine*. Oxford: Oneworld.

Pappé, I., ed. (2015a) *Israel and South Africa: The Many Faces of Apartheid*. London: Zed Books.

Pappé, I. (2015b) "A Brief History of Israel's Incremental Genocide", in N. Chomsky and I. Pappé (eds.), *On Palestine*. Chicago: Haymarket.

Sangster, J. (1994) "Telling Our Stories: Feminist Debates and the Use of Oral History", *Women's History Review* 3(1): 5–28.

Sangster, J. (2012) "Oral History and Working Class History: A Rewarding Alliance", http://www.oralhistoryforum.ca/index.php/ohf/article/viewFile/459/538.

Shaw, M. (2010) "Palestine in an International Historical Perspective on Genocide", *Journal of Holy Land Studies* 1(13): 1–24.

Weiss, P. (2017) "Israel's Efforts to Erase Palestinian History Reflect 'Incremental Genocide', Ehrenreich Says", http://mondoweiss.net/2017/02/palestinian-incremental-ehrenreich.

Yuval-Davis, N. (2006) "Intersectionality and Feminist Politics", *European Journal of Women's Studies* 13(3): 193–209.

PART II
Between epistemology and ontology: Nakba embodiment

3

What bodies remember: sensory experience as historical counterpoint in the Nakba Archive

DIANA ALLAN

A place is not only a geographical area; it's also a state of mind. And trees are not just trees; they are the ribs of childhood. (Darwish 2010: 15)

Mahmoud Darwish's autobiographical prose poem, *Journal of an Ordinary Grief*, opens with a dialogue between the author and his childhood self as he recalls the events that led his family into exile in 1948, first to Lebanon and then as internal refugees in the newly-formed state of Israel. The five-year-old apprehends the scope and meaning of violent dislocation through the growing despair of those around him. He recalls the sound of his mother's melancholy songs of loss, "like primitive psalms" (Darwish 2010: 22), and his grandfather's daily ritual of reading the news to gathered relatives in exile, "a weakness beginning to creep into his voice" (2010: 12) as the months pass. Fragmentary memories, charged with the heightened perception of childhood, evoke the experience of living through the disastrous events of 1948. Darwish's visceral descriptions of places, things and ways of being, and the "ordinary" grief taking hold around him, as it settles into permanence, reclaim the dilatory contingencies and particularities of lived experience. A language of the body shapes intellection and expression, underscoring how social and material worlds are sensed, and how sense matters for communicating experience. At other moments Darwish invokes corporeal knowledge to advance moral and political claims. Later in the text he addresses an imagined Israeli reader: "The true homeland is that which cannot be known or proved. Your ability to manufacture proof does not give you priority of belonging vis-à-vis someone who can tell when the rains will come from the smell of that rock. For you that rock is an intellectual exercise, but for its owner it is a roof and a wall" (Darwish 2010: 39).

This struggle between these two different kinds of knowing – one episte-mological, the other ontological, with the former learned and the latter lived – has its scholarly analogues in the production of Palestinian pasts. The linear, teleological narrative of Palestinian nationhood that reasserts the links between history, identity and territory and enacts a sovereign national consciousness, consistently trumps the more amorphous elements of lived experience and sense perception, what Siegfried Kracauer called "the half-cooked states of our everyday world" (1920, cited in Harootunian 2004). Burdened by the political imperative to document and transcend ongoing, colonial destruction, Pales-tinian historiography and memorial practice have often been conceptualized as tools of resistance that bridge a catastrophic past and a nation yet to come. This suturing of history and nation, as a redemptive purposeful form, has functioned as a category of exclusion, privileging certain events and causal factors – colo-nial forces, political figures, government commissions, traumatic violence and modes of resistance – over accounts of everyday experience, which tend to figure as irreducible and unassimilable.

Predictably, the exclusions have also been gendered (the heroic, "political" sacrifices of men taking precedence over the private, domestic worlds of women) and affective, with expository, event-driven history occluding embodied forms of knowledge and recollection. Affective states often appear at odds with national ones: rooted in highly localized forms of knowing, inscribed in bodied selves, and regarded as irredeemably subjective, they appear out of synch with the urgency of Palestinian politics and scholarship. Scholars are more likely to turn to histor-ical "documents" and sift for "facts" than attend to the complex interplay of experience and expression, subjective and objective reality, or how the senses and emotions inform representation. This hesitancy is perhaps understandable. Media portrayals of Palestinian political culture as violent and impulsive may have inclined scholars to invest agency in more rational, dispassionate actors. It also expresses the desire for an effective and credible counter-narrative, capable of matching, mirroring and disrupting the positivism of the Israeli narrative, what Edward Said (1984) called "permission to narrate". The enduring legacy of

Said's critique of Orientalism (Said 1978) has also contributed to wariness about reinforcing a specious dualism of Western rationalism and Eastern sensualism. Even more broadly, the Cartesian privileging of cognition and speech over the embodied sensorium continues to set parameters not only for analytical rigour and academic value, but for what in informal contexts counts as intelligible and communicable.

While we might intuit why trees for Darwish are "the ribs of childhood", the phenomenological intimacies of attachment that underpin allegorical imagery and sentiment in Palestinian narratives are more often assumed than analysed. What might a study of how people know the time of rain from the smell of a rock entail? What is distinctive about olfaction, as opposed to touch, and what possibilities does it afford for comprehending and representing experience in this context? How is the act of imagining the smell of stone different from the sensory experience of perception itself? And why might this line of inquiry trigger a twinge of scepticism for many readers? Similarly, affective experience often appears too suffused to be a coherent object of study in and of itself, imagined more like an aggregation of elements on the edge of consciousness. By normative measures of social and political accountability, addressing how Palestinians apprehend and are tethered to the world through their senses seems an epiphenomenal detour that risks deflecting attention away from the political forces at work at precisely the moment they demand close scrutiny. Pre-modern temporalities – along with other preliterate cultural registers and non-word-based forms of knowing that diffract or disrupt the spatio-temporal unity of nation-formation and rational subject-formation – appear problematically opaque. While sensory perception continues to figure prominently in Palestinian literature, with a few notable exceptions it remains understudied in Palestinian scholarship.[1]

This tacit hierarchy has had profound implications for our understanding of Palestinian history and experience as something fundamentally discursive rather than embodied, eventful rather than durational. It posits agency as an attribute of conscious mind, while affect is located in the body, beyond interpretive reach. Despite a growing recognition that Palestinian memory and history are sites of struggle and contestation, with greater attention given to regional and economic diversity, and to groups hitherto marginalized in Palestinian historiography (women, peasants, Bedouin, poor city dwellers, refugees), this revisionism has not extended to a more radical rehistoricizing of historical experience itself.[2] Embodied experience – the "felt immediacies"

(Desjarlais 1997) of everyday life – is rarely explored as historical sense. Instead, polyvocality often stands in for those "semi-raw" elements of the past and their complex, lingering affects in the present. "Structures of feeling" add colour or depth to historical narrative more often than they constitute subjects of study in and of themselves. The body, however, is not only a bio-political subject but a locus of knowledge, both in its individual particularity and as a shared "common sense". Habit, routine and embodiment are modes of knowing that shape how people comprehend and ascribe meaning to their material and social environment over time. While Darwish's staged encounter of what is felt with what is "known" mobilizes sensory registers for ideological ends, his poetry also underscores the significance of corporeal experience for rethinking established historical genres and, more broadly, our categories of truth and plausibility. The affective intensities of sense perception – what Lauren Berlant (2011: 53) calls the "elsewhere to sovereign consciousness" – which shape all aspects of subjective life and connect individuals to each other, represent another point of entry and site of inquiry.

It was the experience of working on the Nakba Archive in the Palestinian community in Lebanon that led me to recognize the importance of embodied knowledge and the relative impoverishment of analysis of the senses.[3] Recording interviews on film with Palestinian elders revealed the gravitational force nationalist narrative exerts on individual recollection (Allan 2007, 2014), and the tensions and synergies between embodied and discursive forms of meaning-making. As a medium, the indexical properties of film afforded different possibilities for exploring the affective and sensorial registers lost or distorted in transcription, and the role non-verbal modes of expression play in communicating experience.[4] As the ethnographic filmmaker and theorist David MacDougall (2006: 1) insists, "seeing not only makes us alive to the appearance of things but to being itself". Watching elders speak and listening to their stories, rather than reading them in text, altered my understanding of how experiences are lived, remembered and represented, their complex texture and acute affectivity. As oral historian Alessandro Portelli (1991) observes, meaning emerges in oral narratives as much through the metacommunicative energies of performance as through linguistic content. Recorded narratives had their own velocity and force. Rhythm, gesture, tone and inflection were often as important for communication and apprehension as what was said. Pivotal events could be described in moments, while seemingly incidental occurrences could take hours. An interview recorded in 2005 with Said Otruk, an elderly fishermen from Acre, is dominated by lengthy and evocative descriptions of long days at sea, the fish he caught – the peculiar marvel of "boneless fish" found off Acre's coast that were "all flesh" – nets and particular fishing techniques, and his relations with his crew.[5] His description of his flight into exile in April 1948 is reduced to a single, repeated sentence: "And we got on the boat."[6]

While Otruk's descriptions of line fishing and purse-seining techniques – *jarjara*, *sharak* and *jaroofi* – might at first sight seem insignificant, or at least lack the moral imperative that would lead to broader historicizing reflection, they are bound up with other genealogies of knowing. His accounts of the material and social world of work at sea reveal an orientation to place rooted in everyday relations and routines of labour. When Otruk describes the tug on the fishing line as "beautiful" and mimics the action of the sinking float with his hand, we sense the "social aesthetics" (MacDougall 2006) recalled in that gesture and feel the pleasure it evokes. Thought becomes kinaesthetic as memories are recalled in the muscles, illustrating the tactility of knowledge (indeed, metaphors of comprehension through contact abound: we grasp meaning, are touched, struck, moved and so on). Daily routines also figure as the site where Otruk's relations with Jewish settlers were played out. He recalls Jewish families living in a nearby coastal settlement who would come to the beach and watch them work ("never bother[ing] us").[7] In such moments, other ways of conceptualizing the relation between Palestinian "self" and Israeli "other" – beyond the paradigm of national–ethnic partition – come into view (Azoulay 2013).[8] As the Palestinian struggle is re-conceptualized as a project of decolonization, pre-statist imaginaries of land, self and society embedded in customary practices and habitual ways of life offer alternative avenues for conceptualizing social relations and what it means to belong to a particular place.

If a cartographic imaginary of nationhood and native sovereignty have rendered some experiences more valuable than others, how might we reclaim remaindered forms of historical sense? For Jean Genet, another chronicler of Palestinian life, affect and the senses are central for rendering experience. "I'm not an archivist, or a historian or anything like it", Genet confesses at the outset of *Prisoner of Love* (1986), which describes the nine months he spent with Palestinian *fedayeen* fighters in the Jordanian desert in 1970. He continues with the disarming admission that he had failed to understand the Palestinian revolution he witnessed. "If the reality of time spent among – not with – the

Palestinians resided anywhere", he writes, "it would survive between all the words that claim to give an account of it" (Genet 1986: 5). The acknowledgement of a reality beyond and between words is neither paradox nor mere rhetoric but rather a call for a different order of engagement. The embodied world of the military camp he conjures seems suspended, untethered to chronology, to plotlines partisan or otherwise; he catches the spirit of revolt mid-moment, in the gestures and body language of military commandos. Genet gives us fighters playing cards with an imaginary deck, through carefully choreographed gestures, or singing to each other across hills, competing with the "voice" of stream below; the rituals of washing and shaving; banal moments of listlessness and boredom. Bodies – Genet's and those of others around him – are instruments of perception and inscription, "a general setting" that "co-exists with the world", in the manner envisaged by the phenomenological philosopher, Maurice Merleau-Ponty (1962: 250).

Said once described Genet's account of Palestinian experience as seismographic, "drawing and exposing the fault lines that a largely normal surface had hidden" (cited in Soueif 2003: xiv). Genet was indifferent to the success of the national project and keenly aware of the threat posed by statist and institutional ideologies.[9] His close examination and interpretation of everyday life in Ajloun is concerned with causal structures rather than with the moment captured, and offers a generative model of sensory poetics. It is embodied and intensely felt. If event-driven historical narratives have constrained our ability to engage the affective complexities and contradictions of indigenous pasts, sensory poetics may suggest alternatives. "Accounting for what duress looks like needs the poetics of thought to make its case", observes Ann Laura Stoler (2016: 36), highlighting the importance of sensate bodies for accessing pasts. "Sensorial insights", Stoler continues, are "crucial to the critical impulses that hover unarticulated on our tongues and that flourish in what some are already saying and others of us cannot hear". By circumventing familiar representational strategies and methods of inquiry, embodied experience and poetics may introduce new possibilities for scholars of Palestine.

DISPLACED PASTS

Not long after I began research in Shatila in 2002 I was drawn into a discussion that seemed to perform the intergenerational transmission of memories of the expulsion that I had come to Beirut half-expecting to find. I was sitting drinking tea with Umm Mahmud and her husband Munir on the roof of their home between lines of billowing laundry when we were joined by their elderly neighbour, Abu Hamadi. After more tea and banter, it became clear that he had come to us to escape domestic turmoil. His son was visiting from Berlin with his German wife, and she had refused to travel to Nahr el-Bared camp, in north Lebanon, to see relatives. "When I was young marriage was not for love like nowadays", complained Abu Hamadi, alluding to the fact that his lovesick son had lost all ability to reason with his wife. "You know how I met my wife?", he asked:

> When I was eight years old I got beaten up at school. A boy in my class defended me and we became good friends. Later he suggested we swap sisters. How could I say no? I was engaged at thirteen. After the events [1948] I risked my life to bring my wife to Lebanon. I returned a year later to get her. She had not left with me, but remained with my mother in Nahef [a village in the Northern Galilee]. When I came to Lebanon I first lived in Bint Jbeil [in south Lebanon]. It took me a day and a night to walk to Nahef. I walked through the mountains in the dark … There was no border then, it was open, you could move freely … I remember feeling very thirsty. There was no water anywhere – no rivers or streams to drink from. In the morning I collected dew from the leaves and small puddles. I found fruit to eat and I slept in snatches. It was cold. All I had with me was my coat – I pulled up the collar like this [gestures with his hands]. At one point some Jews that were camped in the woods saw me, and they started shooting. I ran, zigzagging, through the trees to dodge the bullets [laughs, mirroring the movement with his hand]. I was too swift, I flew!

At this point, Munir leant forward and exclaimed, "Uncle, you're a hero!" [ya battal!] You were strong then – not like now. You could run fast, you knew the way!" Abu Hamadi laughed and continued:

> I arrived in Nahef the second night. I followed the stars. Our house was at the edge of the village so I took the path through the orchards without being seen [Israeli soldiers were patrolling villages to prevent refugees from returning]. I knew the hidden paths, the trees that marked our land and the places where I could hide; my feet led me. I spoke to my mother

through the window at the back of our house. I told her to tell my wife to meet me on the hill above the village that night. Then I hid and waited for her in that place. She came with my mother – they called to me … What can I tell you? [pauses]. My mother embraced me. "Why are you leaving me a second time? Who will look after me?" "Yamma", I said, "I'll come back and look after you, don't worry."

Abu Hamadi struggled to maintain his composure and was unable to continue. We sat silently, stunned by the story's abrupt and painful conclusion.

"People in those days were courageous", Munir reflected, after Abu Hamadi left. "Look what they did and how they suffered." Turning to me, he added, "Look how *we've* suffered". Sensing my discomfort, Umm Mahmud quickly interjected: "My parents' generation was uneducated and they didn't under-stand. They were like Tarzan – strong but ignorant. When they left they had no idea what would happen, that they would not return. Our generation is different." She went on to anticipate what the loss of this generation and their stories would mean for the community. "Who will remember?" she lamented. "Sometimes when I listen to Abu Hamadi or to my parents talk about Palestine I realize they will soon be gone. When I remember this I feel life has stopped."[10] This sense of proleptic nostalgia for the imminent loss of ontological connection to the material and social worlds from which these stories emerge, which one hears often, lends a predictable intensity to such moments and forms the implicit backdrop of first-generation narratives. It also gestures to the complex tempo-rality of refugee experience, as the exigencies of the present are experienced both as the continuation of a traumatic past and the past of some diminishing future. As statelessness and deepening deprivation revives and revises the erasures of 1948 in camp communities, past, present and future tenses overlap, challenging normative sequential chronologies of rupture in complex ways (Jayyusi 2007; Khouri 2012).

Much could be said about intergenerational dynamics at work in this exchange – the pervasive sense of guilt that hovers over it, and the particular social context of remembrance. Munir's assertion that Abu Hamadi's story illuminates communal suffering highlights how individual biographies are affectively expe-rienced and collectively interpreted. The story introduced me to the concept of *mubadale* (the practice of "swapping" sisters which allowed poorer families to avoid onerous dowries). It also highlighted the permeability of borders in the aftermath of 1948, as refugees found ways to return to their homes and lands (and the efforts by Israeli forces to prevent return), and navigated the radical discontinuities of their condition.[11] It revealed the gaps in our understanding of these events. Why did Abu Hamadi's mother and wife stay behind? (This detail goes against the grain of official histories of the 1948 expulsion, which often foreground fear of violence towards women as one of the primary reasons villagers fled.) What factors determined who left and who stayed?[12] At the time I was struck by the way Abu Hamadi's painful account of returning to Nahef surfaced in a mundane conversation about a domestic dispute, and by the failure of narrative to bridge past and present. As with many accounts of the expulsion, it underscored the extent to which emotion structures recollection and is elemental to its illocutionary force: here experience is communicated not only through language, but in the sudden curtailing of speech.

"To comprehend", writes Merleau-Ponty (1962: ii), "essentially means to describe what we know of the world and how we know. And we know not through our intellect but through our experience." Drawing on Merleau-Ponty's phenomenological insights, Lena Jayyusi coined the term "*in-vivo* subjectivity" for states of being in which Palestinians experience, recall and make meaningful former ways of life through reference to the body. "It is in and through this (mindful) body that we are in 'place'", writes Jayyusi (2007: 121), and "it is through this relationship to the body that [place] is remembered and narrated". In Abu Hamadi's narrative, remembrance of place is firmly grounded in bodily experience, just as the material environment of exile and old age shape the act of recollection and its reception by others. As he spoke his hands instinctively traced his movements across hills, over rocks, between trees, down paths, spatializing memory through a "corporeal lived geography" (Jayyusi 2007: 125). The thirst quenched by dew gathered from leaves and the feet that find their way home reveal knowledge charged with the cumulative force of lived experience. Descriptions of climbing over mountains and the agility with which he dodged Israeli bullets intensify and accrete meaning in the cramped setting of the camp: each inflects the other. They also suggest a mobile and dynamic relation to landscape, where attachment to place is inscribed through habitual activity and movement (Ingold 1993).[13] If nationalist teleology streamlines the past, organizing experience according to linear narrative logics that unfold towards a conclusion, embodied memories are recursive, collapsing time through repetition and unsettling the temporal boundaries separating past and present.

As Samera Esmeir (2003: 45) argues, the elliptical and truncated quality of many expulsion narratives enact "the doubling of witness". They convey not only the historical details, but also how these events continue to be felt in the lives of those who lived them.[14] In Abu Hamadi's account we feel the density of grief that resists formulation. When Umm Mahmud's mother, Umm 'Ali, sang of a woman newly displaced to Bint Jbeil who entreats a bird to fly over the mountains to find her lost child, she was unable to finish. As soon as she began singing, the moment of impasse was anticipated, and when it came, the others present would also weep.[15] In the moments when language fails, experience is communicated as an affective charge that is culturally constituted and constitutive, connecting speakers and listeners in both predictable and unexpected ways. The expression of emotion and the triggered physiological response is, arguably, another means by which the continuity of valued lifeworlds are sustained as "simultaneously historical, figurative and biographically bodied" (Jayyusi 2007: 130). Affective modes of expression, which are first and foremost felt, draw upon the affective energies simmering in the substrata of camp life that "push a present into composition" (Stewart 2011: 452).

Elders sometimes actively resisted speaking about the past. In certain cases this resistance seemed connected to a residual fear that committing memories of pre-1948 Palestine to the historical record was in some way to recognize them as past and over, imposing finality on a story still unfolding and unresolved. However, the repeated refrain in many interviews – "What can I tell you?", "What can I say", "This is what I know", or, in Otruk's case, "What can I remember? What *should* I remember?" – also suggests a lack of conviction about the purpose and usefulness of recounting these events at all. Recalling the battle to liberate the village of al-Birwa in 1948, Mahmoud Hajja describes how, after a long and valiant fight, the village was handed back to Zionist forces by the Arab Army of Salvation. Hajja trembles and looks away from the camera, the pain of betrayal still keenly felt. "You're clearly an educated man", he says, turning to the interviewer, "*you* study what happened … *This* is history, and history is merciless." He raises his hand to emphasize that there is nothing more to say. Here, again, somatic and affective registers accentuate verbal meaning while simultaneously marking its communicative limits. Hajja's challenge that the interviewer measure the distance between resistance and betrayal for himself inverts the assumption that he should *want* to give an account of his experiences, or recruit them to a moral position. He seems to question storytelling as a reconstitutive tool, or a means of bearing witness. By extension, he also implicitly questions the project of archive – the unequal power relations and imperial logics and complicities it instantiates, and the conceit that documenting histories of dispossession can bring justice for victims, or alleviate suffering.

GENEALOGIES OF LABOUR

When the Nakba Archive was established in 2002, almost no Palestinian oral history had been recorded on film. In turning to film the aim was to document the social and material contexts of remembrance, and to take seriously the embodied and performative dimension of these narratives. At the most literal level, audio-visual media affirm the corporeal dimension of human experience. More than any other medium, film manifests the sensory expression of experience through experience (Sobchack 1992). Film grounds signification in embodied language as an instrument of expression and site of meaning-making, and challenges the primacy of language for understanding. Its power as a medium lies in its immediacy, its ability to reach the body and emotions of viewers directly, circumventing intellectual understanding and proscriptive categories, and enabling imaginative faculties.[16] More broadly, film makes visible the intersubjective and enactive dynamics at work in human communication and the central importance of performative context. Because filmic meaning-making emerges as a result of responsive, dialectical processes, which implicate subject, viewer and filmmaker, it resists interpretive closure, introduces ethical dimensions and complicates *telos*.[17]

While the primary goal in building the archive was to create a historical resource, in reviewing the collection as it has grown over the years, I have come to see the possibilities of a phenomenological study of its contents. Descriptions of labour, childhood, sociality, pain, joy, love, poetic performance, and so forth, archive the past in bodily practice, disrupting the trim lines of event-based histories, and even historicality itself. Like Otruk, most of the elders interviewed were of peasant origin or poor city dwellers and illiterate. Many had lived and worked as farmers and herders in Palestine, and it was chiefly through descriptions of work (and its associated matrix of relationships, places and practices) that they would remember the towns, villages and social worlds they had left behind. Recollections of fishing, tending flocks, sowing and harvesting, and the domestic economy articulate – and bring into alignment – the people, land, routines and affective ties formed through them. The labour involved in maintaining a household, bringing up children or working the land reveals the seasonal rhythms and richness of familial and communal life that fulfilled social, biological and existential needs. Narratives of labour are generative for thinking about the senses as "both sensible and sense-making" (Sobchack 1992: 7), because they reveal and thematize embodied consciousness realizing itself in the world. In the context of performance we become aware not only of a psychic labour of remembrance replacing the physical labours recalled, but also the sensory labour involved in "making something of things" (Stewart 2011: 447).

While individual actions are instinctively understood to be the expression of spontaneous choices, they invariably draw on a reservoir of embodied experiences and cultural conventions that are passed down but not always recognized (Fassin 2007).[18] The reproduction of the past through bodily practice, which records its own history of sensation separately from the mind, can be knowing or unconscious, explicit or implicit.[19] When Umm Wissam, an elderly relative of Umm Mahmud's, described for me the domestic chores she performed as a young girl in Sufsaf, she recalled shaking out the mattresses during the summer months when the family slept outside to make sure no snakes were coiled inside. If she came across one she would talk to it: "Let us treat each other well, you go your way and I'll go mine and no one will be harmed." As she recounted this story, she mimicked the action of peeking between the folds of cloth, noting how she still continued to shake the rugs in the same way she had been taught as a child. When I recalled this conversation after her death, her daughter noted how she herself vigorously shook the rugs the same way each morning, reflecting that it was in such everyday gestures that she kept the memory of her mother alive. Beyond its intimate dimension, the action of shaking out bedding also connected her daughter, if not always consciously, to a more distant past in rural Palestine that she had never experienced. Although inherited bodily memories and habits lose their experiential referents over time, they continue to carry overtones of their original meaning, while producing new ones that, in turn, may be materially inscribed and passed down.

Said Otruk's interviews also reveal how bodies remember and filter experience. A complex picture of attachment rooted in work emerges. "Palestine", to the extent that it figured at all in his narratives, appeared to signify a constellation of material and embodied practices and social relations connected with fishing as much as an iconic, place. Fishing, and the communities of practice it sustained, knitted together cities and villages along the coast stretching up to

Latakia, making social and spatial configurations fluid. When I asked if he had ever visited the border by boat in his many decades of exile, he responded that he no longer had the right nets to fish in those waters, making such a trip futile and meaningless. While my question was informed by an abstract and sovereign logic of maps and borders – Palestine as seen from above – his response charted the corporeal coordinates of a fisherman at sea. For Otruk, Palestine was inseparable from the experience of fishing in particular waters with particular nets. It was also tied to the embodied experience of youth. Describing a photo of himself as a young man reclining in his boat on Acre's waterfront as capturing the "golden age", Otruk appears to gesture as much at the splendid figure of his own youth as at the halcyon days of pre-1948 Palestine: the loss of Palestine appears lyrically convergent with the felt loss of bodily vitality. Such accounts of everyday material and affective life do not simply constitute the narrative tissue connecting more significant events, but emerge as the very ground of social and political life, its embodied *habitus*. We begin to comprehend, *pace* Darwish, how place is not simply geography but a state of mind.

"TWO KILOS AND A BOX OF SONGS": ARCHIVE AND POETIC OPACITY

Sa'da Kayed, a Bedouin Palestinian from the clan of 'Arab al-Hayb, living in Bourj el-Shemali, recalled tending camels as a child: the sound of their bells, their speed when running, the pastures where they grazed, the games she played while working. When her family fled to Lebanon by camel in 1948, thenceforth "moving among strangers", the sound of their bells took on a forlornness, symbolizing the traumatic loss of a way of life but also, paradoxically, its continuity. Camels and bells – like fishing lines for Otruk – functioned as touchstones of memory that connect generations and places across space and time.[20] In her narrative, loss and longing are made meaningful through descriptions of a world rich with sensory and affective experience, mediated through poetic formula. Kayed was first introduced to us as a gifted singer of *'ataba*, a traditional form of lament, largely associated with Bedouin culture. While *'ataba* is a carrier of social memory, values and cultural allusions, the short verse units afford considerable creative latitude. Verbal formulae are interwoven with improvised phrases integrating different temporal registers, linguistic and non-linguistic elements. Her songs are history in another form: describing daily life, work and courtship, they represent a mode of historical consciousness that reproduces cultural patterns rooted in a social somatics of practical activity and verbal play. As pre-literate oral memory they are another form of archive, one that draws upon and enriches a deeply embodied tradition of oral epic.[21]

The laments recorded with Kayed are about love, loss and struggle – themes affectively connected in performance. Recalling a lament she sang during a funeral procession for the resistance fighter Sheikh Izz ad-Din al-Qassam, Kayed admits that she could not remember the year it took place, or how old she was. "I wasn't married then – I was still a young girl", she explains, describing how she walked in the procession "all the way from Haifa to Balad al-Sheikh".[22] Later she sings the groom's song, "Zareef al-Toul", which she concludes by vigorously cursing Arab governments: "It's a loss that Israel took our homeland, but the shame and disgrace is with the Arab Kings." She laughs and adjusts her scarf, as if taken aback by her own forthrightness, but also emboldened by the affirmation she receives from other family members who are listening. In the background a baby cries: "See, even Nassir's daughter wants to curse them!", she teases, shifting focus to the present realities of camp life and redirecting discourses of blame and responsibility to host governments in exile. Desire and betrayal are routed through each other, knitting together histories of violent expulsion and protracted exile, colonial pasts and a "(post) colonial" present (see Stoler 2016).

When Kayed is asked if she used to dance dabkeh at weddings, she responds effusively. "And how ... *Yeee!* We were singing for the flute players":

If you were a golden ring I would hide you,
And put you between my eyes [laughs and covers her mouth]
Play your flute, play!
Your height is admired,
Let those who hate you become sick, blind and mad!
Ala dal'ouna, Ala dal'ouna,
The beloved has left without bidding us farewell.
Oh birds, fly together,
Let us exchange sad times for happy ones.
I wish I were a garden planted with date palms,
And let my parents not give me to anyone by you! [Laughs and looks away]
She put on her kuffiyeh and corduroy dress,

And on the inside her heart is burning.
May God avenge women like us

… There were many songs [pauses]

I have two kilos and a box of songs,
Those that are on my lips are different from those in my heart.

This variation on the well-known song "Dal 'Ouna" (literally, "Let's go and help", from the word *ta'awon*, "cooperation") was traditionally sung to ease the tedium of physical labour in agricultural work and encourage collective effort.[23] The rhythm of the refrain-like stanzas are said to mimic the sound of a scythe cutting wheat, or stamping feet compacting dirt and straw in building work.[24] While Kayed's performance renders these kinetic registers forcefully, the images and syntactical constructions appear confusing and opaque, more like a stream of consciousness. Tense shifts and inconsistent use of pronouns ("I", "she", "us") make it hard to locate the speaking subject, while her assertion that "the songs on my lips are different from those in my heart" communicates incompleteness and experiences that resist inscription, or will not be shared. In performance, the non-linear quality seems to mimic the intensities of grief and desire – "a reenactment of what the senses do when they're catching up to something" (Berlant 2011: 59).

Meaning emerges through vocal pitch, gesture and Kayed's extraordinarily mobile facial expressions. The moments when she laughs ebulliently, turns her head, covers her mouth with her hand, looks down, or suddenly appears melancholy and exhausted tell us something else. As her voice rises and falls, vibrates and extends, her words take on a kind of incantatory power whose meaning is no longer tethered to language, but is intensely visceral. (I have watched this interview countless times and it always makes my hair stand on end and my throat tighten.) We sense the erotic charge and longing of the phrase "And put you between my eyes", just as we feel the weight of grief contained in "Two kilos and a box of songs". These are moments when we see and hear bodies remembering, but also where we become aware of the autonomy of subjects to redirect, interrupt or confound conventions of signification through a liberated lyricism of gesture and poetic practice.

DEAD LETTERS

While the Nakba Archive may have helped preserve the narratives of a passing generation, its modes of mediation, transmission and selection have also contributed to the encoding of representational forms. Converting spoken narrative into text is not without its risks, chief among them a disregard for how oral performance "lives by its fluidity" (Harris 2002: 84). Inevitably, the filmed testimonies recorded for the archive will outlive the vitality of their performance. What happens to embodied memory at this point of transition from history as lived to history as text? How is it affected by capture – what is lost? Hannah Arendt (1998) cautioned that the cost of reifying remembrance – of turning it into a "worldly thing" – is paid for in the "dead letter", which replaces a sense of history as lived experience, practice and possibility. Umm Mahmoud was perhaps alluding to this when she compared the loss of these stories as a lived component of everyday life to a kind of death. As lived experience is inscribed as text and "events" are sutured to narrative, vitality as potentiality is lost. "My feeling of belonging was no longer instinctive", writes Darwish (1973: 17). "It became more mature, and the content of the dream, not its eruption, became my cause." Raja Shehadeh has similarly described how narratives of national attachment alter – and paradoxically compromise – his sense of relation to place:

> Sometimes when I am walking in the hills, say Batn el-Hawa, unselfconsciously enjoying … the smell of thyme and the hills and trees around me, I find myself looking at it, it transforms itself before my eyes into a symbol of samidin, of our struggle, of our loss. And at that very moment, I am robbed of that tree; instead, there is a hollow space into which anger and pain flow. (Shehadeh cited in Parmenter 1994: 86–87)

Palestinians are in this way doubly dispossessed.

Archives create the illusion of distance and transcendence that are both lacking in refugee camps. To understand the full scope and significance of the events of the expulsion for Palestinians in Lebanon is to recognize that they are not only remembered discursively but embodied, passed down not only historically but existentially. When Palestinians say "the Nakba is still happening", they speak on two levels. The Palestinian refugees newly displaced from Yarmouk, Daraa, Neirab and the other Palestinian camps in Syria to Lebanon, Turkey and elsewhere, form simply the latest chapter in a history of displacement that began in 1948. The meaning of the Nakba is not stable, nor can it be disconnected from performative context: attunement to the past necessarily entails engagement with the present and future, as histories of violent dispossession and exclusion are anticipated as much as remembered. As Jayyusi (2007: 110) notes, any discussion of Palestinian memory has to be understood in cumulative terms and in relation to "the continuing figure of erasure and denial that marks the contemporary Palestinian condition". A friend born and raised in Shatila put it simply: "I know about the Nakba because I live in Shatila" (Allan 2014: 51). These narratives suggest a historicity not linear but recursive and open-ended. As with many other sites of (post-)colonial study, Palestinian pasts demand "recursive analytics" characterized by an "unsettled, contingent quality of histories that fold back on themselves, and in that refolding, reveal new surfaces" (Stoler 2016: 26).

In a recent email exchange about the "archive fever" (Doumani 2009) taking hold in Palestine studies with a friend – a scholar of Palestinian history, and herself Palestinian – she writes: "Something anarchic in me finds the invisible so much more desirable because everything is being claimed ... We are a settler colony now and everything has to be indexed through this analytical/political frame." She continues: "I think about the desire I have to shield the gesture and the illegible from the hunger to capture, acquire, incorporate." As scholars of Palestine return to historical sources with different plotlines in mind, broadening our frameworks of inquiry in search of new political and social formations through which to conceptualize the past and imagine the future, it is perhaps worth pausing to consider her note of caution. In a similar vein, the cultural critic Édouard Glissant (1997: 11) advocates what might be called intimacy without transparency: "We preserve difference by granting opacity to others, which is to surrender power." More important than the right to difference (which he says is exhausted) is the right *not* to be understood. Opacity recognizes the stubborn, and potentially empowering, irreducibility of otherness. "I claim the right to opacity for everyone, which is not a withdrawal", writes Glissant. "I do not have to 'understand' anyone, an individual, a community, a people to 'take them with me' at the price of stifling them, of losing them in an amorphous totality" (cited in Murdoch 2013: 886).

Inevitably, any effort to render the embodied and affective complexity of refugee experience through verbal description will fall short.[25] The will to take seriously the idea that "bodies remember" does not translate to certainty of insight into what elders *actually* feel in these moments. The subjective nature of interpretation does not, however, invalidate the project. These constraints can be productive, inviting us to engage in another reality, one that, in Genet's (1986: 3) words, is "fertile in hate and love; in people's daily lives; in silence, like translucency, punctuated by words and phrases". They enable us to perceive commonalities of experience and larger political forces as they manifest in individual bodies and lives, "formulat[ing], without closing down, the investments and incoherence of political subjectivity and subjectification" (Berlant 2011: 53). In the gestures, dispositions and idiosyncracies of speech and voice, we apprehend – however inadequately, and partially – the forces and pressures of world-historical processes; we recognize loss, and all that is enfolded in that word, as something embodied and lived, whose meaning continues to evolve.

Azoulay reminds us that as witnesses to the ongoing destruction of Palestinian society we too are complicit. She exhorts us to attend to the relationship between politics and aesthetics (in its old, etymological sense of sensuous perception), and to the role sensory experience might play in the (re)ordering of relations of power, resistance and the "distribution of the sensible" (Rancière 2001). Politics determines what can be seen, said and heard in the public sphere; aesthetics can in turn resist and disrupt that regime.[26] In this sense, filmed interviews are both objects of study and instruments for rethinking the privileging of the verbal and the national, and truth and value (as transparent given categories, rather than contingent ideological constructions). Much that is meaningful is only communicable in non-verbal form. The affective intensities of performance, silence and refusal reveal different ways of "speaking". As MacDougall suggests, foregrounding "knowledge as meaning" over "knowledge as being" has prevented scholars and filmmakers alike from actively inhabiting what they see, hear and feel. If an emotional and visceral response to our subjects feels analytically awkward, it is also an ethical imperative. Perceiving more attentively, in ways that neither compromise historical and political claims, on the one hand, nor cast aside sensory, embodied experience on the other, requires a perceptual untethering. Recovering the complexity of lived experience demands that we disconnect subjects from the larger ideological narratives to which they are often tied, and refer back to the ordinary sensory worlds people inhabit, past and present.

NOTES

1 See Allen (2009), Esmeir (2007), Jayyusi (2007) Salih (2017) and Sayigh (1997, 1998a, 1998b). Much of the scholarship that has engaged the body and senses as sites of meaning-making has tended to focus on traumatic rupture, rather than more routinized forms of embodied experience.

2 Early interventions came from the social historians Salim Tamari (2001) and Beshara Doumani (1992: 6), who called for "a live portrait of the Palestinian people, especially the historically 'silent' majority of peasants, workers, women, merchants and Bedouin".

3 The Nakba Archive is an oral history archive I co-created with Mahmoud Zeidan. Since its inception in 2002 it has been run as a collaborative project in the twelve official UN refugee camps in Lebanon. Over the course of six years we were able to record around 475 interviews with refugees from 135 Palestinian villages and towns, mainly from the northern Galilee and the coastal cities. The archive is currently housed at the American University of Beirut and has been developed into an online database under the direction of Kaokab Chebaro and, formerly, Hana Sleiman. For more information: http://www.nakba-archive.org.

4 Because the vast majority of Palestinians who fled in 1948 were illiterate peasants, refugee accounts are vitally important and can compensate for an incomplete written record that has been dispersed or destroyed. The interviews recorded for the archive unearthed many details about the events of the expulsion that had not been part of the official historical record.

5 A number of the audiovisual recordings under discussion here can be viewed online at www.nakba-archive.org

6 Otruk is also the subject of an ethnographic film I directed, *Still Life* (2007). http://store.cinemaguild.com/nontheatrical/product/2482.htm.l

7 The narrative of coexistence between Palestinians and Jews prior to 1948 is a recurring element of many of the interviews recorded by the Nakba Archive. Friendships seem to have been particularly strong between women, often forged through the give and take of neighbourly ties. The interview recorded with Hamdeh Jouma in 2004, which recalls her Jewish comrade and "blood sister" Fifa Hadeve, who advised her on matters of love and marriage, is one example.

8 Ariella Azoulay's theory of "potential history" derives precisely from such forgotten moments of alliance, which allow a speculative return to an "archival zero point" (2013: 551), before enmity between Arabs and Jews seemed inescapable, reconnecting histories that have grown rigidly separate

9 Genet made clear that should the Palestinians ever achieve statehood, he would lose interest in their case.

10 Sayigh (1979) has described how in the early years of exile, refugees described the experience of displacement in similar terms, as non-existence and "paralysis".

11 I heard similar stories about surreptitious returns to Palestine, a practice that continued until Israel's occupation of the West Bank in 1967, when border controls began to be rigorously enforced.

12 Like a number of other villages, half of Nahef's residents remained.

13 Tim Ingold's (1993) theory of "taskscape" – the socially constructed nature of land-scape, formed through human activity – is helpful for conceptualizing the temporal dimensions of people's relations to place as something processual rather than static and immutable.

14 "Death generates present absence and nonexistence", writes Esmeir (2003: 45). "It is something that lives on with its survivors … Incoherence, contradictions and absences should be understood as signifiers of something that is still present."

15 The discomfort of these moments was such that Umm Mahmoud would often entreat her mother not to sing. "Although my parents used to speak a lot about Palestine when we were young, I don't like hearing these stories now … Sometimes when my mother sings to my children about Bint Jbeil and how families were separated when they came to Lebanon, it makes us cry … These memories are too painful for her and for us" (Allan 2014: 50).

16 "When we look, we are doing something more deliberate than seeing and yet more unguarded than thinking", observes MacDougall (2006: 7). "We are putting ourselves in a state that is at once one of vacancy and heightened awareness. Our imitative facul-ties take precedence over judgment and categorization, preparing us for a different kind of knowledge."

17 Azoulay's project of recovering potential histories through a close reading of archival photographs is generative for analysing the Nakba Archive. She scrutinizes the gestures, bodily comportment and gaze of Palestinian men and women living under colonial occupation and reminds us that as witnesses to the destruction of Palestinian society, we too are complicit. As viewers, we are called upon to see the politics at work in these images, and to reflect on the power relations they inscribe.

18 Didier Fassin (2007) has recently argued for the need to restore the thick materiality (and contingency) of the past in the present. Exploring how histories of exclusion and oppression are physically and psychically inscribed in AIDS patients in South Africa, Fassin (2007: 177) argues that it is through these gestures and ticks that "the past is embodied in the present but also, more materialistically, that our individual and collective history is embodied in what we are".

19 Remembrance enacted in bodily dispositions rather than represented in speech recalls Pierre Bourdieu's (1977) theory of *habitus*.

20 Salih (2017) describes this interweaving of discourse and everyday sensory perception as constitutive of meaning in narratives of 1948 among elderly Palestinian women in the camps in Jordan. Women remember "through the body and what [that] body endured", writes Salih. "Their ways of narrating … are inscribed in a plot made of ordinary domestic interruptions, affective ties and relations, bodily experiences of place in times of war."

21 Recounting the hilltop improvisation of "warrior musicians" in Ajloun, Genet (1986: 47) describes these forms of sung poetry as a kind of pre-conceptual cultural knowl-edge: "The Palestinians were inventing songs that had been as it were forgotten,

that they found lying hidden in themselves before they sang them ... not so much something discovered as something that re-emerges from where it lay buried in the memory, inaudible as a melody, cut in a disc of flesh".

22 The militant preacher and leader of the resistance against the British and Zionists in the 1920s and 1930s.

23 Now one is more likely to hear Dal 'Ouna sung at Palestinian cultural events, where *dabkeh* and other peasant traditions symbolize cultural tenacity and nationalist sentiment.

24 The rhythm is instantly recognizable to Palestinians, and listeners will often join in, revealing an instilled visceral attunement – a bodily response to sound and rhythm – that taps into cultural tradition and nationalist practice.

25 Furthermore, because bodily registers of knowing and remembering are invariably bound up with speech they should not be understood as a counterpoint to the verbal.

26 Rancière (2004: xi) writes, "a delimitation of spaces and times, the visible and invisible, of speech and noise, that simultaneously determines the place and stakes of politics as a form of experience".

REFERENCES

Allan, D. (2007) "The Politics of Witness: Remembering and Forgetting 1948 in Shatila Camp", in A. Sa'di and L. Abu-Lughod (eds.), *Nakba: Palestine, 1948, and the Claims of Memory*. New York: Columbia University Press.

Allan, D. (2014) *Refugees of the Revolution: Experiences of Palestinian Exile*. Stanford, CA: Stanford University Press.

Arendt, H. (1998) *The Human Condition*, 2nd ed. Chicago: University of Chicago Press.

Azoulay, A. (2013) "Potential History: Thinking through Violence", *Critical Inquiry* 39(3): 548–574.

Berlant, L. (2011) *Cruel Optimism*. Durham, NC: Duke University Press.

Bourdieu, P. (1977) *Outline of the Theory of Practice*. Cambridge: Cambridge University Press.

Darwish, M. (2010) *A Journal of Ordinary Grief*, translated by I. Muhawi. New York: Archipelago Books (first published 1973).

Desjarlais, R. (1997) *Shelter Blues: Sanity and Selfhood Among the Homeless*. Pittsburgh: University of Pennsylvania Press.

Doumani, B. (1992) "Rediscovering Ottoman Palestine: Writing Palestinians into History", *Journal of Palestine Studies* 21(2): 5–28.

Doumani, B. (2009) "Archiving Palestine and the Palestinians: The Patrimony of Ihsan Nimr", *Jerusalem Quarterly* 36: 3–12.

Esmeir, S. (2003) "1948: Law, History, Memory", *Social Text* 21(2): 25–48.

Fassin, D. (2007) *When Bodies Remember: Experiences and Politics of AIDS in South Africa*. Berkeley: University of California Press.

Genet, J. (1986) *The Prisoner of Love*. New York: New York Review of Books.

Glissant, É. (1997) *The Poetics of Relation*, translated by B. Wing. Ann Arbor: University of Michigan Press.

Harris, V. (2002) "The Archival Sliver: Power, Memory, and the Archive in South Africa", *Archival Science* 2: 63–86.

Harootunian, H. (2004) "Shadowing History: National Narratives and the Persistence of the Everyday", *Cultural Studies* 18(2/3): 181–200.

Ingold, T. (1993) "The Temporality of the Landscape", *World Archaeology* 25(2): 152–174.

Jayyusi, L. (2007) "Iterability, Cumulativity, and Presence: The Relational Figures of Palestinian Memory", in A. Sa'di and L. Abu-Lughod (eds.), *Nakba: 1948 and the Claims of Memory*. New York: Columbia University Press.

Khouri, E. (2012) "Rethinking the Nakba", *Critical Inquiry* 38: 1–18.

MacDougall, D. (2006) *The Corporeal Image: Film, Ethnography, and the Senses*. Princeton, NJ: Princeton University Press.

Merleau-Ponty, M. (1962) *Phenomenology of Perception*, translated by C. Smith. London: Routledge & Kegan Paul.

Murdoch, H.A. (2013) "Édouard Glissant's Creolized World Vision: From Resistance and Relation to Opacité", *Callaloo* 36(4): 875–890.

Parmenter, B. (1994) *Giving Voices to Stones: Place and Identity in Palestinian Literature*. Austin, TX: University of Austin Press.

Portelli, A. (1991) *The Death of Luigi Trastulli, and Other Stories: Forms and Meanings of Oral History*. Harlan County, KY: SUNY Press.

Rancière, J. (2001) "Ten Theses on Politics", *Theory & Event*, 5(3).

Rancière, J. (2004) *The Politics of Aesthetics: The Distribution of the Sensible*. London: Bloomsbury Academic.

Said, E. (1978) *Orientalism*. New York: Vintage.

Said, E. (1984) "Permission to Narrate", *Journal of Palestine Studies* 13(3): 27–48.

Salih, R. (2017) "Bodies that Walk, Bodies that Talk, Bodies that Love: Palestinian Women Refugees, Affective Memories, and the Politics of the Ordinary", *Antipode* 49(3): 742–760.

Sayigh, R. (1979) *The Palestinians: From Peasants to Revolutionaries*. London: Zed Books.

Sayigh, R. (1998a) "Gender, Sexuality, and Class in National Narrations: Palestinian Camp Women Tell Their Lives", *Frontiers: A Journal of Women Studies* 19(2): 166–185.

Sayigh, R. (1998b) "Palestinian Camp Women as Tellers of History", *Journal of Palestine Studies* 27(2): 42–58.

Sobchack, V. (1992) *The Address of the Eye: A Phenomenology of Film Experience*. Princeton, NJ: Princeton University Press.

Soueif, A. (2003) "Introduction", in *The Prisoner of Love*. New York: New York Review of Books.

Stewart, K. (2011) "Atmosphere Attunements", *Environment and Planning D: Society and Space* 29(3): 445–453.

Stoler, A.L. (2016) *Duress: Imperial Durabilities in Our Times*. Durham, NC: Duke University Press.

Tamari, S. (2001) *Reinterpreting the Historical Records: The Uses of Palestinian Refugee Archives for Social Science*. Beirut: Institute for Palestine Studies.

4

The time of small returns: affect and resistance during the Nakba[1]

LENA JAYYUSI

[T]he Nakba is a share of death for a human being (*qisma mnil mawt li-bani Adam*). It affected us as though it were a share of death, of death, it took half of our lives and left half.[2]

Hajja Halima Hassan's words, both their substance and more significantly the tonality (and gestural stance) with which they are enunciated, communicate a memory still affectively lived in the here and now; they speak of the unhealed scar of events experienced, still painful in the present, a testimony to a traumatic passage never transcended. When people contest memories of events, the contestations are often centred on the details of concrete actions and outcomes ("facts"), but it is the affective and emotional (expression of) memory, whether spoken explicitly or only gestured, that is the marker of the event's phenomenal significance. It is the affective expression that configures the event's relational meaning: how it bears on the narrator. Here, Hajja Halima's words signify a momentous, even cataclysmic, transformation: a death in life.

Yet in the numerous accounts produced of the events of 1948 in Palestine, which saw the establishment of the Israeli state and the dispossession of the Palestinians as a people, little of this affective and existential reality is manifest: this death in life,[3] the actions and agencies that brought it about, and the experiences and losses it represented are all excised or radically occluded. Consider for example the following statement that appears in a review of a book about the history of Israel, a review that whilst highly positive nevertheless picks out significant omissions:

> This is not to say that "Israel: A History" is without flaws. There are curious omissions. Arthur Ruppin, largely forgotten today except for some street names in Israeli cities, was more than just another early Zionist leader, as one would think from reading Shapira's book.
>
> Ruppin was the visionary who was the first to articulate the need for a majority of Jews in Eretz Yisrael; was the first to insist that land purchase was crucial to the survival of the Yishuv in Palestine – a "no-brainer" later, but radical when it was first asserted by Ruppin. (Chanes 2013)

What could "the need for a majority of Jews in Eretz Yisrael" have consisted of as a project? What course of action or policy could possibly produce that outcome? What would it mean, in practice, for that unspoken constituency which is discursively submerged in this text, present but absent, who would thus be transformed into a minority, at best, in the land of their birth? Indeed, in the naturalness and unselfconscious ease with which this proposition is given, and in which the subsequent proposition is also indicated as a "no-brainer", lies the depth and volume of the radical erasure, not merely of the process and outcomes that were the organic result of such an idea (a "need" for a majority of Jews in a land which held only a Jewish minority), but of the real human cost of the Zionist project. By a trick of syntax, the two propositions together, each perhaps formally correct in its depiction of Ruppin's position, may construct a particular universe of meanings which occludes how things in the actual world happened: they might suggest to the novice reader that the outcome (a majority of Jews) was produced by "land purchase", as though it were ever possible for an entire people to sell off its land of habitus, its entire patrimony in life.[4] The Palestinians, in this syntactically predicated projection, are here potentially represented as possessing a peculiar lack of affect and reason. Indeed, every time the claim is made that the Jews had bought the land (entitling them to the country), this denial of mundane affect and reason to the Palestinians is implicitly accomplished. This claim is an element in the process of dehumanization of Palestinians in Zionist and pro-Zionist discourse that has increasingly taken place over time.

ACCOUNTING FOR THE NAKBA

The silences and structuring figures in Chane's text above are all too frequent in the standard academic and popular (Western) narratives of the engendering of Israel as a state.[5] Too often, these do not stop to question the actual process that unfolded to produce the outcome that emerged at the end of the 1948 war: a country largely (and to all intents and purposes permanently) emptied of most of its indigenous inhabitants within the space of less than a year. Problematic tropes and occlusions also irradiate the accounts of revisionists like Benny Morris (2004).[6] In his Introduction to *The Origins of the Palestinian Refugee Problem Revisited*, Morris cautions:

> In general, it cannot be stressed too strongly that, while this is not a military history, the events it describes, cumulatively amounting to the Palestinian Arab *exodus, occurred in wartime* and were a product, direct and indirect, of that war, a war that the Palestinians started. The threat of battle and battle itself were the immediate backdrop to the various components of the *exodus*. (Morris 2004: 7; italics added)

The language itself signals the conclusions to be taken away, and transmutes the moral implications of the story. Hayden White's discussion of the ways that the language of historical narratives prefigures the meaning of the events themselves[7] thus finds a potent example in Morris' account, even as he displays his detailed knowledge of the attacks by Jewish forces and of the evictions of Palestinians from their towns and villages. The moral grammar of "exodus" rather than "expulsion", which runs through the account and consistently frames his narrative, constructs a specific epistemic and normative space. Yet the process that amounted to "the Nakba" took many months, and involved multiple "waves", as Morris painfully demonstrates in his book. Moreover, not allowing the Palestinian villagers to return to their homes after the events of 1948 was, after all, not a neutral and docile sequel to "war". It is in this cumulative context that Pappe (2006) confronts Morris' paradigm of "war" with that of "ethnic cleansing".[8]

But what of the Palestinian and Arab accounts? Where are they in this? The Palestinian sources were too often ignored as partisan, propagandistic and at best unreliable and untrustworthy. The people who had endured the radical uprooting could not be held to be telling their experience with any authority or authenticity. Thus the uprooting from land and place was compounded with (indeed sealed by) the uprooting and excision from symbolic and communicative space, from historical representation; it was coeval with the denial of "permission" to narrate, as Said (1984) so aptly expressed it. The problem, however, is deeper than the appropriation of the right to narrate: at a fundamental level it resolves into the effacement of both human affect and reason from the figure of the colonial subject: that "they", the Third World community, could not be trusted to tell it as it was means that they cannot see matters for what they really are, or that the affective narratives they tell could not have real grounds. This involves the implicit non-recognition of the existential and experiential nature of the events of loss of home and country, and the consequent affective and moral trauma; a systematic disjoining of events from consequences and of affect from event that is repeatedly visible in the colonial paradigm. The grounds for intersubjective identification are already unmoored within this position. The story is rigged from the outset.

Yet when one examines oral histories of the Nakba, one discovers a range of small narratives that embody the resistance to dislocation, to loss of land and home, and the emotional and affective dimensions of that loss: its enormity and its rejection at the same time, each a function of the other. In the affective recounting of the events, we can discern the affective ecology of these events as lived. The stories themselves exhibit a recollection (a narratological rendition) suffused with feeling and emotion, and enable us to locate and perceive an affective subject in the recollected past.

In part, the affective dimension of the lived, unfolding Nakba can be traced and located within the resistance to dislocation summoned up in the stories, manifest in various actions, ranging from attempts by village communities to fight back to attempted returns to the original sites. One can also trace a "pattern" of flight which itself confirms that affective tie, the insistence on it and the resistance to its severing. In account after account, it becomes clear how people fled from their homes to the outlying vicinity, trying to maintain a connection with their place of origin. It was not a linear flight, as represented in the many compacted and aggregated accounts (including many Arab accounts), except where it was forced into that form by expulsive forces, as in Lydda.

In light of these narratives, accounts that refer to the Palestinians as simply fleeing "war" (rather than direct attack or threat of direct attack) are, at best, reductionist and occlude the actual history of the violent encounter between armed Jewish settlers in Palestine and the Palestinian population, struggling to hold on, if not to place, then at least to communal space, to vicinity as a lived affective and phenomenal field. Claims that Palestinians left willingly at the behest of their leaders in order to make it easy to get rid of the Jews reconstruct the Palestinian from the outset as a coldly calculating creature lacking recognizable human emotional lineaments,[9] a figure of the colonial imaginary. It is itself a sign of, as well as a move in, the racialization of affect (and thought) in colonial discourses. Whilst (pro-)Zionist narratives speak fluidly of the "attachment" of the Jews to their "ancestral lands", such that their "return" (2,000 years later) is conceptualized as natural and moral, and affectively consonant with what any normal human being might feel or desire, Palestinians are deprived even of this in the master narratives of the colonial order. The attachment to an imagined ancient past, turned into a potent mobilizer for contemporary conquest, is produced as more real and realistic, more morally justified and entitled, than the attachment to a current lived habitus, and to generationally accrued patterns, networks and rooted relationships.[10] In such renditions of the colonial subject we can see the radical nature of the colonial: a stance excising the most commonplace lineaments of the human from the roots.

ASYMMETRY AND THE GEOGRAPHY OF DISPOSSESSION

In the narratives, told by Palestinians from very different locales and towns in 1948 Palestine, a pattern emerges of a population suddenly sensing an existential threat – one that becomes highly visible and mutates into a living concern with the Partition Resolution of 1947. A number of accounts, moreover, reconstruct and project a new affective landscape that emerged explicitly after the Partition resolution: a contrast or disjuncture between Palestinian communities and the Jewish settlements often in close proximity. This is indexed in the narratives by the accounts of the dancing and singing that could be heard in the settlements after the resolution, as well as of increased and more audacious attacks by Jewish settlers on Arab villages. That these are noted in a number of accounts expresses their affective valency, both as then experienced and as now remembered.

At this point, the efforts to obtain arms for self-defence and protection of the villages and towns of Palestine seem to have become pronounced. In interview after interview, Palestinians recount in detail the urgent but under-resourced attempts to secure arms for self-defence, and often to secure money for arms in the first place, the women on many occasions selling their gold jewellery so that rifles could be bought.[11] Benny Morris (2004: 7) describes the conflict as being between Jewish militias and Arab militias. Yet there were perhaps only two forces that might properly be given the title of an Arab militia, and that was al-Jihad al-Muqaddas, the irregular defence force led by Abd al-Qadir al-Hu-sayni, and the irregular forces of the Arab Liberation Army (ALA, also known as the Arab Salvation Army) led by Fawzi al-Qawuqji. However, these irregular forces were often enmeshed in a competitive, non-cooperative relationship, and the ALA was repeatedly subject to the pulls and pushes of various Arab heads of state and their territorial ambitions which were not necessarily served by a vigorous defence of Palestinian towns and villages.[12] Thus they were hardly poised or able to defend all the locales of Palestine. According to the accounts, defence committees were established in most villages and towns, composed of the local men, their job being to guard against attack, especially at night, and sometimes to procure arms. Account after account provides specific names of persons who were officially and unofficially entrusted with this latter mission: for example, Adnan al-Shami, Subhi Khadra, an uncle of Ahmad Ali Hajir and others. Some went to Lebanon for the purpose, some to Syria and some to Egypt. Yet the narrative that emerges, both singularly and collectively, is a narrative of asymmetry.[13]

The attempts to procure arms were, for the most part, not very successful, except on the occasions where people were able to raid nearby army bases (as in the testimony of Ahmad Ali Hajir from Tirat Haifa). Either the arms they bought were old and often useless, or they were denied them. Ahmad al-Samad Abu Rashid, from Tirat Haifa, fifteen years old at the time, shakes his head as he recounts that the arms were often "no good": "something to make one cry, they turned out no good". Moreover, the arms obtained were for the most part relatively few and basic. Rajih Kayed 'Uwais from al-Manshiyya (Acre region) recalls that six men from his town, he among them, went out to buy arms. He only had 110 pounds, and each rifle cost 45 pounds without its bullets. They nevertheless managed to obtain sixty-five rifles. Shahira Sadiq from Deir al-Qasi (Acre region) remembers many of her townsfolk going to Syria to get arms and being unable to. Omar Atallah from Saris (Jerusalem region) recalls that they had no more than ten rifles. Ahmad Ali Hajir from Tirat Haifa relates that his brother was given money by his mother and he went to Syria and came back with sixty pieces and 1,000 bullets. Tirat Haifa was able to resist far longer than other towns.[14] Many narrators mention identificatory details on the arms, such as the date (1918), as an indication of the condition they were in and their inability to counter the Jewish attacks effectively. Compared to the mortars, cannons and planes that Jewish forces had, they could as well have been using "sticks" to confront machine guns, as in the case of some of the first skirmishes in Ijzim (Haifa region), recounted in an ironic manner by Ahmad Hassan: "When the Jews used to come to Ayn Ghazzal to attack before, some would go with sticks, with sticks, and the women behind them with water, ululating".

Khadir Dirbas from Tirat Haifa remembers that the men of the town stayed behind to resist after the women and children were evacuated. There were then multiple attacks for weeks, but they refused to surrender when given the choice by Jewish forces. However, the final attack was by air and with mortars. Dirbas says: "can a rifle resist a cannon? A machine gun?" It was then that most of the men who had remained to defend their homes withdrew. It was late at night, and they walked out through the mountains and made their way to nearby 'Ayn Hawd. But 'Ayn Hawd was also under attack, so they went to Ijzim, which was in a similar plight. They therefore left Ijzim, and walked off in the direction of Nablus.

Qasim Darawsheh of Ijzim asks: "What do you want: a rifle to resist an airplane?" Hajja Halima from Saris, near Jerusalem, explains: "My dear, people were unable to resist ... to resist tanks and to resist canons, and to resist ... people would flee". Shahira Sadiq from Deir al-Qasi remembers: "they came and hit us often with the planes, people knew there was no use". Khazna al-Ghadban, originally from Kwaykat, recounts that she left Sheikh Dawud (Acre region), her husband's village, with her children, while he stayed behind. They went to Mi'aar, a mountain village (in the Acre region), and stayed there for three months. "[W]e stayed but the tanks and planes [hit?] us, we had not expected that." When Mi'aar, already swollen with refugees from the Acre district, was attacked, many of them fled to al-Buqei'a, a Druze village, where they stayed under the trees. Then they went to Kufur Sumei', another Druze village, but there were attacks on Tarshiha (Maalot today) and in Suhmata, nearby. After fighting broke out between two Druze villages, Khazna al-Ghadban left for Lebanon, desperate to protect her five children. Hajja Maliha Muhammad Husayn from Saris exclaims: "What, did we leave of our own accord?! We fled of our own accord?! The bullets were crackling around our heads".

NARRATIVES OF A MOVING TRAIL

Already the accounts above reveal a reluctant and piecemeal departure. Collectively and singularly the narratives and testimonies index this within the particulars recounted, describing the circumstances under which people left *and* their affective state.

Zarifa Jaber Wishah, Beit ʿAffa (Gaza district), relates how Jewish forces came into the village and entered their homes, forcing them to leave. They sat outside for a long time, unwilling to depart. Then:

> we left Beit ʿAffa for Karatiyya then to al-Majdal, and in al-Majdal we remained for three months and celebrated the Adha feast in al-Majdal, then they evicted us from al-Majdal and they were behind us and we arrived to Deir al-Balah [Gaza] walking on foot, and the planes were shooting at us.

Ali al-Mughrabi from Muʿthir, a village in the Tiberias area, recounts that the villagers took refuge first in Dishon (Safad region), until it was taken, then in al-Malkiyya, al-Harawi and finally Jerusalem.

Omar Atalla, from Saris, ten years old at the time, remembers that when the Jewish attack came, "at night", the "resistance men ... said get the families out of the houses, or it will be Deir Yassin".[15] Atalla left the village with the women and children, and the men "stayed to fight". They "fought till ammunition went", then, "near dawn the fighters withdrew, 'the town is gone'; they were saying and weeping". The men followed their families. They spent one night in the caves, "and then to Kasla on foot". The refugees then moved from Kasla to Beit Sassin, where they stayed for "1–3 months".

He continues, "then the journey of torment began". Beit Sassin became a target, and so they trekked to the north, carrying their empty rifles. They were at Jaljoul for 10–15 days: "we would hunker down in people's houses". After that it was a village called Allar (Jerusalem area), where they stayed for three months, sheltering under the trees. Even the language used is affect-laden, communicating an experience and fate that was in various ways emotionally traumatic, already suffused with the terms of a radically altered and vitiated condition.

Hajja Halima Hassan from Saris recounts a similarly long trek, punctuated by periods of staying in various villages, along an arc that was ever widening under the force of the attacks:

> We continued to be displaced in the mountains until we got fed up
> ... under the olives, under the sky and open air we slept. And they did

not get off our backs, chasing us ... the town that they would find, they demolished Beit Sassin, they demolished Beit Jiz.

As she speaks these names, she "counts" on her fingers:

they demolished near [Rafat?] ... what town they came to they would demolish. And people forced to leave ... fleeing, fleeing, fleeing until we settled, my girl, in a town called 'Ishwa, 'Ishwa is two or three towns away from us. We sat in it for about a week, then again they overtook it. Then we went and got to Deir 'Aban, then to Beit Natif, in those mountains, wherever they get to they uproot a few villages that flee ahead of them.

Saris fell in April 1948; but Hajja Halima explains:

We fled from Saris ... and we continued to walk and walk ... we continued until, you might say, the end of November ... and we arrived to Kufr Aqab ... and the demolition behind us, wherever they would appear in villages they would demolish. Where are human beings to go?

"Where are human beings to go?" The narratives talk of a widening arc of dispossession, a trek initially thought local, within an affective vicinity, becoming increasingly distanced from the point of origin, such that people became bereft of not only material sustenance but also affiliative sustenance and support, sending them on "the journey of torment".

When concerted attacks took place, or after nodal events like the massacres at Deir Yassin or Tantura, it was often the women and children who were evacuated to nearby areas – a neighbouring village, or surrounding woods or mountains – while the men stayed to defend the village or town. Even when the entire village fell, after a deadly and concerted assault, or because the Jewish forces had actually entered and instructed people to depart using acts or threats of extreme violence, they often went to nearby woods or caves, or to neighbouring villages. It was usually the nearest site that was chosen: some people from the same town went to different proximate locales (e.g. from Saris some people first went to Beit Mahsir, others first to Kasla). Narrators often mention the presence of relatives or acquaintances in these places, or relationships between the villages, that led to their choice of refuge. But as Hajja Halima says: "and they did not get off our backs, chasing us".

It was then a continually re-enforced departure, shaped and driven by attack, panic and fear, not one marked by a calculated decision to leave so that the Arab armies could prevail. The departures from the immediate site, the place of habitus, may have been relatively sudden, but they were cumulative and unfolded over time from the space of homeland: of habitus and habitual connection. Even in the language of the narratives and the descriptions, the recognition of some form of common space, of connectedness, emerges.

One might here recall the descriptions of the German invasion of France during World War II, when France, with one of the most powerful armies in Europe at the time, capitulated within six weeks, during which it seemed as though half of France was at one point on the move – people fleeing from the invading forces, also set upon by mortars and planes, and moving from one locale to another in search of safety and refuge, with French forces themselves also in retreat.[16] Relatively few French found refuge in neighbouring countries, as the Palestinians were ultimately forced to do. The Germans were all over the adjoining countries anyway; and in any case they wanted a subject population, not an absent one. But there is another difference between the French experience as recounted in these records and that of the Palestinian villagers: numerous accounts of the fall of Paris describe Parisians leaving en masse, in anticipation of the German occupation. Though they left relatively hurriedly, many did by some accounts nevertheless attempt to take various valuables with them (china, crystal, jewellery). This has more parallels with the early flight of some of the Palestinian middle classes from the larger cities, though even this constituency did not all depart in advance. In the villages of Palestine, perhaps as in many French villages, most people did not leave in anticipation; they left under duress. There is clearly a class dimension at play in this.

SMALL RETURNS

It is in the very patterns of the search for safety and finally of flight, the movement from the home place to another, detected in listening to multiple oral narratives, that the attempt to maintain a relationship to land and home are evident. From these accounts, it is clear that the villagers oriented to a *vicinity* – the vicinity of the home town – a relational and affective "neighbourhood", within which they attempted to remain. Moreover, while there were chains of attacks and thus departures that took people further and further afield, many still returned for various purposes. The multiple returns themselves evidence a particular structure of affect, expectation and connectedness, and index the fundamental resistance to dispossession.

Routinely, when the women and children were evacuated for their safety (though many women also stayed with the fighting men to make food and so on) they would return during the day to work on land or crops, across periods of weeks, even months. This was the case for the women from al-Abbasiyya (Yafa/ Jaffa region) who stayed in nearby Deir Tarif for about two months, according to Rayya Abu Himaid, returning regularly to harvest in their hometown, which was being defended by the men. Al-Abbasiyya was another town which did not fall quickly. Even when a town had fallen decisively, people made various returns or attempts to return, at least during the initial period before they were driven further away. Fayad al-Sheikh Yousif, from Umm al-Zaynat (Haifa), for example, recalls that "my father went by car, back to the town, he went back and died". Arifa Musa Abd al-Rahman Sarhan from al-Kafrayn (Haifa) talks of going back and finding "a ruin": "my brother and I would go and the Jews would shoot close to us". She says:

> we walked, we walked we went to a khirba near our town they call it Buwayshat. We stayed in it nearly 2–3 months, I mean this was close to our town and we would go and bring whatever we wanted from our house, I mean we want a bowl, we want some molasses, we want eggs from our chickens, we went to go check on our chickens, we would go check them and bring them.

Only after that comes the fateful trek: "the Jews were behind us ... *khalas*, there was no return".

Hussein Ahmad Rabi', from Lifta (Jerusalem), also returned repeatedly to his village: "we would go back and steal in at night take a donkey, load it carrying a quilt, a mattress and come ... I went back a lot, I used always to go back, I used to bring a lot of clothes". Umm Tawfiq Abu Rahme from Shefa-'Amr (Haifa area) had left for Lebanon with her six children.[17] She decided to try to return, and loaded a donkey with a basket carrying her baby son, took her five small daughters with her, and stole back into the country and into her hometown. She was one of the lucky ones who was able to do this successfully. Muhammad

Nawfal al-Azzeh, from Beit Jibrin (Hebron district), recalls that many disabled people had remained in the town after the townsfolk had been forced out by heavy aerial bombardment. "A number of our folks from Beit Jibrin returned to the town, to take revenge, to check on people, get things they needed; they found some of them still alive, some dead and they buried them." No one had been killed before they left, "but after we left and they started to return a number of people from our family were martyred, and from the townsfolk also another larger number".

Perhaps one of the most poignant markers of affective attachment that embodied the resistance to final departure is al-Azzeh's account of his own trips back to Beit Jibrin:

> I returned from Ithna three times a day … used to go from Ithna to Beit 'lam north east to a wood I knew, it had some of the old trees, and I would try to walk so I could see our house which was in the northernmost part of the town. About 7km there were, I would walk these 7km and then crouch during the day opposite our house and look to the southern window of our house which was blue … I would just watch that spot, and if I got weary I would climb upward to see the police station of Beit Jibrin, or veer a little to see my school, the Beit Jibrin school.

Later he recounts how he sold his brother's cows in secret in Hebron in case his brother were to be killed, as the only pasture close by was in the occupied land, and the Jews always shot at him when he slipped in there. Here, in that existential landscape, we encounter the emergence of a new category that was deployed by the colonial power, that of "infiltrators": this is the emergence of a practico-moral and epistemic space that re-writes the original attachment and rights of people to their homes and villages.

These accounts then raise a double set of issues: on the one hand they tell us that the *finalized* absence (which led to formal "refugee" status) was due not simply to the "battle", but to a policy (regardless of when it was initially formed or formulated) of chasing people continuously as far out as possible, and of not letting people return. On the other hand, they demonstrate the expectation of, and the desire and sense of entitlement to, return. The two sides of the issue emerge here: on the one side, the affective and resistant mode of action, and the strength of the attachment; and on the other side, the persistent attempt to alienate a population from its lands and home, the very policy that at the time ultimately enabled the emergence of a Jewish majority in Palestine, now named Israel.[18]

THE AFFECTIVE ECONOMY OF DISPOSSESSION

The affective rejection of loss is the underlying text of these narratives, and it is the fabric of connectedness, and the affective states that are embedded in it, that is displayed in the stories. The story of Muhammad al-'Azza from Beit Jibrin above, recounting how he would trek daily from Ithna to his village, and sit for hours looking at his house, speaks of an immensity of emotion, a heavy affective load, that clearly united need and desire, sorrow and attachment. It is this very kind of affective action, disconnected from practical or instrumental considerations, and solely grounded in attachment, that is cited by Haim Hanegbi in his account of how he became an anti-Zionist. In the film *Matzpen*, by Eran Torbinol (2004),[19] he talks of his encounter with the category of "infiltrators":

> I was the kind of weirdo who'd say, you see this ... there was a village here, here was Saris, here was Colonia ... up there [pointing up screen right] was Qastal, this here was Lifta [points screen left] ... you walk a few hundred metres and see a village, houses still standing to this day. Abandoned. Holes in the roof [gesturing], but houses and fruit trees. Where did the people go [leaning forward in bodily emphasis of the question]. Then you grow up and the memories which used to be riddles combine with the daily news. You're in high school, you read about infiltrators, in the 50s ... infiltrators, infiltrators [gesturing to signify repetition] – an existential threat to Israel. Who were these infiltrators? [Pause]. The infiltrators were *fallaheen* [peasants] who ran away or were driven out [gesturing vehemently, tone vehement], and were trying to go back to their homes. And when they realized that they couldn't get their homes back, they'd sneak in to *steal* their fruit, some even sneaked in just to see the house [touching finger to eye], not to steal or rob, certainly not to murder. Thousands of them were killed.

Hanegbi offers this mode of action (temporary or "small" returns) precisely as an embodiment of connection and entitlement. This, in turn, stands as evidence of the forceful and violent dislocation and disconnection imposed on the Palestinian population. These small (and desperate) returns are affective modes of action that express the relationship to lived place, and to its promise and potentialities. In this context they are read and readable as resistant acts.

The expressions of affect and the descriptions that bespeak and communicate emotions that were felt at past points in time tell a story in themselves, a story that spills beyond the *factual* details of past events even as it conjures them before our eyes. Listen to the words of Hajja Maliha from Saris,[20] describing what they saw on the road as they were fleeing: "I swear by God, by God we saw young men, their hair like an alluring young girl, killed, slain" ("*wallahi, wallah, shufna shabab mitl albint al-ghawiya shu'urhen, maqtulin, madhbuhin*"). In the voiced description, the tone, the bodily posture and the image projected, one can detect the sense of shocked tragedy. The emphatic oath that begins the description frames what is to come as something of great magnitude: almost unbelievable were it not true. Whilst there is no single emotion that can be definitively located or identified exogenously, it is an affective environment that is summoned: grief, horror, loss, enormity, shock. Which of these might be identified explicitly by someone, or experienced in that moment, can never be determined from an outside vantage point. What one can do is locate the intersubjective grounds for these kinds of attribution or avowal, and it is precisely these grounds that are offered in the narrative: beautiful young men, whose hair was like that of a beautiful maiden, killed at the roadside. The image draws a contrast between project and outcome: aspiration and end, life and youth on the one hand, and undeserved death and treachery on the other. It is in these contrasts that the grounds for avowing, or attributing, shock, horror or grief lie. This after all is an idiomatic way of expressing horror or sorrow at the death of the young: "*shabb mitl al-fulla*" ("a young man like a jasmine flower" – meant to convey someone at the peak of beauty and potentiality unexpectedly cut down).

"Contrasts" contain the very material of tragedy, and can underpin the ironic mode of narration. The contrast between what was then and what is now, between what could or should have been and what in fact transpired, between expectation and outcome, entitlement and fatality, and so on, explicitly or implicitly pervade Palestinian narratives, constituting their affective and moral grammar. The affective dimension of the narratives is nevertheless multi-layered: the affective condition, and the emotions that are alluded to, implied or noted, are represented as being within that past (fear, shock, sorrow), but their expression and marking indexes a present affective condition (regret, guilt, the sense of having been betrayed, the sense of trauma or enormity of the events). These are, of course, read and readable in and through the narration, and are located precisely in the connection between detail given, and the known upshot of the past's unfolding, now topicalized in a present that is thus rendered as the summation and vanishing point of that past. Past emotions are themselves often the grounds for distinct emotions in the present. In the difference and simultaneous relationship between within-event emotions and post-event emotions, we can mark the affective afterlife of past emotional states and the ways they can become grounds for contemporary action and orientation. In some respects, this is a feature of both trauma and resistance.

Hajja Halima: "and that was our departure" ("*U hadi tal'etna*"). Her expressions, bodily posture, voice, gestures, all express a stance of dramatic irony towards the past. She laughs as she describes how her townsfolk spent time covering the threshed grain before they left the village in which they had taken refuge after leaving Saris: "they were afraid the townsfolk would steal it". In the laughter, one detects the sentiment, the judgement: how foolish they were, how little they knew what was to be, what was to come; how fixed to the here and now they were, unable to grasp the enormity of what was unfolding; how small their fears and imaginings turned out to be compared to reality. It is in that fixity that the persistence of the expectation of continuity is evidenced, and the grounds that index the sense of the "catastrophic" are made clear.

As Umm Yusif from Lifta talks to her interlocutor, walking down the path to the village (on one of many subsequent post-Nakba returns to Lifta), she talks of the terror that made people leave their village after the Jewish attacks became serious:

> they killed seven from Lifta, just like this. Then came Deir Yassin and the people left, you know how? Don't you want to protect your child? Everybody wanted to protect himself. And then people were dispersed, everybody living in a different place, some in Lebanon, some in Amman, and the people were lost.[21]

For Umm Yusif, it was the final dispersal, the diaspora into Lebanon and Jordan that constituted the catastrophic moment: a moment when "the people were lost". Here the sense and meaning and coherence of life (inter-braiding individual self and collective being) are implicated in the idea of continuity and relationality of home and place. The overwhelming mood of her talk is that of the subjunctive:

the lament about having made the wrong move, and the lack of foresight in the moment of terror: "A week or two we thought, or a month. I wish they had left us in our homes. Now they are demolished, I wish they had left us in our village". Umm Yusif says this as she walks through the ruins of Lifta on the slopes of the Jerusalem mountain. It is clear as they walk and talk that most of the houses were not actually *demolished*, though some of them had been left as semi-ruins (as Hanegbi's talk above also indicates). Is this discursive slippage, the use of repeated phrases and ideas as a generic representation that stand in for the particular? Or is this talk of the "phenomenal" houses: that is, their living tie to them, their lived entitlement, their continuity? Is she saying that "their" houses were demolished, rather than the houses themselves, gesturing to the deep grammar of relationality that organizes the narrative stance in the everyday?

We can similarly detect the deep grammar of Hanegbi's description earlier, of "infiltrators": "they'd sneak in to *steal* their fruit", he says, continuing two seconds later, "not to steal or rob". Again, clearly the acting of stealing "their [own] fruit" is not phenomenally or morally isomorphic with "stealing" or "robbing": the apparent contradiction in his words operates only at the surface level. At the deeper level of moral grammar, the two are not identical. This relationality, the relational history of social actors, is part of our routine moral and ethical assessments in mundane life. More than anything, this summons the painful history in which colonial power, stripping people materially of their lands and resources, also needed to strip them of their lived and symbolic relationship to these, and transformed them discursively into "interlopers", "intruders", "infiltrators" and "terrorists".

The very language of the narratives, and their shape, map out an affective landscape, and an economy of expectations and mundane entitlements. In (pro-)Zionist narratives, the language itself, the categories used, efface this entire economy and replace it with a collapsed de-natured geographic universe, gutted of "human" lineaments: these are the colonial tropes, which re-figure the humanity of the landscape of the colony into one that is flat, de-natured, empty of recognizable human life, and fill it in with a substitute text, locating human moments and dimensions only in the colonist's world.

AFFECT AND THE IDIOMS OF COLLECTIVE MEMORY

One of the most salient features in the narratives of 1948 is the subjunctive mood, people voicing the expectation they had at the time that the dislocation from land and home would only be a few weeks, a few months at most. It evidences the depth of the sense of entitlement people had, and their trust that the rightful response to their plight would be finally enacted and implemented. This expectation of a reciprocal orientation to what is seen as patently right and rightful was fractured irremediably in the aftermath of the Nakba, as silence, complicity and betrayal came to be the patterns detected in the modes of action and response they encountered, both regionally and internationally. This repeated refrain or motif in the narratives emerges as an *idiom* of Palestinian collective memory, articulating and crystallizing a shared affective and corporeal experience and a reciprocal recollection: namely the sense of betrayal, the complete surprise at the outcome, and the idea of an entire world lost and undone. "And the people were lost."

This idiom is entangled with another motif, attesting to the unexpected and relatively sudden nature of the Nakba moment and the experience of dislocation: Umm Yusif of Lifta:

we left with nothing. I tell you, the people here did not take with them anything. We just took the children and left. We were thinking to come back, no? We had the keys with us, I showed them to you, no? We had the keys with us, we were planning to return. We left everything as it was.

"We left everything as it was": so many of the accounts reproduce a similar affectively loaded detail and specify its particulars: Hajja Halima from Saris talks of the grain that was left on the threshing floor, others of the grain about to be harvested that was left untouched; Amina Jamal from Balad al-Sheikh (Haifa) reminisces that "our house was stuffed full" (*mahshieh hashi*); Omar Atalla from Saris says of the moment of departure that "my mum had just freshly baked some bread". Such quotidian details often striate the narratives, indexing the unexpected character of the initial departure and its contingencies. Umm Ibrahim, also from Saris, remembers the plenty they left behind in their homes:

Everything remained in them. Everything remained in them, everything
… from the cupboards to the beds, from food to drink, the granaries
were full of corn flour and corn, the clay pots of olive oil, the sugar, the
rice, everything that was in the house, all of it stayed in its place my girl,
by God no one carried anything with them … thanks be to God that a

woman was able to carry her child, only![22]

This gap between the tableau of an organized life, plentiful in both its concreteness *and* its continued potentiality (its unfinished trajectory), and its sudden unexpected loss together with the meagre scale of existence left open to them, it is this contrast that is an index of the enormity of the Nakba, the measure of the catastrophe. The Nakba was about an entire life-world upended. That is why this kind of expression is repeated, detailed in various modes, all amounting to the same sentiment in the present. They are not merely expressions of an "idyllic memory" so often produced of the past; they express the affective valency of details as signifiers of a distinct condition that has been undone. These expressions too therefore become affective idioms of collective memory.

The asymmetry of arms and the inability to withstand the Jewish assault, discussed above, surfaces as another idiom in such memory work. This particular idiom within the narratives condenses and evidences perhaps a blend of regret, guilt and realism that infuses these repeated words: Qasim Darawsheh's rhetorical question, "What do you want: a rifle to resist an airplane?", is mirrored in most of the accounts. It may, in part, be an index or symptom of a cumulative yet shared experience over years of being a refugee in other countries: the repeated attacks and accusations levelled at the dispossessed Palestinians (especially in Lebanon) that they had chosen to leave their country, or even that they had "sold it". The affective tone of the present is saturated with the qualities of the affective landscape of the past; but that landscape of the past is now seen through the eye of the present, a present that has not overcome the troubles of that past and its consequences.

Emotions (affect in general) are indices of the "moral": an intersubjectively shared and acknowledged feature of the grammar of the "human" as constituted in daily practice and life. Affect, as an orientation and potentiality, as a relational valency towards the lived outside of oneself, the lived and human environment, and feeling or emotion as an immediate response to that environment and events within it, are deeply embedded in the way that agents and their actions are described, appraised and judged (sometimes deciphered) and thus in the mode of relationality towards these agents (and their actions) that is in turn legitimized or justified. In other words, the very constitution of "intersubjectivity", and the reciprocity of perspectives that is its implicit scaffolding, is intimately adjoined to, and embedded in, the mutual recognition/ality of affect and emotion. It is not a trivial matter that the worst kind of judgement of a person's humanity (or lack thereof) is the absence of emotion in the face of great events.

It is perhaps for that reason that colonial discourses extirpate and excise the emotions of the colonized subject from their accounts, except where they may be represented as having a negative valency. Thus the understanding of the colonial complex needs to pay attention to the constitutions, ascription and avowal of affect, as Laura Anne Stoler's important work demonstrates so well (see e.g. Stoler 2008a, 2008b). The various significant sites of human action and encounter, such as the reception or infliction of death, pain and loss, are where criterial emotions and sentiments are experienced and displayed. In the violence of colonial practice and policy, it is these sites which must be sanitized: if the victim of violence is perceived as affectless, then the materiality of the violence seems to be placed in doubt: this is the mode through which "violence" becomes seen as anything other than violence.[23]

So the colonial subject is made out not to feel the same emotions and affective states, at the same kinds of experiential moments, or ever to the same degree, as the colonizer's community. They are not affected in the same way. There are, of course, encounters when the colonial power and its spokespersons did not particularly care or need to do this – or inflicted death and pain not as a means but as an end (to set an example or inflict punishment). In the case of the Zionist project, however, "affect" and "emotional need and conditions" were central to the construction of colonial entitlement, indeed to the explicit denial of a colonial nature to the Zionist enterprise.

BETWEEN FACT AND MEMORY WORK: A METHODOLOGICAL NOTE

Memory, as we know, is not the simple reflection of the world as it unfolds; it has its absences, its truncations, its cross-overs, its ellipses, its inversions, its conflations and its affective sites. All these represent points of possible interference, and can work to produce an inflected refraction of past events. But they can also signify much of importance in the human experience of events, and in our understanding therefore of the lived stream of those events.[24] Whilst oral testimonies, and witnessing, cannot be the final and objective course to particular "truths", they have irremediably been constituents of the navigational practices of "truth-finding" in various cultures and societies, from the classical world to the modern. What varies extensively, however, is whose memory and/ or testimony counts, to what extent, and who makes the call as to whether it counts. As Kurt Danziger (2008: chapter 7) elaborates, which "memories" were trusted, and which were not, depended on the period and social context: some people's memory was privileged over others', some treated as authoritative, others as systematically suspect (women, children). This knot between account, account giver and judgement of legitimacy is, at each point, contingent on the practico-historical standards of the time or the group that has the power to make the call. It necessarily remains open to revision as historical contexts and standards change.

It is important to note, however, that historical "records" themselves do not offer a pristine reflection of the world as it unfolded either. Are they not also subject to institutional (and state) interests, classifications that bow to particular epistemic and moral frames, to mistakes, blind spots and self-conscious omissions?[25] Are historical statistics, for example, not unavoidably an outcome of historically situated classificatory practices: do they not often involve procedures of averaging, discounting or aggregating? Are there not matters to which access is blocked or not available, where lacunae are managed by various remedial practices? In other words, documentary records are themselves outcomes of social practices of one kind or another, rather than transparent indices of an objective truth.

Both kinds of material are irremediably situated in human and social contexts and trajectories of action. To ignore an entire corpus of testimonies, such as the Palestinian oral histories, is to prejudice (and risk) the outcome of an inquiry. This is precisely Joel Beinin's critique of Morris' historiography.[26] It is clear that both species of material (where available) are significant for any inquiry into a question of contemporary history (whether autobiographical or collective). Indeed, from the Nuremberg Tribunals to the International Criminal Tribunal for the former Yugoslavia and others, both kinds of material have been *conjointly* used, one checked and triangulated against the other. Though oral testimonies and documentary records each oblige a distinct methodology, in both cases the analyst needs to be attentive to the specific issues of their situated production, and to treat them as both topic and resource. Both need to be treated as topic and resource simultaneously, and to be conjointly read through and against the grain at the same time.

NOTES

1   The oral narratives that provide the materials for this paper are drawn, with thanks, from the following sources: Palestine Remembered (http://www.palestineremembered.com); al-Jana – Arab Resource Center for Popular Arts in Beirut (http://al-jana.org; Badil Resource Center for Palestinian Residency and Refugee Rights in Bethlehem (http://www.badil.org/en/); the Lifta interviews were collected by Mohammad 'Adarba and Lena Jayyusi; *Searching for Saris* film by Jinan Coulter (2013).

2   Interview by Jinan Coulter, Qalandia Camp, 2010, in the film *Searching for Saris* (2013), produced and directed by Jinan Coulter, co-produced by Enjaaz (a Dubai Film Market initiative), executive producer Tariq al-Ghussein. All translations of interviews are made from the transcript of the unedited rushes, and may therefore differ slightly from the translations that appear in the film.

3   Rosemary Sayigh (1979: 107) notes very similar experiential expressions that refugees used of the Nakba.

4   According to John Ruedy (1971: 134), on the eve of the proclamation of the state of Israel in May 1948, "88 [by British figures] to 91 per cent [by Zionist figures] of the cultivable soil was neither owned nor leased by Jews".

5   For example, Medding (1990); Blumberg (2013); Cavendish (1998); BBC news site, last updated 6 May 2008, on the occasion of the sixtieth anniversary of the establishment of the state/the Nakba http://news.bbc.co.uk/2/hi/middle_east/7381315.stm. There are scores of films, videos and other popular cultural sources which reproduce the same kind of narrative using similar kinds of devices, figures and silences.

6   See Ilan Pappe's (2006) critique of Morris.

7   Hayden White (1976: 32–33) writes that "The plot-structure of a historical narrative (*how* things turned out as they did), and the formal argument or explanation of *why* 'things happened or turned out as they did' are prefigured by the original description (of the 'facts' to be explained) in a given dominant modality of language use: metaphor, metonymy, synecdoche, or irony."

8   Pappe (2006) draws on archival materials as well as oral testimonies to ground the relevance of this paradigm.

9   Erskine Childers (1971) researched this much publicized claim, and found it to have no basis in fact. Benny Morris (2004) also confirms that he found no real evidence of this in his extensive research.

10   Hence the constant talk among hardline Zionists, especially those of the settler movement in the West Bank, that the Palestinians are simply itinerants passing through.

11   On the issue of the loss of gold jewellery, see Humphries and Khalili (2007: 213–215, and 223–224). See also Sayigh (2007: 151). They discuss the painful loss of gold in the events or aftermath of the dispossession; lost, taken, buried for safe keeping and never retrieved, sold for food etc. In the testimonies I am referring to, the gold is used as a means of raising money for arms: the act is experienced and recounted both as an index of need and of collective cohesion and solidarity, and at the same time of the harshness and extremity of the situation that demanded such a sacrifice.

12 See for example, Landis (2001: 178–205). Landis argues that the government of Shukri al-Quwwatli at the time had already become convinced that the Palestinian Arabs could not be rescued, and was trying to keep Abdullah of Transjordan from claiming "greater Syria". The forces under the command of Fawzi al-Qawuqji as a result were not necessarily invested in defence of Palestine. This is interesting in the light of the repeated references in various narratives to "betrayal" by al-Qawuqji.

13 The issue of asymmetry becomes more poignant when set against the powerful motif of betrayal and complicity in Palestinian oral histories. It is a theme whose rendition within the narratives awaits more detailed and sustained inquiry.

14 Tirat Haifa held out until 16 July 1948, though the attack order against it came on 14 May (see Pappe 2006: 132, 155 and 161).

15 The village of Deir Yassin was the site of a brutal massacre by Irgun forces on 9 April 1948, and is repeatedly cited in Palestinian memory accounts as being a focal point in the spread of terror among Palestinians. Tantura, a village in the Haifa region which also saw a massacre by the invading Alexandroni Brigade on 22 May 1948, is often cited by villagers from the Haifa area. For more on the Deir Yassin massacre, see McGowan and Ellis (1998). On the Tantrua massacre, see Pappe (2006: 133–137).

16 See for example the description in EyeWitness to History.com "Thousands of civilians fled before it. Traveling south in cars, wagons, bicycles, or simply on foot, the desperate refugees took with them what few possessions they could salvage. It wasn't long before the roads were impassable to the French troops who were headed north in an attempt to reach the battlefield" (http://www.eyewitnesstohistory.com/francedefeat.htm, 1). A wonderful literary text is Irene Nemirovsky's *Suite Francaise* (2014).

17 Personal communication, Shefa-'Amr 1984.

18 In her sharply honed demographic analysis of the Arab/Jewish population balance by the end of 1946 (practically the eve of the Partition Plan), Janet Abu-Lughod (1971: 154) shows that according to figures prepared jointly by the Mandate's Department of Statistics and the Jewish Agency, Jews constituted a numerical majority in only one sub-district of Palestine, the twin-city area of Yafa (Jaffa)–Tel Aviv. She concludes that "force of arms accomplished within little more than a year what decades of [Jewish] migration had decisively failed to do, namely, to effect a complete demographic transformation in the lion's share of Palestine".

19 The film was shot in Israel, Palestine, Jordan, the UK and Germany between 1999 and 2003. Video, 54 min., Hebrew, English and Arabic. DVD subtitles: Hebrew, Arabic, English, French, Spanish, Russian, German, Polish. The excerpt quoted here is available at https://www.facebook.com/BDSBarkan/videos/1816167635290762/. The film is available at https://www.youtube.com/watch?v=upoACIfPIzs.

20 Interview with Jinan Coulter in *Searching for Saris* (2013).

21 This is an English transcript of the interview; provenance unknown, but most likely from Badil Resource Centre, Bethlehem. It is interesting that the transcript of the English translation (which is what I worked with) has the phrase "and the world was lost" instead of my retranslation here as "the people were lost". The former translation

connotes an even greater sense of loss and trauma. However, it does not accord as well with the likely idiomatic colloquial Arabic expressions that use the term "*al-'Alam*", which is usually a reference to "people" – in the feminine – rather than to "the world".

22 Interview by Jinan Coulter, *Searching for Saris* (2013).

23 In *Hearts and Minds,* the award-winning film on the ravages of the Vietnam War, by Peter Davis, General Westmoreland says in interview, "the Oriental doesn't put the same high price on life as the Westerner. Life is plentiful, life is cheap in the orient" (see https://www.youtube.com/watch?v=rXjeQ8TEkc4). The juxtaposition of shots of Westmoreland saying this with scenes of Vietnamese mourning the loss of loved ones was criticized by some as manipulative. This criticism is perhaps itself an index of the discomfort of some with the "outing" of colonialism.

24 For the productive reading of silences, elisions and conflation in oral testimonies, see the work of Alessandro Portelli (especially 1991, 2003).

25 See, for example, Benny Morris' (1995) inquiry into Israeli official records.

26 Beinin (2005: 6) argues that "the exclusion of Arab voices and sources of evidence, especially in the work of Benny Morris, limited the extent of that revolution and situates some of the new history close to traditional Zionist categories of knowledge".

REFERENCES

Abu-Lughod, J.L. (1971) "The Demographic Transformation of Palestine", in I. Abu-Lughod (ed.), *The Transformation of Palestine: Essays on the Origin and Development of the Arab-Israeli Conflict.* Evanston, IL: Northwestern University Press.

Beinin, J. (2005) "Forgetfulness for Memory: The Limits of the New Israeli History", *Journal of Palestine Studies* 34(2): 6–23.

Cavendish, R. (1998) "Foundation of the State of Israel", *History Today* 48(5), http://www.historytoday.com/richard-cavendish/foundation-state-israel.

Blumberg, A. (1998) *History of Israel.* Westport, CT: Greenwood.

Chanes, J. (2013) "One Nation Under God", *Forward,* 5 February, http://forward.com/culture/170240/one-nation-under-god/.

Childers, E. (1971) "The Wordless Wish: From Citizen to Refugee", in I. Abu-Lughod (ed.), *The Transformation of Palestine: Essays on the Origin and Development of the Arab-Israeli Conflict.* Evanston, IL: Northwestern University Press.

Danizger, K. (2008) *Marking the Mind: a History of Memory.* Cambridge: Cambridge University Press.

Humphries, I. and L. Khalili (2007) "Gender of Nakba Memory", in A.H. Sa'di and L. Abu-Lughod (eds.), *Nakba: Palestine, 1948 and the Claims of Memory* New York: Columbia University Press.

Karsh, E. and R. Miller, eds. (2013) *Israel at Sixty: Rethinking the Birth of the Jewish State.* Abingdon: Routledge,.

Landis, J. (2001) "Syria and the 1948 War in Palestine", https://faculty-staff.ou.edu/L/Joshua.M.Landis-1/Syria_1948.htm.

McGowan, D. and M.H. Ellis, eds. (1998) *Remembering Deir Yassin: The Future of Israel and Palestine*. New York: Olive Branch Press.

Medding, P.Y. (1990) *The Founding of Israeli Democracy, 1948–1967*. New York: Oxford University Press.

Morris, B. (1995) "Falsifying the Record: A Fresh look at Zionist Documentation of 1948", *Journal of Palestine Studies* XXIV(3): 44–62.

Morris, B. (2004) *The Birth of the Palestinian Refugee Problem Revisited*, 2nd ed. Cambridge: Cambridge University Press.

Nemirovsky, I. (2014) *Suite Francaise*, translated by S. Smith. London: Vintage.

Pappe, I. (2006) "Preface", in *The Ethnic Cleansing of Palestine*. Oxford: Oneworld Publications.

Portelli, A. (1991) *The Death of Luigi Trastulli and Other Stories: Form and Meaning in Oral History*. Albany, NY: SUNY Press.

Portelli, A. (2003) *The Order Has Been Carried Out: History, Meaning and Memory of a Nazi Massacre in Rome*. Basingstoke: Palgrave Macmillan.

Rogan, E. and A. Shlaim, eds. (2001) *Rewriting the Palestine War: 1948 and the History of the Arab-Israeli Conflict*. Cambridge: Cambridge University Press.

Ruedy, J. (1971) "The Dynamics of Land Alienation", in I. Abu-Lughod (ed.), *The Transformation of Palestine: Essays on the Origin and Development of the Arab-Israeli Conflict*. Evanston, IL: Northwestern University Press.

Said, E. (1984) "Permission to Narrate", *JPS* 13(3): 27–48.

Sayigh, R. (1979) *Palestinians: From Peasants to Revolutionaries*. London, Zed Books.

Sayigh, R. (2007) "Women's Nakba Stories: Between Being and Knowing", in A.H. Sa'di and L. Abu-Lughod (eds.), *Nakba: Palestine, 1948 and the Claims of Memory*. New York: Columbia University Press.

Stoler, L.A. (2008a) "Affective States", in

Stoler, L.A. (2008b) "Epistemic Politics: Ontologies of Colonial Common Sense", *The Philosophical Forum* 39(3): 349–361.

White, H. (1976) "The Fictions of Factual Representation", in A. Fletcher (ed.), *The Literature of Fact*. New York: Columbia University Press.

PART III
Archiving the Nakba through Palestinian refugee women's voices

5
Nakba silencing and the challenge of Palestinian oral history

ROSEMARY SAYIGH

In making Zionism attractive – that is, making it attract genuine support in the deepest sense – its leaders not only ignored the Arab; when it was necessary to deal with him, they made him intelligible, they represented him to the West as something that could be understood and managed in specific ways. Between Zionism and the West there was and still is a community of language and of ideology, and the Arab was not part of this community. To a very great extent this community depends on a remarkable tradition in the West of enmity towards Islam in particular and the Orient in general (Said 1979: 25–26).

Late modern colonial occupation differs in many ways from early modern occupation, particularly in its combination of the disciplinary, the bio-political and the necro-political. The most accomplished form of necro-power is the contemporary colonial occupation of Palestine. Here the colonial state derives its fundamental claim of sovereignty and legitimacy from the authority of its own particular narrative of history and identity. The narrative is itself underpinned by the idea that the state has a divine right to exist; the narrative competes with another for the same sacred space. Because the two narratives are incompatible and the two populations are inextricably intertwined, any demarcation of the territory on the basis of pure identity is quasi-impossible. Violence and sovereignty in this case claim a divine foundation: peoplehood itself is forged by the worship of one deity, and national identity is imagined as an identity against the Other, other deities. History, geography, cartography and archaeology are supposed to back these claims. As a consequence, colonial violence and occupation are profoundly underwritten by the sacred terror of truth and exclusivity (mass expulsions, resettlement of "stateless" people in refugee camps, settlement of new colonies). (Mbembe 2003: 27)

INTRODUCTION

If the details of Zionism's expulsion of the indigenous inhabitants of Palestine in 1948[1] had not been transferred through family and community memories, the Nakba would be little more than a single event in the transformation of the Ottoman empire into a set of nation-states on the Western model. The Nakba's disastrous consequences for the people of Palestine would be suppressed in well-oiled colonial terms such as "population exchange" or "re-settlement". True, the documents existed from which to fill out the factors that crowned the Zionist movement with statehood in 1948 (Morris 1987; Masalha 1992). But entirely missing from this record is the experience for the people of Palestine of the 1948 expulsions, leading to collective consequences that I conceptualize as "damaged lives". This concept has primarily been used in relation to health, family, sexuality and the individual, but I propose to extend its meaning to any collectivity displaced or expropriated by the international power structure. The expulsions of 1948 damaged the Palestinians by reducing them from potential citizens of a sovereign state for which Britain was assigned by the Mandate to prepare them, under article 22 of the League of Nations Covenant, to a situation of disenfranchisement, partial dependence on international charity and host state toleration. Economic interventions by the Great Powers such as the establishment of the United Nations Relief and Works Agency (UNRWA) merely reinforced separation from their homeland and entrenched their loss of national recognition (Pappe 1994). Around 156,000 Palestinians who remained inside the territory controlled by Israel were differentiated by sect and assigned second-class citizenship (Zureik et al. 2011).

The importance of the Nakba as rupture in Palestinian lives and history is incontestable. Displacement meant loss of homes and land, archives, libraries, public buildings, archaeological treasures, and the rupture of national institutions and identity under construction since the late Ottoman Empire. Whatever their class, residence or status, it damaged Palestinian lives to some degree, and none more than those who were forced by destitution to settle in camps. Their reaction to dispossession has been well described by Davis:

> the destruction they experienced in 1948 has resulted in continuous assertions in writing, oral accounts, and everyday conversations of their indigenous presence on the land; of their connections to the surrounding cultures and heritages; and of the long history and ties to the land of Palestine, the land of their ancestors. (Davis 2011: 19)

NAKBA SILENCING

The violence used in silencing the Nakba is demonstrated both in the multiplicity of means employed, and the extent of institutional investment in them, stretching beyond the Israeli state to Zionist organizations worldwide, and to the United States. Among these means, a central one has been ensuring the commemorative primacy of the Nazi Holocaust. Holocaust remembrance is funded and supported by a host of sources, most prominently by Jewish organizations, Israel and the United States. The success of the campaign to keep the Holocaust in the forefront of world consciousness is demonstrated by a number of signs: Jewish and international associations that have been established to secure Holocaust remembrance, for example the Shoah Foundation for education on the Holocaust and other genocides, the Task Force for International Cooperation on Holocaust Education, Remembrance and Research.[2] Holocaust denial is illegal in fourteen European countries plus Israel and Australia; criminalization of Holocaust denial has been discussed in the United States and the United Kingdom but not put into law; in some countries jurists consider that Holocaust denial is covered by laws against "hate speech".[3] A EU Framework Decision on Racism and Xenophobia says that Holocaust denial should be punishable by all member states, but leaves compliance open.[4] All the countries of the Organisation for Security and Cooperation in Europe (OSCE) have Holocaust memorials (OSCE 2015).[5] The United Nations Educational, Scientific and Cultural Organisation (UNESCO) and the George Eckert Institute for International Text Book Research have undertaken a project to investigate world school curricula to assess if and how the Holocaust is dealt with.[6]

Much of the aid raised for victims of the Holocaust is said to have found its way back into Holocaust remembrance funds, with US backing (Finkelstein 2000: 130, 131). When the Polish parliament tried to limit compensation, Elan

Steinberg of the World Jewish Congress denounced this as "fundamentally an anti-American act" (Finkelstein 2000: 131). Finkelstein notes further that:

> Apart from Holocaust memorials, fully seventeen states mandate or recommend Holocaust programs in schools, and many colleges and universities have endowed chairs in Holocaust studies. Hardly a week passes without a major Holocaust-related story in the *New York Times*. (Finkelstein 2000: 143)

Holocaust museums have been established in as many as thirty countries around the world, and twenty-five in the US alone, seven of them in New York, with the largest in Washington on the national mall.

American hyper-memorialization of the Holocaust raises questions of motivation: is it designed to keep the eye of censure on Germany for war crimes in World War II, obscuring those committed by the Allies, such as Hiroshima and Nagasaki, or the fire-bombing of Dresden? Or is it to divert attention from genocides against indigenous peoples committed by European colonizers in America and elsewhere? Or to bury slavery and its contemporary sequels in order to avoid real compensation? Whatever the motivation, Holocaust museums in the US and the pedagogic programmes attached to them maintain an idea of Israel's existence as recompense for unparalleled suffering, as well as creating support for an alliance that costs American taxpayers dearly.[7]

The American alliance that protects Israeli violence from censure surely has many components, among them a similar origin in colonial expropriation, and a shared biblical tradition that exhorts its followers to destroy their enemies. The violence of biblical language has been noted by several scholars, for example Masalha (2013: 75). Using text analytics software, Osborne (2016) found the Old Testament to be more than twice as violent as the Quran.[8] The term "Judeo-Christianity", increasingly used since the 1940s to define America's "civic religion", differs notably from the previously common term "monotheistic religions" by excluding Islam.[9] The US and Israel also share interests in control of Arab oil, exclusion of non-Western influences and prevention of Arab unity. Recent research has put a question to the long-standing idea of US neutrality between Arabs and Israel until the demonstration of Israel's military superiority in the "Six Day War", by revealing that Zionist–US alliance building began before Israel's establishment (Gendzier 2016).

A major strategic advantage Zionism possessed in its diplomacy to the West – and even beyond – was the Bible. From the first century AD Christian missionaries carried the Bible to all part of the world. Notions of the "Holy Land" disseminated by Western scholars and travellers helped justify Zionism's claim to ownership by extracting Palestine from the Arab/Muslim east and attaching it notionally to Europe. Moreover, the "Holy Land" concept was basic to the construction of "Christian Zionism", precursor to Jewish Zionism and its most important source of international support. The disposition of Protestants in general and evange-lists in particular to advocate for Jewish "return" to Palestine is well substantiated (Sharif 1983). Evangelists such as Falwell and Robertson in the US preach strongly for Israel.[10] Even in Africa evangelical Christians support Israel.[11]

It goes without saying that the Nakba has not been commemorated in the way the Holocaust has. Indeed, a primary factor suppressing the Nakba in the global awareness is the power of Holocaust commemoration. The influ-ence of the global north over education systems worldwide, whether through UN development aid or publishing power, renders full coverage of the Nakba unlikely even in textbooks on the Middle East. The spread of human rights curricula incorporating the Holocaust as a major violation is another factor in the suppression of the Nakba. This linking has universalized Holocaust teaching to an exceptional degree, illustrated in a bizarre attempt to introduce it in UNRWA schools in Gaza in 2009. That this project was under serious consider-ation by UNRWA's Gaza field director John Ging is evident from contemporary media reports in which Ging is quoted as saying: "No human-rights curriculum is complete without inclusion of the facts of the Holocaust, and its lessons" (MacIntyre 2009). Given that Gaza is besieged and continually attacked by Israel, and that 43.5% of Gaza's population is aged under fourteen, this initiative can surely be classified as symbolic violence.

Silencing the Nakba has had the effect of representing the Jewish takeover of Palestine as a legitimate reward for victimhood rather than as an act of colonialism consciously projected along European lines, and intended to support Western hegemony over the Arab east (Said 1979: 29; Masalha 2012: 34). The power of Holocaust commemoration suppresses not only the Nakba but also the causal connection between the Holocaust and the Nakba, just as a building constructed over another buries the history embodied in the first (Trouillot 1997). Indeed, the siting of Israel's extensive Holocaust museum, the Yad Vashem, on the lands of Deir Yassin, renders the ruined massacre site invisible to all but those who know of its presence. Yad Vashem is "a vast, sprawling complex of tree-studded walkways leading to museums, exhibits, archives, monuments, sculptures and memorials ... 62 mil pp of docs, 267,5000 photos, thousands of films and video-taped testimonies ... 3.2 mil names of Holocaust victims" (Masalha 2005: 6, 7). The Kfar Shaul mental hospital established in 1951 covers homes ruined during the massacre. The graves of those who died in Deir Yassin are unknown and unmarked. Forests established by the Jewish National Fund cover the ruins of villages destroyed during 1948 (Pappe 2006: 229–234).

The Deir Yassin massacre is not forgotten but the form of its commemoration highlights the contrast in resources between Israel and the Palestinians. The annual gathering of massacre survivors and descendants near the ruins of the village on the anniversary, 8 April, is characteristic of modes of Nakba commemoration.[12] These people form one of many Palestinian "communities of mourning" that remember specific tragedies as part of a Nakba that continues and expands. It is through such coming together on commemoration days that Palestinian history is formed, in a highly variable mingling of the personal, familial, local and national.

Such events punctuate the calendars produced by Palestinian villages, political parties and non-governmental organizations (NGOs) across the diaspora, a form of history-making that binds local communities to the broader frameworks of "people" and "nation". These calendars give evidence of the way place and political context diversify Nakba commemoration. While the Nakba and other tragedies such as the massacre of Tal al-Za'ter in 1976 were among the main events marked by Fateh calendars during the period of armed struggle, this changed after Oslo, but not everywhere equally: while a third of events on a Fateh-affiliated NGO calendar in Lebanon in 2002 were massacres, Fateh calendars in the West Bank highlighted events connected with state-building, cutting down on massacres (Khalili 2007: 163). Since Oslo, diversity between regions in terms of Nakba remembrance has grown: semi-ignored in areas under the National Authority until the fiftieth anniversary in 1998, when Arafat declared a national Nakba Day, with appropriate political and cultural manifestations;[13] followed ritualistically in Lebanon;[14] while in Israel young Palestinians are marking the fall of individual villages in 1948 as part of vigorous campaigns of reclamation (Hawari 2014).

Adding to the variability of Nakba commemoration over time and between diasporic regions is the number of other tragedies that have punctuated Palestinians' post-1948 history, the massacres and sieges from Deir Yassin to Yarmouk camp, each more immediate in local experience than the original catastrophe. As annual repetition fades Nakba mourning, new technology permits the virtual reconstruction of disaster-stricken communities. In a recent instance, survivors of the Tal al-Za'ter massacre of 1976 in Lebanon have created "afterlives" on Facebook (Yaqub 2015). Segmented by geography, diverse educational systems and political affiliations, and in the absence of a forceful liberation movement, the Palestinians find in local communities the best vehicles for transmitting Palestinian history as they experience it.

Among Israeli measures to silence the Nakba are decrees banning use of the term in school books on pain of withdrawal of state funding (Strickland 2015).[15] Police force has been used to remove Nakba Day demonstrators, and to target Zochrot, an Israeli NGO that records Nakba memories (Horowitz 2012). Yet more powerful than Israeli interdicts has been American silencing. As Abu-Lughod and Sa'di point out, "The debilitating factor in the ability to tell their stories and make public their memories is that the powerful nations have not wanted to listen" (Sa'di and Abu-Lughod 2007: 11). It was not until the 1990s that American university presses began to publish research-based Palestinian studies (e.g. Slyomovics 1989; Peteet 1991; Swedenburg 1995). The 2007 publication of *Nakba: Palestine, 1948, and the Claims of Memory*, edited by Ahmad Sa'di and Lila Abu-Lughod, with its use of the hitherto censored term Nakba as its main title, was a breakthrough that marked full "permission to narrate".

In relation to the Palestinian Nakba we are faced with a paradox: on the one hand there was rapid understanding that this rupture was of the utmost political seriousness for the Arab region as well as the Palestinians. This awareness generated a large number of political studies, of which the best known is Constantine Zurayk's *Ma'na al-Nakba*.[16] Zurayk wrote:

> The defeat of the Arabs in Palestine is no simple setback or light, passing evil. It is a disaster in every sense of the word, and one of the harshest of the trials and tribulations with which the Arabs have been afflicted throughout their long history – a history marked by numerous trials and tribulations. (Zurayk 1956: 2)

Yet on the other hand we find an absence of interest on the part of Palestinian cultural institutions in recording Nakba experience. These post-Nakba institutions were directed by an elite to whom oral history was not only unfamiliar but also suspect in giving voice to the "ignorant". Moreover, conveying Nakba suffering was not a priority for directors who aimed at convincing the "international community" that support for Israel damaged Western interests in the Middle East. As Mahmoud Issa remarks, the *fallaheen*:

> are almost totally absent from history writing … Not only men's voices, but women's too are absent, neglected and marginalised … the Palestinian nationalist narrative was always an elite narrative; until recently we have only heard the voices of Palestinian elite groups, urban notables and official spokespersons, on the one hand, and Israeli versions of the events and the orthodox Zionist discourse, on the other. (Issa 2005: 180)

In 1996 Palestinian political scientist/historian Saleh Abdel Jawad, who had trained at Columbia in oral history methods, put forward a plan to record interviews with expulsees from all regions of Palestine. He called it "Race Against Time". His project was declined by the Institute of Palestine Studies on the grounds of lack of funds.[17]

THE CHALLENGE OF PALESTINIAN ORAL HISTORY

A host of initiatives have partially filled the gap left by the national institutions, notably Birzeit's "Destroyed Village" series, undertaken by the university's Centre for Research and Documentation of Palestinian Society (CRDPS); Al-Jana's collection commemorating the Nakba's fiftieth anniversary (1998); the website PalestineRemembered initiated by Salah Mansour in 2000, with interviews recorded in Syria, Jordan, Lebanon and Gaza;[18] the Nakba archive recorded by Diana Allan and Mahmoud Zeidan in 2002 in Lebanon with over 650 survivors from over 150 villages and towns;[19] the Oral History Centre in the Islamic University of Gaza (Catron 2013); the Nakba Museum Project of Memory and Hope (Washington, DC);[20] and a still growing number of Palestinian village histories, using oral history in varying degrees (Davis 2011). The absence of a central plan means that regional coverage of the Nakba and the *shatat* is highly uneven. Palestinians in some parts, for example Lebanon and Jordan, have been intensively recorded, while in others, for example Iraq, Kuwait, Saudi Arabia, Israel and the United States, little or no work has been done, and the histories of these communities remain relatively unknown.

The Nakba stimulated an intense outpouring of poetic, literary, autobiographical and artistic production in the Arab region, from figures such as Emil Habibi, Ghassan Kanafani, Mahmoud Darweesh, Samih Kassem, Tawfiq Ziyad, Fawaz Turki, Samira Azzam, Ismail Shammout, Tamam Akhal, Joumana Husseini, Mustafa Hallaj and Suleiman Mansour. The celebrated Lebanese singer Fairooz sang about Jerusalem and the refugees in the mid-1960s, and about Beisan and the hope of return. The anger and grief that was being expressed in poetry, fiction, music and painting found its parallel at the popular level in stories refugees and exiles told to each other. As Abu-Lughod and Sa'di observe: "many Palestinian refugees of the Nakba generation told their stories over and over, to their children and to each other" (Sa'di and Abu-Lughod 2007: 11), forming, as they remark "dissident memory, counter-memory ... a counter history" (Sa'di and Abu-Lughod 2007: 6). Masalha (2008: 136) comments: "Story telling and oral history was deployed in the post-1948 period by the Palestinian refugee community as an 'emergency science'"; and Feldman writes that "maintaining a refrain of home" helped Palestinians survive the Nakba.[21]

For Salman Natour, a dissident Palestinian citizen of Israel, remembering was an obligation: "If we lose our memory, hyenas will eat us". Natour wrote his memories in a trilogy, *Memory*, *Travel Over Travel* and *Waiting*, which "move[s] back and forth between fiction, nonfiction and oral history documentation" (Hassan 2016). The memories contained within scattered Palestinian communities eventually became accessible to researchers and NGOs as recording technology became more widely available, leading to studies presenting personal experiences as well as a number of oral history collections. This trend was supported by the rise of academic interest in memory in the 1980s.

It was in the mid-1980s that an institutional appreciation of oral history developed at Birzeit's CRDPS, impelled by concern to document the villages destroyed by Israel during 1948.[22] The Centre was first directed by anthropologist Sharif Kanaana, recorder of Palestinian folk tales (Muhawi and Kanaana 1989), and later by political scientist Saleh Abdel Jawad. Both scholars used oral testimonies, though in dissimilar ways (Al-Hardan 2016: 44). A similar centre was established at the Islamic University of Gaza in 1998. Rochelle Davis attributes this surge of popular interest in remembrance to the forced evacuation of the Palestine Liberation Organization (PLO) from Lebanon to Tunis in 1982, a setback that turned Palestinians towards:

local and personal resources, memories, personal records, and documents held within their own families and communities. The sudden flourishing of the village books in the later 1980s reflects this fundamental shift in where Palestinians are investing their voices. No longer are they relying on a distant and compromised PLO leadership to represent and define them; rather they are creating elaborate dossiers in the form of village books to tell who they were, who they are today, and why their histories are important. (Davis 2011: 251)

As a predominantly rural society until 1948 Palestinians possessed a highly developed oral culture, in which all kinds of knowledge – methods of farming, property boundaries, genealogies, proverbs, folk poetry and stories, songs, myths, history – were transmitted orally. Wandering storytellers, the *hakawati*, kept audiences aware of current as well as past events (Masalha 2008). Although oral history as a method of history-making did not develop in Palestinian research and publishing institutions until many years after their establishment, the first Palestinian oral historian we know of, albeit an amateur, appeared on the cusp of the Nakba. A man called Ibrahim Abu Higleh is recalled by Shafiq Ghabra, a Palestinian resident in Kuwait, as systematically taking notes at Palestinian gatherings on a range of topics, "by listening and recording carefully what is said during gatherings" (Ghabra 1988: 2). Both Abu Higleh and his notes seem to have disappeared without trace, though since his village of origin is known it is not impossible that his work may one day be recovered.

In the early 1970s, with the PLO in control of the camps in Lebanon, a professional oral historian, Palestinian Nafez Nazzal, carried out a study on the Nakba as part of a doctoral dissertation at Georgetown University under the supervision of Hisham Sharabi. Nazzal interviewed over 100 refugees between Lebanon and Syria, aiming at discovering what had forced them to leave their villages.[23] His book, *The Palestinian Exodus from Galilee: 1848*, was published in 1978 by the Institute for Palestine Studies in Beirut. In his Foreword, historian Rashid Khalidi remarks that Nazzal's study "provides irrefutable evidence that the foundations of the state of Israel was accompanied by, and indeed conditional on, the wholesale expulsion of the Palestinian Arab majority of the population from their homes and property" (Nazzal 1978: x).

Ted Swedenburg and Sonia el-Nimr at Birzeit University were among the first scholars to use oral history methods in Palestinian research (el-Nimr 1990;

Swedenburg 1995). Swedenburg (1995) used oral history, as did Bayan al-Hout for her PhD study (1981), and for her later book on the Sabra/Shateela massacre (2004). Sam Bahour (1994) achieved wide coverage of Occupied Palestine and the diaspora in his oral history with the Lynds. Randa Farah used oral history for her PhD, and for a study of identity in al-Baq'a refugee camp (1997). Sherna Berger Gluck (1994) used oral history in Palestine for advocacy. Adel Yahya formed an oral history archive at el-Bireh, and used it to write books on the refugees and camps (Yahya 1999). Faiha Abdulhadi (1999, 2006a, 2006b) has recorded three generations of Palestinian women on their engagement in national struggle. Saleh Abdel Jawad (2007) recorded 450 survivors from eighty-six villages for his study of Nakba massacres. Mustafa Kabha (2013) combined oral with documentary sources in his book on the Palestinians. The life stories of sixteen Palestinians from various backgrounds living in different parts of Occupied Palestine have been recorded and published by Malek and Hoke (2015).

Researchers interested in Palestinian history, politics, identity, refugees and women have moved in the direction of oral history through intensive use of the interview. This category is too large to include instances here, but I note that the surge in women's studies that began in the 1970s brought subjectivity and speech to the fore in work with Palestinians (as in Peteet 1991; Najjar 1992; Moors 1995; Abdo and Lentin 2002; Fleischmann 2003; Shalhoub-Kevorkian 2009; Abdo 2014), and in a number of personal memoirs (e.g. Sakakini 1987; Shahid 2000; Karmi 2002). An increase in reportage on Palestinian communities also brings "ordinary" people to the foreground, quoting, naming and contextualizing them (e.g. Sayigh 1994; Slyomovics 1989; Pearlman 2003; Yahya 1999; Tabar 2007; Hammami 2010; Omer 2015).

The recent establishment of the Palestinian Oral History programme in the Library Archive of the American University of Beirut gives hope that smaller collections may be replicated and made more accessible to researchers.[24] The tragedy of Syria and the destruction of Palestinian communities there reminds us that the consequences of the Nakba are still being played out. Syria was the host country where Palestinian NGOs such as Wajeb (Palestine Return Community) were most active in commemorating and recording village histories (Al-Hardan 2016: 199 fn 4); and Yarmouk was the site of Al-Shajjara, publisher of many village histories until the death of its founder Ghassan Shihabi in 2013 at the hands of a sniper. The Ibrahim Abu-Lughod Institute of International Studies at

Birzeit has a varied oral history holding. Other small local collections are known to exist but do not so far figure on any central register.

There have been a number of critiques of oral history by scholars engaged in work with Palestinians. Yezid Sayigh lists among its defects:

> the effects of weak or selective memory, lack of imprecision of concrete historical detail, ideologically driven portrayal of past events, personal self-promotion, and adaptation or outright distortion of responses in accordance either with the perceived aims and prejudices of the interviewer or with the current political agenda of the interviewee. (Sayigh 1997: xvi)

The Israeli historian Benny Morris has expressed scepticism about the reliability of Palestinian memory of 1948: "My limited experience with such interviews revealed enormous gaps of memory, the ravages of aging and time, and terrible distortions or selectivity, the ravages of accepted wisdom, prejudice and political beliefs and interests" (Morris 1987: 2). But later research has revealed the inadequacy of Morris' documentary sources, for example in underestimating massacres, rapes (Abdel Jawad 2007) and, most importantly, intentionality on the part of the Zionist/Israeli leadership. Pappe notes:

> As he exclusively relied on documents from Israeli military archives, Morris ended up with a very partial picture of what happened on the ground ... The picture was partial because Morris took the Israeli military reports he found in the archives at face value or even as absolute truth. Thus he ignored such atrocities as the poisoning of the water supply into Acre with typhoid, numerous cases of rape, and the dozens of massacres the Jews perpetrated. He also insisted – wrongly – that before 15 May 1948 there had been no forced evictions ... Had Morris and others used Arab sources or turned to oral history, they might have been able to get a better grasp of the systematic planning behind the expulsion of the Palestinians in 1948, and provide a more truthful description of the crimes the Israeli soldiers committed. (Pappe 2006: xv)

Rosemarie Esber, who recorded with Palestinians in Lebanon and Jordan in 2001, justifies using oral history on the basis of the illiteracy of the older generation, making orality the "only choice". But she adds that "Palestinian oral interviews in the aggregate are supported by a wealth of independent sources, are internally and externally consistent, and provide a credible means of contributing to the reconstruction of events" (Esber 2008: 400).

ACTIVIST ORAL HISTORY, REPARATIVE HISTORIES

Up to this point I have been writing as if the major rationale of work in Palestinian oral history is to challenge the exclusion of the Nakba from world knowledge. While such an aim is justified by the international community's complicity in Zionist colonialism (Cronin 2011), there is more crucial work that Palestinian oral history work can carry out. The Nakba is not past but ongoing, manifested in the occupation itself, settlement construction, in killings that are not investigated or punished, illegal detention, torture, home demolitions, land grabs and community evictions.[25]

In an essay comparing Palestinian and Zapatista resort to law, Linda Quiquivix notes that Zapatistas engage with law "as a particular form and structure for the exercise and circulation of power", one based in modern Western political thought that sharply divides ruler from ruled. While Zapatistas act outside state law to assert their rights, Palestinians wait for self-determination to be "granted by a small group of actors in the carefully controlled arenas of courts and legislatures". This writer admits that legal appeals have increased sympathy for the Palestinians in the West, yet "the situation on the ground continues to slip further into the most dire" (Quiquivix 2013–2014: n.p.). This analysis underlines the need for more radical forms of anti-colonial struggle.

A crucial point in Zapatista strategy, according to Quiquivix, is their takeover of schooling in areas they control. For Palestinians to achieve a more effective liberation strategy they need a different kind of history from those offered by UNRWA and Arab education systems: histories that tell about their resistance. Though histories of Palestine invariably mention the Great Revolt of 1936–1939 as a major challenge to British domination, there has been little study of its modes of organization and popular participation. Even Ghassan Kanafani's booklet "The 1936–39 Revolt in Palestine" (n.d.), valuable though it is for political analysis, lacks the details that only participants could give. Working much later in Lebanon, Zeina Ghandour (2011) sought out survivors of the revolt in the camp of Baddawi, and recorded their memories. Maryse Ghandour's film about the Great Revolt, *The Land Speaks Arabic* (2007), includes testimonials by militants from Balad al-Sheikh and Safsaf. But there were many other episodes and forms of resistance against both the British government and the Zionist colonizers. Traces of these may remain in Palestinian memories, post-memories and oral traditions, and can be sought out by researchers and activists. As an example of popular resistance I offer this extract:

> Somebody told the Ingleez that there are revolutionaries hiding in al-Birweh. The British captured them and took them to an open space with *subayr*. It was July. They told the youths to pick the cactus fruits. Then they threw the cactus branches on top of the *shabab* and stepped on them. They made another group carry heavy stones and soil in their *kumbaz* from one place to another ... They came to the houses of the rebels to take clothes, mattresses and grains to burn them. I rescued the mattresses and took them to the *bayara* ... people asked me to take water to them. The Ingleez tried to stop me. I grabbed a soldier's rifle and threw it down. The soldier said, "I'll shoot you", but I went on with the water to my son and the others among the olives. They were black, black, you couldn't recognize them. My son was crying, he said the other *shabab* are dead under the cactus. I poured [water] into my son's mouth. I said, "No, my dear, they are alive. Share the water among you".26

As a people whose lives have been damaged by imperialist/colonialist power, Palestinians are in need of reparative histories. Reparative histories are of a kind that restore agency:

> reparative history is about more than contemplating injury or apportioning blame. It is about agency, and it can be wedded to a form of memory energised by the emancipatory activism, solidarity and political struggles of the past ... The concept of the reparative ... enables the work of mourning to be connected to the politics of material redress by refusing to understand the history of "race", imperialism and slavery from the vantage point of contemporary reason and progress. *The point here is to excavate histories of resistance, solidarity and collectivity as vital for the now.* (Bergin and Rupprecht 2016: 12; italics added)

People with "damaged lives" need full knowledge of the capacities and methods of resistance their forefathers and foremothers employed in the past, so as to revive and adapt them for "the now". They need to sustain their anger and desire for restoration. Reparative history "is concerned with grievance as the starting point of politics, with no easy relation to a restorative project, but recognising grievance and rage as the agent of history" (Bergin and Rupprecht 2016: 12). It will replace narratives founded in liberal universalism with "those founded in rage, resistance and redress" (15).

Close to seven decades after the Nakba, Palestinians are still refusing to forget. Yet access to their past is constrained by the educational programmes to which they are subjected. As noted earlier, resistance during the Mandate has not been fully researched, and questions have not been asked about informal modes through which, after 1948, the expulsees remembered Palestine, nor how they adapted to the *shatat* without abandoning their Palestinian-ness. The little investigated history of life in the *shatat* would certainly yield testimonies of how people coped from day to day with "damaged lives".

Currently the Nagab is a target area for displacement, with Israel planning 1,195 new settlements and renewing attacks on Bedouin villages.[27] Recording attacks and resistance to them would make oral history more relevant to Palestinians, as well as developing its original aim of challenging the narratives of the powerful. As Thayer Hastings writes:

> While recording stories of Palestinian elders who witnessed the Nakba is more urgent than ever, oral history also has the potential to amplify community struggles to defend against current displacements by documenting protests, legal battles, and cultural expression. This provides a space for a counter narrative that is particularly useful to Palestinian communities living under Israeli rule, whether in the Occupied Palestinian Territory or in Israel, or for Palestinians marginalized by other governments. (Hastings 2016)

Hastings adds:

> Two communities in urgent need of oral history as an activist practice are the neighboring villages of Attir and Umm al-Hiran in the northern Naqab. These villages immediately south of the Green Line of the West Bank are home to around 1,000 residents and are under immediate threat of expulsion, much like the nearby South Hebron Hills villages including

Susiya. A recent Israeli High Court ruling has slated Attir and Umm al-Hiran for demolition and replacement with a Jewish-only town and a Jewish National Fund forest.[28]

Hastings crucially links activist oral history practice to the future, and to the right of return as target point for Palestinian cultural activism:

> Working outside of and in opposition to the legal discourse highlights the law's limitations and affirms indigeneity in the face of settler colonial law. It therefore also extends forward, creating alternative narratives and opens the space for planning how to implement the right of return. (Hastings 2016)

CONCLUSION

The vast size of work in Palestinian oral history compared with the rest of the Arab east suggests the degree to which the Nakba has impelled "ordinary" Palestinians to remember, reflect upon and speak about the historic disaster that separated them from their homeland, ruptured their history and forced them to lead "damaged lives". Orality is an important part of their struggle against colonialist erasure, displacement, siege, oppression and impoverishment. An important part of the new activism will be campaigning to get Palestinian oral history introduced into history curricula, since the power of the Zionist narrative erases or deforms understanding of the Nakba. This is especially critical now that Israeli state archives are about to be closed, which will restrict research into the production of the Nakba.

Current reflections on Palestinian oral history suggests that we are at a moment of radical transformation in conceptualization and practice. Central to this transformation is the idea that oral history recording should be activist and political rather than academic in its aims and method. The historical context for this change is intensification of Israeli violence, decline in hope of international intervention, and co-optation of the national leadership in its form as the PLO.

There is growing awareness of the role oral history can play in connecting Palestinian communities to each other across the *shatat*, and to the international solidarity movement. Mobilizing to protect local communities against displacement is central to the new conceptualization, based in awareness that these communities are living archives of resistance histories. An activist praxis of oral history takes community building as an aim through fulfilling needs for localized knowledge.

Cultural activism also implies democratization of oral history practice, as in: (a) giving back oral histories to the communities and individuals that offer them; (b) addressing issues that concern marginal communities; (c) conducting oral history teaching workshops in such communities; (d) mobilizing to establish cultural centres and archives in them; (e) adopting changes in technology, such as more use of visual media to show speakers' homes and neighbourhoods, or the use of mobile phones for ease of access to testimonies compared with university collections.

NOTES

1   Convention pins the mass expulsion of Palestinians to 1948 but in fact it began in 1947 and continued afterwards, particularly in the Nagab (Pappe 2006: 55–60; Maddrell 1990: 6–8).

2   Its name was changed in 2015 to the International Holocaust Remembrance Alliance.

3   http://en.wikipedia.org/wiki/Laws_against_Holocaust_denial.

4   http://en.wikipedia.org/wiki/laws_against_Holocaust_denial.

5   The OSCE is a mainly European setup that includes Turkey.

6   https://en.unesco.org/news/new-report-maps-global-status-holocaust-education-o?language=en.

7   "Israel is the largest cumulative recipient of foreign assistance since World War 2. To date, the United States has provided Israel $124 billion dollars … In bilateral assistance" (Sharp 2015). Israel also receives funds from annual defence appropriations.

8   "Violence more common in Bible than Quran, text analysis reveals", *Independent* 9 February 2016. Osborne used Odin software.

9   https://en.wikipedia.org/wiki/Judeo-Christian.

10 http://en.wikipedia.org/wiki/Christian_Zionism.

11 "Natanyahu to Kenya's Christian Zionists: "We have no better friends in the world than you" (Mandlowitz 2016).

12 Exceptionally, an international human rights organization has sited a memorial to Deir Yassin in Geneva (McGowan 2003).

13 The fiftieth anniversary in 1998 was exceptionally commemorated in Ramallah, with a special issue of Nakba memories in a local paper. In May 2016, sirens sounding sixty-eight times showed the National Authority defying Israeli diktat.

14 An UNRWA teacher complains that Nakba commemorations are made meaningless by the repetition of nationalist songs – "It should be about struggle": F.M., Shateela, 1 November 2014.

15 "Israel bans 'catastrophe' term from Arab schools", Reuters, 22 July 2009.

16 The quotation here is from the English translation, published in 1956.

17 See interview with Saleh Abdel Jawad in *Al-Jana* (2002: 30–34).

18 http://palestineremembered.com/MissionStatement.htm. The interviews are drawn explicitly into the realm of activism through a section titled "The Conflict 101".

19 http://www.nakba-archive.org.

20 http://www.nakbamuseumproject.com; Blau (2015).

21 "It was acts of holding onto and retelling memories, of returning to their villages to retrieve their possessions, of stealing things from Israelis, or engaging in militant actions that helped to keep the tragic realities of Palestinian history from utterly destroying Palestinian community and political life" (Feldman 2006: 40).

22 The number of villages destroyed varies. Khalidi (1992) suggests 418 but excludes Bedouin settlements, hamlets and city neighbourhoods. *Haaretz* gives wider coverage: 601 villages, based on Zochrot mapping: http://www.haaretz.com/israel-news/.premium-1.668820.

23 Nazzal (1978: 3) deviated from oral history practice in that he did not record his interviews but reconstructed them from notes and memory.

24 http://www.aub.edu.lb/ifi/programs/poha/Pages/index.aspx.

25 For daily details see *Addameer*; *Adalah*; *Al-Awda-News*; *Electronic Intifada*; *Mazin Qumsiyeh*; *Mondoweiss*.

26 Umm Muhammad Sa'd, recorded 21 July 1992 in the Old Peoples' Home, Sabra.

27 http://www.ameinu.net/blog/current-isses/inconceivable-population-transfer-the-Bedouin-village-of-umm-al-hieran/. See also Amnesty: http://www.amnesty.org.il/en/cat/817.

28 Hastings (2016) adds that Attir and Umm al-Hiran are particularly important sites for activism because Palestinian communities of the Naqab do not receive the attention and support that those of the West Bank and Galilee do.

REFERENCES

Abdelhadi, F. (1999) *Bibliography of the Oral History of Palestinians: With Emphasis on Women*. Ramallah: Idarat al-takhtīt wa-al-tatwīr [in Arabic].

Abdelhadi, F. (2006a) *The Roles of Palestinian Women in the 1930s*. Al-bīrah: markaz al-mar'ah al-Falastīnīyah lil-abhāth wa-altawthīq; Paris: UNESCO [in Arabic].

Abdelhadi, F. (2006b) *The Roles of Palestinian Women in the 1940s*. Al-bīrah: markaz al-mar'ah al-Falastīnīyah lil-abhāth wa-altawthīq; Paris: UNESCO [in Arabic].

Abdel Jawad, S. (2007) "Zionist Massacres: The Creation of the Palestinian Refugee Problem in the 1948 War", in E. Benvenisti et al. (eds.), *Israel and the Palestinian Refugees*. Berlin: Springer.

Abdo, N. (2014 *Captive Revolution: Palestinian Women's Anti-Colonial Struggle within the Israeli Prison System*. London: Pluto.

Abdo, N. and R. Lentin, eds. (2002) *Women and the Politics of Military Confrontation: Palestinian and Israeli Gendered Narratives of Dislocation*. Berlin: Berghahn Books.

Al Hardan, A. (2016) *Palestinians in Syria: Nakba Memories of Shattered Communities*. New York: Columbia University Press.

Al-Jana (2002) *File on Palestinian Oral History*. Beirut: Arab Resource Centre for Popular Arts.

Bahour, S., et al. (1994) *Homeland: Oral Histories of Palestine and Palestinians*. Northampton, MA: Interlink.

Bergin, C. and A. Rupprecht (2016) "History, Agency and the Representation of 'Race': An Introduction", *Race and Class* 57(3): 3–17.

Blau, K. (2015) "Untold Stories; First-ever US Nakba Museum Opens in Washington DC", *Mondoweiss*, 12 June.

Catron, J. (2013) "Gaza Researcher Determined to Record Nakba Generation Before Time Runs Out", *Electronic Intifada*, 23 October.

Cronin, D. (2011) *Europe's Alliance with Israel: Aiding the Occupation*. London: Pluto Press.

Davis, R. (2011) *Palestinian Village Histories: Geographies of the Displaced*. Stanford, CA: Stanford University Press.

Esber, R. (2008) *Under the Cover of War: The Zionist Expulsion of the Palestinians*. Alexandria, VA: Arabicus Books and Media.

Farah, R. (1997) "Crossing Boundaries: Reconstructions of Palestinian Identities in Al-Baq'a Refugee Camp, Jordan", *Palestine, Palestiniens: territoire national, espaces communitaires*. Beirut: CERMOC.

Feldman, I. (2006) "Home as a Refrain: Remembering and Living Displacement in Gaza", *History and Memory* 18(2): 10–47.

Finkelstein, N. (2000) *The Holocaust Industry: Reflections on the Exploitation of Jewish Suffering*. London: Verso.

Fleischmann, E. (2003) *The Nation and its "New" Women: The Palestinian Women's Movement 1920–1948*. Oakland, CA: University of California Press.

Gendzier, I.L. (2016) *Dying to Forget: Oil, Power, Palestine and the Foundations of US Policy in the Middle East, 1945–1949*. New York: Columbia University Press.

Ghabra, S. (1988) "Palestinians in Kuwait; the Family and the Politics of Survival", *Journal of Palestine Studies* 17(2): 62–83.

Ghandour, Z. (2011) *A Discourse on Domination in Mandate Palestine: Imperialism, Property and Insurgency*. London: Routledge-Cavendish.

Gluck, S.B. (1994) *An American Feminist in Palestine: The Intifada Years*. Philadelphia, PA: Temple University Press.

Hammami, R. (2010) "Qalandiya: Jerusalem's Tora Bora and the Frontier of Global Inequality", *Jerusalem Quarterly* 41: 29–51.

Hastings, T. (2016) "Oral History as a Tool to Defend Against Displacement", *Al-Shabaka*, 15 September.

Hassan, B.Y. (2016) "Preserving Memory and a War that Still Rages", *Electronic Intifada*, 22 February.

Hawari, Y. (2014) "Young Palestinians Protect History and Heritage in Galilee Villages", *Electronic Intifada*, 30 October.

Horowitz, A. (2012) "Israeli Police Barricade and Arrest Activists Attempting to Commemorate the Nakba", *Mondoweiss*, 25 April.

al-Hout, B.N. (2004) *Sabra and Shatila: September 1982*. London: Pluto.

Issa, M. (2005) "The Nakba, Oral History and the Palestinian Peasantry", in N. Masalha (ed.), *Catastrophe Remembered: Palestine, Israel, and the Internal Refugees*. London: Zed Books.

Kabha, M. (2013) *The Palestinian People; Seeking Sovereignty and State*. Boulder, CO: Lynne Rienner.

Karmi, G. (2002) *In Search of Fatima: A Palestinian Story*. London: Verso.

Kanafani, G. (n.d.) *The 1938–39 Revolt in Palestine*. Committee for Democratic Palestine.

Khalidi, W. (1992) *All That Remains: The Palestinian Villages Occupied and Depopulated by Israel in 1948*. Washington, DC: Institute of Palestine Studies.

Khalili, L. (2007) *Heroes and Martyrs of Palestine: The Politics of National Commemoration*. Cambridge: Cambridge University Press.

MacIntyre, D. (2009) "UN to Teach Children about the Holocaust", *The Independent*, 5 October.

Maddrell, P. (1990) *The Beduin of the Negev*. London: Minority Rights Groups.

Malek, C. and M. Hoke (2015) *Palestine Speaks: Narratives of Life Under Occupation*. London: Verso.

Mandlowitz, A. (2016) "Amidst the Sounds of the Shofar, Natanyahu thanks Kenya's Christian Friends of Israel", *BreakingIsraelNews*, 6 July.

Masalha, N. (1992) *Expulsion of the Palestinians: The Concept of "Transfer" in Zionist Political Thought*. Washington, DC: Institute of Palestine Studies.

Masalha, N. (2005) *Catastrophe Remembered: Palestine, Israel, and the Internal Refugees, Essays in Memory of Edward W. Said*. London: Pluto.

Masalha, N. (2008) "Remembering the Palestinian Nakba: Commemoration, Oral History, and Narratives of Memory", *Holy Land Studies* 7(2): 123–156.

Masalha, N. (2012) *The Palestine Nakba: Decolonising History, Narrating the Subaltern, Reclaiming Memory*. London: Zed Books.

Masalha, N. (2013) *The Zionist Bible: Biblical Precedent, Colonialism and the Erasure of Memory*. Durham: Acumen.

Mbembe, A. (2003) "Necropolitics", *Public Culture* 15(1): 11–40.

McGowan, D. (2003) "Remembering Deir Yassin", *Electronic Intifada*, 24 September.

Moors, A. (1995) *Women, Property and Islam: Palestinian Experiences 1920–1990* Cambridge: Cambridge University Press.

Morris, B. (1987) *The Birth of the Palestinian Refugee Problem, 1947–1949*. Cambridge: Cambridge University Press.

Muhawi, I. and S. Kanaana (1989) *Speak, Bird, Speak Again: Palestinian Arab Folktales*. Oakland, CA: California University Press.

Najjar, O. with K. Warnock (1992) *Portraits of Palestinian Women*, Salt Lake City, UT: University of Utah Press

Nazzal, N. (1978) *The Palestinian Exodus from Galilee, 1948*. Washington, DC: Institute of Palestine Studies.

El-Nimr, S. (1990) "The Arab Revolt of 1936–1939 in Palestine: A Study Based on Oral Sources". PhD thesis, University of Exeter.

Omer, M. (2015) *Shell-Shocked: On the Ground Under Israel's Gaza Assault*. New York: OR Books.

Osborne, S. (2016) "'Violence More Common' in Bible than Quran, Text Analysis Reveals", http://www.independent.co.uk/arts-entertainment/books/violence-more-common-in-bible-than-quran-text-analysis-96863381.html

OSCE (2015) "Holocaust Memorial Days: An Overview of Remembrance and education in the OSCE Region", 4th ed., January, http://www.osce.org/hmd2015?download=true.

Pappe, I. (1994) *Britain and the Arab–Israeli Conflict, 1948–51*. London: MacMillan and St Antony's College.

Pappe, I. (2006) *The Ethnic Cleansing of Palestine*. Oxford: One World.

Pearlman, W. (2003) *Occupied Voices: Stories of Everyday Life from the Second Intifada*. New York: Nation Books.

Peteet, J. (1991) *Gender in Crisis: Women and the Palestinian Resistance Movement*. New York: Columbia University Press.

Quiquivix, L. (2013–2014) "Law as Tactic: Palestine, the Zapatistas, and the Global Exercise of Power", *Badil Publications* 55: n.p.

Sakakini, H. (1987) *Jerusalem and I: A Personal Record*. Jordan: Economic Press Co.

Sa'di, A.H. and L. Abu-Lughod, eds. (2007) *Nakba: Palestine, 1948, and the Claims of Memory*. New York: Columbia University Press.

Said, E. (1979) *The Question of Palestine*. New York: Times Books.

Sayigh, R. (1994) *Too Many Enemies: The Palestinian Experience in Lebanon*. London: Zed Books.

Sayigh, Y. (1997) *Armed Struggle Search for a State: The Palestinian National Movement 1949–1993*. Oxford: Institute of Palestine Studies and Oxford University Press.

Shahid, S. (2000) *Jerusalem Memories*. Beirut: Naufal.

Shalhoub-Kevorkian, N. (2009) *Militarisation and Violence Against Women in Conflict: A Palestinian Case Study*. Cambridge: Cambridge University Press.

Sharif, R. (1983) *Non-Jewish Zionism: Its Roots in Western History*. London: Zed Books.

Sharp, J. (2015) "US Foreign Aid to Israel", *Congressional Research Service*, 10 June: 1–39.

Slyomovics, S. (1989) *The Object of Memory: Arab and Jew Narrate the Palestinian Village*. Philadelphia: University of Pennsylvania Press.

Strickland, P. (2015) "Israel Continues to Criminalize Marking Nakba Day", *Al-Jazeera*, 14 May.

Swedenburg, T. (1995) *Memories of Revolt: The 1936–1939 Rebellion and the Palestinian National Past*. Minneapolis: University of Minnesota Press.

Tabar, L. (2007) "Memory, Agency, Counter-narratives: Testimonies from Jenin Refugee Camp", *Critical Arts* 21(1): 6–31.

Trouillot, M.-R. (1997) *Silencing the Past: Power and the Production of History*. Boston: Beacon Press.

Yaqub, N. (2015) "The Afterlives of Violence Images: Reading Photographs from the Tal al-Za'ter Refugee Camp on Facebook", *Middle East Journal of Culture and Communication* 8: 327–354.

Yahya, A. (1999) *The Palestinian Refugees: 1948–1998. An Oral History.* Ramallah: The Palestinian Association for Cultural Exchange.

Zurayk, C. (1956) *The Meaning of the Disaster*, translated by B. Winder. Beirut: Khayat.

Zureik, E., D. Lyon and Y. Abu-Laban (2011) *Surveillance and Control in Israel/Palestine: Population, Territory and Power.* London and New York: Routledge.

6

Shu'fat refugee camp women authenticate an old "Nakba" and frame something "new" while narrating it

LAURA KHOURY

The scene of a married middle-aged woman with a knife walking to the checkpoint of Shu'fat refugee camp in 2015 is not what Umm Shadi dreamed her daughter would do when she was expelled from Beit Tool village in 1948. She said, "my one daughter is in prison not for what she has done but, when you think about it, it is what we have instilled in her, to love and protect her land and family". It turned out that her daughter's son had been taken to prison the day before for throwing stones at Shu'fat refugee camp checkpoint. She was so angry and upset: "This is what the Nakba did to us women!", she said. "The worry of ever losing anything anymore!" This was not the first statement I recorded in which a connection between the Nakba and today's misery is made. What interests me most is the logic embedded in her statement; it is the social residual impact not the psychological impact that concerns me.

I offer an indigenous feminist reading of the memorization of the Nakba by Palestinian women of the Nakba generation living in refugee camps, as they transmit some of the past, the enduring social framework, both consciously and subconsciously, to the present, creating continuity and transcending the present. The transcendence means going beyond but staying within the realm of the experience, and the continuity encompasses assertions that the scars of colonialism, alienation, as well as the accompanying pride, despite the dehumanization, made those memories not a simple recitation for oral histories, but something else. What is under scrutiny here is what was not disrupted: something "old" that transformed into something "new". New in its effect or its use, new in terms of formulating new activism and situating it in the present. Collective memory emerges when people exchange remembrances of events and draw on others' memories (Zelizer 1995: 226), and "both the medium and the outcome of social configurations" (Olick 2007: 118). It is social, not just cognitive, and it brings forth women's voices, like "the diamonds of the dust heap" (Woolf 1954: 7).

Refugee Nakba-generation women circulating their stories permeated everyday life as an "everyday practice" (Allan 1995: 48). Coming from semi-agricultural societies, where land was their source of livelihood and their work was mainly in the fields, authenticated it and transmitted its logic to other generations. In terms of gender relations, what has been negotiated between men and women then also transcended because:

> The dynamics of gender in each society or region operate not through grand revolutionary upheavals but through the ongoing negotiations between men and women both at the individual and collectively organized levels. Masculinity and femininity exist not simply in opposition but equally in relation to each other. (Mohammed 1994: 32)

Additionally, "patriarchy under capitalism takes a specific form that is different under feudalism" (Federici 2004: 25); therefore, whichever patriarchal logic existed then, at the time, when they were peasants, was retrieved as they shared their stories collectively. But this is a two-sided process as the logic itself shapes memory making, but also the opposite, and in turn their shared memories sustain that logic.

This chapter exposes the desire of the Nakba-generation refugee women to consolidate pre-1948 Nakba memories for the purpose of transcending constellations of societal meanings that allow for continuity and resistance. This involves relationality to knowledge frameworks of the times:

> Once memory items are sufficiently bound so as to determine what they are, they can be related to one another forming the higher-order systems of relationships that give memory its value. It is only in relation to other objects, events, or ideas that memory items contribute to knowledge,

because then it becomes possible to surf between memories and to bring learned information to bear in different situations. The webs of associations the relater element establishes can be useful in themselves, and they also serve as the organized substrate from which generalized, stable memory is consolidated. (Anastasio et al. 2012: 124)

Relationality makes "memory items (mental representations of objects, facts, events, ideas, etc.) meaningful because of their objective connections to other items" (Anastasio et al. 2012: 106) and consolidation is best understood as a process that continually reshapes "less changeable" memory in a constant, recursive loop of reconstruction (recall) and reconsolidation (reformation) (Anastasio et al. 2012: 251). Sartre (2004: 5) asserts that the image and perception differ but that the image operates thinking. Women applied their imagination to the fullest but they created an "existence-as-image" (*L'existence en image*) or a mode of being. The association women make is important to our work here, especially when discussing their collective imagination.

"MEMORY IN THE GROUP": AN "OLD" LOGIC REASSIGNED AS "NEW"

Collective memory is the experience of creating and producing meaning in the present by referencing the past. Though memory may imply a complex web of intersecting messages about society, I suggest that it, principally and ultimately, implies consolidating an "old" logic of thinking, a certain arrangement that sounds comfortable and fit for the present. Re-experiencing memories unconsciously and emotionally suggests experiencing harmony, but at a fundamental and conscious level it reinvigorates a social framework. In other words, "societal logics shape memory making and the reproduction and reconstruction of history itself" (Ocasio and Mauskapf 2016: 4). So Umm Imad in 1948 told her husband "we are not leaving Palestine"; her word was final, but she is still the decision maker in her household.

As a starting point, conceptually, scholars using old categories to understand women in their work made that work useless and "conceptually unclad" (Mackenzie 1989: 56). In fact, using Western-imposed binaries implants a divided mentality, which I refrain from advancing. I argue that there are, at times, negotiated gender-related categories especially when they are tied to the social framework of the old times. A memory theory that can be considered constructionist is that of Halbwachs, who coined the term. It provides insights about a "memory in the group" not "of the group". His work investigates many forces, such as social interactions, familial ties, time and especially social structure. Collective memory, to him, is also based on lived experience. He wrote: "Our memory truly rests not to learned history but on lived history" (Halbwachs 1980: 57). He studied the transformation of memory over time to show how the images a community makes of itself are slowly transformed and that: "[W]hat is essential is that the features distinguishing it from other groups survive and be imprinted on all its content" (Halbwachs 1980: 87).

Halbwachs rejects concepts that are connected to the psychology of the individual and argues directly against psychological notions about the origin of memory. I agree that "the individual mind is ultimately incapable of producing memory by itself; rather, the individual mind succeeds only in storing memory images" (Halbwachs 1992: 41). These images, when isolated from society's influence, "have no consistence, depth, coherence, or stability" (Halbwachs 1992: 44). These stored images cannot be recalled or constructed as memories without a number of social frameworks that influence the different groups to which an individual belongs. Therefore, Halbwachs offers us a new venue for analysing the social framework. I wonder how women independently construct today's lived experience in very creative ways by building on "old" social framework.

Palestinian refugee camp women's uprooting testimonies gave them strength to overcome their alienation in the refugee camp (Khoury 2005). Their imagination and pre-Nakba memories are both produced and a product to be consumed for continuity and to overcome alienation. In fact, something "new" develops when social space is both a field of action and a basis for action. "Social space can be shown to be a medium and outcome of social practice" (Brenner and Elden 2009: 372). The practice of sharing memories and remembrances of events, at times involves drawing on others' memories, narrating their past and conveying it as part of the present. During the Third Intifada of October 2014, I witnessed women coming together, creating a strong sense of community and a resistance model of lived experience. The specific themes that surfaced in their narratives were not different from much of what other scholars explored.[1] However, how and why did they reassign the "old" social framework and transform it into something "new"? This cannot be answered using Western-imposed binaries, because they implant a divided mentality.

THE NAKBA GENRE: MEMORIES OF MEMORIES

I find it useful to engage in Olick's (2007) investigation of the "memory of memory", applying Bakhtin's (1963) dialogism that unfolded particular dialogues in time and through time. Bakhtin, made a distinction between influence – awareness of texts – and genre that possesses an organic logic or the sharing of a common "way of seeing". Genres are used as a system of dialogue to better understand the past through the lens of the present. "A genre lives in the present, but always remembers its past, its beginning" (Bakhtin quoted in Olick 2007: 121). The beginning for most refugees is tied to the Nakba genre, which possesses a logic and a way of seeing. An indigenous approach is an epistemology or a different way of knowing (Smith 1999); this epistemology is relational in nature, acknowledging the interconnectedness of the physical, mental and emotional.

The settler-colonial scheme remains the best interpretive paradigm. It allows for viewing the Nakba as a process of elimination of the indigenous people by seeking land but also replacing aboriginals with settlers, with attention to its counter-hegemonic implications.[2] Nonetheless, for lack of a better descriptive model to explain the Zionist movement's colonization of the land of Palestine since 1948 (Khoury et al. 2013b), this particular colonization scheme allows for understanding the development of new layers of resistance, and how refugee women's "memory is neither something pre-existent and dormant in the past nor a projection from the present, but a potential for creative collaboration between present consciousness and the experience or expression of the past" (Boyarin 1994: 22). There is another "level of colonialism" that refugees face in "the extent to which a colonizing power installs economic, political, and socio cultural institutions in a colonized territory" (Mahoney 2010: 23). Judaization, a complex amalgam of exclusion/transfer/wiping out, is one other level of colonialism. Its artefacts are: erasure of the memory including changing the names of towns, villages and cities; the removal of people through genocide, eviction, transfer, or wiping their identity; and the depletion of archaeological sites (see Masalha 2012).

Field (2012) explains how oral history is not a supplement to historical research and research does not collect oral histories but creates them, so the stories are not waiting to be discovered by historians; the conditions of possibility that allow for negotiation of dialogues about memory are open-ended. Memories are reminiscences of the past that link people to their nation.[3] Memory work is:

the process of framing visual and emotional traces of the past into forms of memory, narrative, and other representations … Memory work has the potential to integrate thinking and feeling about one's own past in an unattainable fantasy … "Imagining memories" in a form of memory work that frames sensory inputs and creates frameworks that are central to sustaining self-cohesion and identity formation over time. (Boyarin 1994: 179)

Both "collective memory" and "collective identity" are the effects of intersubjective practices of signification that are constantly re-created within the framework of marginally contestable rules for discourse (Butler 1990: 145).

This work analyses the self-reflexive awareness process women undergo when they narrate the Nakba, contributing to the movement of writing history from below – and it is a type of dialogue towards developing a new subjectivity. Precautionary premises informed this work: I avoid the faults of writing about national traumas, in psychological terms (like the memory industry), in which victimization becomes the overwhelming courier, but approach it as a socio-historical process in which the "Nakba" genre overwhelms the analysis. Against a uniformity of the tale, I sought the variety of lived experiences. I concede indigenous scholarly theorization that decreases Eurocentric system of thought.[4] I employ the method of listening without engaging, aware of romanticizing memory (see Stoler and Strassler 2000), or the threat of "erasure" of sensual tales, but mostly aware that memory is shaped by the present (Dana 2017), and that nationalistic narratives silenced any uncomfortable memories, and acknowledge the inconsistencies of witnesses and testimonies when the memories have to do with massacres (for example Esmeir 2007 on the Tantura massacre).

Methodologically, inspired by indigenous feminist research practices, I used "ground-truthing"[5] to be able to explore women's journey. This is the practice of using field observations and interpreting, analysing and verifying remotely sensed information about the physical features of an area (Carp 2009) to understand the different modes of relationships between women while they construct a reflexive critical knowledge. In particular, as they liberate their everyday routine lives, they act on their sensory knowledge and their experience in pre-1948 lived experience, and re-evaluate it based on the "now" of their lives. Also, exploring how women in fact perceive their roles as women as an extension to their previous village experience and the logic prevalent at the time.

Lastly, "If we don't expose the despotism against Indigenous women, then most non-Indigenous people would quickly dismiss Indigenous feminism as meritless" (Mouchref 2016: 90). Elderly Palestinian refugee women's collective memories are rooted in indigenous feminism and embedded in the historical experience of colonization. It is an epistemology or a different way of knowing (Smith 1999). It values their voices and holds women in equal status with men. Collected narratives on Palestinian women as authority figures, as in the seminal volumes that Abdul Hadi (1999–2001), have been produced in an attempt to change the traditional and stereotypical image of peasant women. This work supports the idea that they are able to make oppression visible, that they are authority figures, whether or not they are aware of this. Lastly, I adopt the premise that "collective memory of imperialism has been perpetuated through the ways in which knowledge about indigenous peoples was collected, classified and then represented in various ways back to the West, and then, through the eyes of the West, back to those who have been colonized" (Smith 1999: 1–2).

THE PERSISTENCE OF REASSIGNING A SOCIETAL LOGIC AND SOCIAL FRAMEWORK

How did women of the Nakba generation position themselves in their stories (see Table 6.1)? What were they fetching or coding as they recited their ways of doing things before the Nakba? How did they become the guardians of that social framework of the time? I identified many occasions when they saw themselves as strong, and that the whole family was dependent on them, though the chores they did were not easy to begin with. In this section, their narratives will speak of all that. Sayigh has long called for archiving and collecting Nakba narratives, but in her current work (Sayigh 2015), as she deconstructs the systematic silencing of Nakba sufferings, she posits that simple narrative collection may not be sufficient because what is vital and efficient is creating central collection mechanisms. The right of return requires a collective effort in order to achieve a holistic view of the Nakba experience and integrate it into public knowledge and school books. Sayigh wondered what women wish to pass on to their children. The following selected testimonies (before their discussion) suggest some of what women insist should be passed on and aids understanding of how important it is to truly integrate their narratives into public knowledge – as marginalization of refugee-ism is increasing.

Table 6.1 Wiped villages of interviewees: date, population at time, number of refugees created and amount of land lost

Interviewees	Age	Village location*	Day/month wiped	1948 population	Refugees created	Land lost dun.
Umm Shadi	83	Beit-Tool*	1/4/1948	302	1,852	4,205
Umm Ziad	73	Beit Muheiser*	10/5/1948	2,784	17,097	15,428
Umm Saad	78	Kherbet al-Loz*	13/7/1948	522	3,206	4,495
Umm Hussein	84	Sarees*	1/4/1984	626	3,847	3,769
Umm Nidal	79	Al-Dawaymeh **	29/11/1948	4,304	26,429	60,561
Umm Walid	74	Beit Natif**	21/10/1948	2,494	15,315	32,760
Umm Na'el	88	Deir Ayoob***	6/3/1948	371	2,280	4,500
Umm Ali	81	Al-Walajeh*	21/10/1948	1,914	11,754	17,708
Total: eight women intensively visited	Average 80	Mostly in Jerusalem	All villages wiped in 1948	Ranges 100s and 1,000s	Ranges 2,000–25,000	Ranges 4,000–60,000

* Jerusalem   ** Hebron   *** al-Lydd and al-Ramleh

"Deir Ayoob was facing the bridge"

Umm Na'el, eighty-eight years old, from Deir Ayoob, has much to talk about, but her narration and nostalgia were spatially focused on what faced their destroyed village: the bridge facing their home:

> We are from Deir Ayoob (village). We used to sleep in Yalo and return in the morning to Deir Ayoob, spend the day then return to Yalo at night, from fear. I was a strong (*qawiyya*) girl. Yalo is so beautiful. It is near Bab al-Waad, do you know where Bab al-Wad is? Near Bab al-Wad there is a bridge, right in front of our village (*baladna*). We used to go by foot to al-Ramla, Al-Lydd, and Yafa to bring all types of things we need. I used to go with my girlfriends (*rafikaty*) to bring our market needs and come back. They used to bring the oranges from Akka – west of us. The oranges from Aker were mounted as high as a car in front of the mosque. We used to buy every twenty oranges with one shilling. I remember most when I used

143

to cut and collect timber and fallen branches (*ba-hatteb*) from the forest and I came back hungry and I ask my mom for food, she used to tell me here eat oranges! I remember that very well.

Because our homes were in front of the bridge they demolished them all. The British demolished the whole line of homes because they were in front of the bridge. The revolutionaries used to come from that bridge. We saw the revolutionaries who cut the telephone wires next to Bab al-Waad. The English men said: "common common fuck in". Deir Ayoob is very tiny, there were about only fifty families. So, we went to Yalo and we were dispersed since that time. The English kicked us out like sheep to Beit Sira – at the borders of Deir Ayoob – and said: "Yallah common to Beit Sira". They drove us out like sheep. God destroy their homes. Like how did they know about Beit Sira. There were traitors!

After Yalo, came the Jews, right by the main entrance of Yalo, they appeared. We were still girls in Yalo but Yalo was a tabooed area. For a while we used to go to Yalo at night to sleep and spend the day in Deir Ayoob. All other areas were taken: Beit Nuba, Yalo, Deir Ayoob, they all were taken. The women from al-Ramleh and al-Lydd were kicked out too with us, I swear they were barefooted. I saw a woman with only one sock on one foot. But we left with our clothes on, we were not barefooted like al-Lydd women. We were humiliated. We all sat under the olive tree, tightly because the place was so tight. We took the keys with us but we do not know where they are now.

They kicked us out and we went to Beit Nooba, we did not stay long there, then we went to Kharabtha, and we stayed long there, my mother, my brothers and one sister she was forty days old only. People were scared. They put all the people under the olive trees. We would put a blanket and sleep there. Everyone, all the people from all over were there: from al-Lydd, al-Ramleh, plenty of people were there. They were not our relatives. We were on one side and they were on the other.

We went back and forth between Yalo and our village. Deir Ayoob was beautiful, it was in front of the bridge. There were grapes and figs. Our village was beautiful as it stands in front of the bridge. I swear, I still remember it until this day. We used to take the basket and go bring figs, the fig was that big [she opened her hand and showed how big it was]. We went to visit recently, now it is all made out of streets and cars go back and forth, it is near Imwas and tourists go there. They took our homes. God break their homes.

"Water springs make anything alive"

Umm Shadi, an eighty-three-year-old widow from Beit Tool, constantly emphasized how water was fundamental to their daily lives. As she tells of the dispossession of their land and village, first by the British Mandate, then by the Zionists, she relates every aspect of her life to the need for water:

I left when I was old from our county, I was fifteen years old. Then, we stayed in Yalo, near al-Latroun. My brother left to the United States and sent us some remittances so we built a house and stayed there. Yalo was better than Beit Thoola twenty times. Our village, Beit Thoola, was very mountainous, you cannot find a piece of land without rocks on its pasture. There was very little land for people to grow plants due to the rocks, and lots of cactus and there is no water spring. I remember it well. I remember everything.

The Jews began demolishing our houses. The town that they entered they demolish its houses and do the things that are not right and immoral just like what they did in Deir Yassin [massacre] but even much more!!! Abu Ghosh was adjacent to our village about 6 kilometres. They told us not to run away but from the nearby village they used to say take your girls and run away. We also fled to al-Mizra' al-Sharqyeh [north of Ramallah].

After four months we returned to Yalo and my father wanted to get some figs from Beit Thoola but the land was planted with bombs. He left with his cousin on a donkey but the road was evil. The camel broke its leg and my father's leg was broken too. He started screaming until his uncle heard him but he told them to be careful as the land was planted with bombs.

Later the Jews colonized Yalo, Umwas and Beit Thoola in one day, so we returned to al-Mizra' al-Sharqyeh and stayed there 3–4 years then again back to Yalo. We stayed one year but they came to us and we ran away. We went to Beit Anan and I was nineteen then. But, there was no place for us to stay and we stayed near the oil machine – God saves you from this evil. We did not find water wells or water springs, so after a month we went to Haret al-Yahoo inside Jerusalem walls. In there in the Hosh with our cousins, the family of X, the family of Y, the family of A and the family of B [she recalls the families' names] were all stacked next to each other.

Until today, I still go to Yalo and I pick almonds, oregano and everything. There are trees of all kinds because there is water there. In front of the house we have a pomegranate tree, grapes, apple tree, almond and I pick from all of them every year when I go. We had all sorts of trees. It is beautiful, *water makes anything live*.

"The place was a butchery"

Although the significance of this massacre has not been a focus of attention, Umm Nidal, from al-Dawaymeh, remembers the butchery in al-Dawaymeh. She remembers the exact day that it happened (29 October 1948). She stayed in touch with the only woman who miraculously survived the massacre with her two children. She remembers seeing butchered bodies too:

It was a Friday the 29th of October 1948. All what the Arabs had was a "*mikanizm*" [Turkish word for a gun]. They had real guns. What do you expect? They butchered everyone. The massacre was worse than Deir Yassin's massacre.

Al-Dawaymeh was very spacious, people from all over come there. They used to come to the market on Fridays. There was something called Friday's Market. From al-Lydd to Ramleh, from the north and the south meet there, in Friday's Market day. They shop because everything was cheap there.

The only survivor that day was a woman with her two kids as they hid under the hay with her. She heard everything and saw everything.

People come from all over, were one family from every county. Al-Dawaymeh used to gather people from all over. We met many people there and made friendships. In fact, when we were kicked out from our village my father went to a friend that he met in the Friday market and we lived in al-Khalil for few years with them. People loved to come to al-Dawaymeh as they can socialize there. Women used to go to the market every Friday and they would sell their products.

al-Dawaymeh was about to become a municipality on its own. It was too wide of a land. They built all the infrastructure for the roads, it was all planned, it had a future in the market, all what was left then was just the asphalt road. al-Dawaymeh would have become a big city by now. A beautiful city. Everything was all set and prepared just the asphalt. This is why the Jews took it, they do not want it to become a big city.

Not even one person remained alive, they killed every man and woman, there were 203 people slaughtered in the butchery of al-Dawaymeh. Many tried to walk there but were killed because they infiltrated bombs on the way there, *we used to see bodies butchered, the place was a butchery.*

DISCUSSION: WHAT DO NAKBA-GENERATION WOMEN WISH TO PASS TO THEIR CHILDREN?

Umm Nidal was a bit younger than both Umm Shadi and Umm Na'el but her story describes the hopes of the village to become a city. Also, other women liked her because she was from al-Dawaymeh, which was about to become a big city. What has she carried with her all these years? She has carried the idea that she had lived in a place that made little distinction between men and women, as they all went to the market and they all socialized with other villagers, and their role in transmitting not only goods, but also values and traditions. This was cultural capital for a large village that was on the verge of becoming a city. The reputation of al-Dawaymeh with its popular markets and wealth and community ties is what Umm Nidal wished to transmit to her grandchildren.

Reading al-Aref (1956), the renowned historian of the 1948 war and battles of Jerusalem, it is evident that the bridge which Umm Nidal highlighted was not just a bridge, it was where the fighting was most intense in 1947. It was a lifeline for the colonizers. He writes:

> this passage in Bab al-wad was tying the valleys of Palestine with the mountains of Jerusalem. There was a need to capture this bridge and the areas surrounding it of villages, highlands to save Jerusalem [from the enemy] … This passage has throughout history a strategic significance and whoever controls it dominates Jerusalem … fighting there was the fiercest in all Palestine. (al-Aref 1965: 491–492)

Umm Na'el knew very little about history and facts about the revolutionaries; however, in her description of the bridge, she explained that there were always young men there, though she probably could not exactly identify why they were always there. What she wished to pass to her children was how things weighed at the time, how it felt like colonization, and the pride in these young revolutionaries without exactly knowing what they accomplished at the time.

Women and younger girls travelled to cities like al-Ludd and al-Ramlah to go to the market. They did things together as *rafayek* (good friends). Their visits to the city were memorable to them, as were the oranges piled as high as the car. For example, Umm Shadi recalled going to collect wood. There was clearly a strong appreciation of nature, the forest, water springs, figs and grapes. Umm Shadi has shared many stories with the women who constantly visit her. Umm Shadi is well known for telling Nakba stories and she intentionally brings women of all ages together so they can hear and retell stories. I return to this point below.

Umm Shadi told the story of how *qawyah* she was; she meant that she did all the necessary work (*t-hatteb*) in the fields and later when they were dispossessed she worked as a water transporter in Haret al-Sharaf. She had a history of skilled labour. It is not clear if she picked up other types of work and became skilled again, but having many children tied her to housework. Umm Imad also told us that she was *qawyah* when she was young. When she grew up and after she was married she remained strong-willed:

> We stood in front of the buses in Bab-al-Amood. There were buses
> taking people to Beirut, al-Sham (Syria), and Jordan. The bus driver would
> call out and Abu Imad said: "Come let us get on the bus with the people".
> I told him: "you want to go God ease your way. I do not want to go, you
> go; I want to stay in the country". Bus drivers wanted to fill their buses and
> go. I had two kids and I refused to go. Many years after, when Sabra and
> Shatila massacres took place, I told my husband: "You see, if I agreed to go
> we would be killed by now".

Umm Imad was determined to decide where she would live. In times of despair and loss, she knew what she wanted. Umm Imad being the only daughter, was treated like her brothers, and thus grew up making decisions just like a boy. She said she even controlled the kind and amount of food in the household.

Umm Imad used to knit Palestinian peasant dresses. She would put her small children to sleep and begin knitting traditional dresses that peasant women still wear (she was wearing one and it was colourful). She said: "My father used to tell me that I will lose my sight". She used to be paid 20 pennies for each ball of thread, which was a lot at the time. Umm Imad was proud of her paid labour. She also showed me her wedding dress, which she had cut and put in a frame to hang on the wall.

Most of the women showed their strength and determination to contribute to their households in one way or another. Some women expressed how *qawiyya* they were, while others presented their life stories, which reveal much about their strength. Umm Saad from Beit Nuba said: "When women want to wash their clothes near the water spring they used to do that at once. All of them together". She said that they would occupy the streets for ten days for wedding ceremonies and it became their territory. They would dance and entertain themselves for long days. Their agency is grounded in everyday experiences. Umm Waleed, from Beit Nateef said: "Women used to get together by the water fountain and sometimes play games with water". She explained that women would bring the water home but when they were by the fountain, men disappeared. "I enjoyed playing with the girls my age, but we had to go back because my brothers and father are waiting to take a bath."

The gender division of labour was not based on narrow specialization. The division between public and private spheres was not clear, as in the simple pre-capitalist peasant mode. Mies (1998: xvii) suggests looking for what was better in the past, in non-industrial societies, and argues, like many others who are attempting to write history from below, that it was the bourgeoisie that established the gendered division of labour as a characteristic of capitalism. She wrote: "They withdrew their women from the public sphere and shut them in their cozy homes" (Mies 1998: 104). History is written based on diaries of the Victorian middle classes (Coontz 2000).

Umm Ziad, from Beit Mehseer, believed that men have the right story about what happened during the deportation. (Some scholars contend that men had the role of telling stories: Humphries and Khalili 2007, Sayigh 1998.) But in telling the story she chose certain parts over others, intentionally or unintentionally, because this was what she wanted to pass on. Umm Hussein, eighty-two years old, from Sarees, was relaxed when talking about her village. It sounded as though she had selective amnesia regarding certain lived experiences. Umm Hussein did not have amnesia, as her granddaughters said; she was selecting the stories and memories. And although these were of a place where she spent the shortest time in her life (eighteen years), these were the stories that she wished to relive. Therefore she still returns to Sarees as if it is in her dreams.

THOSE DECLARED VULNERABLE ARE IN FACT RESISTING

Butler exposes the logic behind vulnerability/invulnerability of how those in power strategize to present themselves as vulnerable. This suggests that it is politically produced and suggests moving behind the human rights framework (which negates the capacity for those declared vulnerable to act politically). Thereby, Butler asserts how all this gives value to collective resistance (Butler et al. 2016). Refugee women, who are vulnerable, are resisting by "claiming the right to public space ... or continuing to exist, and or breathe" (Butler et al. 2016: 26). "Being while Palestinian" is ultimately an "everyday revolution" (see Khoury 2012), because inherent in rejecting the colonizer is refusing to submit to the colonizer's state. Women's contribution to political movement has always been crucial (Abdo and Lentin 2002). Public space, the colonizer's tool of domination, was a site of women's actualization, of breaking out of gender constraints, offering resistance to gender hierarchies; it provided an alternative configuration that could be used to subvert the oppressor–oppressed paradigm (Wrede 2015: 10).

The dialogue between women included imaginative re-creations of the villages, displayed sentimental attachment to their villages and re-created an idyllic peasant life.[6] They exhibited an ability to devise new layers of resistance. Some clearly perceived themselves as resisting, while others did not. The home remained a "site of commemoration that celebrates Palestinian history, heritage and culture" (Kassem 2012: 195), but the way they structured it and designed it was based on their desire to reassign "new" societal experience. Keeping culturally specific spatial practices like cooking, attending to the needs of the neighbours, caring for each other, displays how they practised "resistance through imagination". Their lived space became a meeting place (locality) that embodied social relations to talk about the times and social frameworks before the Nakba.

As the women recounted their memories, it was a reflective practice by which they related to themselves and others in a form of a dialogue. Even though most women's memory of the Nakba is based around the experience of loss of community (see Humphries and Khalili 2007: 216; but also Sayigh 1998, 2007),[7] it is the space of interaction where their resistance is most needed and critical. They tell themselves about how the refugee camp is standing like a discarded island, and that it should remain as a space of resistance, a site for the right to return. Thus women revived those memories to keep the struggle alive.

Ultimately, the colonial space is contested and resisted by reinstating a sense of community, which they have transmitted from their past lived experience in the village. They have reinstated the social framework of the past so that they could transcend it.

The awareness that refugees have constantly been subjects of memory and knowledge opened the way to giving more weight to the unspoken words. It is indigenous knowledge, from "the conceptualization, formulation, and eventually the knowledge produced" (Al-Hardan 2014: 63), and women's unspoken words reveal what has been underscored. This work dovetails with Sayigh's (2015) investigations into what women wish to pass on to their children. Umm Shadi sometimes openly encouraged women to tell their Nakba stories to their grandchildren, recounting and creating a knowledge base to yield a continuity in the struggle as they revive their collective memories, also extending the societal logic that existed in pre-1948's gender relations and structure. Along with other women, they constructed a reflexive critical base connecting the past to the present and the space in the diaspora with the space in the village. This is what Umm Shadi wished to pass on to the younger generation.

Colonial space remains a field of controversy due to variations in the modes of resistance. Refugee spaces are controlled and disciplined (Hanafi 2008). Foucault (1979: 196) viewed resistances as distributed in an irregular fashion, with "the points, knots, or focuses of resistance ... spread over time and space at varying densities". The irregularity is present in Shu'fat refugee camp because "[T]here is no single locus of great refusal, no soul of revolt, source of all rebellions, or pure law of the revolutionary. Instead there is a plurality of resistances" (Foucault 1979: 95–96). Today, the sites of oppression and discrimination have turned into spaces of resistance (Pile and Keith 1997).

As women recounted pre-Nakba and Nakba tales, they framed newer concerns asserting the resistance option (as opposed to the concession option that the PA chose). They tackled many concerns, from overcrowding, to pollution, to raids, to check-point intimidation, to fear for their children, which signify care for the community.[8] The collected narratives displayed how they identified themselves as strong and active in public life. Their characterization is based on Sayigh's (1998) tellers of the Palestinian present, where half (four) had the "struggle personality", with strength and courage, two were "*sit fil beit*" (women who stay at home) and two had the "challenge" and "confrontation" personality, attempting to challenge gender norms historically (Umm

Hisham). None wanted their maternal sacrifice to become a symbol of loss, a passive identification (as identified by Sayigh and Peteet 1986). Johnson (2009) also found "struggle personality" and "*sit fil beit*" self-identification in al-Amari refugee camp.

Refugee women, the Nakba generation, positioned themselves in a routine collective memory practice revealing slightly different symbolic meanings – like guardians. As they told their stories they displayed an ability to practise some power. For the first time, there appeared to be an attempt to position themselves as village women with a knowledge base (see Hatoss 2012).[9] Positioning, as a concept, facilitates the thinking of social analysis in such a way that the use of "role" – which is static, formal and ritualistic – may be limited linguistically (Davies and Harre 1990). This positioning by Nakba-generation women was enhanced through using the ground-truthing approach, because it permitted the events to be narrated by constructing an old social framework (relations of production per se) to a new place at a different time. In other words, their social (lived) space became women's field of action and simultaneously the basis for their action too. Thus, Umm Shadi's attachment to her village was narrated as the story of abundance of water in wells or springs but simultaneously as a source of power.

CONCLUSION: DEMYSTIFYING THE NEUTRALITY OF SOCIAL DIVISIONS

The study breaks away from a long tradition of scholarship that submits to blind binaries of male/female, active/passive, public/private and victim/agent, but without sacrificing the intersected forces that shape subjectivity. It looks a bit beyond the thinkable frame of reference (monolithic thinking) to enable a reflexive framing of memory in the form of a dialogue. It abandons the Westernized notion of agency (see Mahmood 2005; Khoury and Da'Na 2013) because it found agency to be grounded in everyday experience. I also agree with Hanafi (2008) that camps are not boundless spaces with an ongoing process of assimilation into the urban fabric. I see the camp space as a colonial space par excellence, where spatial colonial practices make them places in the making. I see camp residents resisting spatial domination from within the old structures. Women have the agentive capacity of making their own histories (as in Sayigh 1998). Women cannot live an ordinary life under colonization. They recreated camp space as a site of a new type of resistance that corresponds with the new levels of colonialism. They made the camp a space of inclusion, when it was intended by the colonists to be one of exclusion.

Anderson (2010: 89) suggests that women organizing is an indigenous thing: "our pre-colonial societies were sustained by women's work". Even though women are generally excluded from memory politics (Sa'di and Abu-Lughod 2007; Peteet 1992, 2005; Sayigh 1998, 2002), the dialogues explored here evoked a wealth of knowledge about the past and displayed an outstanding ability to win little battles in their everyday lives. They actually developed a shared language, sustained a resistance culture and negotiated their vulnerability as women, as refugees and as colonial subjects. In other words, in an analysis of their discursive practices, their vulnerability was a source of power. Their discourses were an action, not merely a representation. Even though most women's memory of the Nakba circled around the experience of loss of community (see Humphries and Khalili 2007: 216; but also Sayigh 1997, 1998, 2007), but also because the camp is isolated, facing attempts at eroding it as a space of resistance, the tales about loss of community need to be revised. Similar to Humphries and Khalili (2007), who found refugee women to be uncertain whether their knowledge is authoritative, apart from two women the rest fell into this category. More importantly, women consolidated memories and made associations between then and now in such a way that the social framework of that pre-Nakba time was activated and sustained the previously negotiated status in regard to men and society. As Umm Shadi reminded her husband, who wanted to flee in 1948: "see if I followed you we would have been slaughtered now in Sabra and Shatilla massacres".

I found a pattern of Nakba-generation women who were directly involved in decision making and had a strong presence in the public space in the pre-Nakba period (working on the land, fetching water and so on). In the women's reflections I found knowledge of the history of practices in their community (history is thus extended in practice), invoking an ability to produce and re-appropriate their selves through many epochs as they framed the old into something "new". This attests to the notion that what came to be known as public vs private spheres was a creation of the capitalist system, not part of the peasant structure in pre-Nakba Palestine. I am not suggesting that gender hierarchies did not exist or that there was the absence of a system of oppression based on patriarchy, but identification with Western forms of feminism is problematic. Refugee women of the Nakba generation are constrained by tradition and as they reinvigorate that social framework they also revive traditions. I argue, along with Naber (2006), that they face multiple oppressions, but the imposition of the binaries which constrain them further is what I critique (see Khoury et al. 2013a). Some scholars shed light on how women became the main enemies of colonial rule (Federici 2004); other indigenous feminist researchers dismissed feminism, emphasizing the difficulties indigenous people face when attempting to identify with Western forms of feminism (Anderson 2011). Palestinian refugee women of the Nakba generation are able to make oppression visible. This, to them, is an everyday revolution (Khoury 2012). It is "existence-as-imaged" in reflective experience, a mode of being (Sartre 2000).

NOTES

1 Brand (2009) summarizes some traits that my research methodology holds back from engaging in about women and their collective memory, because I avoid questions framed in a Western lens. I truly believe that even the way the question is posed reveals Eurocentric tendencies, and conscription to Western modernity. For example: Do women see things in the eyes of their husbands? Are they only supporting men in their struggle? Did they glorify the past, idealize their villages, remembered it as living happily, in Paradise? I posit that using Western-imposed binaries implants a divided mentality.

2 Busbridge (2017: 1) says that the settler-colonial paradigm has counter-hegemonic implications for reframing Israel-Palestine in its prescription for decolonization. It is in the context of decolonization that the limits of the settler-colonial paradigm become most apparent.

3 There exists an impressive amount of research on memory regarding the Palestinian refugees (Sa'di and Abu-Lughod 2007), some are ethnographic accounts (Sayigh 1997, 1998, 1995; Farah 2006; Khalili 2008) and others focus on gender (Sayigh 1981; Peteet 1992, 1994).

4 Zoe Todd (2016: 15) explains how, "with the wave of the post-colonial wand, many European thinkers seem to have absolved themselves of any implication in ongoing colonial realities throughout the globe. And yet, each one of us is embedded in systems that uphold the exploitation and dispossession of Indigenous peoples".

5 I combined field observations of camp space spanning three years 2013–2016, in-depth participation and visitations with eight Nakba-generation refugee women (see Table 6.1) spanning almost a year – from soon after the third Intifada started – October 2015–August 2016, and a content analysis of media messages and women's gatherings over the three years. Six months after the end of the collection period (December 2016 and February 2017) I revisited the women to follow up on some interviews and

witnessed new colonial spatial practices that helped shape the work. This will appear in a larger project.

6   Khalili (2007) captures the social invocation of past events, places and symbols in various social contexts and analyses mnemonic practices; and Davis (2007), in her content analysis of the memorial books written by villagers themselves about the history of their village, identified "[t]he past that is mapped consists of memories and idealizations". I identified some other moments that are peculiar due to the methodology of ground-truthing employed.

7   Most research about women came to this realization.

8   I did not discuss the role of NGO's due to its irrelevancy here but does not mean that they are not playing a role in how camp women are represented.

9   While Hatoss (2012) was studying refugees she used semi-structured interviews and found out how refugees had a strong ethnic self-concept.

REFERENCES

Abdo, N. and R. Lentin, eds. (2002). *Women and the Military Confrontation: Palestinian and Israeli Gendered Narratives of Dislocation.* New York: Berghahn Books.

Abdul Hadi, F. (1999–2001) *Al tareek al-shafawi: Adwar el-mara' al-Filasteenyah* [The Oral History: The Roles of the Palestinian Woman]. Center for Palestinian Studies, Archiving and Researching, Lebanon [in Arabic].

Al-Hardan, A. (2014) "Decolonizing Research on Palestinians: Towards Cultural Epistemologies and Research Practices", *Qualitative Inquiry* 20(1): 61–71.

Allan, D. (1995) "Mythologizing al-Nakba: Narratives, Collective Identity and Cultural Practice Among Palestinian Refugees in Lebanon", *Oral History* 33(1): 47–56.

Anastasio, T.J., K.A. Ehrenberger, P. Watson and W. Zhang (2012) *Individual and Collective Memory Consolidation: Analogous Processes on Different Levels.* Cambridge, MA: Massachusetts Institute of Technology Press.

Anderson, K. (2011) *Life Stages and Native Women: Memory Teachings and Story Medicine.* Winnipeg, Canada: University of Manitoba Press.

Bakhtin, M.M. (1963) *Problems of Dostoevsky's Poetics.* Moscow: Khudozhestvennaja literature [in Russian].

Boyarin, J., ed. (1994) *The Politics of Timespace.* Minneapolis: University of Minneapolis Press.

Brand, H. (2009) "Palestinian Women and Collective Memory", in M. Litvak (ed.), *Palestinian Collective Memory and National Identity.* London: Palgrave-Macmillan.

Brenner, N. (1998) "Between Fixity and Motion: Accumulation, Territorial Organization and the Historical Geography of Spatial Scales", *Society & Space* 16: 456–481.

Brenner, N. and S. Elden (2009) "Henry Lefebvre on State, Space, Territory", *International Political Sociology* 3: 355–377.

Butler, J. (1990) *Gender Trouble: Feminism and the Subversion of Identity.* London: Routledge.

Butler, J., Z. Gambetti and L. Sabsay, eds. (2016) *Vulnerability in Resistance*. Durham, NC: Duke University Press

Busbridge, R. (2017) "Israel-Palestine and the Settler Colonial 'Turn': From Interpretation to Decolonization Theory", *Culture and Society*, http://journals.sagepub.com/doi/pdf/10.1177/0263276416688544.

Carp, J. (2009) "Ground-truthing: Representations of Social Space: Using Lefebvre's Conceptual Triad", *Journal of Planning Education and Research* 28: 129–142.

Coontz, S. (2000) *The Way We Never Were: The American Families and the Nostalgia Trap*, 2nd ed. New York: Basic Books.

Dana, S. (2017) "Palestinian Revolution: The Limits of Anti-Colonial Imagination", in *Al-Nakba* Ramallah: Masarat, Palestinian Center for Political and Strategic Research [in Arabic].

Davis, R. (2007) "Mapping the Past, Re-creating the Homeland: Memories of Village Places in Pre-1948 Palestine", in A. Sa'di and L. Abu-Lughod (eds.), *Nakba: Palestine, 1948, and the Claims of Memory*. New York: Columbia University Press.

Davies, B. and R. Harre (1990) "Positioning: The Discursive Production of Selves", *Journal of Theory of Social Behavior* 20: 43–63.

Al-Aref, A. (1956) *Al-Nakba and the lost paradise*, Vol. 3. Lebanon: Al-Asreyeh Library [in Arabic].

Esmeir, S. (2007) "Memories of Conquest", in A. Sa'di and L. Abu-Lughod (eds.), *Nakba, 1948 Palestine and the Claims of Memory*. New York: Columbia University Press.

Farah, R. (2006) "Palestinian Refugees", *Interventions* 8: 228–252.

Federici, S. (2004) *Caliban and the Witch*. New York: Autonomedia.

Field, S. (2012) *Oral History, Community and Displacement: Imagining Memories in Post-Apartheid South Africa*. London: Palgrave Macmillan.

Foucault, M. (1979) *The History of Sexuality: The Will to Knowledge*. London: Penguin.

Hanafi, S. (2008) *Palestinian Refugee Camps: Disciplinary Space and Territory of Exception*. CARIM Analytical and Synthetic Notes, http://cadmus.eui.eu/bitstream/handle/1814/8631/CARIM_AS%26N_2008_44.pdf?sequence=3.

Hatoss, A. (2012) "Where Are You From? Identity Construction and Experiences of 'Othering' in the Narratives of Sudanese Refugee Background Australians", *Discourse and Society* 23(1): 47–68.

Halbwachs, M. (1980) *The Collective Memory*, edited and translated by F.J. Ditter and V.Y. Ditter. New York: Harper & Row

Halbwachs, M. (1992) *On Collective Memory*, edited and translated by L.A. Coser. Chicago: Chicago University Press,.

Humphries, I. and L. Khalili (2007) "The Gender of Nakba Memory", in A. Sa'di and L. Abu-Lughod (eds.), *Nakba: Palestine, 1948, and the Claims of Memory*. New York: Columbia University Press.

Johnson, P. (2009) "What Rosemary Saw: Reflections on Palestinian Women as Tellers of the Palestinian Present", *Journal of Palestine Studies* 38(4): 29–46.

Kassem, F. (2012) *Palestinian Women: Narrative Histories and Gendered Memory*. London: Zed Books.

Khalili, L. (2007) "Heroic and Tragic Pasts: Mnemonic Narratives in the Palestinian Refugee Camps", *Critical Sociology* 33(4): 731–759.

Khalili, L. (2008) "Incarceration and the State of Exception: al-Ansar Mass Detention Camp in Lebanon", in R. Lentin (ed.), *Thinking Palestine*. London: Zed Books.

Khoury, L. (2005) "United States of America: The Struggle for Economic Citizenship", in J.M. Billson and C. Fluehr-Lobban (eds.), *Female Well-being: Social Change around the World in the 20th Century*. London: Zed Books.

Khoury, L. (2012) "Being While Black: Resistance and the Management of the Self", *Social Identities* 18(1): 85–100.

Khoury, L. and S. Da'Na (2013) "Geopolitics of Knowledge: Constructing an Indigenous Sociology from the South", *International Review of Modern Sociology* 39(1): 1–28.

Khoury, L., S. Dana and G. Falah (2013a) "Palestine as a Woman: Feminizing Resistance and Popular Literature", *The Arab World Geographer* 16(2): 147–176.

Khoury, L., S. Dana and I. Abu Saad (2013b) "The Dynamics of Negotiation: Identity Formation among Palestinian Arab College Students inside the Green Line", *Social Identities* 19(1): 1–19.

Mackenzie, S. (1989) "Restructuring the relations of work and life: Women as environmental actors, feminism as geographic analysis", in A. Kobayashi and S. Mackenzie (eds.), *Remaking Human Geography*. Boston: Unwin Hyman.

Mahmood, S. (2005) *Politics of Piety: The Islamic Revival and the Feminist Subject*. Princeton, NJ: Princeton University Press.

Mahoney, J. (2010) *Colonialism and Postcolonial Development, Spanish America in Comparative Perspective*. Cambridge: Cambridge University Press.

Masalha, N. (2012) *The Palestine Nakba: Decolonizing History, Narrating the Subaltern, Reclaiming History*. London: Zed Books.

Mies, M. (1998) *Patriarchy and Accumulation on a World Scale*, 2nd ed).London: Zed Books.

Mohammed, P. (1994) "Gender as a Primary Signifier in the Construction of Community and State among Indians in Trinidad", *Caribbean Quarterly* 40(3–4).

Mouchref, M. (2016) "Representations of Indigenous Feminism and Social Change", *Cultural Intertexts* 6: 88–101.

Naber, N. (2006) "The Rules of Forced Engagement: Gendered Inscriptions of Terrorism on Arab Muslim Bodies", *Journal of Cultural Dynamics* 18(3): 235–267.

Olick, J.K. (2007) *The Politics of Regret: On Collective Memory and Historical Responsibility*. London: Routledge.

Ocasio, W. and M. Mauskapf (2016) "History, Society, and Institutions: The Role of Collective Memory in the Emergence and Evolution of Societal Logics", *Academy of Management Review* 41(1): 1–24.

Peteet, J. (1992) *Gender in Crisis: Women and the Palestinian Resistance Movement*. New York: Columbia University Press

Peteet, J. (1994) "Male Gender and Rituals of Resistance in the Palestinian 'Intifada': A Cultural Politics of Violence", *American Ethnologist* 21: 31–49.

Peteet, J. (2005) *Landscape of Hope and Despair: Palestinian Refugee Camps.* Pittsburgh: University of Pennsylvania Press.

Pile, S. and M. Keith, eds. (1997) *Geographies of Resistance.* London: Routledge.

Sa'di, A. and L. Abu-Lughod, eds. (2007) *Nakba: Palestine, 1948, and the Claims of Memory.* New York: Columbia University Press.

Sartre, J.-P. (2004) *The Imaginary*, translated by A. Elkaim-Sartre. London: Routledge.

Sayigh, R. (1995) "Palestinians in Lebanon: Harsh Present, Uncertain Future", *Journal of Palestine Studies* 25(1): 37–53.

Sayigh, R. (1981) "Roles and Functions of Arab Women: A Reappraisal", *Arab Studies Quarterly* 3: 258–274.

Sayigh, R. (1998) "Palestinian Women as Tellers of History", *Journal of Palestine Studies* 27(2): 42–58.

Sayigh, R. (2002) "Remembering Mothers, Forming Daughters: Palestinian Women's Narratives on Refugee Camps in Lebanon", in N. Abdo and R. Lentin (eds.), *Women and the Politics of Military Confrontation: Palestinian and Israeli Gendered Narratives of Dislocation.* New York and Oxford: Berghahn Books.

Sayigh, R. (2007) "Women's Nakba Stories: Between Being and Knowing", in A. Sa'di and L. Abu-Lughod (eds.), *Nakba: Palestine, 1948, and the Claims of Memory.* New York: Columbia University Press.

Sayigh, R. (2015) "Silenced Suffering", *Borderland*, 14(1): 1–20.

Sayigh, R. and J. Peteet (1986) "Between Two Fires: Palestinian Women in Lebanon", in R. Ridd and H Callaway (eds.), *Caught up in Conflict: Women's Response to Political Strife.* London: Macmillan.

Smith, L.T. (1999) *Decolonizing Methodologies: Research and Indigenous Peoples.* London: Zed Books.

Stoler, A.L. and K. Strassler (2000) "Casting for the Colonial: Memory Work in 'New Order' Java", *Comparative Studies in Society and History* 42: 4–48.

Todd, Z. (2016) "An Indigenous Feminist's Take on the 'Ontology' Turn: 'Ontology' is Just another Word for Colonization", *Journal of Historical Sociology* 29(1): 4–22.

Woolf, V. (1954) *A Writer's Diary: Being Extracts from the Diary of Virginia Woolf*, edited by L. Woolf. San Diego, CA: Harcourt Brace.

Wrede, T. (2015) "Theorizing Space and Gender in the 21st Century", *Rocky Mountain Review* 69(1): 10–17.

7

Gender representation of oral history: Palestinian women narrating the stories of their displacement

FAIHA ABDUL HADI

The paper is based on highlighting the voices of Palestinian women who were displaced from Palestinian cities and villages in 1948 as a primary source,[1] adopting the methodology of oral history from a gender perspective.

This multidisciplinary perspective is premised on the interaction between the researcher and the narrator (Tonkin 1995), and a deep knowledge of women's psychology (Gluck and Patai 1991); at the same time, it acts on deconstructing the dominant values, which fail to recognize the experiences of women as a major component in history making. Thus a new set of values would be formed, allowing the integration and harmonization of the experiences of women and men (Hoda 1999: 168).

By telling their stories, women become visible and their voices are raised to express what they experience, know and go through. When we listen to the voices of women we can discern what is common in their stories regarding the "year of displacement", as well as the differences emanating from their different social class and the different human experience they had in each town that they were displaced to. By listening to the hidden, honest and unheard voice of women, we can also understand the power relations between men and women and among the women themselves.

In order to allow the hidden voices of the narrators to emerge, and in order to listen to their honest and true opinions regarding what had happened to them from the year of displacement until the date of recording the interviews, the research adopted the gender perspective whereby the researchers listened patiently and attentively to the women. They observed and recorded the elements surrounding the narrators, and documented the body language: the eyes, the mouth, the lips, the hands, the feet and their eyebrows, in addition to documenting the long and short moments of silence. They shared with the narrators the concerns, dreams and pain that they experienced with the same sense of intimacy as when the narrators talked about the suffering of the past. While it is true that the researchers followed a research questionnaire, this served only as an outline that helped them probe some critical issues regarding the question of displacement. However, what was central to the methodology was its interest in allowing the narrators the opportunity to start talking from the angle that they preferred when remembering the past, so that their choices would help reveal which experiences and feelings were major and central to the past for them (Al-Dajani and Soliman 1995).

This interaction and communication between the researchers and the narrators is what could contribute to the generation and building of shared knowledge regarding the displacement in 1948, which might sometimes be aligned with the written Palestinian narrative and differ at other times, but certainly and necessarily adds new dimensions to it.

THE LIVING MEMORY OF PALESTINIAN WOMEN

The Palestinian women narrated their memories regarding the displacement of 1948. Through their eagerness to render a very accurate and detailed account of the events, the women described every detail of what affected their families. They described their efforts to secure food, water, clothes, other means of comfort, things they left behind when they were displaced. They focused on the impact of what had happened to them and their families, which contributes towards deconstructing the Zionist narrative claiming that Palestinians left voluntarily in 1948, surrendering their country without resistance.

The women's stories agreed that the Zionist militia resorted to the systematic expulsion of the women and their families through various means. They killed by shooting civilians directly, and by them bombing from the air. They also spread terror among Palestinians with shelling, bombs, explosions, tanks and massacres, the most prominent of which was the massacre of Deir Yassin. They did not only claim responsibility for these massacres, they also intention-

ally exaggerated them,[2] confirming that what happened was ethnic cleansing par excellence.[3]

Thurayya Yaseen Alya'qoubi, displaced from Majdal Asqalan[4] and currently residing in Rafah city,[5] described the events in Al Majdal in 1948 when planes were dropping bombs over the residents of the city in a clear attempt at displacement: "The planes used to strike three times a day, then we started fleeing to Ni'lia,[6] which was a village that did not attract attention, but because it was Al Majdal, the Jews told the displaced: go, go to Al Majdal, go to your 'Paris' meaning Al Majdal." [7]

Rasheedeh Hasan Fdalat, displaced from I'raq Al Manshiyyah[8] and currently residing in Al Baqa'a refugee camp,[9] described what happened to her and the residents of her village on the day of their displacement, when the Hagana gangs used the most heinous methods to terrorize them and force them to leave:

> Each night there were bombs fired by Zionist militia and where would they fall? They would primarily fall among the cattle at my grandfather's house, right inside the house! From the morning, they would fire ten [she counts on her hands], ten and twenty at a time. One day my uncle's wife took a knife, and my grandfather did not know, and said, I want to slaughter one or two of the cattle so that we can eat them. I swear to God, the meat of the cattle at my grandfather's house was blown away to the next neighbourhood [pointing with her hand to a place far away] from the impact of the airstrikes. This is something I heard with my own ears, and saw with my own eyes. My mom was always counting the bombs, and she would miscount! [She hits her leg with her hand], one bomb after the other, boom, boom, and where would they fall? They would fall on our town, how could I describe it? Let us say it was something like Al Baqa'a refugee camp. My mother started saying: [she holds her head and starts scratching it violently with her hands] my children, my children, my sons my daughters, my children my children [she claps] the next thing I saw was that her head had all turned white, white, she had white hair.[10]

Sana Kamel Aldajani, who was displaced from Yafa (Jaffa)[11] and currently resides in Cairo, talked about the fear and horror that was caused by the bombs the Zionist militia fired towards the houses in order to force their residents to leave. She explained that the intention of the Palestinian families at the time was to leave temporarily, seeking safety away from the bombs and shelling:

> It was almost around this time, exactly on 28 April 1948, when I and five of my siblings together with our parents were home. We would wake up terrified in the middle of the night to the noises of bombs shaking our house. It seems like on that night the plan was to target Yafa [Jaffa] in particular because it was the first harbour city and was very important for Palestine and the whole of the east Mediterranean coastal area. Yafa had always played a prominent role for Palestine and hosted many of the leaders who played a tremendous role in the years that preceded the displacement and beyond. I was eight years old, as I mentioned. Together with my siblings, we would run to my parents' room only to find them as terrified as we were. The decision was quick that night as I remember clearly: get dressed children and let us go to the house of my grandparents from my mother's side, which was off the sea and the seacoast a bit. There we found a large number of the family members. Suddenly we were a very large family all of us, my grandparents, uncles, my grandmother and aunts, my cousins, we were all there! Gathered at my mother's great grandfather's house, in the large garden, recounting many stories that Zionist militia has utilized the element of surprise during the attack and a timing when the people are at their houses.[12]

Ameeneh Abdelhameed Ataba, displaced from Saffourieh[13] and currently residing in Nazareth,[14] talked about the tanks that barged into the streets and fired their shells at the time of breaking the fast during the month of Ramadan and forced people to flee:

> It was during the month of Ramadan. People were just breaking their fast. Suddenly, they saw the tanks. Two tanks barged into the town. Our house, that is our land, was close to the street. The residents of Saffourieh, the gardeners, once they saw the tanks entering the town started saying: there are barrels behind them and others would say, there is something happening, we do not know! They could hear the tanks, they started shouting, they entered and it meant occupation. The gardeners backed away, they backed away. They hid amidst the pomegranate trees. My

mother was pregnant in her ninth month and I was a little girl. They grabbed us and took us to hide amidst the pomegranate trees.[15]

Lateefeh Ahmad Uthman Mtair, displaced from Bir Ma'in village[16] and currently living in Qalandya refugee camp,[17] identified the time of the aggression and the violent manner in which the Zionist military entered the village that led to their displacement: "We remained in Beit O'ur Il Tahta,[18] and then we moved a bit further up from Beit O'ur Il Tahta. There were fig trees named: the figs of Abu Nsseir and we sat underneath them. If only you saw the scene, the ground and the sky were on fire."[19]

Labeebeh Rasheed Aleesa, displaced from Saffourieh and currently residing in A'in Al Helweh refugee camp,[20] confirmed that people were forcibly displaced by the bombing and that the residents did not have any weapons to fight back:

We were in Saffourieh, I don't know, there were airstrikes against the town. People went out and their intention was just to hide under the olive trees. We went out under the bombing, the planes bombed the town and the Palestinians had neither planes nor anything else for that matter! The Jews were firing at the people, at the children, at the babies, they fired at everyone and the planes would bomb everywhere. People were not armed at the time, they had nothing.[21]

In describing the displacement process the women used expressions indicating that they were seeking safety and refuge from imminent death for a limited period and that they never thought of leaving their towns or villages permanently. On the contrary, they refused to use the term immigration: "It was not a decision to leave, it was a decision to avoid the aggression and the massacres";[22] "we experienced a state of fleeing";[23] "the people fled as a result of that";[24] "suddenly it felt like it was the end of days";[25] "We left with the idea that we would return";[26] "and what forced us to flee except for the bombing of the country and the killings? What forced us to be displaced except for fear?"[27]

Khadeejeh Khalil AbuIsba, displaced from Salamah[28] and currently residing in Amman, came up with a special term, through which she expressed her refusal to describe her departure from Palestine as immigration. Instead, she used a very specific word, "elevation", to indicate a temporary move out of one place to another:

First they let the women go out before the men and the revolutionaries
[she refutes the idea that the family immigrated. In the preliminary
interview, she answered the question about immigration angrily: "we
did not immigrate; we were elevated, meaning we left temporarily
until we were able to return". She repeated several times: "no, no, we
did not immigrate"].

When we left Salamah had fallen on 25 April 1948 [she insists on the
date when Salamah was occupied, her eyes staring and her expression
hardening]. What did they do? The Jews besieged the town from all four
sides, where would the people leave. The Jews kept an opening as if to
say, come on, leave, we have opened the road for you to leave through the
valley that separates our town from Yazour.[29] The valley was there between
our town and Yazour. Therefore, when my brother and cousin left with
their cars, which belonged to the dairy company, they were unable to drive
down the valley. They parked the cars and swam. When they came out of
water, they had reached Al-Lydd.[30]

WOMEN'S EFFECTIVENESS: PARTICIPATION IN THE ECONOMY

Since the early days of the first displacement in 1948, the management of the
family's economic affairs constituted a primary concern for rural women. These
women thought of the most important items to carry with them as they left their
houses: they carried: some cooking utensils,[31] grains and mills,[32] some poultry
and donkeys,[33] money,[34] jewellery,[35] embroidered items[36] and identification
documents.[37] They took pillows, duvets and mattresses,[38] as well as the keys to
their houses.[39] They sold their gold, which they had saved, grew their own food
and took up paid work. Despite the very harsh living conditions, the women
insisted on an education for their children. Women left the private sphere and
entered the public sphere in order to contribute towards securing their family
finances. They sold their homemade products in the market, worked in the
fields, worked at sewing and embroidery.

Rasheedeh Hasan Fdalat talked about the displaced women's work in
cutting and gathering wood to be used for cooking, first in order to feed the
family and also to contribute towards supporting their families by selling the
wood. She talked about having to work at a young age gathering wood, and
her insistence on going to school at the same time despite her youth. She then
talked about her determination to learn how to sew in order to find a paid

job and be financially independent. Through her story, the suffering becomes apparent at all levels: social, psychological, economic and health:

> We went to Al Arroub refugee camp. Every ten days the United Nations Relief and Works Agency (UNRWA) would distribute one kilogramme of flour per person, each person would get one kilogramme of flour. Sometimes, they would distribute fish, or cheese [she draws a circle on her palm to show the shape of the cheese], or dried eggs in packets like this. You would take the contents of the packets, stir it in water and eat it with bread. Yes, we would eat it. It was a miserable life; there were no markets or shops, nothing of the basic elements for life. We only had water, we would go fill the clay jugs and put them in the tent. How can we manage? What shall we do? Women started going out to collect wood. The baker and his name was Abu Mohammad would tell them: bring the wood to me. Instead of going here and there trying to sell it come to me and I will buy the wood from you for the bakery. Initially, I used to go to school. At the school, they brought together all the girls, all of them and I was studying at the school. Some of our relatives started collecting wood. My mom told them: take Rasheedeh with you and she will make a bundle of wood for me and one for her and we would go back home. Praise be upon Prophet Mohammad, we put the wood here like this and there came the baker. He asked my mom, would you sell the wood "Umm Ismail"? She said, we use them for cooking, [she starts counting on her hands] we need fire to cook, for washing the clothes, for bathing, all in this tent, in this tent. They had given us a small tent because we were a small family: myself, my brother, my mom, and my sister. We were four sleeping in the tent. A small tent with one pole [she raises her hand making the shape of a pole] one pole. How much did he want to pay for the wood? He wanted to pay 75 dimes! 75 dimes, but at the time that was a good amount of money. With one dime, you could get what you wanted. If you wanted [and she started counting on her hands] tea you could get it with one dime, but there were no shops then yet. My mom was not used to go out to collect wood or even get out into the non-built-up area. The Fdalat family particularly, and I say that to everyone, their women never went out to the fields, never participated in the harvest, or anything of the sort. It is true they owned shops and the women would sit at the shops to help their husbands but that was it.

Here, she said, make the bundle bigger and I will meet you half way. She started to meet me half way and carry a bundle of wood on her back, on her shoulders but could not carry it on her head. Gradually, she started to meet me and take off some of my burden. We were barefooted, walking on the thorns, did not have anything to protect our hands, had thorns on our heads. We would go and start removing the thorns [she moves her fingers on her hand as if she is taking out the thorns] and we would take out the thorns of each other's hands. There was no soap or "Tide" [washing detergent] like these days for people to use for cleaning themselves.

People suffered even from lice! They suffered from lice and the Americans came, took lice from people's heads, and put them in jars! This was how poor people were. There was nothing that could be used as cleaning detergents. You would go to wash the clothes [she moves her hands as if rubbing a piece of cloth] like this; you would wash your son's head with water sometimes. We did not have the basic necessities of life. When father did not come back and no one brought us any news about him, whether he died or recovered or anything, my mother said: until when will I sit still like this? So she started to also go out with us, we would go out to collect wood together. We were kids, we remained in the camp. I used to go to collect wood and go to the teacher. She would tell me: Where were you? Why were you absent "Miss" Rasheedeh? I would tell her: I was collecting wood my teacher. She would tell me listen; you go to either collect wood or come to school! But to do both it does not work out. I used to come back from collecting wood at 10 o'clock; the girls would have had all the lessons. My classmates would feel sorry for me, one of them would write to me saying, answer this way [she writes on her hand], and another girl would write something, and they would pass the paper to me through the boys. One time, I wrote maybe two words on my paper, but I was unable to write everything, just what the girls sent me. The teacher said, hand in your papers, and we did. Peace be upon Prophet Mohammad, the teacher wrote, where is the rest of the answers "Rasheedeh"? Each one of you should write their names on their paper. Then I took out that paper, the one that my friends wrote to help me. I got ten out of ten, a full mark.

The teacher was surprised and said oh, excellent. Then they opened a place to teach girls sewing. They started to do this gradually for the refugee camps. They brought a tent next to the school's tent. We were in tents. We would study in tents, wearing our regular clothes (she points to her clothes), just the way we were dressed, there was no uniform, no special clothes, no shoes. I did not even have slippers or anything. We used to walk back and forth barefooted in the same dress. We did not even have any underwear. They said, they teach sewing.

My mother said, go "Rasheedeh" go and learn how to sew, forget about school. I went there. They taught us how to sew. The clothes would come cut and ready and we would just sew them manually [she moves her hands as if she is sewing], a machine stich. We learned sewing and it benefited us when we grew older. They taught us how to knit using knitting needles. However, I was always busy, as I told you: I would go to collect wood and come back only to find that the girls took all the lessons and the same applied to sewing. I would go to collect wood only to come back and find out that the girls learned everything. I would go and when I return I would find that they have learned everything about weaving and I would know nothing. I would come always late and the girls would be waiting impatiently to finish and go home, they would not want to stay behind to show me what they learned. My mom – May she rest in peace – took me with her and went to some of our neighbours. At the end we remained, we remained in the refugee camps. There was a teacher called Miss "Zakiyyeh", she used to teach us and the male teachers would teach the boys. They would give them for each student they teach, or maybe there was another way to figure that out, one kilogram of flour. Every ten days, they would give them one kilogram of flour. But they showed patience and perseverance, they remained steadfast and continued to teach the students.[40]

Unlike women displaced from the villages, discussed above, women displaced from the cities carried with them some money,[41] some pictures and the family documents,[42] clothes, silver and carpets,[43] jewellery,[44] wooden boxes containing embroidered items,[45] embroidered wedding dresses,[46] embroidered handker-chiefs, and a special kind of embroidered covers and sheets.[47]

Some of the women had to contribute towards their families' financial costs, primarily by becoming teachers or learning sewing. Many of them had received a good education and learned some technical skills that allowed them to obtain paid jobs. Some of them worked in hosting countries and some of them had worked in the Gulf.

Regarding city women who became refugees, "Sana Kamel Aldajani" spoke about Palestinian women's work in teaching following their displacement in order to support their families:

> When we were evacuated, many Palestinian women provided for their families financially. They went to teach in all the Arab countries. The women helped their husbands; they were completely different from who they were in their country after the displacement. Sometimes they took the responsibility for their families alone and on their own. I have a very good example for women who took the full responsibility for their families. I will never forget Mrs. "Mufeeda Al Dabbagh", a very respectable woman from Yafa who comes from a well-known family. She and her sister left for Saudi Arabia right after the displacement. She was my school principal in Yafa and that is how I know her. Anyway, she went to teach, that was her and her sister's weapon. She was chosen to teach the king's daughters, my God how much she benefited from that! How much they loved her! How productive she was! She was the first to open a girls' school there and she called it "Al Hanan" [Tenderness]. The school exists until this day, the school of Mrs. "Mufeeda Al Dabbagh" from Yafa and her sister Mrs. Kamleh, may they rest in peace. They were the first to open the Al Hanan School for the royal family and then the school was open for everyone in Riyadh. I just gave this as an example of what our girls and women were able to do, particularly in the field of teaching. It was the biggest and most comprehensive field of work that allowed women to stand by their men at the time of their displacement until now.[48]

Firyal Hanna Abuawad, displaced from Beit Jala[49] and currently residing in Santiago, Chile, talked about her and her siblings' work in sewing after her displacement, which helped in securing her family's livelihood:

> I was responsible for the female workers. I was sixteen years old and I was responsible for all the female workers at the factors. My sister was responsible for the designs. She was a seamstress working in Jerusalem. When she came here [to Santiago], she was the fashion designer. My

brother "Faisal" used to cut the clothes and do different tasks. My father bought this big house. He bought a very, very big house. It was originally a school before they rented it out. It used to accommodate 140 workers. I was not married then. At the time here was between twenty and twenty-five workers and I was their supervisor.[50]

ELEMENTS OF STRENGTH

Through the women's stories about the details of their journey of displacement, two juxtaposed images emerge that combine strength and weakness, steadfastness and suffering. There is the image of the woman as the victim who was subjected to systematic violence and experienced various forms of pain, various forms of economic, social, psychological and physical suffering. In addition there is the image of the woman as fiercely fighting for her right and the right of her family to a dignified life. The woman who fights through all possible means for her people's right to freedom, and who is aware of the importance of education, the media, music, folkloric songs and the arts in general in people's lives.

Ameeneh Mahmoud Alafghani described the horrific journey of displacement from Yafa to Nablus. She also described how she smuggled her husband's weapon (a gun) from Yafa:

We were just going about our regular life, my husband was working and we were happy. Suddenly, hell broke loose, some of the neighbours fled, cars stopped moving. We were afraid. My husband worked for Jews as a guard. We took our mattresses and ran away. We went to a neighbourhood called Tal Al Reesh. My mother had a house there and we stayed in it. I stayed there; we packed the mattresses and the clothes. I cooked "Mloukhiyya" with fava beans [a dish called Bissara]. I served the food, only to hear my husband saying, go, everyone is at the house, they have all gathered here. The women had run away. I ran away with my little sister. At night, I told him: I want to go. He told me: come, let us go, I want to take you to Saknah. I had a great fall; it was night time and very dark. I could not see from the darkness and the sense of fear. My husband told me: I want to help you escape. We left and crossed through the groves to avoid being detected by the binoculars.

We went to my sister's house. She was married and lived there and we spent the rest of our night there. In the morning, we ran away. Where to? He told me: I found a house in a neighbourhood called Saknet Al Ghazazweh. It is empty there is no one there. We went, my little sister, and me alone. My brother went to his work, and my mother had not left yet. I was afraid all night and the cats were mewing all the time.

There was no water and no light. I kept my eyes open until the morning. I could not wait for the morning to arrive. In the morning, my mother came; my mother, my dad, and my brother came. We remained with them for a while. We would eat and drink together. Then my husband said we have to go to Nablus. I tried to convince him otherwise, but he said, no the neighbourhood is empty, no one is here, there is no water and there is no food, there is nothing here.

We went to the sea, together with the people who remained with us. There we thought we would ride a boat like the others. They told us people were taking the boats, and would be in the sea for seven days but then they go back to the shore. We were afraid that we would face the same fate. We went back to Nablus. We arrived there in the evening. My husband had a gun that I smuggled with me. We were desperate to bring it with us.[51]

Labeebeh Rashid Aleesa talked about the resistance by Saffourieh's women; how they faced the conspiracy of displacement, and how they confronted and clashed with the soldiers:

They forced them all out of Saffourieh, by force. There was one woman related to us. She said that the soldiers would come to force them out of the town. The women would go out to beat them and shout at them. One woman had beaten a soldier and had taken away his helmet and his weapon, and ran away. They told her: the soldiers will come now and arrest you. She told me, I was really sent to prison. She went, took a bath, and changed her clothes. Soon after, the soldiers were asking about her, and then they took her and put her in jail. Her name was Suad, "Suad Saeed", if I remember correctly.[52]

Through the testimony of Samiyyeh Abdelrahman Altaji, displaced from Al-Ramleh[53] and currently residing in Amman, women worked at polishing the bullets that resistance fighters used to confront the occupiers and resist the displacement:

They sent us weapons from Egypt but it was all rusted. All the bullets that came for the guns were rusted. I would sit together with my mother-in-law, sisters-in-law, and later my brother-in-law's wife, the five of us women the whole night polishing the bullets so that they can use them for the weapons.

Ultimately, the Jews came; when they entered, they told us: it is time for you to leave. My father-in-law told them: I want to remain here; they told him the entire town's residents could remain except Sheikh "Mustafa Al Khairi" because when there were problems in the villages surrounding Ar-Ramleh, they would come to my father-in-law to rule between the parties, my father-in-law would decide on the cases like a judge and would help parties to reconcile. The people did not resort to the British government and the Jews hated him because they knew he was the "ruler" of all Ar-Ramleh villages as well as Al-Lydd's villages. He told them eventually: I am staying here and I will not leave and you have to allow me to remain here.[54]

The role of women emerges not only in resisting displacement but also in trying to stop some of the massacres. Maryam Muhamad Noufal, displaced from Hleiqat[55] and living in Jabalia refugee camp,[56] talked about the women[57] who managed to stop the Dayaymeh massacre by shouting in the faces of the aggressors:

Everyone was standing for prayers at the mosque; they killed them, yes they killed them! My aunt "Hadyyeh" from her family, they started shouting with the mayhem of people, the officers went in and forced the Jews to leave after they killed all those who were in the front row. If they had left them there, they would have continued killing the people. The women started shouting, they came, and the women started running. There are no women like the women of Dawaymeh.[58]

The role of women as partners of men in resisting the aggression emerges through the testimony of Rasheedeh Hasan Fdalat:

They were resisting, resisting, men and women alike. Yet, Umm Rabah would sit amidst the sacks on the roof of the house. She would sit and watch where the shooting was coming from. When she saw her husband feeling tired, she would tell him: go down and I will go up to replace you. They would alternate roles. All our women were resisting alone, they did not receive any training or anything! They were alone. You could say that they were able to communicate with the Egyptian army and were able to understand each other. Therefore, they would watch things at least or pass weapons! They would give them water and food in the trenches. The Egyptian soldiers had dug trenches in the town, and the women would go and serve them food and water, and sometimes weapons if possible.[59]

Through the testimonies, the strength of Palestinian women emerged in several ways. Women in villages, towns and refugee camps showed an interest in education. They showed a capacity to learn, including the use of technology, and demonstrated political awareness. City women who had the opportunity to learn at foreign schools were able to speak languages fluently and were able to learn skills such as metal working and playing the piano, while women from villages and refugee camps were characterized by their ability to improvise poetry and sing folkloric songs.

The testimonies of Ameeneh Abdelhamid Ataba and Samiyeh Abdelrahman Altaji provide us with the best examples of Palestinian women's awareness of the importance of education and their insistence on overcoming the obstacles that faced them despite the differences in social conditions and class. They also indicate the different forms of suffering related to the social class to which these women belonged.

Ameeneh spoke about her mother's insistence on teaching her despite the difficulties of life and living conditions. Her story shows the strength of her mother, who would take a donkey and lead them back and forth between Aylout and Nazareth to guarantee her children's education:

What brought us from Aylout to Nazareth? My mom was worried about us, but more so about me, that we would not go to school and continue our education. I went to Kindergarten, then to grade one. Do you know who used to feed us the most? You know I remember, you know, they used to care for the orphans [the nuns]. They set up tents on the fields for those displaced from Saffourieh. They used to distribute milk, as well as cookies oil; this is how they called it cookies oil. They would distribute milk, biscuits, cheese, and sometimes they would give us dried milk. They used to call them the White Sisters. My late husband used to work for them; he did the gardening work for them. They used to come, as you know to give us shots and treat us. The nuns have always played a good role in our lives. They would bring us clothes. We used to walk barefooted, where would we get the money from to buy shoes? They used to bring us cardigans, they really cared. I attended Kindergarten and grade one at Aylout. Then one day we were returning from school, the donkey was not there. The donkey was very important for us; it would bring us to Nazareth. My mom would put us on the donkey, just like a car nowadays. Can anyone do it? My mom would ride the donkey to bring us back. That is how the streets of Aylout were. My late mom would put me and Muhammad [her brother] on the donkey and we would come to Nazareth.[60]

Samiyyeh talked about her own personal suffering because of being unable to continue her education, and her insistence on not giving in to her father's will. She talked about her artistic talent that helped her return to school:

I learned metal work. I did many things for the house, for me, for my house that is for my future. I did all of that at St. Joseph. The metal would be brought in and there would be items from crystal that we would add metal to. I did plates as well as a piano cupboard to put my piano books in it. I did a chair with a leather seat. When I got engaged, my dad said: you will not go to school anymore. I cried and cried, and sobbed. I stopped eating or drinking for a few days. My brother then came and told me dear sister, why cannot we take this picture of our dad, remove this terrible wooden frame and replace it with metal from your work? He added to it Abdelrahman Nafeth Altaji and the year it was made. I did that and took it to my dad. He said, where were you the last three or four days. I answered: I was laying in my bed because I want to go back to school and you refuse to let me. So he asked me, what do you want in return for this frame in terms of a gift? I told him: I want to go back to school for one year. He said, go talk with the sisters and tell them you are going back. I talked to the sisters and told them that I am going back and that I want to stay at the school for another year. They said, you are most welcome; the whole class is at your disposal, just like the way you want. I remained there for a year. That year, my dad allowed me only to sit for the piano exam and then I sat for Brevet.[61]

Awareness of the importance of media and history, as well as the capacity to use social media platforms, were things about Rasheedeh Hasan Fdalat that drew our attention:

> My uncle Muhammad Eid was a martyr. The British caught him; he was with the revolution together with a friend of his called Yousef Abutayeh. I want to mention these two because they are heroes and I wish someone would talk about them in the West Bank or through radio or TV stations, or in the newspapers. They were with the revolution; he was my mom's cousin, so he is my uncle (from my mother's side). He had been married only for two months and he would attack the British, but they had taken harsh measures against us! They started to impose heavy taxes on people, anyone who was found to carry a pocketknife would be put in jail, anyone going out for a walk at night they would arrest him for interrogation. Britain controlled our lives a lot. This young man together with a number of other young men were called revolutionaries, not freedom fighters as they would call them nowadays. He planted a landmine for the British, but they were caught and put in prison. I was still a baby; this was like seventy-five years ago. I posted this on Facebook. Anyway, he was in jail for six months, and then they executed them and allowed no one to see them. They did what they wanted with them, put them in wooden coffins and brought them to the town on British tanks. This should go down in history, this story.[62]

Layla Nusaybeh-Altaji Alfarouqi, displaced from Al Ramleh and residing in Amman, talked about the supportive role of her pioneer aunt Zulaykha Shihabi, who was able, through the Women's Union, to help other women whose husbands or sons were martyred. She talked about the humanitarian role of the pioneer Hind Husayni when she established Dar Al-Tifl Al Arabi to care for the children of martyrs following the Deir Yassin massacre:

> I know from my aunt Zulaykha because she used to help women whose children or husbands have joined the revolution or were martyred. They worked through the Women's Union and charitable organizations that supported the families of the revolutionaries. Hind Husayni, for example, who after the Deir Yassin massacre started on a personal initiative and

using her big house – and status, you know we're talking about Alhusayni family and their status – that was located in Herod's Gate[63] opposite the Orient House[64] and the house of Ismaeel Baik Alhusayni too. She went and brought the children of Deir Yassin and housed them in the first floor. She brought with her all children and sick people, who were not killed, she saved them, brought them, raised them up, and established Dar El-Tifl.[65]

Firyal Hanna Abuawad talked about the role of female teachers and nurses in supporting the resistance:

There were women teachers and nurses and everything else. They used to bring them fabric to make things that the revolutionaries would need. They worked at the convent, at the hospital; they would make quilts and bedding for the hospitals. The nurses used to help a lot. They helped us a lot. There were many of them from our town. The women were very good.[66]

Poems and songs hold a special status among Palestinian women, for they have long constituted an element of strength and an effective weapon in confronting obstacles and hardships, and in remembering those bittersweet moments, as remarked in the stories of Thurayya Yaseen Alya'qoubi,[67] Rasheedeh Fdalat,[68] Fatima Hijazi[69] and Khadeejeh Khalil Abuisba.[70]

Songs also were a source of support for the revolutionaries who were defending their country against displacement and uprooting, as explained by Khadeejeh Khalil Abuisba.[71]

CONCLUSION

The testimonies of the women based on the methodology of oral history from a gender perspective reveal that Palestinian women had not given in to their oppressive circumstances, nor did they surrender to sadness and lamentation following their displacement in 1948 and their changing social conditions. Palestinian women rather fought back courageously and played an effective and vital role in the Palestinian social, political and economic life at home and in the diaspora.

From day one of their displacement, Palestinian women rose to the challenge in order to meet the needs of their families, firstly to keep them alive and then to improve their living conditions, recognizing the importance of education and work. While urban women resorted to the education they had acquired through joining the official education system, rural women resorted to their intelligence and awareness of the importance of developing their capacities. Rural women were keen to get an education for themselves and their family members; these women were also forced to enter the paid labour market, making use of their experience in growing food and their ability to learn.

Palestinian women carved out their own terminology, emanating from their views on politics and life. They rejected the Zionists' term "Hijra Taweyya" (voluntary leaving), and insisted on a narrative based on their personal experience, of being displaced and forced to leave. None of the displaced women wanted to leave their house, village or country, as is evident in the fact that they left their houses with everything intact, and carried with them only the minimum that would help them survive until they were able to return home. They used various terms, such as expulsion, transfer, displacement, forced displacement and elevation, all of which help enrich the Palestinian discourse and narrative, which is a counter-narrative to the false Zionist story.

NOTES

1   For the purposes of preparing this paper, I utilized the archives of the Project on 1948 Palestinian displacement carried out by Alrowat for Studies and Research (2012–), http://www.alrowat.com. It might be useful to add here that I am the founder and director of Al Rowat. I am supervising an ongoing project on displacement since 2012, with the help of fifteen field researchers who have so far collected 104 narratives. Fifty-seven documented narrations have been used in this paper, recorded from displaced Palestinian women aged 73–96 years, thirty-seven of them are widows. The fifteen researchers who conducted the interviews are located in the areas of research: West Bank, Gaza, 1948 areas, Jordan, Lebanon, Egypt and Chile.

2   A massacre took place in the village of Deir Yassin, located 5km west of Jerusalem. The village was fully ethnically cleansed on 9 April 1948. Mordachai Ra'nan, the leader of Etzel (Ergon) in Jerusalem, was the first to exaggerate the number of Deir Yassin martyrs, settig it at 245. This information was delivered during a press conference that Ra'nan held on Friday 9 April. The BBC confirmed this figure. However, the number is more accurately estimated as 100 martyrs, mostly women, the elderly and children (Al Khaldi 1999: 124–125).

3   The Commission of UN experts had defined ethnic cleansing in a report submitted to the Security Council (United Nations 1994) in 1993 as "making an area ethnically homogenous by use of force or threats to uproot individuals who belong to specific communities in the region". The Commission's final report issued in May 1994 added the following crimes: mass killing, ill-treatment of civilian prisoners, and prisoners of

war, use of civilians as human shields, destruction of cultural property, dispossession, attacks on hospitals, medical teams, Red Cross and Red Crescent sites carrying their logos. The international law also addressed the issue of systematic expulsion of civilians and the barbaric acts associated with it following World War II. Article 49 of the Fourth Geneva Convention of 12 August 1949 prohibits "individual or mass forcible transfers, as well as deportations of protected persons from occupied territory to the territory of the Occupying Power or to that of any other country". These acts are considered grave legal violations of the Fourth Geneva Convention. War crimes are particularly grave in nature.

4   Located north-east of Gaza. It was fully ethnically cleansed on 4 November 1948.

5   Located 30km south of Gaza.

6   Located 19km north-east of Gaza. It was fully ethnically cleansed on 4 November 1948.

7   Interview with Thurayya Yaseen Alya'qoubi (1930), Rafah. The interview was conducted by researcher Na'eemeh Abu Hmeid on 12–14 May 2015, p.21.

8   Located 32km north-east of Gaza. It was fully ethnically cleansed on 1 March 1949.

9   One of the largest Palestinian refugee camps in Jordan. It is located at the north-western borders of the city of Amman on the Amman–Irbid road.

10 Interview with Rasheedeh Hasan Fdalat (1935), Al Baq'aa refugee camp, Amman. The interview was conducted by researcher Muna Ghosheh on 4 May 2015, pp.10, 11.

11 One of the oldest and most important cities of historic Palestine. It is located approximately 555km to the west. Yafa was ethnically cleansed on 26 April 1948.

12 Interview with Sana Kamel Aldajani (1940), Cairo. The interview was conducted by researcher Alia Okashesh on 17 April 2014, pp.1–3.

13 Located 6km north-west of Nazareth. It was fully ethnically cleansed on 16 July 1948.

14 One of historic Palestine's major cities. It is located approximately 105km to the north of Jerusalem. It was occupied on 6 July 1948.

15 Interview with Amineh Abdelhamid Ataba (1942), Nazareth. The interview was conducted by researcher Zeina Al Zu'bi on 10 March 2015, pp.1-3.

16 Located 14 km east of Al Ramlal, and home to 592 residents in 1948, it was fully ethnically cleansed on 15 July 1948.

17 Qalandia refugee camp was established in 1949 to the east of Jerusalem airport.

18 The village is located west of Ramallah.

19 Interview with Latifah Mteir (1921), Qalandia refugee camp. The interview was conducted by researcher Asmaa' Al Kilani on 16June 2015, p.2.

20 A'in Al Helweh refugee camp. It was established in 1948 and is located within the boundaries of the coastal city of Sidon (Saida), south of Lebanon.

21 Interview with Labiba Rasheed Al Issa (1939), 'Ein Al Helweh refugee camp, Lebanon. The interview was conducted by Amneh Al Khateeb on 18 January 2016, p.3.

22 Interview with Sana Kamel Aldajani, Cairo, mentioned previously, p.8.

23 Interview with Rasheedeh Hasan Fdalat, Al Baq'aa refugee camp, Amman, mentioned previously, p.1.

24 Interview with Labiba Rasheed Al Issa/ 'Ein Al Hilweh refugee camp/ mentioned previously, p.3.

25 Interview with Ameeneh Mahmoud Al Afghani (1923), Old City, Nablus. The interview was conducted by researcher Nida'a Abu Taha on 25 June 2014 and 26 April 2015, p.1.

26 Interview with Kamleh Sari Hashash (1942), Balata refugee camp, Nablus. The interview was conducted by researcher Sumayya Al Safadi on 30 August 2014 and 19 March 2015, p.1.

27 Interview with Fatima Mohammad Hijazi (1928), Al Baqaa' refugee camp, Amman. The interview was conducted by researcher Sireen Musleh on 2 October 2013 and 30 April 2014, pp.10–13.

28 The town is located 5km east of Yafa. It was fully ethnically cleansed on 25 April 1948.

29 Located 6km east of Yafa. It was fully ethnically cleansed on 1 May 1948.

30 Al-Lydd is located 5km north-west of Al-Ramla. It was occupied on 10 July 1948. Interview with Khadeejeh Khalil AbuIsba (1933), Amman-Jordan. The interview was conducted by researcher Haifa Irshaid on 5 September 2012, pp.19–20.

31 Interview with Mariam Mohammad Nofal, Jabalia refugee camp, mentioned previously, pp.9 and 11.

32 Interview with Rasheedeh Hasan Fdalat, Al Baqaa' refugee camp, Amman, mentioned previously, p.20.

33 Interview with Lutfeyyeh Mteir, Qalandia refugee camp, mentioned previously, p.7.

34 Interview with Kamleh Samri Hashash, Balata refugee camp, Nablus, mentioned previously, pp.3 and 5.

35 Interview with Thurayya Yaseen Alya'qoubi, Rafah, mentioned previously, p.34.

36 Interview with Othmana Saleh Ass'ad (1925), Qaddoura neighbourhoods, Ramallah. The interview was conducted by researcher Asma'a Al Kilani on 31 August 2015, p.16.

37 Interview with Labiba Rasheed Al Issa, 'Ein Al Hilweh refugee camp, mentioned previously, p.2.

38 Interview with Labiba Khalil Ma'arouf (1920), Mar Elias refugee camp, Beirut. The interview was conducted by researcher Amneh Al Khateeb on 11 January 2016, p.10.

39 Interview with Zakyyeh Mahmoud Salem (1920), Umm Al Faraj-Akka. The interview was conducted by researcher Amneh Al Khateeb on 21 January 2016, p.22.

40 Interview with Rasheedeh Hasan Fdalat, Al Baqaa' refugee camp, mentioned previously, pp.21–25.

41 Interview with Fardous Al Taji Al Khairy (1932), Ramallah. The interview was conducted by researcher Asma'a Al Kilani on 14 April 2015, p.5.

42 Interview with Laila Nusseibeh (Al Taji Al Farouqi), Amman, Jordan, mentioned previously pp.22, 32.

43 Interview with Samiyyeh AbdelRahman Al Taji (1919), Amman, Jordan. The interview was conducted by researcher Muna Ghosheh on 23 December 2014 and 15 April 2015, pp.9 and 12.

44 Interview with Intisar Faheem Al Farkh (1938), Amman, Jordan. The interview was conducted by researcher Hanan Al Turk on 20 April 2014 and 1 March 2016.

45 Interview with Sana Kamel Aldajani (1940), Cairo, mentioned previously, p.11.

46 Interview with Firyal Hana Abu Awad (1942, Santiago, Chile, The interview was conducted by researchers: Jida Homd Hamam and Dima Abu Ghazaleh on 15 June/2012 and 11 November 2012mentioned previously, pp.5 and 22.

47 Interview with Nadia Al Tarazi (1935), Ramallah. The interview was conducted by researcher Haifa Irshaid in Amman on 13 August 2013, p.36.

48 Interview with Sana Kamel Aldajani, Cairo, mentioned previously, pp.15–16.

49 The city is located 2km north-west of Bethlehem.

50 Interview with Firyal Hana Abu Awad), Santiago, Chile. mentioned previously, p.7.

51 Interview with Ameeneh Mahmoud Al Afghani (1923), Old City, Nablus, mentioned previously, pp.2 and 7.

52 Interview with Labiba Rasheed Al Issa, 'Ein Al Hilweh refugee camp, mentioned previously, p.9.

53 One of the largest and oldest historic Palestine cities. It is located 38km north-west of Jerusalem. It was occupied on 11 July 1948. Soon after the city's occupation, the Zionists made an agreement with its inhabitants that they could stay. Soon after, the Zionists reneged on their promise and detained over 3,000 men in a concentration camp, and on the same day they started looting the city. On 14 July 1948, the city's inhabitants were ethnically cleansed (forcible expulsion) from the city. Out of the 17,000 Palestinians who used to call al-Ramleh home, only 400 people were allowed to stay.

54 Interview with Samiyyeh Abdelrahman Al Taji, Amman, Jordan, mentioned previously, pp.11–12.

55 Located 20km north-east of Gaza. It was fully ethnically cleansed on 12 May 1948.

56 Established in 1948 and located north-east of Gaza city.

57 It is located 18km north-west of Hebron. It was fully ethnically cleansed following the horrific massacre that the Israeli army committed on 29 October 1948.

58 Interview with Mariam Mohammad Nofal (1930), Jabalia refugee camp. The interview was conducted by researcher Na'eemeh Abu Hmaid on 5 Junr 2014, p.12.

59 Interview with Rasheedeh Hasan Fdalat, Al Baqaa' refugee camp, mentioned previously, pp.13–14.

60 Interview with Ameeneh Abdelhamid Ataba, Nazareth, mentioned previously pp.29-31.

61 Interview with Samiyyeh Abdelrahman Al Taji, Amman, Jordan, mentioned previously, pp.4–5.

62 Interview with Rasheedeh Hasan Fdalat, Al Baqaa' refugee camp, Amman, mentioned previously, pp.3–6.

63 Herod's Gate in Jerusalem. It is a gate in the northern walls of the Old City of Jerusalem. It adjoins the Muslim Quarter, and is a short distance to the east of the Damascus Gate.

64 The Orient House was the headquarters of the PLO between 1980 and 1990. It is located in Jerusalem and was originally built in 1897 by Ismail Moussa Alhusayni.

65 Interview with Laila Nusseibeh (Al Taji Al Farouqi) (1935), Amman, Jordan. The interview was conducted by researcher Hanan Turki on 11 November 2013, pp.29–30.

66 Interview with Firyal Hana Abu Awad, Santiago, Chile, mentioned previously, p.19.

67 Interview with Thurayya Yaseen AlYa'qoubi, Rafah, p.18.

68 Interview with Rasheedeh Hasan Fdalat, Al Baqaa' refugee camp, Amman, mentioned previously, pp.44–45.

69 Interview with Fatima Mohammad Hijazi, Al Baqaa' refugee camp, Amman, mentioned previously, pp.2, 9 and 10.

70 Interview with Khadeejeh Khalil Abuisba, Amman, Jordan, mentioned previously, pp.21, 22 and 26.

71 Ibid., pp.3 and 10.

REFERENCES

Al-Dajani, M. and J. Soliman (1995) "Dr. Rosemary Sayegh: Between Anthropology and Oral History", *al-Jana* (Beirut), No. 3 (August): 17–22.

Elsadda, H. (1999) "How to Make Use of Feminist Literature in History Writing", in F. Abdulhadi (ed.), *The Palestinian Women and Memory*. Ramallah: Ministry of Planning and International Cooperation.

Gluck, S.B. and D. Patai, eds. (1991) *Women's Words: The Feminist Practice of Oral History*. New York and London: Routledge.

Kalildi, W. (1948) *Dayr Yasin*, 9 April. Beirut: Institute for Palestine Studies, 1999.

Tonkin, E. (1995) *Narrating our Pasts: The Social Construction of Oral History*. Cambridge: Cambridge University Press.

United Nations (1994) Report of the UN Security Council, S/1994/674, 27 May: 1–36, http://www.icty.org/x/file/About/OTP/un_commission_of_experts_report1994_en.pdf.

PART IV
The Nakba and 1948 Palestinians

8
The ongoing Nakba: urban Palestinian survival in Haifa
HIMMAT ZUBI

History is written by the victors. Cities are likewise built by the victors; and the history of Haifa, "the city of peace and coexistence", has been blotted out by the victors who have silenced the story of the Arab Haifa and the narratives of its original residents.

In the absence of a Palestinian archive, the oral history methodology has become of utmost importance for the documentation of the Palestinians' life before and throughout the Nakba, especially the life of the marginalized communities.

This chapter is derived from the argument that the Palestinian Nakba did not end in 1948 and that it has been a systematic practice rather than a single event. To better comprehend its continuous reality, special attention should be paid to those who remained in Palestine following the occupation.

As in historical narratives based on oral history, this study addresses a specific subject in terms of time and space, and presents the experience and lives of urban Palestinians who remained in Haifa after the Nakba. It does not attempt to portray pre-Nakba and post-Nakba life in Haifa. Yet by shedding light on the lives of the remaining townspeople, as portrayed in their memories, it contributes to historicizing the different aspects of this population's life, that are still absent from Palestinian and global studies.

This study is based on the explicit and concealed contents of the oral testimonies of twelve Palestinian residents of Haifa, in addition to a few other published testimonies. As well as archival documents, this chapter tells the story of Haifa from the perspective of its indigenous Palestinian residents. It places a special emphasis on the meaning of the Nakba that their city has gone through; why they decided to leave/stay and the ways they resisted the attempts to eliminate them during and following the Nakba. Moreover, the study divulges the reality of their lives, highlighting the changes that occurred in their everyday life from their own perspective, and the present–absent "silence box"[1] of their stories.

THE ONGOING NAKBA

The Zionist project carries within it features of the settler-colonial project (Masalha 2012; Wolfe 2006) and is mainly based on the concept of elimination and effacement that does not necessarily relate to genocides (Wolfe 2006).

In 1948, the Zionist movement expelled 750,000 Palestinians, 90% of whom were townspeople. Moreover, 420 villages were evacuated and destroyed (Khalidi 2006). This was followed by the declaration of the establishment of the State of Israel upon the ruins of the Palestinian people.

The 1948 Nakba did not mark the end of the attempts to remove the Palestinians. It was the beginning of the elimination of the physical space and of the Palestinian body, which continue. The Nakba is not merely a memorable historical event. It is an ongoing tragedy; a limitless disaster in terms of time and space (Khoury 2012). It is a continuous trauma for the refugees, and for the Palestinians in the occupied territories (within the 1948 and 1967 borders) (Masalha 2012). The ongoing Nakba is accompanied by continuous attempts to efface and expel the Palestinians from history and time.

Studies about the pre-Nakba period are of immense importance, for there is documented evidence of the Palestinian existence on this land before they were uprooted. Moreover, socio-historical studies, especially those which used oral testimonies as a liberal methodology (Masalha 2012), have greatly contributed to reintegrating the Palestinians, including the marginalized populations, into history (Sayigh 2002; Masalha 2012; Zu'bi 2012; Sa'di and Abu-Lughod 2007).

However, the history of those who remained in their homeland after the Nakba, particularly the urban Palestinians, and the impact of the ongoing Nakba on their daily lives, are still absent from the field of research generally, and from Palestinian studies particularly.

The Nakba of the Palestinian cities

The Palestinian cities did not survive the Nakba. While some Palestinian villages remained safe from collective displacement and total destruction (Manna 2016), the Zionist military forces conducted a semi-complete effacement of the vast majority of Palestinian cities (Rashid al-Haj Ibrahim 2005).

The Palestinian cities were targeted directly after Operation Nachshon.[2] It was the first operation in Plan Dalet,[3] and special attention was paid to the main cities in Palestine (Pappé 2006: 103). Following the Deir Yassin massacre on 9 April,[4] and further to the implementation of Plan Dalet, Zionist military forces violently targeted the Palestinian cities. This led to their fall between mid-April and late May[5] 1948 (Khalidi 2008). The occupation of the Palestinian cities included the semi-complete evacuation of their Palestinian residents.

Israeli statistics reported in official correspondence during 1948–1949 indicate that only 26,000 Palestinian civilians, out of 202,000, survived expulsion during the Nakba.[6] Another document details the number of survivors in each city, based on a report issued by the Minorities Ministry and entitled "News of the Arabs in Israel and the Occupied Territories". The document included the hand-written word "classified", and indicated that according to reported data of the Minorities Ministry, dating back to 23 August 1948 and referring to the number of non-Jews, 4,000 Arabs remained in Yafa, 600–800 in Al-Lydd, 150 in Ramlah, 4,500 in Haifa, while not one Palestinian remained in Safad and Tiberias.[7]

These figures were modified at a later stage,[8] particularly after conducting a preparatory survey prior to the elections to the Constituent Assembly.[9] Despite the slight modification of the numbers,[10] these figures demonstrate the semi-complete ethnic cleansing of the Palestinian cities, as the percentage of the remaining Palestinians did not exceed 10% of the original residents.[11]

The Nakba and the fall of Haifa

As in other Palestinian cities and villages, the city of Haifa witnessed anger and tension following the declaration of United Nations Partition Plan in November 1947. Further to the strike declared by the Arab Higher Committee in response to the Partition Plan, the Arab city witnessed violence, and bombs were thrown by the Zionist forces.

The attacks continued throughout the months that preceded the occupation of Haifa. They resulted in many killed and wounded, and evoked fear among the Palestinians, many of whom fled the city. The displacement had particularly increased in the second month of 1948, and Palestinians fled the city, although since its establishment in December 1948 the National Committee of Haifa[12] had repeatedly called on the residents of Haifa to remain in the city (Khalidi 2008).

The events in Haifa caused some Palestinian leaders to flee the city (Pappe 2006). Some left Haifa, heading to the Arab countries to consult the Higher Arab Committee or the military leadership, as was the case with Rashid Al-Hajj Ibrahim. He left Haifa on 8 April 1948, for an urgent meeting with Amin al-Husseini in Cairo, and with President Shukri al-Quwatli, along with members of the military committee in Damascus. However, Haifa fell before his return, as indicated in his memoirs (Rashid al-Haj Ibrahim 2005).

The Haganah attack on Haifa started early on 21 April 1948,[13] and ended the next day, upon the fall of the city to the Zionists. The attacks had been a combination of bombardments with heavy machine guns and mortars and psychological warfare through continuous noisemaking through the evening until midnight (Rashid al-Haj Ibrahim 2005: 30).[14] The exodus of the Palestinian residents of Haifa, which started on 22 April, was a spontaneous reaction to the tactics of the Haganah.

EVERYDAY LIFE IN HAIFA FROM ITS RESIDENTS' PERSPECTIVE

Based on interviews with native Palestinians in Haifa, this section addresses the experience of Haifa's Palestinian residents before and after the city's fall. Interpreting the interviewees' experiences before and during the Nakba, first why did Palestinians leave during the Nakba?

Additionally, using archival and periodical documents, the daily lives of the Palestinian residents in Haifa after the Nakba are illustrated, and why this actuality was concealed from their testimonies is explained.

Haifa before its fall

Compared with other major Palestinian towns, Haifa is a relatively newly established city, whose history of development dates to the second half of the eighteenth century.[15]

Haifa had entered a phase of rapid growth following the construction of a branch line for the Hejaz railway, connecting the city to the main line between Damascus and Medina. Haifa's port became a reception point for Mecca's pilgrims, and a main site for wheat exports; hence it served many regions (Al-Bahri 1922; Mansour 2006).

The British forces occupied Haifa in 1918. The first fifteen years of the British Mandate constituted a significant stage in the city's development. During that period, the Mandatory government invested special efforts to develop the city in a way that reflected its policies and political aspirations (Seikaly 2002). Despite the aspirations of the British mandate, and its military interests and collusion with the Zionist forces, the Arabs had benefited from these developments and prosperity. The Palestinian contributions to the city transformed it into the biggest industrial centre in the region, and it benefited from the establishment of the new port and the oil refineries in the early 1930s. Haifa entered a new phase of industrial prosperity that attracted thousands of new residents, seeking employment (Yazbak 2010; Seikaly 2002).

Haifa Umm El-a'mal (Haifa the mother of labour)
Due to the aforementioned reasons and the difficult economic situation facing peasants, resulting from the British policy regarding the lands (Faris 2014; Seikaly 2002; Abdo 1987), the city of Haifa had witnessed an 80% increase in its Arab population in the period between 1931 and 1944. This is a significant increase when compared to other Palestinian cities at that time[16] (Yazbak 1988).

Thousands of Palestinians had arrived in Haifa from various localities (Faris 2014). While the clear majority of Haifa's Arab inhabitants came from inside Palestine, the city also hosted migrants, from the adjoining Arab regions such as Syria and Lebanon (Seikaly 2002: 48), as indicated by Abu Raed's[17] testimony:

We are originally from Afghanistan; my grandfather was a Sheikh and one of the "People of the House". He lived in Haifa. We had two houses at Sirkin Street, leading to the market. He [my grandfather] was wandering throughout Greater Syria to heal and help people. During his wanderings, he met my grandmother, and they got married in Damascus. My grandmother is a descendant of the Horani family from Syria.

Abu Raed's family was not the only family with relations in Arab and Muslim regions. The interviews conducted with the Palestinian residents of Haifa who remained after the Nakba demonstrate that many of them have family ties with adjoining Arab localities, especially on the wife's part. As Umm Nour stated:

I am originally from Haifa, but I was not born there. My mother gave birth to me in Lebanon, in Batroun [village]. After their wedding, my mother and father lived in Haifa. However, prior to [my] delivery, my mother was going to her parents in Lebanon. Nothing could be compared to the woman's experience of delivery alongside her parents.

In this regard, Haifa was not very different from other coastal Palestinian cities (Ziadeh 2010; Tamari 2008). Like Ziadeh's (2010) Tripoli, which hosted different groups, thus enriching the landscape with a sort of diversity, Haifa had also featured such demography. It had a diverse society, where long-standing inhabitants coexisted with Muslim and Christian immigrants from inland towns (Seikaly 2002).

The city's port and open borders contributed to Haifa's economic prosperity and diverse markets (Seikaly 2002). The markets' names demonstrate that the city was an integral part of the Arab sphere; and the inhabitants' testimonies are an indicator of the city's lifestyle and of its relationship with its Arab neighbours on the one hand, and with other countries on the other:

> My father was a fabric merchant; he was importing fabrics from Europe, the Greater Syria and the Muslim countries, but mainly from the Greater Syria. He had a shop in Al-Shwam [Greater Syria] market, where he also had an associate. That market was overcrowded, like the old market of Nazareth, but it extended over a big area. (Umm Elias)

The open borders and being an integral part of the Arab world was also clear in Umm Nabil's testimony:

> I remember the fabric shop of Abu Fadel in Al-Shwam market. He had English fabrics [imported from England]. It was for men's fabrics. There was also 'Azam's shop for women's fabrics; they used to bring the fabrics from Europe. When my mother wanted to sew us clothes for the holidays, she used to go to Al-Shwam market. I used to go with her to see the throng in the market. There were also spices and seasonings. Al-Shwam [the Syrians] were bringing everything.

Those who did not move from the countryside to the city had also benefited from Haifa's markets, where they sold their rural products, as Salwa testified:

> The vegetables were brought from the villages around Haifa: from Shefa-'Amr, I'billin and Tamra. The most important products were the eggs and the

dairy products. The Bedouin women used to bring eggs, chickens and milk from the nearby villages to sell them in the market early in the morning.

Prosperity was not limited to the markets for fabrics and food. It also included the construction industry. Describing his family business, Abu Raed said: "My father had two trucks and a quarry. All the stones of which the houses in Abbas Street were built were brought by my father from Qabatiya and Jenin".

Haifa's economic progress and prosperity were reflected in the establishment of national institutions (Hasan 2008). For example, on 1 July 1919, a chamber of commerce was founded in Haifa to run the city's economy, facilitate trade and represent the traders to the government in all trade-related procedures, through twelve members, including a president, whom the traders elected once every two years (Al-Bahri 1922).

The diary of Rashid al-Hajj Ibrahim (2005) points to the establishment of many social, educational and cultural Arab institutions in the city. For example, there was the Orthodox club where literary, scientific and political lectures were held. The Islamic Association (1992) and the Arab Orphans' Committee (1940) were also established in the city (Rashid al-Haj Ibrahim 2005: 227).

The press was also strong in Haifa, especially after the Ottoman counter-coup of 1908 in Istanbul, which obliged the Ottoman sultan to grant more freedom. In consequence, various journals and newspapers were established (Al-Bahri 1922).[18]

Within the framework of this cultural and intellectual prosperity, the city also hosted theatre plays performed by great actors of the Palestinian theatre in Haifa and Yafa.[19] During that period, it was common for Haifa, like other Arab and Palestinian cities, to host Arab artists. The most outstanding performances were by the musician Farid al-Atrash and his sister Asmahan. Oum Kolthoum also performed in Al-Inshirah Theatre in the city (Hasan 2008; Mansour 2011).

There had been other manifestations of urban life reflecting the modern space. Haifa also had a nightlife. The city had two different styles of nightlife: cabarets and nightclubs for men, and artistic soirees for families and the middle class:

My mother says that Abdel-Wahab came to Ein Dor Cinema; the one they destroyed. There was a woman who kept saying Oh My Love ... Oh My Love. Her husband told her if he is your love, I am divorcing you. Oum

Kolthoum and Farid Al-Atrash also came to Ein Dor ... Central Café was in Al-Abyad market; they danced there for the whole night. All the Egyptian dancers performed in Central Haifa. It started at eight o'clock in the evening and lasted until one after midnight. There was an Egyptian dancer called Ne'amat. A man from the city fell in love with her, and took her as a second wife. His first wife burnt herself, and then died. Ne'amat married him, and lived in our neighbourhood, behind the churches' neighbourhood. It seems that she left with the others, at the outbreak of the war. (Interview with Zahra Khamra, quoted in Igbarieh 2010: 223)

Why did indigenous Palestinians leave Haifa? The Nakba from the perspective of Haifa's people

While historical studies (e.g. Khalidi 2005) rightly highlight the military and political reasons behind the Palestinian displacement, Palestinian family ties, and being an integral part of the Arab world, as the following argument suggests, were among the motives for Haifa's residents to leave the city following the escalating confrontations between the Palestinian Arabs and the settler Zionist residents in the city. These family ties, I also argue, were crucial for the return of some Haifa families after their displacement.

The displacement of Haifa's residents followed the 1947 Partition Plan had increased following the terrorist attacks against them early in 1948:

I remember that we were frightened, especially after they shot the priest in the church's yard, while he was walking around reading the Evangel. Following that event, the situation did not calm down; instead, the attacks increased, and that enhanced fear. We used to go to Lebanon, to my maternal uncles, once a year and stay there for three months, regardless of the war. In 1948, we left earlier. My father told my mother, take the kids to your parents [in Lebanon]; and you will come back when the situation calms down. (Abu Nour)

In this regard, Samira related:

when the shooting towards the building started, the building in which we and my uncle's family lived ... My uncle used to live in Haifa because he was a railroad employee. When the shooting started, he [my uncle] returned to my grandparents' [his parents'] house in Bethlehem region. We went to my maternal grandparents; I mean to my maternal uncles in Nazareth.

These findings are consistent with those of Faris (2010); he indicates that the rural women joined the groups that left Haifa before its fall:

The Palestinian farmers had first sent the women out of Haifa towards their villages. For example, the residents of Silwad village gathered their wives and children; who rode big trucks. Some managed to take some goods, while others left everything behind. The vast majority of the rural women thought that they would return. (Faris 2010: 74)

Another testimony by Abu Jeryis, a ninety-three-year-old interviewee, high-lights the impact of the family ties, especially women's ties, on the decision to leave and on the destination they headed to:

We are originally from Shefa-'Amr; we came to Haifa in the twenties, because of my father's work. We were nine siblings, all living in Haifa. During the confrontation, my siblings and I moved to Shefa-'Amr, but my brothers whose wives were from Lebanon moved to Lebanon; their wives are from there [Lebanon], and they insisted on going to their parents.

The role of family ties in the displacement of Haifa's indigenous Palestinian residents, intending to return in due course, is further asserted by the fact that this was not the only time they had made such a decision. However, it was the last time, after which they could not return; thus, they paid a very high price.

The Nakba had been preceded by World War II, when Haifa was bombarded. During that period, as in all times of war, fear caused people to leave their houses and take refuge with their families in various regions in Palestine and its neighbouring Arab countries:

During the war [World War II] we were very frightened – Haifa was bombarded by airplanes. We left the house and went to Ramallah. We stayed there for about two years. My parents stayed there and enrolled me in a boarding school. I studied in the Sisters' school for two years. (Umm Elias)

This was echoed in Umm Nabil's testimony:

> During the great war [World War II] I studied in the Sisters' school in Isfiya. We were children and we were frightened. My mother took me and my sister out of Haifa's school and enrolled us in Isfiya Sisters' school. I stayed in Isfiya for a year and returned to our house in Haifa after the war ended and the situation calmed down.

The same applies to Abu Roni's family:

> We are originally from Zamrin [Arabic for Zikhron Ya'akov]. During the Great War, we were living in Haifa; we came to Haifa because my father found work there. But during the war [World War II] my parents took us back to Zamrin until the situation calmed down.

The Nakba was not the only crime committed by the Zionist institutions. There was also the Zionist authorities' decision banning the refugees from returning. That was explicit in Ben Gurion's letter to Abba Hushi, dated 2 June 1948, declaring: "I have just learnt that Mr. Marriott[20] is interested in the Arabs' return. I do not know how he is interfering; but until the end of the war, we are not interested in the enemy's return, and all the institutions have to follow this line".[21]

This was also evident in a report sent by Ya'acov Salomon to Ben Gurion, entitled "The Liberation of Haifa":

> I am the legal counsel of the Patriarch Hakim, so in some way, we are kind of friends and we talked on current affairs ... He (Patriarch Hakim) just came back from Beirut inquiring into bringing Christians Palestinian refugees back to Haifa ... I told him my opinion (emphasizing it is my personal opinion), during wartime no refugee will be allowed to be back[22].

Why did the Palestinians remain/return? The nation, the homeland and the home
The indigenous Palestinians of Haifa did not remain idle or passive in the face of the policies that attempted to eliminate their physical existence. They achieved this by staying in their homeland or by doing almost everything they could to return. As endurance is deemed an act of resistance for the Palestinians in exile

(Allen 2008), their return and the original residents of Haifa remaining was an act of resistance against attempts at physical elimination.

As mentioned previously, the people did not expect the borders to be closed; they intended to stay in Haifa or to return to it. Samira talked of the reasons behind their staying:

> I will tell why we stayed here; here we have our home and our land; it is our homeland and we were born here. In the 2006 Lebanon war,[23] my daughter told me to go to Nazareth, she said I would die if I stayed in Haifa. I told her that we left in 1948 and our house was taken away. I prefer to die here than leave my house. During the Nakba we went down to the church and stayed there; later on, we went to the port. I do not remember why we left the church; but what I know is that the British were encouraging the people to take small boats and go to Beirut. My mother said no, we are not leaving: I want to go to Akka and then to Nazareth. I want to go to my parents' house. I will not leave my homeland and my parents, no matter what happens. We left our house, but we stayed in our homeland and among our family.

Infiltrations and "illegal" border crossing have always been ways of resistance for indigenous people; a way to re-live the lives they had before being forcibly fragmented (Ghanim 2015). When the indigenous Palestinians of Haifa learnt that Israel intended to close the borders and prevent the refugees from returning to their homes, they were ready to face all hazards in order to return. The Arab countries that hosted them were considered like a homeland; yet Haifa was the "Home" to which everyone wanted to return, even if "infiltration" was necessary.

> As in the novel *Bab Al-Shams*,[24] my father was daily going to Yaroun [in Lebanon]. People were calling my mother to go and see him. My grandmother used to tell my mother, beware Nejma! they might kill him tomorrow. You'd better go to your husband, return to your home. That is how we escaped back. They put us, the small kids, in boxes, and we were "smuggled" back home at night. (Umm Nour)

This story was repeated in Abu Nour's testimony:

We went to Lebanon and my father was constantly visiting us. Later on, they closed all the ways while he was still in Lebanon. He infiltrated the borders back home, and then he filed a request to bring us back.

Following the declaration of the establishment of the State of Israel, the families of Haifa fought for the return of their relatives. Those who had previously sent their children away until the war ended wanted them to return directly after the fall of Haifa. Despite the harsh conditions in Haifa during that period,[25] they insisted on going back:

I left, while my mother, father and eldest siblings stayed. I left with my paternal uncle, aunt and grandmother to Lebanon. In Lebanon, we stayed with people who had previously worked at my father's quarry. They gave us a house, and in the first three months, they did not ask for rent. After the war, my father wanted to bring me back from Lebanon; it took a while. After a year and a half, I obtained a permit and returned via Ras an-Nakura. I was a little boy and the whole family was living in Haifa. That's why they [the authorities] approved my return. (Abu Raed)

The story of a communist leader in Haifa, Tawfik Toubi,[26] better demonstrates this. Tawfik Toubi struggled first to bring his family members back through "legal" means. On 5 October 1948, he sent a demand to the Minister of Labour and Construction (Mordechai Bentov) to allow the return of his two brothers (Shafik and George), his sister (Maggie) and his paternal aunt (Jawhara Toubi). He also demanded the return of the wife and daughter of the other communist leader Emile Habibi: Nada (twenty-four years old) and Juhaina Habibi (fourteen months old), in addition to the wife and son of Ahmad Kawwas: Samira Kawwas (nineteen years old) and Basem Kawwas (thirteen months old). He indicated in his request that the authorities had approved the return of the family of Shehadeh Shalah[27] (deputy mayor of Haifa) from Lebanon.[28]

On 11 November (a week after filing the request), the Minister of Labour and Construction sent a letter to the Minister of Minority Affairs (Bechor Sheetrit) recommending the approval of Toubi's request. He indicated that he knew Toubi personally and that the latter was an employee at the labour and construction bureau in Haifa's branch. On 31 November, the Minister of

Minority Affairs, Sheetrit, addressed a letter to the Minister of Defence (Ben Gurion) and to the Minister of Foreign Affairs recommending the approval of the request, based on the recommendation presented by the Minister of Labour and Construction.[29]

Archival documents indicate that the authorities rejected Tawfik Toubi's request. In a letter from Yaavoc Shimoni of the Middle East department in the Ministry of Foreign Affairs, dating back to 9 November 1948, to the Minister of Minority Affairs, the former wrote "I do not find a reason for handling this request inconsistently with the decision that prohibits the return until a full agreement is reached". He added: "when we approved the return of the family of Shehadeh Shalah, we had strongly emphasized that the present case cannot be handled like the preceding one".[30]

Despite the rejection of the official request, the family's will to return was undiminished, as testified by Maggie (the sister of Tawfik Toubi):

Following Tawfik's visit to us, that lasted for a week, and his return to Palestine, my mother decided that we should return at any price; she could not leave Tawfik alone. Some people were running away through the Galilee, from the last Lebanese village near the borders, Rmaich. We took our clothes (we did not have anything) and came to Rmaich by bus. At Rmaich we had to pay money to people who helped us escape from one village to another. We arrived from Rmaich to Hurfeish. We, my mother, siblings and I, walked during the nights from Hurfeish to Kafr Sumei, and from Kafr Sumei to Julis. Every night, the (Druze) residents of these villages were accommodating and feeding us. We were walking the whole night; my siblings were riding a donkey, while my mother and I walked after them. From Julis we arrived to Kafr Yasif. We stayed in Kafr Yasif for two months. The registration in Abu Snan was still in process. We went there to get registered, as if we had never left the country. After a month, Tawfik succeeded in bringing us back to Haifa.[31]

Despite the harsh conditions in Haifa, its original residents insisted on returning home:

When I returned, my neighbour told me, from now on you will be dreaming of eating an apple [an indication of the lack of resources]. I told him what matters is that we returned to our homeland. I am Palestinian, and I do not have another land. (Abu Nour)

THE ISRAELI MILITARY GOVERNMENT

The Palestinian Nakba did not end in 1948, as the Zionists remained hostile towards the Palestinians who remained in their homeland. The expulsion continued after the Nakba; hundreds of Palestinians were uprooted and expelled from the territories that Israel had occupied.[32]

The Palestinians who remained in the occupied areas were subject to military government until the end of 1966, following a decision made by the Provisional State Council. During the 1948 war, specifically on 19 May 1948, it was determined that in wartime a state of emergency should be declared in certain regions, based on the recommendations of the commander-in-chief, and the approval of the Minister of Defence (Ozacky-Lazar 1996; Salomon 1980: 284).

The constitutional authority of the military government was based on the mandatory defence regulations that applied to the state of emergency (1945), adopted by the Provisional State Council. It implemented five out of 162 articles of the emergency regulations.[33] The military government was also based on the Israeli Defence Laws 1949 (Security Zones) enacted by the Minister of Defence. In addition to the Mandatory Emergency Regulations, these regulations allowed the authorities to expel residents from a certain district by order of the Minister of Defence (Jiryis 1968: 20).

The military government system was established in the "Occupied Territories"[34] in September 1948. It included three areas in which 755 of the country's Arab inhabitants lived: the Galilee, the Triangle and the Naqab, in addition to the cities Ramlah, Al-Lydd, Yafa (Jaffa) and Asqalan (Ashkelon) (Masalha 1992; Jiryis 1968; Ozacky-Lazar 1996).

Implementation and enforcement was assigned to the military governor, according to a "fixed command" distributed to all military governors on 17 March 1950. This command gave the military governors broad authority to enforce these regulations where necessary (Ozacky-Lazar 1996: 71).

Although the Mandatory Defence (Emergency) Regulations (1945) were imposed on the whole State of Israel, they were actually implemented only in the areas that were subject to the military government. These regulations empowered the military government and the military governor to intervene in all the affairs of Palestinian society, without any supreme civil authority and with limited judicial authority (Jiryis 1968: 27).[35] However, the boundaries of the military government areas and the closed areas were not precisely known, except by the military government administrators, and the Palestinians could only identify them through daily practices (Jiryis 1968: 24).

Despite the impact of this period on the lives of the Palestinians who remained in their homeland, studies on this subject have been scarce; and they have been mainly conducted by Jewish scholars (Ozacky-Lazar 1996; Bauml 2007; Lustik 1980; Korn 2000; Pappe 2013).[36] These studies have focused on analysis of the military government's policies and their implications for the Palestinians and their status in the Jewish state. They were mainly based on various official Israeli documents, without giving a voice to the Palestinians or researching their experiences dating back to that period.

There have also been some Palestinian studies addressing that period. Most of these studies did not give voice to ordinary Palestinians, focusing on the implications of that period for different aspects of Palestinians' status (Mustafa 2014; Khamaisi 2014; Kabha 2014; Abdo 2011).[37] The studies by Ghanim (2015), Hawari (2011) and Ghanayem (2014) differ, as they placed an emphasis on people and their experiences,[38] interviewing Palestinians who lived through that period.

The military government and the Palestinian city: the case of Haifa

Despite the importance of these studies and their contribution to demarcating this phase in Palestinian history and its implications for various aspects of life, they have largely marginalized the Palestinian city. None of these Palestinian studies has addressed the reality experienced by the residents of these cities during that period, although it greatly contributed to destroying the process of Palestinian urbanization.

During the Nakba, the cities were almost totally emptied of their original residents. The cities of Al-Lydd, Ramlah and Yafa were officially subject to the military government.[39] The remaining residents of these cities were put in ghettos: Yafa's residents were all gathered in Al-'Ajami, Al-Lydd's were all put in a ghetto at Al-Kaneesa (the church) neighbourhood. The remaining residents of Ramlah were obliged to move to the Ghetto neighbourhood[40] (Nuriely 2005; Yacobi 2009).

While Haifa was not among the cities officially subject to the military government,[41] its indigenous Palestinians were gathered in Wadi Nisnas (Ghetto) and were subjected to the same policies practised towards the Palestinians who were under official military government in Yafa, Al-Lydd and Ramlah.

In the first week following the occupation of Haifa, 3,200 Palestinians were obliged to live in just two areas: Wadi Nisnas and Wadi Salib. To guarantee tight surveillance, the authorities established two "information and guidance" offices for the remaining residents of the city: the first was at 130 Al-Iraq Street, the house of Muhammad Abdel Hafiz, while the other one was at 35 Allenby Street, in the Archbishop's house.[42] Although these bureaus were given a civil name, their main mission was to issue permits to move out of the areas in which the Arabs were allowed to live.[43]

Within less than two months, the Arab space had been further reduced. On 1 July 1948, the Haganah commanded that all the Arabs who remained in Haifa should be grouped together in Wadi Nisnas "ghetto". The command did not include non-Arab foreign residents, hence the outrage and objection of the original residents. Still, despite the objection of the Palestinians and the Temporary Arab Committee, and although the neighbourhood suffered severe lack of water and electricity, the decision was implemented in less than a week.[44] In November 1948, it was decided that the remaining Palestinians still living outside Wadi Nisnas should be transferred to the ghetto.[45]

Subjectification of the colonizer's archives
The original residents of Haifa returned to a reality in which they were detached from the Arab world and from the surrounding villages. The city they had known had been destroyed; though not subject to formal military government, they found themselves under systematic surveillance and control that applied to all the Palestinians who remained in their homeland (Sa'di 2014; Cohen 2010; Lustik 1980).

The Palestinians who had survived in Haifa shared with me comprehensive details of the circumstances of their daily lives, before and during the Nakba, but not their daily life experiences in the city following its occupation.

Interviewees were asked to share the effect of the new reality on their lives; how did daily life change and how was it to return, or to stay, while almost everything had changed: landscape, community life and social bonds. Additionally, they were asked to portray how they adjusted to the new daily reality of settler-colonialism.

Almost without exception, interviewees refrained from going into everyday experience and did not share their ordeals during that time. I needed to understand what prevented urban Palestinians who had stayed in their homeland from sharing this side of their story. What does this "silence box" mean about individual memory and collective memory? And what does it tell us about the military government imposed on the urban Palestinians?

Before answering these questions, and in the absence of daily life experience in the testimonies, I will draw a picture of the urban Palestinians' daily lives under military government based on counter-readings (Penelope 2010) of the Zionist archival documents and periodicals of that time. I argue that these resources, while historicizing the victory achieved by the colonizer, provided an indication of the indigenous daily life, and the details that the Palestinian memory chose to efface. Reports of "Shai-Arab" unit[46] include detailed information regarding the check-points in the city and the way borders operated: "all passers-by had to go through these checkpoints. The Jews could pass, while the Arabs and the foreigners were interrogated. If found 'eligible', they were allowed to pass".[47] Other documents refer to the restrictions imposed on the movement of Haifa's original residents and the number of requests filed to the "communication bureau" to leave the ghetto.[48]

The colonizer's press provides an additional source for understanding the reality experienced by the Palestinians at that time. Despite the objectives of the Zionist press reports, mostly written to glamorize the image of the newly estab-lished system, a critical review of them provides a description of the Palestinians' reality in Haifa at that time, and helps in solving the "absence box".

In a report published in *Davar* newspaper, on 6 May 1948, the journalist describes his visit to Haifa, and mentions the checkpoints and the permits. He reports:

> This is the checkpoint of the Hebrew military government, through which the Arabs pass. They all hold crossing permits issued by the Haganah in Arabic and Hebrew. The permit includes details of the residence place and the regions they are allowed to move in. On the margins, it is indicated whether the permit holder is allowed to have any luggage.

One can learn about the difficulty of obtaining a permit, and the attitude of the "guidance" bureaus towards the Palestinians, from a report published in *Al HaMishmar* newspaper:

> The permit issuance is not easy. Sometimes it requires waiting for a long time, and involves indecent attitude towards the Arabs in the bureaus.

Some treat them properly, but others show resentment towards them [the Palestinians]. Even when looking for weapons, the executive bodies do not make any effort to prevent damage to the property. Let alone the thefts committed in the Arab localities.[49]

The archival documents provide information regarding the control and surveillance techniques and the ways "Good Arabs" (Cohen 2010) were shaped through facilities being granted to those who were "loyal". They simultaneously divulge methods of resistance adopted by the Palestinians. As indicated in one report of the "communication bureau", dating back to the beginning of September 1948, "the villagers are freely moving between Isfiya and Daliyat al-Karmel. The Druze buy vegetables from the villagers (from Ijzim village) and sell them in Haifa after they get official permits. We should reduce permits issuance, except for some who demonstrate loyalty to us".[50]

This provides insight into the daily life of Palestinians in Haifa following its occupation. This is of utmost importance, especially considering its absence from the testimonies of Haifa's residents.

The ongoing Nakba and the "silence box"

For Palestinians, the Nakba is still deep-rooted in the present existential condition of every individual, affecting multiple aspects of their lives (Sa'di and Abu-Lughod 2007: 10). Recent Palestinian work on historicizing the Nakba legitimized narrating life before the Nakba and the Nakba itself. However, accounts of the everyday lives of the Palestinians who stayed in their homeland following the Nakba (the 1948 Palestinians) are still being muted.

The trauma of the Nakba was immediately followed by the military government, which interfered in every aspect of the daily lives of the Palestinians. Palestinians were subject to systematic surveillance and control that has lasted long after the military government was officially ended (Sa'di 2014).

In some cases, as in the cities, Palestinians were evicted from their homes and were concentrated in one Arab neighbourhood "ghetto". Some of them lived, and still live, literally in other Palestinians' houses (Palestinians who became refugees).

Auerbach (1971) argues that remembering the past depends on having a detached perspective in the present through which one can look at one's past (Auerbach 1971). Palestinians, who are still living the dispossession and the destruction of their city and community, find it hard to narrate their "past", as this past is neither distant nor yet over (Sa'di and Abu-Lughod 2007).

Additionally, the small number of Palestinians who stayed in Haifa made remembering more complicated. Following Maurice Halbwachs' (1992) work, historians and cultural theorists largely agree that individuals remember, through dialogue with others within social groups. To remember, one needs others with whom one will be able to tell the story, to think collectively. When the urban society has vanished, family members have been split apart, and the "site of memory" has been changed dramatically, thinking collectively or socially and recollecting memory becomes almost unimaginable.

Furthermore, in recent decades Palestinian social historians, sociologists, activists and artists have been politicking the collective memory of the Nakba as a major means of Palestinian cultural resistance and the struggle for self-determination (Masalha 2012). Concentrating on the Nakba of 1948, despite its importance, has left less room for individual and collective memory of the continuing Nakba, especially for the Palestinians who stayed in their homeland.

As indicated in the first part of this chapter, the interviewees talked of precise details of their daily lives in Haifa before the Nakba. They mentioned their neighbours, school friends, the shops where "almond candies" were sold, the places where the women bought goods for the weekly reception, the best tailors, the fabric shops and the places these fabrics were imported from. They remembered the places of entertainment, the coffee shops, the nightlife and Café Central.

They also shared details of the Nakba: the murder of the priest in the church-yard and sobbing over dropping a shoe while climbing into the refugees' boat: "I remember that incident as if it happened today; I cried because these were my brother's shoes, and I was afraid he would be angry with me", Samira said.

On the other hand, none of them "remembered" the daily life during military government: not the permit lines, or the checkpoints; Umm Nour, for instance could not recall how she got the permit to travel to Nazareth Hospital in order to study nursing. Nor could Abu Emile recall who helped him get the permit for a job in the Kibbutz.

Zerubavel (1996) argues that "Remembrance" is socially constructed and is filtered by social environment. Memory, she asserts, is regulated by social rules of remembrance that tell us what we should remember and what we can or must forget (Zerubavel 1996: 286).

Examining everyday life under the military government regime in Haifa shows the absurdity and complexity of the day-to-day reality of survival, a reality that challenges the binary of heroism and weakness, collaboration and resistance, alienation and familiarity.

Soon after the war, settlers ceased to be external (Esmeir 2007), and the military government facilitated permanent settlement in Palestine. New settlers also lived in Haifa, and some of them settled in the Arab "ghetto", where they occupied the territory and space of indigenous Palestinians, including living in refugees' houses. They became the privileged "neighbours" with whom Palestinians were compelled to interact daily.

While settlers were enjoying freedom of movement and did not need permission to work, matters relating to Palestinians' ordinary lives, such as job search, doctor's visits and attendance at weddings or funerals outside Haifa, or outside the ghetto's borders, necessitated dealing with the Israeli authorities.

This, combined with the denigration of the individual, made narrating their stories very painful. The procedure of seeking permission, as shown earlier, had involved maltreatment on the part of the soldiers in the "guidance" bureaus and at checkpoints.

Palestinians have had to regularly seek the settlers' approbation for conducting their everyday lives. They have had to discipline themselves, and to act "correctly" in order to be permitted freedom of movement.

National narratives usually make the past seem more complete and comfortable than it was, through nostalgia for an idealized and pastoral past and by reluctance to expose complicity, culpability and collaboration (Sa'di and Abu-Lughod 2007). Consequently, the memory of the reality of daily life during the unofficial military government in Haifa, apart from its individual psychological aspects, might be perceived as a disfigurement of Palestinian collective memory.

While not challenging the collective memory, and at the same time protecting themselves from their memories' ghost, Haifa's indigenous Palestinians omitted the memory of the military government and concealed it in a "silence box".

In recent decades, oral history has presented a very important methodology of decolonizing hegemonic history. By exploring the history and voices of suppressed or marginalized narratives, it constructed alternative histories and memories (Masalha 2012: 211; Sayigh 1979). However, investigating hidden substance and concealed content of colonized groups has not been addressed.

CONCLUSION

The military government period cannot be deemed a transient event in the lives of Palestinians. It has had a great impact on them and shaped their relationship with the Jewish state.

The absence of the city from the Palestinians' life has greatly contributed to deforming the development of Palestinian society in Israel. Moreover, the marginalization of the survivors' stories has contributed to silencing a significant episode in the history of the Palestinian people.

The presence of the "silence box" which contains stories of personal humiliation still produces fear among this group of Palestinians, who still endure the unpleasant feelings of surveillance and control in their relationship with the colonial system.

It took the Palestinians a long time to open the Nakba defeat box. Despite being a very painful memory, Arab and Palestinian researchers have played a major role in opening this box by conducting interviews with survivors of the Nakba, and documenting the Nakba's events from their perspectives, through the studies and through cyberspace.

Due to the absence of such studies and of an oral history regarding the experiences of the Palestinians who remained in their homeland after the occupation, Palestinians' experiences during the military government remained outside the history of the Palestinian people; they kept them hidden in the "silence box", not daring to share them.

NOTES

1   The term "absent box" is inspired by Elias Khoury's recent novel: *Awlad el-ghetto. Esmi Adam* (The Children of the Ghetto. My Name is Adam), 2017.

2   An operation started on 1 April, aiming to build a road from the coastal city of Tel Aviv to inner Jerusalem. During this assault, many Arab villages were destroyed and occupied, until the battle of Al-Qastal, which took place on 11–13 April (Khalidi 2005).

3   That enhanced the confidence of the Jewish leadership regarding its ability not only to take over all the areas allocated to the Jewish state by the United Nations, but also to conduct ethnic cleansing there. For further information on Plan Dalet, see Khalidi (2005).

4   The Deir Yassin massacre had a significant impact on the Palestinians who heard of the massacre, which claimed the lives of ninety-three victims, thirty of whom were children (Pappe 2006). This had increased fear and caused many to flee, fearing similar massacres.

5   The offensive was first directed towards Tiberias, which fell on 16 April (Tiberias was occupied during operation Yiftach that aimed to cleanse Eastern Galilee of Arabs and to establish a connection between Tiberias and Safed). This was followed by Haifa's fall on 22 April, which had had a further significant impact on morale in the other Palestinian cities. It did not take long until Safed's occupation on 29 April, in addition to the Arab Jerusalemite neighbourhoods. The city of Acre fell on 6 May, followed by Yafa's occupation on 13 May.

6   The state Archive, Minorities' Statistics, File No. 3554/15, Document No. 0801, "A table summarizing the number of the Arab civilians in the Arab localities between 1946–1948/49".

7   The State Archive, Minorities Statistics, File No. GL-15/3554, Document No. 273/0801.

8   The reported number of Palestinian Arabs remaining in Ramallah was 1,549 out of 16,380 in 1946, while the reported number in Al-Lydd was 1,056 out of 18,250 in 1946. The State Archive, Minorities' Statistics, File No. GL-3554/15, Document No. 0801.

9   It was started on 8 November 1948 and completed in February 1949, following the occupation of the Galilee (letter from the bureau of the Prime Minister's advisor and entitled "Arabs in Israel-Estimates", 13 May 1953. The State Archive, Minorities' Statistics, File No. GL-3554/15.

10   This modification was probably conducted for different reasons: the inaccuracy of the first survey conducted a few months following the Nakba or due to the refugees who fled to the cities from other parts of the country, in addition to the return of some Palestinians during that period.

11   The cleansing efforts excluded Nazareth, where the population of 1,949 increased from 15,540 to 16,800, as the city hosted refugees coming from nearby villages.

12   Following the declaration of the Partition Plan, the Arab Higher Committee advised local leaders in the Palestinian villages and cities to establish national committees. The Arab Higher Committee prepared a binding system for these committees, through which they should operate under the supervision of the Higher Committee, and within the framework of the National Charter (Rashid al-Haj Ibrahim 2005).

13   The military operation during which Haifa was occupied was called Operation Misparayim, after the military plan that aimed to "dismember" the Arab city, separating each part of the cities from the two others. Later, the name was changed to "Be'our Hamets" (removal of leavened bread), since it was conducted on the eve of Passover. This naming refers to the removal of leavened bread, preceding Passover, following God's command, which forbade Jews to eat leavened bread during the Jewish exodus from Egypt. According to Jewish customs, search for leavened bread is conducted in Jewish houses the night before Passover, and if found, it is collected and burnt the next day, before noon. The occupation of Haifa was of military significance, since it was a meeting point between the eastern and southern lines of the Jewish settlements. Moreover, it was the most important harbour in the Eastern Mediterranean after Alexandria, and was the terminal point of the oil pipeline from Iraq. It was also a key communication centre for rail and road transport (Khalidi 2008: 6).

14 It was also the result of the Anglo-Zionist collusion that was continued even after the fall of the city (Khalidi 2008).

15 In 1764–1765, the governor of acre, Dahir al-Umar, laid waste to the older hamlet of Haifa al-Atiqa, located some one and a half miles to the west of the modern site, and transferred the population to a new site, which he had surrounded by a protective wall (Seikaly 2002).

16 While the period from 1922 to 1931 witnessed a 41.1% increase in the Arab population of the cities, the increase in the Arab population in Haifa during that period was 46.1% higher.

17 All names of the interviewees have been changed to protect their confidentiality, unless stated otherwise.

18 The most important being "al-Nafā'is al-'asriyyah" (The Modern Treasures) of Khalil Beidas; "Al-Carmel" of Naguib Nassar; "Al-Nafir" of Elia Zakka; and "Al-Zahra" of Jamil al-Bahri (Al-Bahri 1922).

19 Haifa had had a national theatre group called "Al-Carmel actors group", headed by Iskandar Ayoub Badran. The "Institute of Arab Music" was also established in Haifa, under the management of musician Saleem al-Hilu. Halim al-Roumu pursued his musical education there.

20 Cyril Marriott was British Counsel General designate in Haifa.

21 https://www.haaretz.co.il/news/politics/.premium-1.2644759

22 Minutes of meeting with Patriarch Hakim, Saturday 26 June 1948. The State's Archive, "The liberation of Haifa", P-941/3.

23 The reference here is to the Israeli war against Lebanon, and the response by Lebanese Hezbollah.

24 Drawing on the stories he gathered from refugee camps over the course of many years, Elias Khoury's epic novel *Gate of the Sun* (*Bab Al-Shams*) has been called the first magnum opus of the Palestinian saga.

25 Yaacov Salomon, a prominent figure in Haifa, indicated in one of his letters to Ben Gurion that he would not advise any Arab to return to Haifa, even if it were his closest friend. Letter by Yaacov Salomon about his meeting with Patriarch Hakim on 26 June 1948. The State's Archive, Special Files, P-7/931.

26 Elected later as a Knesset member for the Israeli Communist Party.

27 Shelah himself returned to Haifa from Beirut in June 1948 with Patriarch Hakim. The State's Archive, Special Files, P-7/931.

28 The State's Archive, Bureau of the Ministry of Minority Affairs, File No. G-299/34.

29 Ibid.

30 A letter from the Ministry of Foreign Affairs, the Middle East department, to the Minister of Minority Affairs, State Archive G-299/43.

31 At that time, the borders were not completely closed by Israel, and the northern area was still in a state of war.

32 The villages of Al-Majdal, Iqrith and Bir'im were among these villages (Manna 2016).

33 Article 109: expulsion from certain regions; Article 110: Police supervision and exile;

Article 111: administrative detention; Article 124: imposition of curfew; Article 125: closure and restricted access to/from certain regions (Ozacky-Lazar 1996: 84).

34 The territories that were occupied in 1948, and that were supposed to be within the borders of the Arab state, per the 1947 Partition Plan.

35 The military governor established court-martials empowered to rule on breaches and non-compliance with the regulations. The judges of these court-martials were not necessarily qualified in the field of law and the judiciary. On the other hand, the High Court of Justice power of intervention with respect to the martial law was reduced. At the outset of the 1950s, the High Court ruled that it could not intervene in the decisions of the military governor, as his conduct was derived from security motives. It was determined that the court cannot investigate military governors on security issues, as this type of investigation would undermine the national security (Jiryis 1968: 21).

36 Some have researched the motives of the military government (Ozacky-Lazar 1996), its implications for the economic status of Palestinians (Bauml 2007) and their legal status (Lustik 1980; Korn 2000). Other studies have addressed the history of Palestinians in Israel, and their relationship with the Jewish state (Pappe 2013).

37 Muhammad Mustafa (2014) discussed Palestinian political organization in that period. The contribution of the military government in planning the space and restraining the urbanization process among the Arab population in Israel was the focus of Khamaisi's (2014) study. While Mustafa Kabha (2014) examines the Arab press under the military government. In addition, Nahla Abdo (2011) discussed implications of this permit regime for Palestinians' economic status.

38 Areen Hawari (2011) wrote about the impact of that period on masculinity, its development and variations in the Palestinian society based on interviews conducted with men and women who lived through that period. Hunaida Ghanim (2015) wrote about the lives of the residents of Al-Marjeh village, near the Green Line, under martial law. Mahmoud Ghanayem (2014: 119) researched the relationship between fiction and the reality experienced by the Palestinians under the military government, and how Arabic literature attempted to write a historical testimony that was not devoid of a political position. Based on the oral testimonies and the stories told by the residents, Ghanim (2015) researched the tools that they developed to deal with the new reality following the Nakba.

39 Military government in the cities ended one year after its fall (around July 1949).

40 Ramallah residents still call the neighbourhood a ghetto up to this day.

41 Upon the occupation of the city, the supreme national institutions declared on 5 May 1948 that the city shall not be subject to martial law; the civil responsibilities were assigned to "Va'adat ha-Matasav" (a special committee established by the Yishuv leadership to set the preparatory steps for establishing the mechanisms of the state). The responsibility for security issues was assigned to the Haganah forces.

42 *Al HaMishmar*, 27 April 1948.

43 Al HaMishmar, 4 May 1948.

44 *Kol HaAm*, 4 April 1948.

45 A letter from Yitach, head of the Minorities Bureau, to Haifa's commander on 19 December 1948, the State's Archive and the Minorities' Book, File No. G- 30968.

46 It was the intelligence arm of the Haganah responsible for Arab affairs.

47 The report also includes the names of two detainees; one was suspected of involvement in the Refinery operation, while the other was accused of "smuggling" Arabs from Beirut (as indicated in the source). "The Participation of Hiram Unit in the search and seizure operation in the German colony and Abbass street on 5 July 1948", The Haganah Archive, File No. 105/260.

48 The Haganah Archive, File No. 105/260.

49 *Al HaMishmar*, 4 May 1948.

50 The Haganah Archive, File No. 105/260.

REFERENCES

Abdo, N. (1987) *Family, Women and Social Change in the Middle East: The Palestinian Case.* Toronto: Canadian Scholar Press.

Abdo, N. (2011) *Women in Israel: Race, Gender and Citizenship.* London and New York: Zed Books.

Al-Bahri, J. (1922). *Tarikh Haifa* [History of Haifa]. Haifa: The National Library in Haifa.

Allen, L. (2008) "Getting by the Occupation: How Violence Became Normal during Second Palestinian Intifada", *Cultural Anthropology* 23(3): 453–487.

Auerback, E. (1971) *Mimesis: The Representation of Reality in Western Literature.* Princeton, NJ: Princeton University Press.

Bauml, Y. (2007) *A Blue and White Shadow: The Israeli Establishment's Plicy and Action among its Arab Citizens: The Formative Years: 1958–1968.* Haifa: Pardes Press.

Cohen, H. (2010) *Good Arabs: The Israeli Security Agencies and the Israel Arabs, 1948–1967.* Berkeley: University of California Press.

Esmeir, S. (2007) "Memories of Conquest: Witnessing Death in Tantura", in A. Sa'di and L. Abu-Lughod (eds.), *Nakba: Palestine, 1948 and the Claim of Memory.* New York: Columbia University Press.

Faris, A. (2010) "Adeeba El helh – Palestinian Rural Women in Haifa 1930–1948", *Jerusalem Quarterly* (10): 66–75.

Faris, A. (2014) "Adeba El-Halah: Lives of Palestinian Rural Women in Haifa 1930–1948", *Jerusalem Quarterly* (17): 66–74.

Ghanayem, M. (2014) "Between Historical testimony and producing a Myth", in M. Kabha (ed.), *The Palestinian Minority in Israel: Military Rule and Its Legacy.* Haifa: Mada-AlCarmel.

Ghanim, H. (2015) "Borders and the Secret Life of Every Day Resistance: Al-Marjih Village as a Case Study", *Journal of Palestine Studies* (102): 121–142.

Halbwachs, M. (1992) *On Collective Memory*, edited and translated by L.A. Coser. Chicago: University of Chicago Press.

Hasan, M. (2008) *The Forgotten: Women and the Palestinian City, and the Struggle for Memory*. Tel Aviv: Tel Aviv University.

Hawari, A. (2011) *The Construction of Masculine Identity among the Palestinian Citizens of Israel, in the Context of the Political, Judicial, and "Security Related" Practices During the Military Regime Period*. Ramat Gan: Bar Ilan University.

Igbarieh, H. (2010) *The Telling of Haifa: Haifa Narrated by its People*. Haifa: The Social Development Committee of Haifa.

Jiryis, S. (1968) *The Arabs in Israel*. Beirut: Institute for Palestine Studies.

Kabha, M. (2014) "The Arab Press under the Military Rule (1948–1966)", in M. Kabha (ed.), *The Palestinian Minority in Israel: Military Rule and its Legacy*. Haifa: Mada-AlCarmel.

Khalidi, W. (2005) "Why Did the Palestinian Leave", *Journal of Palestine Studies* 34(2): 42–54.

Khalidi, W. (2006) *All That Remains: The Palestinian Villages Occupied and Depopulated by Israel in 1948*. Beirut: Institute for Palestine Studies.

Khalidi, W. (2008) "The Fall of Haifa Revisited", *Journal of Palestine Studies* XXXVII(3): 30–58.

Khamaisi, R. (2014) "The Role of the Military Rule in Planning and in Restricting Urbanization among Palestinian Arabs in Israel", in M. Kabha (ed.), *The Palestinian Minority in Israel: Military Rule and its Legacy*. Haifa: Mada-AlCarmel.

Khoury, E. (1997) *Bab al-Shams* [Gate of the Sun]. Beirut: Dar al-Adab.

Khoury, E. (2012) "Rethinking the Nakba", *Critical Inquiry* 38: 1–18.

Korn, A. (2000) "Military Government, Political Control and Crime: The Case of Israeli Arabs", *Crime, Law & Social Change* (34): 159–182.

Lustik, I. (1980) *Arabs in The Jewish State: Israel's Control of a National Minority*. Austin: University of Texas Press.

Manna, A. (2016) *Nakba and Survival: The Story of the Palestinians who Remained in Haifa and Galilee (1948–1956)*. Beirut: Institute for Palestine Studies.

Mansour, J. (2006) "The Hijaz–Palestine Railway and the Development of Haifa", *Jerusalem Quarterly* (28): 5–21.

Mansour, J. (2011) *Haifa: Name that Soliloquizes with the Moon and Talk to the Sea*. Haifa: The Social Development Committee Haifa.

Masalha, N. (1992) *Expulsion of the Palestinians: The Concept of "Transfer" in Zionist Political Thought, 1882–1948*. Beirut: Institute for Palestine Studies.

Masalha, N. (2012) *The Palestine Nakba: Decolonizing History, Narrating The Subaltern, Reclaiming Memory*. London and New York: Zed Books.

Mustafa, M. (2014) "The Political Activism of Palestinians in Israel during the Military Rule", in M. Kabha (ed.), *The Palestinian Minority in Israel: Military Rule and its Legacy*. Haifa: Mada-AlCarmel.

Nuriely, B. (2005) "Strangers in a National Space: Arab-Jews in the Palestinian Ghetto in Lod", *Theory and Criticism* 26: 13–42.

Ozacky-Lazar, S. (1996) *The Crystallization of Mutual Relations between Jews and Arabs in the State of Israel: The First Decade, 1948–1958*. Haifa: University of Haifa.

Pappe, I. (2006) *The Ethnic Cleansing of Palestine.* Oxford: Oneworld.

Pappe, I. (2013) *The Forgotten Palestinians: A History of the Palestinians in Israel.* New Haven, CT and London: Yale University Press.

Penelope, E. (2010) "Unpacking Settler Colonialist's Urban Strategies: Indigenous People in Victoria, British Columbia, and the Transition to Settler-Colonial City", *Urban History Review* 38(2): 4–20.

Rashid al-Haj Ibrahim, K.W. (2005) *Defending Haifa and the Problem of Palestine: The Memories of Rashid al-haj Ibrahim, 1981–1953.* Beirut: Institute for Palestine Studies.

Sa'di, A. (2014) *Thorough Surveillance: The Genesis of Israeli Policies of Population Management, Surveillance and Political Control towards the Palestinians.* Manchester: Manchester University Press.

Sa'di, A. and Abu-Lughod, L. (2007) *Nakba: Palestine, 1948 and the Claims of Memory.* New York: Columbia University Press.

Sayigh, R. (1979) *Palestinians: From Peasants to Revolutionaries.* London and New York: Zed Books.

Sayigh, R. (2002) "Remembering Mothers, Forming Daughters: Palestinian Women's Narratives in Refugee Camps in Lebanon", in N. Abdo and R. Lentin (eds.), *Women and the Politics of Military Confrontation: Palestinian and Israeli Gendered Narratives of Dislocation.* London: Berghahn Books.

Salomon, Y. (1980) *In My Own Way.* Jerusalem: Edanim Publisher.

Seikaly, M. (2002) *Haifa: Transformation of an Arab Society, 1918–1939.* London and New York: I.B. Tauris Publisher.

Tamari, S. (2008) *Mountain against the Sea: Essays on Palestinian Society and Culture.* Oakland, CA: University of California Press.

Wolfe, P. (2006) "Settler Colonialism and the Elimination of the Native", *Journal of Genocide Research* 8(4): 387–409.

Yacobi, H. (2009) *The Jewish-Arab City: Spatio-Politics in a Mixed Community.* Abingdon: Routledge.

Yazbak, M. (1988) *The Arab Migration to Haifa.* Nazareth: Alqabas Library.

Yazbak, M. (2010). "The Arabs in Haifa: From Majority to Minority Processes of Change (1870–1948)", *Israel Affairs* 9(1–2): 121–148.

Zerubavel, E. (1996) "Social Memories: Steps to a Sociology of the Past", *Qualitative Sociology* 19(3): 283–299.

Ziadeh, K. (2010) *City on the Mediterranean.* Beirut: Shorouk Press.

Zu'bi, H. (2013) "The Effect of Nakba on Socio-economic Status of Palestinian Women: Internally Displaced Women from Saffouri Village as an Example", *Journal of Palestine Studies* 95(24): 108–134.

9
Saffourieh: a continuous tragedy
AMINA QABLAWI NASRALLAH

I am Amina Ahmad Ibrahim Qablawi Nasrallah. I was born on 6 March 1954 in Saffourieh in Galilee, five kilometres from Nazareth. Below I recount the experiences of my family during and immediately after the Palestinian Nakba of 1948 and my own encounters and memories of that period. This was a deliberate choice to draw on early memories which remain vivid in my mind and unobstructed by more mature political discourses used to adapt to young adult life as an internally displaced Palestinian refugee in Israel. The following account recalls events of two types. Firstly, events which I directly inherited and otherwise learnt about through my immediate and extended family. Secondly, events which I experienced personally.

THE NAKBA OF 1948
I have been told by my paternal grandmother, Radeyah Abdelhamid Abd Alhadi Abu Elne'aj (herein "Radeyah" or "my grandmother"), that on 15 July 1948 she was in her house preparing an Iftar meal for the breaking of fast during the holy month of Ramadan. On that day, like the rest of Saffourieh's residents, she was surprised by the Israeli planes which began bombing the town indiscriminately. Radeyah was a widow, her husband Ibrahim Qablawi having been mysteriously killed earlier in the 1940s, his body found close to the British military camp a short distance from his house. Radeyah said that they were shocked and horrified, because it was the first time in their lives they had been bombed by a plane. Many were killed and injured, and the residents ran in different directions without knowing where to go or where they could find shelter. Some ran towards a nearby town called Shefa-'Amr, while others ran towards Nazareth.

My grandmother, her eight children and other family members escaped towards Al Reineh, a village north of Nazareth. Radeyah and my family left their Iftar meal cooking in the pots, ready to be served, and fled hungry and thirsty. They found Al Reineh packed with refugees from other villages, who were all talking about the terrifying dangers they faced. My grandmother recounts that they were worried about being massacred by the Israelis, as had happened in other places in Palestine, especially Deir Yassin, Al Lydd and Ramla and the nearby village I'llut. The stories they had heard about the mass killings of people shook them and filled them with even more terror. They decided to keep walking north, away from the fighting, without knowing where they would end up. My grandmother and family had also fled with my great grandmother Amina Mifleh Al Amin. She was old and unable to walk for long distances, and therefore remained in Al Reineh. The family walked day and night until they reached the town of Bint Jbeil in South Lebanon.

Bint Jbeil was crowded with Palestinian refugees from other parts of Galilee. There, they heard from other refugees that Damascus was safer. After spending some time in Bint Jbeil, the family continued walking until they reached Damascus.

My grandmother used to say they thought their ordeal would be short and that they would return to Saffourieh within two to three weeks.

In Damascus they entered into a state of shock on two levels: firstly, as refugees having lost everything and, secondly, the new experience of residing in a "big city". Damascus was known for its rich history and civilization, grand buildings and large colourful markets, the Souk Al Hamediyeh in particular. My grandmother described the city's wide streets, which she found unfamiliar and difficult to cross due to heavy traffic. They spent hours in the Ummayad Mosque and were fascinated by its beauty and the kindness of those in charge of it. My grandmother spoke about her visit to Salahuddin Al Ayyubi's tomb inside the mosque, the great warrior who defeated the Crusaders in the battle of Hittin in 1187, a short distance from Saffourieh. This was poignant for her as Salahuddin had a special place in the hearts and minds of all Arabs, and the Palestinians in particular.

My grandmother spoke about the open-minded and liberal women of Damascus, who were free to leave their houses alone, without male minders. She realized after seeing Damascus in all its glory why some Palestinians named their daughters Sureya, the Arabic name for Syria.

During her stay in Damascus my grandmother became tired and demoralized by the search for accommodation. Eventually she found a derelict house in poor condition without proper doors, where they spent several months waiting for salvation and a return to Palestine.

In Damascus my grandmother was accompanied by her three daughters, Khadra, Amina and Huda. Her eldest daughter, Khadra, was pregnant at the time, and was married to her cousin, Mohammad Ali Hussein Qablawi. Together they had an eighteen-month-old son called Salim. Amina was married to Salim Mo'ed from Saffourieh, and Huda, who was engaged prior to becoming a refugee, later married her cousin in Damascus.

My grandmother also fled Saffourieh with her three sons, Ahmad, Saeed and Muhammad-Yaser, and her youngest daughter, Yosra. My grandmother looked after all of them. In that miserable and desolate house in Damascus, Khadra delivered her second child, Sami. My grandmother nursed Khadra while looking after the rest of the family. Soon Khadra fell ill and later died, leaving behind her two children in the care of my grandmother. My grandmother recalled burying her daughter Khadra in Damascus and described a feeling of deep sadness which remained with her for a long time after. Salim, Khadra's eldest child, later developed an eye infection, causing him to lose sight in one eye.

My grandmother realized there was no sign of any immediate solution to the Palestinian refugee problem. She therefore decided to return to Palestine, no matter the risks. She decided to split the family into two parts, one returning to Saffourieh and the other staying temporarily in Damascus until she had assessed the situation at home. She intended to give the others instructions to follow her later. Radeyah returned home with her three sons, two daughters, Amna and Yosra, and two grandsons. In Damascus she left her brother Muhamad Abu Alne'aj and his wife, her two other daughters, Amina and Huda, with their husbands and her other son in law, Muhammad Ali, Khadra's husband.

My grandmother repeatedly spoke about her damaging experience of walking unaided through the rough badlands and mountains with her family on their way home to Saffourieh. To her surprise she found her house and land occupied by a group of people from Saffourieh, led by Muhammad Abd Elhamid. Nothing was left of her cattle, sheep or livestock. My grandmother immediately asked those occupying to vacate the house. They refused, telling her the Israeli authorities had granted her house and land to Saleh Salim Sleiman, the former mayor of Saffourieh. My grandmother forced her way into the house, finding it entirely looted except for two large wardrobes, which were not easy to move. One of the wardrobes, called a *Samandara*, spanned from wall to wall and up to the ceiling. The *Samandara* was used for storing wool quilts and bed covers. The two wardrobes had been crafted by my great-grandfather Abdulhamid as a wedding present for my grandmother. Abdulhamid was a skilful and renowned carpenter specialized in making traditional olive oil presses. He had also made the doors for her house which had been dismantled by the occupiers and burnt in the house for heating and cooking. Despite their attempts, those occupying the house failed to drive out my grandmother and her children. Instead, she forced herself and her family back into their house, eventually sharing part of the house with the occupiers. Similarly with the land, my grandmother managed to share and cultivate part of her land despite the occupiers' presence.

The occupiers and their supervisor, Saleh Salim Sleiman, subjected my grandmother to repulsive treatment. As well as abusive language used towards her and her children, Radeyah was routinely threatened and, on occasions, physically pushed out of her house and off her land. My grandmother arranged a formal meeting with Saleh Salim Sleiman, demanding that he end the occupation of her house and land. She recounted Saleh Salim Sleiman's insistence that he had been granted the house and the land by the Israeli authorities. He was shameless, and told her "Shut up woman! Go back to Damascus and eat Shami apples". The Shami apples were and are famous across Arab countries for their beauty and fine taste.

My grandmother realized that Saleh Salim Sleiman was collaborating with the Israelis in order to displace Saffourieh's residents. It was known that Saleh Salim Sleiman had handed the Israelis all the files of the council and had helped convince Saffourieh's residents to leave their homes for two weeks. Saleh Salim Sleiman said the Israelis had given him guarantees that they would allow the residents to return to their homes no later than two weeks after leaving Saffourieh. It was evident Saleh Salim Sleiman had helped the Israelis to cheat his fellow residents. Many of Saffourieh's residents stayed in the town and refused the Israeli order, among them the Sheikh of Saffourieh, Muhammad Abdel Majid El Azhari, who was also known by the names of Al A'alem (a Muslim scholar) and Al Azhari (having been educated at Al Azhar university in Egypt). Eventually, these returning residents were forcibly removed and internally displaced. Saffourieh's residents have been prevented from returning to their homes. To this day they remain scattered across the north of Palestine, mainly in Nazareth, Shefa-'Amr and Al Reineh.

The Israelis subsequently used Saleh Salim Sleiman to convince large numbers of the Saffourieh residents who became refugees in Nazareth to sign documents giving up their houses and lands in Saffourieh to the Israelis in exchange for small pieces of land in Nazareth. Sheikh Al Azhari led many Saffourieh residents to refuse to sign any such documents. Sheikh Al Azhari also petitioned the Israeli government for many years, albeit in vain, to allow Saffourieh's displaced residents to return to their homes. Due to his stance, Al Azhari was subjected to vindictive treatment and humiliation at the hands of the Israelis and their collaborators. They would leave rubbish on his doorstep and spit at him. My grandmother and her family always stood by Sheikh Al Azhari, aiding and supporting him.

Some Saffourieh residents reluctantly agreed to the offer to sign the documents under heavy pressure from local compradors and Israeli forces. The land they received in exchange was on a large plot called Karm Aljammal in Nazareth, confiscated by the Israelis from the Aljammal family, whose own members were scattered across neighbouring Arab countries as refugees.

The Saffourieh residents had in fact become refugees, both homeless and jobless. Saleh Salim Sleiman was the first to give up his house and land in order to encourage Saffourieh's refugees to accept the transfer. This enabled the Israelis to demolish Palestinian houses in Saffourieh, first using dynamite and then by bringing Jewish settlers to live in the town. The Israelis later granted Saleh Salim Sleiman my family's house and land as a reward. He was also made a member of the Israeli Parliament. Years later the Israelis removed the road sign leading to Saffourieh, which was written in three languages – Hebrew, Arabic and English – and instead put up a sign carrying the name Tsipori in Hebrew and English only.

After her meeting and continued efforts to plead with Saleh Salim Sleiman, my grandmother was in disbelief at his stance and decided to continue her battle. She returned home and encouraged her children to resist the occupiers and help her cultivate the land. Later she sent two of her children to school. Muhammad Yasir attended school in Nazareth. He would return home terrified by the occupier's efforts to prevent his attendance as well as general threats towards him. My grandmother became worried for his safety and eventually stopped sending him to school.

Her youngest daughter, Yosra, was sent to school in the village of Al Reineh, which was still full of refugees. As the school was overcrowded, Yosra was forced to attend classes in the open air, held under the olive trees of Al Reineh. Yosra was subjected to harassment from the same group of occupiers. My grandmother recalled that one day she had given Yosra a lettuce to take to her teacher as a gift, but was prevented from doing so and insulted by the occupiers. They spat at her and snatched the lettuce from her. She returned home in tears. Also worried for her safety, my grandmother stopped sending Yosra to school.

Muhammad Ali, who remained in Damascus after the death of his wife Khadra, sorely missed his children, Salim and Sami, and in 1949 returned to Saffourieh to see them. He was spotted by the occupiers, who informed the Israelis of his return. They ordered a guard to watch him until the Israelis arrived. Muhammad Ali sensed he was being watched and tried to escape. He was stopped by the occupiers, who wanted to hand him over to the Israelis. A physical fight broke out between them. He was fit and managed to escape, leaving his attackers with one of his shoes, which they managed to grab during the altercation. Muhammad Ali managed to reach Damascus and re-join his two sisters in law and their husbands, where they remained as refugees in the Al Yarmouk Palestinian refugee camp.

Muhammad Ali's shoe was used by the Israelis as evidence to accuse my grandmother of harbouring an "infiltrator", a term Israelis attributed to Palestinian refugees returning to their homes. An Israeli military force searched the house and interrogated my grandmother. She explained to them that Muhammad Ali was a citizen of Saffourieh and had returned to see his two children who were under her care. The Israelis ignored her and decided to detain the children. My grandmother refused to hand over the two boys to the Israelis and resisted attempts to arrest them by force. The Israelis abducted both of the young boys, Salim and Sami, handing them over to UN observation officers so they could be expelled to Damascus to join their father. That was the last time my grandmother saw Salim and Sami. The incident broke her heart and she said she wept like never before.

After this incident the Israelis increased the pressure on my grandmother and her family to leave their house and land in Saffourieh. They surrounded the house with a large military force including armoured vehicles. The siege lasted for several months. The soldiers manning the siege restricted the family's movement, making their daily lives miserable.

My grandmother turned to a relative, Mahmoud Afifi, for help. Mahmoud Afifi was married to Radeyah's aunt A'esha, the daughter of Mefleh Alamin, one of Saffourieh's notables. Mahmoud moved from Saffourieh shortly before the 1948 Nakba and settled in Nazareth, where he and his brother Tawfiq Afifi ran a public transportation company. Mahmoud, like the rest of the internally dispossessed Palestinians at that time, was frustrated and demoralized as a result of the Nakba and subsequent events. He was worried for the safety of my grandmother and her children and was wary of the possibility that she could resist Israeli attempts to expel her family. Mahmoud told my grandmother that the Israelis had killed thousands of Palestinians, expelled hundreds of thousands of them and demolished more than 500 towns and villages. My grandmother recalled Mahmoud telling her "Who are you to resist them? We are a small nation while Israelis have the support of all of the world. They will kill you and kill your children".

Initially, Mahmoud advised my grandmother to leave her house and land and move to Nazareth, where he was prepared to help her and her family find a place to live and work. She rejected the idea outright, instead asking him to suggest a good lawyer to file a case before the courts. Seeing Radeyah's determination to fight for her rights, Mahmoud arranged for Radeyah to instruct Palestinian lawyer Hanna Naqara. Naqara, from Haifa, was a communist who was recognized then as the most famous land lawyer in Palestine. He was dubbed "the Land Lawyer" due to his brave defence of Palestinian landowners against Israeli land confiscations, having continued to practise under the Israeli rule. Naqara submitted a complaint to the court in Nazareth against Saleh Salim Sleiman, requesting the eviction of him and his men from my grandmother's house and land. After many sessions the court ordered Sleiman and his co-occupiers to leave my grandmother's house and land. The court also decided that the cultivated land and the house built on it were administratively part of Al Reineh village and did not belong to the newly built Israeli settlement over Saffourieh.

Until this day, further generations of the Qablawi family remain in Saffourieh but are prevented by the Israelis from building homes. They are therefore forced to live in caravans or temporary dwellings without proper roofs. Almost seventy years on from 1948, the Israelis still refuse to connect my family's houses or, more aptly, their besieged compound, to public electricity, water and sewage networks. My family was obliged to purchase private generators for electricity. The adjacent Moshav Tsipori settlement received these facilities immediately after the settlement was built. This was part of a specific Israeli policy intended to inculcate the idea that my family were living temporarily on their land and did not belong there.

With respect to Saffourieh's water supply, my family would carry drinking water in gallon cans from Saffourieh's headspring, having dug a well on our land to extract enough water to irrigate our fields. In the late 1960s the municipality of Nazareth discovered that prior to 1948 it had purchased the right to extract drinking water from the headspring of Saffourieh. The agreement was concluded in secret by Saleh Salim Sleiman, Saffourieh's mayor, without the knowledge of the town residents. As the Nazareth municipality was obliged to lay the water pipes through my family's land, my family was able to secure a fresh water supply.

MY FATHER'S MURDER

Gradually my grandmother began re-building her life by breeding cows, sheep and chickens and cultivating her land. This was to the dismay of the Israeli settlers who were brought to settle in Saffourieh.

Meanwhile, my grandmother's son Ahmad (my father), had turned eighteen and in 1951 had married Radeyah Mou'ed (my mother), also from Saffourieh, but whose family had become refugees in Nazareth. At my father's wedding the best man was Saeed Barakeh from Saffourieh, who became a refugee in Shefa-'Amr, where he still lives with his family.

My mother's father, Hasan Shibli Mou'ed, was killed in 1948 in Saffourieh, after their family were deported to Nazareth. Hasan returned to Saffourieh and was shot dead by the Israelis on the doorstep of his house. He was hastily buried in his house, which was later demolished.

In 1952 my mother gave birth to my eldest sister Khadra, named after my aunt who had died as a refugee in Damascus. On 6 March 1954 I was born and named Amina after another of my aunts who had become a refugee in Syria.

As a result of the court's decision, the Israelis escalated their attempts to expel my family by increasing restrictions on their movements and preventing them from cultivating their land. They brought in Jewish settlers to build houses over the ruins of Saffourieh, creating a new settlement, Moshav Tsipori, part of which was on land confiscated from my family in 1948. To create a pretext for further dispossession, the settlers would provoke my grandmother and her children, alleging that they were trespassing into Moshav Tsipori lands. Other land belonging to my family had been confiscated by the Israelis in 1948 and was granted to the settlers of Moshav Tsipori and Kibutz Hasolelim. Kibutz Hasolelim was also partially built on land confiscated from my family in 1949.

The Moshav's settlers ceaselessly provoked the family. These provocations included blocking the road leading to our house from the western side, forcing my family to open a new access route to their house. The old blocked road was then ploughed and cultivated by the settlers.

To avoid clashes with the settlers, my grandmother and her children refrained from entering into the family's nearby confiscated lands, including the foot of a mountain called Jablat Alnoss. The mountain had been granted by the Israeli authorities to the settlers and was left uncultivated. It was the job of my uncle, Muhammad-Yaser, to look after the family's sheep. My grandmother would tell her children to herd the sheep on the other side of the land close to the main road. One day some of the sheep crossed the southern side of the road, to another piece of land called Wad Al A'ama, which had also been confiscated by the Israelis. One of the Jewish Moshav's settlers suddenly appeared and captured my uncle Muhammad-Yaser, who was only fourteen years old. Becoming extremely frightened of the armed settler, Muhammad-Yaser began screaming loudly asking for help. My father Ahmad, who was at home, heard the screams and rushed to free his brother. Ahmad got into an argument with the settler. My father and the settler did not speak the same language. My father spoke some Hebrew but the settler did not understand Hebrew and spoke what my uncle described as a strange language which neither he nor my father understood. The settler then threatened to shoot my father. Bundling my father onto his horse and carriage, the settler freed my uncle, before riding away. Muhammad-Yaser rushed home to my grandmother to inform her that his brother had been abducted. My grandmother immediately dashed outside to find out what had happened to my father. She found he had been shot, with several bullet wounds to the head. The settler was trying to cover up his crime by dragging the body and throwing it into a nearby well. My grandmother stopped the settler from doing so. She retrieved her son's body and rushed him to a hospital in Haifa, where he was later pronounced dead.

The murder of my father shocked the Palestinians in the towns and villages close to Saffourieh, especially the internally displaced Saffourieh families who had become refugees and who knew my father. They all came to pay their respects and support my family. Others signed petitions which were handed to the Israeli authorities protesting against the murder of my father and requesting that the murderer be put on trial. A group of forty-seven notables from the village of Al Reina signed a petition addressed to the Israeli Government which read:

> We the undersigned ... strongly condemn the murderous crime of the
> late innocent citizen Ahmad Ibrahim Qablawi, who was assassinated at
> the hands of an evil culprit, while close by to his own land in Saffourieh.
> We demand to punish hard the evildoers in order to deter others not to
> commit such ugly crimes and protect the citizens' lives. We demand from
> the Government to abandon its policy of land theft and dispossession
> which encourages those breaching security to commit crimes against the
> villagers seeking to return to and tend to their lands. (See appendix)

Saeed Barakeh, who had been the best man at my father's wedding, told me many good things about him. He said that when he heard that my father had been murdered, he rushed to our house in Saffourieh to pay his respects and support my family. When my grandmother saw Saeed entering her house she cried: "Dear Saeed, why you are coming on your own? Where is Ahmad? Why didn't you bring him with you?"

I was forty days old when my father was murdered. My grandmother told me she loved my father dearly. She, said he offered her great support and helped her during the difficult times. He accompanied her to all of the court sessions in Nazareth. She also told me that my father was a handsome, clever and loving young man known for his generosity and good heart. He was loyal to his family and was loved and respected by everyone knew him she said. He loved singing and danced the *Dabka* (a Palestinian folk dance) professionally. A photograph of him dancing the *Dabka* at a friends' wedding was hung on the wall in our house. My grandmother would look at my father's photograph and say to me "He never hurt anyone in his life, not even his enemies". She used to say that the only comfort she had was that my father was martyred on his own land and not in a foreign country. Our family was prevented from burying my father in Saffourieh. He was eventually buried in Nazareth.

I remember when I was young my grandmother would take my sister Khadra and me to visit our father's grave, especially during our school holidays. We would read the *Surat Al Fateha* from the Quran, dedicating it to his soul, and my grandmother would distribute homemade sweets traditionally prepared for wakes. We would also visit his grave on the annual event traditionally called the Thursday of the Dead and my grandmother, Khadra and I would distribute coloured boiled eggs and homemade sweets to those less fortunate than ourselves.

Soon after my father was murdered my grandmother found herself thrown into a new battle with the Israeli authorities. Keen to assist the settler who murdered my father to cover up and avoid punishment for his crime, the Israeli authorities refused all petitions to put the settler on trial. Instead they put my grandmother under heavy pressure to accept a settlement. The authorities sent messengers to warn my grandmother that unless she accepted a *Sulha*, leaving the settler free of any criminal prosecution by law, she would be expelled from her land and her remaining children would be murdered.

The *Sulha* was an ancient tribal tradition which later became a traditional customary form of Arab dispute resolution. *Sulha* was never understood or practised as a substitute for the enforcement of state criminal laws under Ottoman, British or Israeli occupation. Moreover, it was not credible to suggest that *Sulha* formed part of the traditions of newly settled prominently Western Jewish society in Palestine.

My grandmother believed that the *Sulha* would allow her family to live in peace and on that basis reluctantly agreed. To conclude the *Sulha*, a group of notables drawn from Saffourieh's refugees came to our house together with a few Israeli officials and members of Moshav Tsipori settlement, none of whom my grandmother had met before. After they left, she discovered an amount of cash hidden under one of the mattresses in the sitting room. She took the money to Mahmoud Afifi and asked him to return it to the settlers. Afifi apologized, saying he could not return the money as it formed part of the *Sulha*. Mahmoud warned my grandmother that they would kill her family and drive her out of her home and land. Seeing no alternative, my grandmother invested the money in a small piece of land next to our land and registered it in the names of my sister and me. My family have left this piece of land uncultivated until this day. Once the *Sulha* was imposed on my grandmother, the settler who murdered my father moved on to Haifa.

My beautiful and long-suffering young mother, Radeyah Mou'ed, was arguably the person most affected by my father's tragic murder. She became a widow at twenty years of age, left with two baby daughters. Soon after this tragedy my mother moved to live with her mother Deya, also widowed, and her young brothers and sisters, who had become refugees in Nazareth. As a young widow, she found herself subject to social rules which obliged her a year later to marry to her cousin Akram Mou'ed. Cultural and succession issues arising out of my father's murder eventually caused a rift between my father and mother's respective families. My grandmother, Radeyah Abu Elne'aj, took my sister Khadra and me under her care. It was 1955 and I was then only a year old. As a result of the arrangement, neither I nor my sister saw our mother again until 1985.

ONGOING DISPOSSESSION

Meanwhile, the Israelis continued their attempts to evict my family from their house and lands in Saffourieh.

They erected a pig farm close to our house, intending my family to become trapped between the pig farm and the Mushav settlers, thereby causing us to leave. In building the pig farm, the settlers had violated the tenets of the Jewish religion and traditions, which do not consider pork to be Kosher. The pig farm spread a vile stench and released a stream of stinking waste that was diverted on to our land, destroying our family's vegetation and infesting the area with insects and rodents.

The Jewish owners of the pig farm later dug a waste pool on our land, which caused further clashes with my family. The memory of my father's murder remained on the surface and my grandmother was worried that the farm owners might kill her remaining two sons. She asked her sons not to engage in any confrontations with the farm owners and stay far away from the farm. My family commenced several legal actions against the pig farm owner, which were lengthy and expensive, almost bankrupting my family. Despite receiving a court order in our favour, the settlers continued to dig on our land time and time again.

My family suffered other provocations. On one occasion, the settlers in Saffourieh sent tractors to repeatedly plough parts of our land. My grandmother would try to convince the tractor driver not to plough her land. Whenever he refused she threw herself in front of the tractor to stop him. My sister Khadra, my cousins and I would watch with sadness, anger and disbelief. Other provocations were carried out by the Youth Brigade groups in the Israeli army (the *Gadnaa*). The *Gadnaa* would cross from the middle of our cultivated land wearing heavy boots during their training exercises, damaging the vegetables or other crops. They would also steal cucumbers, tomatoes and other vegetables.

I attended school in Nazareth with my sister and my cousin. We would wait on the main road near our house for the one bus working on that line, which served many villages. Its route started from Sakhnin village, passed through Shefa-'Amr and ended in Nazareth. This bus was frequently behind schedule or did not stop because it was full. So we would try to stop the bus taking Jewish children from Moshav Tsipori to schools in Afula and Nazareth I'llit (the settlement built in upper Nazareth in 1957). The Moshav was at that time too small to have its own school. However, the Moshav bus never stopped for us unless the driver was an Arab. When we had the rare chance to board the Moshav's bus, we would be attacked by the Jewish settler's children. They called us names in Hebrew which we only understood later. Some of the insults they used were "*Aravim Melokhlakhim*", meaning "dirty Arabs", and "*Araboushim*", meaning "Arab rats". I learnt the meaning of these insults from my uncle. Muhammad-Yaser. Eventually, that bus would never stop for us regardless of whether the driver was a Jew or an Arab. It was understood that the drivers were instructed not to stop. Many times we were obliged to walk five kilometres to and from school.

I used to return home from school for lunch and rush out to the fig tree at the back of our house. There I would pick delicious Ghezali figs, put them between two flat biscuits, press them into a fig sandwich and eat it. I used to cry under the fig tree, and call for my father and beg him to come back. But there was never any reply. I would always go back home very angry.

One day I found a guest called Muhammad Rashid Sleiman, who was known as Abu Mahmoud, had come to visit us at home. His donkey was tied outside the house and he sat chatting with my grandmother. She asked me to say hello to him. I refused and hid myself behind her back. My grandmother apologized to Abu Mahmoud, saying "Please pardon Amina, she is unusually upset and does not want to speak to anyone". Abu Mahmoud replied "She has every right to be angry after what they did to her father".

Abu Mahmoud was the uncle of Fahimah, the wife of my uncle Muham-mad-Yaser. He visited us regularly after finishing work in the Mushav Tsipori settlement. Abu Mahmoud was a middle-aged man with wide blue eyes, slightly humpbacked, and had a blond beard and moustache mixed with white hair. He wore traditional Palestinian clothes and looked anxious. Abu Mahmoud's land in Saffourieh had been confiscated and granted by the Israeli authorities to an Eastern European settler named Sando, who then sadistically employed Abu

Mahmoud to cultivate his own land. Sando built his own house on the ruins of Abu Mahmoud's house.

Abu Mahmoud would confide in my grandmother about his internal suffering from having to work on his own land for Sando. One day he was asked by Sando to plant citrus trees in the plot which used to belong to him. He tried to convince Sando to give up the idea because the type of soil on that particular plot was not suitable for citrus trees. Abu Mahmoud carried lifelong experience in land cultivation inherited from his father and ancestors about the nature of their land. Sando refused to listen to his advice.

Abu Mahmoud was obliged to follows Sando's dictate, planting the trees and irrigating them in vain. The trees later died. I recall Abu Mahmoud repeating how he had told Sando, "This is my land and I know it very well".

My grandmother would urge Abu Mahmoud to look for work elsewhere and used to say to him "How could you bear working in your confiscated land?" Abu Mahmoud would reply, "I get comfort while working in my land and smelling its soil, especially after I became a refugee in the nearby village of I'llut". She used to call Fahima and ask her to prepare a cup of Arabic coffee for her uncle. Abu Mahmoud would murmur "Every time I remember my confiscated land I lose the appetite to eat or drink".

Abu Mahmoud was not the only Saffourian to work on his own confiscated land. The settlers employed many Saffourians who had become internally displaced refugees in Nazareth, many of whom I know personally. I would listen carefully to their sad stories during their visits to my grandmother.

Before 1948 we had neighbours close to our house who during the Nakba became refugees in Lebanon and Syria. Their houses were demolished. However, their groves of different fruit trees, especially pomegranate, and their corresponding water wells, remained on their confiscated land. I played with other children in these groves, climbing trees, watching the birds and animals and throwing stones into the wells to measure their depth. I would enjoy the sound of the stones hitting the water. I used to tell my grandmother about my adventures in those groves, and she would recount the names and stories of her neighbours who had lived and worked in these beautiful groves. She spoke with sympathy about her good-hearted and well-mannered neighbours; simple people who respected each other. Sometimes she accompanied me to those groves to identify the ruins of the destroyed houses and to tell me the names of their owners.

Saffourieh's groves of pomegranate trees were very famous in all parts of Palestine. For me these groves were my little paradise. We woke up one day to the noise of Israeli bulldozers deployed to uproot all the trees in these groves and bury the water wells. The Israeli's destroyed the habitat in which the beautiful birds and animals lived. They destroyed my paradise. The uprooted fruit trees were heaped to one side, loaded up on trucks and taken away. Later, tractors came and ploughed the bare land. The scene was grotesque and shocking for me as a child, for which I still feel a deep sadness. I remember seeing many of the internally displaced Saffourian refugees in Nazareth gathering to watch that sad scene, collecting logs for their stoves, while the Israeli settlers stood on the other side relishing the destruction of the groves and the pain it caused.

My father's murder was not something that could be forgotten for long, and we were reminded of it again after an attack on my uncle Saeed. During the period of military rule imposed on the Palestinians inside Israel until 1966, Saeed was severely beaten up by a patrol of the Israeli Military Police while they were passing by Saffourieh. As a young girl I was shaken to see my uncle Saeed lying in bed with serious injuries all over his face and body. The patrol passed by him while he was waiting on the main road for the bus to go to Nazareth. After being beaten up in an indiscriminate and unprovoked attack, Saeed was thrown to the side of the road. I recall he spent a long time in bed recovering.

The Israelis never ran out of ideas of how to visit misery upon my family. The Saffourieh settlers began gradually imposing themselves on my family, by making regular visits. My grandmother would always receive them in a proper manner, serving them food and drinks in accordance with customary traditions of Arab hospitality. One of those settlers was an Iraqi Jew bearing the Arab name Abu Khader. He spoke Arabic with an Iraqi dialect. Years later in 1974, when I went to study at the Hebrew University of Jerusalem I was introduced to an Israeli student called Rinna from Moshav Tsipori. She was amazed to hear that I was from Saffourieh and asked "How could it be that there was an Arab from Saffourieh. There are no Arabs in Saffourieh". I asked her about her family and she eventually told me her father was an Iraqi Jew. I immediately said, "I know him he is Abu Khader, the only Iraqi Jew in Saffourieh". It was clear Rinna did not take kindly to my association or the encounter. We never met again.

Another settler called Shlomo also visited my family. He carried a pistol on his waist and was sometimes accompanied by his wife. During one visit my great grandmother, Amina, started crying and begging Shlomo to help return

223

her only son Muhammad from Damascus. My two uncles held her back and my grandmother explained, "Oh dear mother, Shlomo is only a settler. The decision on this matter is in the hands of big powers not individuals".

During a further visit, my uncle Saeed was nearly killed by Shlomo. This time Shlomo was carrying a rifle and instigated a provocative conversation on a political topic. He spoke nervously and aggressively and did not tolerate my uncle Saeed's views. Shlomo then physically attacked Saeed, drawing his rifle and aiming to shoot Saeed. My grandmother and my other uncle, Muhammad-Yaser, who at the time was busy shearing the sheep, tried to stop Shlomo. During their tussle Shlomo shot a round in the air. The shot frightened all of us, me included. My grandmother often repeated that she had lost half of her life during that incident.

I can never forget the sad stories that I used to hear during my childhood from other Palestinians about their experiences at the hands of the Israelis. I recall the story of a woman named Mayyasa from the village of I'llut, which suffered a horrific massacre by the Israelis, during which Mayyasa's husband was killed. As a child, I would beg my grandmother to let me stay with my aunt Yosra in Nazareth. This was after she married Taha Muhammad Ali, who would later became a well-known poet and writer. My aunt Yosra was a well-mannered, friendly and loving person. She helped me and my sister Khadra greatly. Yosra was highly skilled in cooking, baking cakes and making sweets. She shared this skill with her neighbour Mayyasa, Hayat, Mayyasa's daughter, and her sister in law Sabah who used to live in the same house. Yosra could speak to Mayyasa out of a wide window in her house which overlooked Mayyasa's courtyard. When the window was open they would chat casually in her courtyard, sharing coffee and sweets.

Yosra introduced me to Mayyasa, "This is Amina, my niece. I told you about her and her sister. Their father was killed by the Israelis". Suddenly Mayyasa started crying, telling Yosra about the murder of her husband and other residents of I'llut, as one of many massacres committed against the Palestinians in 1948. I will never forget Mayyasa's description of I'llut's victims; inflated bodies left in the fields as nobody dared to bury the bodies out of fear of repercussions from the Israelis. Mayyasa spoke of how she had escaped with her daughter Hayat and her son, seeking refuge in Nazareth close to my aunt's house. Mayyasa's story was added to the thick file of oral histories from the Palestinian Nakba which I carry with me and which is lodged deeply in my memory.

In 1977 I submitted an application for a passport to the Israeli Ministry of Interior. I was told that I was not a citizen of the country, despite being born six years after the establishment of Israel and bearing an immutable family past spanning hundreds of years, at least, on our land in Palestine., I was told by an Israeli Ministry of Interior employee, who had recently immigrated from somewhere in Europe, that I was not a citizen and had no right to obtain a passport unless I applied for naturalization. I was in total shock and disbelief upon hearing this. It was like reliving my family's catastrophe again. I became very angry and exclaimed to the officer in charge "What are you talking about, my family has existed on this land since the creation". My words did not help and did not explain my case. I understood that I belonged to the category of Palestinian residents in Israel referred to by the Israeli authorities as "Present Absentee". This category of residents was created to define the legal status of Palestinians who escaped the war in 1948 and had returned to their homes. The Israelis applied this law even to the children of those returning Palestinians. After many visits to the Ministry of Interior to submit the application for naturalization, I was granted a passport. I was told that the passport would serve me for one year only, because I was a newly naturalized citizen, and so I would have to renew it every year. I felt very angry after discovering that the Israelis did not recognize me or a vast number of Palestinians who remained on their land, instead considering us as absentees. I realized that the 1948 Nakba was in fact ongoing and affecting all Palestinians wherever they lived. I cried like never before and wanted to shout out loudly for the world to hear.

It was clear for me that the Israeli authorities do not recognize the existence of the Palestinian people and do not want to make peace with them. I realized that we should resist their aggression and expose their crimes and lies. The Palestinians are not able to carry on this task in their own; they need help from the international community.

APPENDIX:

Petition by Palestinian notables to the Israeli government, condemning the murder of Ahmad Qablawi (my father)

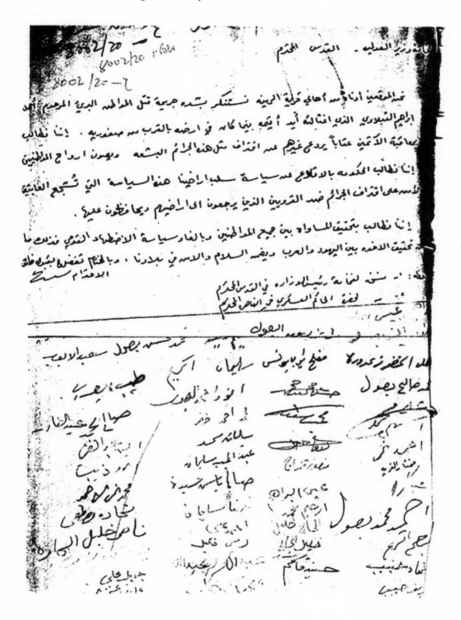

10
The sons and daughters of Eilaboun

HISHAM ZREIQ

During the filming of my documentary *The Sons of Eilaboun*, in the spring of 2006, I interviewed more than twenty people who had witnessed the events of the Nakba in Eilaboun. I also conducted other interviews with historians, such as Ilan Pappe, on the same subject.[1] To my amazement, I found the testimonies of all the people to be almost identical concerning the main events; the difference was basically in some individual experiences of those interviewed. The following text is based on the interviews, along with consultation of Israeli Defence Forces documents, and particularly the report of the United Nations Truce Supervision Observers (UNTSO) on the massacre in Eilaboun.

The interviews were very intense and emotional, and some people cried when they spoke about their lost loved ones. I was also amazed to find this traumatic event continued to affect and touch the people strongly after over fifty-eight years.

The massacre in Eilaboun is but one example of what Palestinians suffered through the policies and tactics of "Plan Dalet", developed by the high command of the Israeli Army to rid the future State of Israel of its Arab inhabitants who were considered by Israel as a threat.[2]

In an interview with Ilan Pappe, he had the following to say about Plan Dalet:

The Jewish leadership, actually the High Command of the Jewish society, the Matkal, later it was called the High Command of the Army, met in Tel-Aviv and decided on the means of implementing Plan Dalet: It divided the future state of Israel into twelve zones and created twelve brigades; each brigade was supposed to cleanse all the area from the Palestinian villages and towns in it. And the plan was very clear on how to do it:

You encircle the village or neighborhood ... occupy it; separate the men – defined as anyone above the age of ten – from the women and the children; expel the women and the children, and take the men you think have a military potential, and send them to the POW camps; and you execute those you suspect were involved in actions against the Jews. This was a standard operational command.

Commands to the Israeli soldiers were clear and demonstrated the intention to "cleanse" the Palestinian areas. This intent was also clear in the following document obtained from the IDF archives, which states: "Do whatever is in your power to cleanse the captured areas, quickly and immediately, of hostile elements, in accordance with the orders that were issued ... Facilitate the movement of the residents."[3]

THE VILLAGE OF EILABOUN

The village of Eilaboun is a Palestinian village in the Galilee; it was composed of two parts assembled around two churches, a Greek Orthodox and Greek Catholic one.

According to United Nations Truce Observers,[4] the village population was 750 Christian Arabs, 600 belonged to the Greek Catholic Church and 150 to the Orthodox Church. The village functioned as an agricultural centre, growing wheat, barley, lentils and olives. Before the Jews attacked the village, it had 400 sheep and goats; 200 cows; five horses; fifty donkeys and 1,000 fowl.[5]

WHEN THE WAR REACHED EILABOUN

In the summer of 1948 Nazareth and the surrounding villages fell into the hands of the Israeli army, and refugees from the area started passing through Eilaboun to Lebanon. After the fall of Tur'an, Bu'eine and Kafr Kanna, Eilaboun became the first defence line of the Arab Liberation Army (ALA).

An air raid and shelling in July and August forced the people of Eilaboun to go and live in the caves near the village. The men continued working the land, as it was harvest time. The Israeli soldiers would shoot at them two or three times a week, to prevent them from working on their land. In the middle of September, the people who had become fed up with living in the caves returned to their homes, despite the danger.[6]

Various people observed that a second wave of refugees passed through Eilaboun, carrying with them stories of killings and massacres that scared many young men, leading some young villagers to leave the village and seek refuge in Lebanon.[7] Most interviewees attested that, "the elders of Eilaboun gathered in the parsonage of priest Morkus, and discussed what to do, and made a decision to stay in Eilaboun, because some of the villagers that lived around Eilaboun were not harmed and were allowed to stay, and they assumed the same will happen to them".[8]

THE FALL OF EILABOUN

"On Friday, 29 October, the Jewish forces at Galilee, in an action generally directed northwards, attacked in particular along the axis: Lubiya, Eilaboun, and Maghar."[9]

The UNTSO reported that "on the eve of 29 October, the shelling intensified, and it was a very frightening experience. The people rushed to hide in the two churches of the village, they were very scared, some left with their sleeping clothes and some did not even wear their shoes". The Arab Liberation Army withdrew from its posts south of Eilaboun without informing the villagers; the volunteers from Eilaboun were forbidden to inform their fellow villagers and families and were threatened with execution if they did, so the people of Eilaboun were left without any protection. The quietness of the posts made the villagers suspicious, so some young men tried to see what was happening and realized that the ALA had withdrawn, and that they were left without any protection, unarmed and unprotected. Some of the young men feared for their lives and ran towards Lebanon, but many others stayed in the churches with their families.

According to several interviewees, "The Elders of Eilaboun prepared to surrender to the invading Israelis, so they raised a white flag on the Catholic Church and a yellow one on the Orthodox Church".[10]

As the UNTSO reports: "In the morning of Saturday, 30 October, between 0500 and 0600 hrs (local time) the Jewish troops entered the village, and the inhabitants (Christian Arabs) immediately surrendered".[11]

The village's four priests surrendered the village, holding a white flag, but the army commander pushed them and ordered them to call everybody to "El Hara", the village square. The village square is adjacent to the parsonage and the Catholic Church, so the people in the Catholic Church started coming out to the square, when suddenly the Israeli soldiers started shooting at them, killing a man from Horan called Azar, who used to work for one of the village families, and wounding two boys, Yousef Slayeh and Butros Matta. The people in the Orthodox Church were called out as well, coming into the square with their hands above their heads. The soldiers separated the men from the women into two groups in the square. What is interesting is that none of the interviewed could remember how long they stayed in the square, but all of them said it was a terrifying period of time; they could not say if it was minutes or hours.[12]

The following testimony, told by Salem Zreiq, expressed the feelings many other interviewees shared:

> We walked until we reached the Hara, which is the main town square. The first thing we saw in the square, a man named 'Azar from Horan, who used to work for Salim Zreiq, was killed in the middle of the square. The bullet had struck him in the head. Until this moment, I ... I see him in my mind. We entered [the square]. "Sit down!" we were told. We sat down. Of course, I cannot say how long – an hour ... two hours. We were tyrannized by fear. We did not feel the difference between an hour, half-an-hour, or a quarter of an hour.[13]

Similar stories were told by many interviewees, as the following narrative shows:

> The Israeli officer chose seventeen men, and ordered the rest of the villagers to march north to the village Maghar (about 7km away from Eilaboun) to be used as a human shield for the advancing forces, in case there were land mines on the road. After the force arrives to Maghar the villagers were supposed to be allowed to return to their village, as they were told. Samira Zreiq, the wife of Badee, one of the chosen men, begged the soldiers to pick up her eighteen-year-old son that was left with his very old great-grandmother, but the soldiers did not let her, and the boy was left in the village with his great-grandmother, and the villagers, instead of returning their village started their march to the unknown. The priests, on the other hand were ordered to go to their homes.[14]

THE MASSACRE

Butros Matta could not walk because of his wounds, so he stayed sitting a few metres away from the chosen seventeen men and the soldiers, making him the only witness to what happened in the square.

According to Butros and others: "The Israeli officer chose five of the men, and ordered them to drive a Jeep in front of the military convoy as a human shield; the rest stayed in the square".[15] He continued:

> The remaining men in the square sat waiting, hands on their heads, while the Israeli soldiers huddled in discussion. An officer stepped forward, "We need three men", he shouted. Three men stood up and were marched off with the soldiers. Moments later, three shots were heard. The soldiers returned, "Three more men", and three more shots. And so on, until only three men remained in the square. The last three were shot with an automatic rifle in the square.[16]

The fourteen martyrs of Eilaboun were:

1. Aazar Msalam, who came from Horan to work in Eilaboun.
2. Badee Zreiq (twenty-four years old), survived by his wife, two daughters and son.
3. Fadel Eilabuni (twenty-two years old), single.
4. Melad Sleman (twenty-one years old), single.
5. Zake Eskafe (twenty-six years old), single.
6. Abdala Shofane (sixteen years old), single.
7. Michael Shame, who took refuge in Eilaboun from Haifa. He was survived by his wife and two sons.
8. Raja Nakhle (thirty-seven years old), single.
9. Muhammad Asa'ad, who took refuge in Eilaboun from Hittin, single.
10. Hanna Ashqar (forty years old), survived by his pregnant wife and eight sons.
11. Naa'im Zreiq (thirty-nine years old), survived by his pregnant wife and five sons.
12. Jeryes Hayek (twenty-four years old), survived by his wife and daughter.
13. Foad Zreiq (twenty-five years old), survived by his wife and daughter.
14. Sema'an Shofane, his son was one of the martyrs too (see above Abdalla Shofany[17]).

The UNTSO report corroborated the killing of thirteen men: "Thirteen men were killed; five bodies in a mausoleum grave were viewed by Captain Zeuty and Major Compoeasso, and had undoubtedly been shot. ... Homes viewed showed evidence of having been plundered; pious images were broken and destroyed" (UNTSO Report).[18][[10.3]]

Information from all the residents of Eilaboun who were interviewed confirmed that the village was looted and left almost empty. Beside the priests, a few children and very old people who could not go to the churches, there was no one left in the village. The remaining villagers woke up to the aftermath to find their loved ones killed in four locations, and had to bury them in a temporary mausoleum.

THE THREE-DAY MARCH TO LEBANON

The residents of Eilaboun started walking in front of the armoured vehicles towards Maghar. When they were about 2km away from Eilaboun, the soldiers shot at them, wounding the boy Tawfiq Ashqar. When they reached Maghar, the soldiers did not allow them to drink, eat or go back to Eilaboun, but forced them to walk farther to the north. When they left Maghar, an old man screamed "People, Eilaboun died!", and the women started to cry.

According to Salem Zreiq,

> The people got tired, and wanted to rest, we sat to take a rest, the minute we sat, they [Israeli soldiers] started shooting at us from a military point that was built by the British in the World War II in case Germany reached there. They started to shoot at us from it, and wounded Tawfiq Hanna Ibrahim, they hit him in the arm.[19]

In the afternoon, the soldiers ordered them to stop for a rest. When they arrived near the village of Kafr 'Inan (about 12km away from Eilaboun), they sat down under a big oak tree.

Kafr 'Inan (population, 418 people) was a Palestinian village that was cleansed and destroyed by the Israelis on 30 October 1948.[20] In my interview with Mr Shqeer, a former resident of Kafr 'Inan, he told me a moving story: "The Israeli soldiers shot my brother Suleiman Shqeer, and wanted to shoot me as well, when my mother jumped and hugged me and told the soldier, 'you took one, leave him to me, and they let me be'". The Israeli soldiers took another seven men and executed them near the village.

The eight martyrs of Kafr 'Inan were: four from the same Shqeer family (Suleiman, Hassan, Fawaz and Gamil), Eisa Kayed, Suad Asa'ad, Abdel Qader Saffouri and Mehyel-Deen Taha.[21]

The people of Eilaboun did not have anything to eat or drink the whole day, so they asked the soldiers for some food. The soldiers gave them some food, but they barely started to eat when a military vehicle came and started shooting at them, thinking they were attacking the soldiers. Sema'an Shofany was killed and some others were wounded. They ran for their lives, together with the people of Kafr 'Inan, up the mountain towards the village of al-Farradiyya. The village of al-Farradiyya (population 777) was also cleansed and destroyed by the Israelis on 31 October 1948.[22]

According to the UNTSO report,

Shortly before sunset, the people of Eilaboun and Kafr 'Inan reached Farradiyya tired, hungry and thirsty. The children slept without having any food. The soldiers gathered the people of Eilaboun and of Kafr 'Inan in a square near the mosque of Farradiyya. In the evening the Israeli soldiers threatened the people of Eilaboun that if they did not pay 100 Palestinian pounds [a lot of money back then], the Israeli soldiers would kill some of the young men of Eilaboun, so the people gathered the money, most of it from one man called Ibrahin Hanna, and paid the soldiers, but the soldiers were not satisfied, they searched the people one-by-one, took their jewellery, whatever money they had, and anything else of value they could find. The villagers stayed the night at the mosque, it was cold and they did not have anything to cover their bodies with.

The soldiers executed men from al-Farradiyya; the number was not known but the people of Eilaboun said they killed a lot of men.[23]

While we were in the square, they told us "people of Farradiyya surrendered". They gathered the young men that gave up their weapons, there is no resistance and no fear, in God's will we will go home. Shooting started, we asked what is wrong, and they said "They killed young men from Farradiyya". They shot young men from Farradiyya after they surrendered and dropped their weapons and the Mukhtar called them from the mountains ... they killed them. (Salem Zreiq)

"Oh God, how many people they killed in Farradiyya."[24]

According to the UNTSO report:

> In the morning the soldiers marched the people of Eilaboun, Kafr 'Inan and Farradiyya to the village square. On the way to the square one soldier spoke with Fadil Eilabuni, a man from Eilaboun, as if he knew him, and then shot him and pushed him down the edge of the road, about 2 metres high. Fadil Eilabuni miraculously survived and went to Lebanon where he spent the rest of his life.

The report adds:

> In the square they separated the men from the women, and took the men to the camp as prisoners of war (POW), and forced the women, children and the old to walk towards the north, a march through the very steep upper Galilee mountains. The soldier shot at them again, and wounded some of them, and they ran scared. Two women left their babies, being exhausted and without food for two days, they could not carry them anymore, one of the babies was retrieved by an old man, the other just disappeared and could never be found.[25]

Here are the voices of some of the Eilabuni villagers:

> "When we climbed this mountain, who can climb mount Eljarmaq (Mirun)? The people reached the top almost dead." (Anise Zreiq)

> "It is good that we are still sane. The agony! Carrying two children and running through Faradiya's slopes, while they were shooting at us." (Milya Zreiq)

> "The march was not easy from Eilaboun to Lebanon through the mountains. We were running while they were shooting at us. We did not walk slowly." (Anise Zreiq)

In the late afternoon the people of Eilaboun reached the village of Mirun (about 24km away from Eilaboun), and rested in the olive grove near it.

Mirun (also spelled Mairun, had a population of 336 people) was a Palestinian village that was cleansed and destroyed by the Israelis at the end of October 1948.[26]

The UN Truce Supervision Observers (UNTSO) Reports:

On October 31 1948, Captain Zeuty, Safad observer, met near Meiroun (1918-2651) women and children who had been expelled from Eilaboun. These poor people told that they had been pushed out of their Village and pushed towards a frontier. No men were left with them: Some had been shot and others kidnapped.[27]

As most of those interviewed attested, the people of Eilaboun were very hungry, they asked the soldiers to be allowed into the abandoned Mirun to look for something to eat. After an hour they came back with some flour and some dried figs. The women prepared some bread to feed the children. During the night it was very cold and they slept in the open without any cover. At midnight the soldiers loaded the people onto trucks and drove them to the Lebanese border. The trucks were crowded, and the ride was rough because of the winding mountain roads. It was so dark that mothers were separated from their children. The atmosphere was of fear and uncertainty: there was the sound of mothers calling for their children, and children crying for their mothers. It was still dark when the soldiers dropped them near the border, and ordered them to walk a narrow and rough gorge, by sunset they noticed that the soldiers were nowhere near them, and they understood they were no longer on Palestinian soil.

They reached a pond near the Lebanese village Rmaych; they were very thirsty, everybody jumped into the pond to drink. In Rmaych men who had fled Eilaboun before its fall informed the villagers that the twelve men chosen by the soldiers in Eilaboun had been executed. They did not stop in Rmaych but continued to Ain Ebel, about 6km away, and there they stayed in the church of Ain Ebel. They stayed in Ain Ebel for three days, and during that time the children had to beg for money and food because of their hunger – a scar carried by many until this day.

Most of the people of Eilaboun were taken to the refugee camp Miyah w Miyah near Sidon, but some who had family members already in Lebanon had a better luck, and went to live with them in slightly better conditions.

IN THE PROCESS OF BECOMING REFUGEES

The people of Eilaboun were scattered across Lebanon from Miyah w Miyah in the south of Lebanon to Batroun in the north of Lebanon.

In the refugee camp Miyah w Miyah, several interviewees attested that "each two families took a tent; they did not have any mattresses or blankets. It was a harsh situation, they had no food, they had nothing". The food was distributed twice a day; each family sent one person to collect it.

In the Batroun, the Zreiq clan (more than fifty people) had to live in one house with five rooms, they did not have anything, no money, and they did not have enough food. My father Salem Zreiq had the following to say:

> We wanted to survive in Batroun, we could not wait for the aid to come, we started to steal, and we went to the farms we stole tomatoes, eggplants, etc. The owner came and told us we are steeling, we said "We are not thieves, we are people that own land and are respected, but we want to survive, we don't want to die of hunger".[28]

As my father relayed, "the people of Eilaboun lost their village, homes, belongings, loved ones and their pride as well".

THE UN TRUCE SUPERVISION OBSERVERS' INVESTIGATION

The following are some extracts from the UN (UNTSO) report, providing an insight into their findings after investigating the events:

> On their own side, the UN Observers in Tiberias led an investigation of Meirun (12-265) on 31 October 1948; Maghar on 5 November 1948; and Eilaboun on 7 November 1948. A special investigation was conducted on 12 November 1948 from 1100 hrs till 1400 hrs, by Lt Col. Sore – Ass't to B-3, Capt. Ratard (French Army) of the Tiberias UN, Observers' Group, accompanied by the Israeli Army Liaison Officer Major Spector.

Their findings: "Thirteen men were killed; five bodies in a mausoleum grave were viewed by Captain Zeuty and Major Compoeasso and had undoubtedly been shot. Twenty men of military age were taken as prisoners of war. Homes viewed and showed evidence of having been plundered, pious images were broken and destroyed." The Report added:

It was not possible to interrogate a Jewish witness about the matter: The troops responsible for those atrocities have left the sector. Those actually in the place know nothing about it [sic]. The extrusion itself was certified by Captain Zeuty, Safad observer who saw in Mairun the women and children expelled from Eilaboun. The evidence from the Catholic curate was given in presence of the Jewish liaison officer. His sincerity cannot be suspected. Having seen how the Jews behaved in upper Galilee, I fear that this curate would be submitted to bad treatments as retaliation.

The Report concluded: "There is no doubt in this observer's mind that the Jews committed murder and plunder in the case".[29]

THE MEN IN THE PRISONER OF WAR CAMPS

The following testimonies were relayed by Farid Zreiq, Yousef Slayyeh and Slim Hanna:

> The men the Israeli militia chose in Farradiyya on 31 October 1948 were taken to Maghar, to a "gathering" place, where they gathered men from many villages. In the night they transported them to Nahlal by buses and gathered them near the police station. The men stayed in Nahlal for forty-eight hours, without any food, and very little water. They had to sleep on a pebble ground, full of insects…
>
> From there, the Israeli soldiers started transferring them to the POW camps. They gathered the men in Atlit near Haifa, and placed them in tents. The ground was full of thorns, but they had to sleep on it. They gave each man a blanket to use as mattress and cover. The Israelis kept the captive men there for one month, before starting distributing the men to other POW camps. The Israelis sorted out the old men and the ill and sent them to Jordan. In the POW camps they tried to tempt the young men with money to leave to Jordan, but the latter refused their offers … The conditions in the POW camps was even worse than before, the men were made to do forced labour.[30]

The following are some testimonies on the conditions for the men in the POW camps:

"Life was terrible on all levels; in terms of food, the way they treated us ... everything." (Yousef Slayyeh)

"It was a very horrible situation, very painful, we did not know anything about the fate of our children, siblings, family and our village." (Salim Ashqar).

"A guy from Farradiyya called some of his friends to bring him food; the guard on the posts shot him and killed him." (Salim Ashqar)

The testimony of Yousef Slayyeh was particularly poignant: "One night a guy went out of his tent, he wanted to pee, a guard thought he wants to run away, he shot at him and the bullet hit another guy sleeping in the tent near ours."

Slayyeh continued:

Every day they used to force us out, in the cold, in the rain, to count us. They grouped us in fours, but not while we were standing. They forced us to squat on the ground, to count us, and each time they made a mistake, they started all over again. The work we were forced to do in the beginning was very harsh. I am sure the work they forced other people to do (forced labour) was much easier than that we had to do. I was a kid (fifteen years old), they took us to warehouses where they stored grains, like beans, lentils and similar produce. Each bag weighed about 100kg. We had to carry the bags from the warehouses to the trucks.

THE RETURN

Return is the dream of all Palestinian refugees, but for the people of Eilaboun it became a reality. This reality was materialized partly through their determination, partly through luck, but mostly because of the exposure of the Israeli atrocities in the village, revealed by Captain Zeuty after the UNSTO report. The villagers met with Captain Zeuty near Mirun, and the latter agreed to put pressure on the Israelis to let them go back, and the efforts of the priests who had stayed in Eilaboun also facilitated the process. However, the story of their return was anything but a smooth one.

Here are some testimonies of the villagers of Eilaboun about their return:

My wife and children had their own story, they [the Israelis] caught them while returning [to Eilaboun], they took them to Akka and after that sent them to Marj Ibn 'Amer (Jezreel Valley) on 15 of March, it was very cold. They [the Israelis] left them [his wife and sons] without any cover, without anything. They took their [his wife and sons'] clothes. She [the wife] had with her five little children … she was alone. Those stories … one can never forget. (Farid Zreiq)

Farid Zreik continues:

The Israelis claimed to allow the people of Eilaboun back, but in reality they did not allow them back, they had to come back secretly at night. Those who were unlucky and were caught were sent to Jenin. Those who stayed, the [Israeli] government allowed to go back. This is not the case; they turned a blind eye, nothing written. Those they caught coming back, the Israelis dropped near Jenin, they did not allow them to go back. My wife and kids are an example for that, they caught them and dropped them near Jenin.

Anise Zreiq corroborated Farid Zreiq's experience saying: "People were terrified when they returned. When we crossed the road between Rmaych and Israel, people used to freeze. We sat like this [freezing without any movement] until we saw the way was clear and ran to the other side, and when they saw us they shot at us" (Anise Zreiq).

Malakeh Eid recounts: "On Christmas Eve while the bells tolled we were in the wilderness … I will never forget this until I die".

AFTER THE RETURN

The villagers of Eilaboun, as recounted above, returned to a looted village. They had no food, no work, they had nothing. While men were still in the POW camps for the first six months after the return, many women had to work hard to provide for their families. It is important also to remember that Eilaboun villagers, like all Palestinians of the forty-eight territories have lived under the military rule that lasted until 8 November 1966, and they needed a permit to leave the village.

Here are some testimonies of Eilabouni villagers' situation after their return to their village:

We returned to our homes. We found nothing, no cows, no goats, no sheep, no mattresses or blankets, no plants … nothing. We wanted to eat and drink, we started to go to the nearby villages, Arraba, Deir Hanna, Sakhnin, and beg for food. (Mere'i Srour)

After the return life was very difficult, no one was able to work, everyone had to have a permit to leave the village. We did not have food. During the night, people were calling each other to go to work in Tiberias. When they were caught, they would be returned, because they had no permits. People wanted to live, to eat, we had nothing. Homes were empty, work was not allowed, you needed a permit to go to Tiberias to work, one needed a permit to go anywhere, and there was no food. (Anise Zreiq)

Milya Zreiq said the same: "After we returned, it was hard, they limited our travel, when children were ill and screamed and cried there was no doctor. It took more than two months until they allowed us to go to Nazareth to treat the children."

Rayah Zreiq had the following to say: "I went to Hittin's olive grove walking, and worked all day for one lira [the Israeli currency back then], to feed my siblings. A year after that I went to the olive groves in Maghar, and worked all day for only one and a half lira, to feed my siblings."

THE BEHEADED SOLDIERS

The Arab Liberation Army soldiers beheaded two Israeli soldiers who were killed in battle, and paraded the heads in Eilaboun, an act that was not accepted by the people of Eilaboun. All of those interviewed emphasized they had nothing to do with this act. They all stressed that the people of Eilaboun did not like what the soldiers did. The priest of Eilaboun protested and stopped the parade.

According to the UNTSO Report, "Father Markus states that one month before the Jews invaded Eilaboun, two Jewish soldiers had been killed by Kawji Fawji [Fawzi Kawakji] troops and their bodies had been beheaded. The heads had been delivered back for burial to the Jews". Still, the Israeli soldiers executed thirteen men, and expelled the people of Eilaboun to Lebanon, using the beheading of the two soldiers and the parade with the heads as an excuse.

According to the UNTSO Report, part of these deeds (the Israeli massacre in Eilaboun) might be accounted for by:

- The parading (by the ALA troops) of the heads of the two Jewish soldiers.
- The resistance put up (by the ALA troops) at Eilaboun and the excitement of Jewish troops.
- Immediate security concerns.
- They cannot be justified on a legal plane. (UNTSO Report)

The people of Eilaboun were punished because the ALA troops resisted strongly, beheaded two Israeli soldiers and paraded the heads in Eilaboun. In other words, they were punished for the deeds of ALA soldiers.

What is even more distressing is the fact that the Israeli soldiers (Battalion 103) used the same excuse to commit another massacre in the land of Arab El-Mawasi (a semi-nomad tribe near Eilaboun), where the Israeli soldiers executed fourteen men and boys on 1 and 2 November 1948:

1. Abd-Alah Ersheed (sixteen years old)
2. Saleh Alramli (thirteen years old)
3. Ateya Ersheed
4. Meqbel Ersheed
5. Meejel Ersheed
6. Saeed Qasem
7. Asaad Qasem
8. Bayer Taha
9. Mohamad Taha
10. Hseen Ahmad
11. Hasan Alwahsh
12. Mohammad Alander
13. Ahmad Alnader
14. Nayef Aleesa

The Israeli soldiers even reported and documented their deeds in Arab El-Mawasi, as the Israel Defence Forces archive document shows:

Subject: Report of patrolling the Arab El-Mawasi area: "Skeleton of the two missing in action soldiers in a previous operation in this area. Their identification was established by their uniforms found near them. They are beheaded. ... Fourteen men were executed. The rest were sent to POW camps".[31]

CONCLUSION

The people of Eilaboun are still traumatized from the events of the Nakba. Today, even after fifty-eight years, the people cry whenever they mention their loved ones who were killed then. They could not understand why the Israelis did that to them, and all the interviewees asked this same question: "Why us, when we did not do anything and were peaceful and unarmed?" They could not understand and could not accept what had happened to them. All interviewees spoke about the massacre in Eilaboun, even those who were already in Lebanon at the time. This was undoubtedly the biggest trauma that inflicted the village since 1948. What makes the trauma so deep, I found, is the fact that the Eilabounis could not then, or now, comprehend why the Israelis did this, despite the excuse given to them by the Israelis. Their trauma has been exacerbated by their witnessing and knowing about the killing of fourteen men from Arab El-Mawasi by the Israelis. All these experiences made it impossible for them to understand, let alone accept.

The hardships faced by the Eilabounis during their expulsion and march to Lebanon was evident in the words, the facial expressions and the body language of the interviewees. The women walking the difficult terrain of the Upper Galilee Mountains, without their husbands, carrying their children, while the Israeli soldiers shot at them, was particularly traumatic. Milya Zreiq's statement: "It is good that we are still sane ... The agony! carrying two children, and running the Faradiya's slope, while they [the Israelis] were shooting at us", expresses it all.

The humiliation they faced in the process of becoming refugees was no less traumatic. In addition to the separation of the women and children from their husbands/fathers and not knowing about their fate, some of the Eilabuni refugees witnessed men being killed, and others dragged off to the POW camp. Those who survived and were able to return found their village looted, emptied, except for the walls, windows and doors, although many were broken. As stated in the UNTSO Report, "Homes viewed showed evidence of having been plundered; pious images were broken and destroyed".

The POW camps left their marks on the men who experienced them. The villagers spoke of the harsh conditions of forced labour and the maltreatment they faced, which was also documented in the UNTSO Report as follows: "The

Arab men were held at Nahlal for two days without food or shelter. There were reported cases of maltreatment of Arabs by Jewish guards at Nahlal."

All of the above, I believe, is not unique to Eilaboun; this is rather the story of most of the Palestinian villages that were cleansed by the Israelis. What is possibly unique to Eilaboun is the return, albeit to an emptied village. Their return was made possible largely by their amazing will to return, combined with the luck of meeting the UNTSO observer near Mirun, which led to the UNTSO investigation.

Before I conclude, I would like to say that the claim that the Israelis treat Palestinian Christian differently (better) than Muslim Palestinians is a myth. This myth was exposed in Eilaboun as well as in various other Palestinian villages such as Iqrit and Kufur Bir'im. And from my own experience as a Palestinian Christian, I admit, I was never treated differently from any Muslim Palestinian. If anything, I proudly say that my village, Eilaboun, defies Israeli attempts at dividing Palestinians on a religious basis. The two Muslim martyrs of Eilaboun are buried in the Zreiq family mausoleum grave along with my uncle, Badee Zreiq (one of the martyrs), my mother, my father and other relatives of mine. This to me symbolizes the unity of Palestinians in victimhood and defiance.

NOTES

1   All interviews were conducted in May 2006 and took place in Eilaboun and Nazareth.
2   The information on Plan Dalet is based on the interview I conducted with Ilan Pappe during the month of research. Here is what Ilan Pappe told me about Plan Dalet, the policies and practices used by the Israelis in displacing the Palestinians during the Nakba: "The Jewish leadership, actually the High Command of the Jewish society, what they called the Matkal, later to be known as the High Command of the Army. The Matkal met in Tel-Aviv and decided on the means of implementing Plan Dalet. The Plan divided the future state of Israel into twelve zones; created twelve brigades and each brigade was supposed to cleanse all the area from the Palestinian villages and towns in it. And the plan says very clearly how to do it: You encircle the village or neighbourhood, you occupy it, you separate the men which they [Israelis] defined as anyone above the age of ten, you separate the men from the women and the children, you expel the women and the children and you take the men that you think have a military potential and send them to the POW camps, and you execute who are suspicious of being involved before in actions against the Jews. This was a standard operational command."
3   IDF Archive 49/715, File 3.

4   The United Nations Truce Supervision Observers conducted an investigation on the events in Eilaboun and published its report on the same. See UN Archive 13/3.1 box 11, "Atrocities, September–November".

5   Ibid.

6   Interview with Nimer Zreiq and Farid Zreiq.

7   Interview with Samira Zreiq, Meree Srur and Nimr Zreiq.

8   Most interviews attested to this, especially Butros Matta, Farid Zreiq and Nimr Zreiq.

9   UN Archive 13/3.1 box 11,"Atrocities, September–November".

10 Interviews with Miriam Eid, Farid Zreiq, Yousef Hayek and Diab Eilabuni.

11 UN Archive 13/3.1 box 11, "Atrocities, September–November".

12 Several interviewees, including Salem Zreiq, Diab Eilabuni and Butros Matta.

13 Interview with Salem Zreiq, corroborated by most others.

14 Interviews with Samira Zreiq, Salem Zreiq, Anise Zreiq and Rayaa Zreiq

15 Interviews with Butros Matta and Farid Zreiq.

16 Interview with Butros Matta.

17 This information was corroborated by all interviewees from Eilaboun.

18 UNTSO Report, UN Archive 13/3.1 box 11, "Atrocities, September–November".

19 Interview with Salem Zreiq.

20 For more information on Kafr Inan, see Palestineremembered @ http://www.palestineremembered.com/Acre/Kafr-'Inan/.

21 Mr Shqeer.

22 For more information on the village of al-Farradiyya see, http://www.palestineremembered.com/Safad/al-Farradiyya/.

23 Interviews with Milia Zreiq, Miriam Eid, Asaad Zreiq, Salem Zreiq and Rayan Zreiq.

24 Interview with Malakeh Eid.

25 See UN Archive 13/3.1 box 11, "Atrocities, September–November".

26 See http://www.palestineremembered.com/Safad/Mirun/.

27 UNTSO, UN Archive 13/3.1 box 11, "Atrocities, September–November".

28 Interview with Salem Zreiq.

29 UN Archive 13/3.1 box 11, "Atrocities, September–November".

30 Interviews with Farid Zreiq, Yousef Slayyeh and Slim Hanna.

31 IDF Archive, 51/957, file 1683, Battalion 103, company C; See also, IDF Archive 5943/49/114, 13 April 1938.

11

"This is your father's land": Palestinian Bedouin women encounter the Nakba in the Naqab

SAFA ABU-RABI'A

We were expelled, meaning we were not allowed to enter our lands. It is forbidden: we used to stand on the fences or on the mountain and we explain to our children: "we used to live here; there was the water well …" it's important for me that my daughters will know how our lives used to be. (Abu-Bader)

Abu Bader's words, narrating her tribe's dispossession of their historical lands in 1948, describe the same reality of Bedouin villages in the Naqab after almost seventy years, where Bedouin are still being expelled from their villages by force. Abu Bader's voice reflects the cry of Yaaʻqob Abualkeaan's mother; he was killed by Israeli police in January 2017, when they were demolishing his home. These female voices narrate the same story: forced expulsion from their lands, denying their historical attachment to the place and presenting them as invaders that need to be re-organized within the Israeli state. Both these voices represent the continuing Nakba in the Naqab, that began in 1948 and continues to affect the Naqab intensively. But it also represents the strength of these women in resisting and facing their forced dispossession, by reviving their attachment to their lands and passing it to their children, as a dominant factor in defining their territorial identity.

As I was writing this chapter, the Palestinian Bedouin village Umm Al-Hiran in the east Naqab was being demolished and its inhabitants were being expelled.

On this same land, Khiran, a new Jewish settlement, was about to be established. Its residents are religious Israeli-Jews, motivated by the ideology that God gave the land of Israel to the Jews. Demolishing homes, confiscating land, expelling Palestinians from their villages and replacing them with Israeli settlements did not end with the 1948 war; nor is it happening only in the West Bank. These practices of displacing Palestinians from their land, physically and consciously, are happening here and now, in the Israel of 2017, and most intensively in the Naqab, among Bedouin Arabs, where the Nakba literally did not end.

The Bedouin in the Naqab suffer from ongoing displacement. Umm El-Hiran is only one of forty-five Bedouin villages in the Naqab, some of which pre-date the 1948 war. Half of these villages are not recognized, regardless of their age, and are under persistent threat of demolition and their inhabitants' eviction.

I would like to present voices that are silenced in both the national Palestinian and Zionist discourse. These are the voices of Naqab Bedouin women from the 1948 generation and their daughters (two generations of the Nakba) and their resistance to the ongoing displacement that Bedouin society has suffered for the last seventy years. My claim is that in these oral and spatial practices, implemented for years by these women, they establish a territorial identity among their children. These practices include narrating their historical experiences in their lands, visiting their historical lands, naming their villages with historical names and continuing a resistance discourse during their exclusion from the space. I will argue that through these strategies, these women establish their sense of belonging to the place, physically and consciously, and educate their children to be owners of the land. These voices reflect how women are re-telling Naqab history and reclaiming their past. This study attempts to assess the shaping of their children's territorial identity.

My research is based on in-depth interviews with Bedouin women as part of my PhD thesis (Aburabia 2013). These women live in recognized and unrecognized villages.[1] They have experienced both life on their lands and being uprooted from it and are able to testify first-hand. The informants' core is a group of the 1948 generation, joined by their daughters and other women from the tribe during the interviews. They tell each other the historical narrative, and this participation reflects how their tribal narrative is shaped and constructed collectively according to their tribal structure.

My methodology is ethnography based on extensive fieldwork in the Naqab (2005–2009). I also conducted observations, visiting women's houses, meeting them on social occasions, to collect data through informal conversations with them and their families.

My methodology is based on a qualitative research paradigm called "grounded theory". This approach uses fieldwork as the main resource to shape theory, and uses interviews to achieve new theoretical insights from the bottom up (Shaked 2003; Spector-Marzel 2010). These methodologies allow these voices to be exposed and documented as oral history, by analysing how these women describe these events as influencing their lives. This methodology relies on a post-colonial feminist approach (Mohanty 1991, 2002; Narayan 2000; Vickers and Dhruvarajan 2003; Spelman 1988) that allows researchers to document Arab women's lives in a way that matches their reality more closely. Particularly when working with illiterate women, these narratives challenge the representation of their lives from orientalist and outsider Westernized perspectives, resisting how knowledge is constructed on behalf of Third World women (and Arab and Muslim women in particular), strengthening the idea of their inferiority. This discourse claims that knowledge about Third World women has been constructed as monolithic and unified, relying on universal and ethnocentric views based on clear power relations between the West and its "Other/s".

These women are thus presented as oppressed, lacking in ability, veiled, isolated, controlled by patriarchy, tradition and religion, with no respect to their differences in status, ethnicity or geographical location. This ethnocentric orientalist approach focuses on "saving" such women, using issues like circumcision and honour killings as the main representations of these women (Abdo 1997; Mohanty 2002; Kandiyoti 1996; Johnson-Odim 1991; Cooke 2001). Using post-colonial feminist methodologies allows me to glance into the private space of Bedouin women and expose their social dynamics.

ISRAELI STATE DISPLACEMENT MECHANISMS: BEDOUIN DISPLACEMENT

I will first introduce the Israeli state displacement mechanisms used to remove Bedouin in the Naqab as part of an intensive process of Judaizing the space. These express the clear agenda of the state to concentrate the Bedouin in fewer spaces and control their movement, meanwhile establishing new Jewish settlements on these same lands. These processes dispose Bedouin on two levels:

physical removal from their lands by legal means, and a disconnection of consciousness, portraying them as nomads with no meaningful link to land, and in need of civilization.

The second part relates to Bedouin women from the 1948 generation and their daughters, showing how they establish a sense of place by strengthening their links to their historical lands and passing these on to their children via oral and spatial practices. These voices challenge the Zionist historical discourse in Israel that excludes Bedouin from the Naqab space, as well as the image of Bedouin women in the academic and public space. This chapter seeks to reveal the dynamic inter-generational lives of Bedouin women, who are active within their tribal spaces to resist their expulsion from their lands, by strengthening their direct and continuous links to them. I aim to stress their significant unique activism as historical agents, within private spaces and among their family members, as an important part of the struggle over the space.

I will begin by describing the main mechanisms used to exclude and dispossess Bedouin from and of the Naqab space; I will also discuss historical discourse, legal, planning and academic practices.

The 1948 war played a significant role in reshaping geographical and tribal reality in the Naqab space. This is expressed in the reduced number of Bedouin and drastic changes in social structure. Before 1948, Bedouin were almost exclusive residents of the Naqab, numbering 90,000–100,000 people from ninety-six tribes. After 1948 and the establishment of the state of Israel, most of them were expelled or escaped to Jordan, Gaza, Sinai and the West Bank. The Naqab population dropped to 11,000 people from seventeen tribes, most of them belonging to the Al-Tayaha tribes (Ashkenazi 1957; Abu-Ras 2006; Al-Aref 1933; Ben-David 1972, 1986; Morris 1997; Falah 1989).

One of the main mechanisms used to control Bedouin in the Naqab (as implemented in all Palestinian societies in Israel after the 1948 Nakba, was military rule, from 1948 until 1966. Bedouin were concentrated within fixed borders in a specific geographic space called "the siege area" located between Arad, Bir Alsabe' (Beer Sheva) and Yeruham. The remainder of the tribes left in Israel were removed by force to this area (Yiftachel 1999). Their mobility was limited to this area; they were disconnected from residual Palestinian populations left in Israel; and, above all, they were prevented from returning to their lands. As land is a fundamental component in defining social structure (due to the fact that land ownership is a precious source of power within

Bedouin society), this had a huge effect on the inner political and social structure of the community.

Alongside the military regime, the state implemented legal and planning means to dispossess Bedouin. The legal system in Israel is active in constructing the Zionist project as a moral narrative that aims to salvage the land from nomadic, un-civilized Bedouin, presented as primitives who do not belong to any given space. This process has made Bedouin invisible in the eyes of the law (Yiftachel 1999; Fenster 1991; Shamir 1996). Bedouin were presented as opposing the law, especially when their ownership of land was based on traditional oral legislation passed from one generation to the other (implemented by these tribes for years). In contrast, the Israeli legal arguments are based on specific documented dates and times, operating on the basis of systematic expropriation of land in the Naqab. In addition, the state has adopted old laws and regulations, among them the Ottoman *mowat* law (1858) and the Dead Lands Ordinance (1921). This means that all the lands of Bedouin Arabs in the Naqab are now classified as uncultivated, and therefore pass into state ownership (Yiftachel 1999). Similarly, the 1953 Land Acquisition Law confiscated a great deal of land, regardless of the possession of ownership documents.

Another mechanism used to weaken the relationship of the Arab Bedouin with their lands is urbanization, namely the establishment of seven Bedouin towns in the Naqab: Tal Al-Sabea, Rahat, Kuseife, Arara, Segev Shalom, Hura and Laqia. The purpose was to concentrate the most Bedouin in the smallest space, thus vacating their lands for the construction of new Jewish settlements. These towns were established without proper design, relying on Bedouin agricultural culture. Today, these towns are in great social distress, and suffer from poverty, unemployment, crime, social tensions and lack of economic infrastructure. Approximately 50% of the Bedouin Arab population lives in these towns, and others continue to live as they did before the establishment of the state, still waiting for planning regularization. These communities are not recognized by the state of Israel and so lack economic and social infrastructure. Their inhabitants are under constant pressure, including the destruction of their homes and spraying of their crops to force them to leave their land (Nathanson et al. 1999; Lithwick 2002; Almi 2003; HRA 2004). For years, government programmes have been formulated to re-settle the Naqab (Negev) Bedouin.[2] To limit the movement of Arab Bedouin in the region and accelerate their concentration in the permanent settlements, special bodies were established, including the

Bedouin Administration, "Green Patrol", the National Unit of Building Inspection at the Ministry of the Interior and a police unit (*Rotem*) whose function is to focus on crime among the Arab Bedouin in the Naqab (Yiftachel 1999; Svirski and Hason 2005).

At the same time, academic research has also shaped the image of the Arab Bedouin in the Naqab as lacking any affinity to land, constructing them under two orientalist categories of knowledge: Nomadism (Epstein 1933; Ashkenazi 1957; Ben-David 1986; Bar-Zvi and Ben-David 1978; Marx 1956, 1967, 1974); and Modernism (Bar 1980, 1985; Dinero 1997; Jakubowska 1992; Soen and Shmueli 1987; Meir 1997). These categories portray them as ahistorical, nomadic and primitive: a society that needs to be civilized by Israelis, who will "save" them from their own culture (Aburabia 2014).

Research analysis suggests that in this period the Bedouin were excluded from historical discourse in general, and discourse about the Nakba in particular. From 1980 onwards, academics (especially from Israeli-Palestinian and Jewish backgrounds) began developing a new critical discourse,[3] arguing that government policy has deepened the plight of Arab Bedouin by misidentifying their social and cultural needs, and that evictions and relocation of Bedouin relates to the Zionist agenda to Judaize the Naqab. It is clear that academic research is another institutionalized mechanism (along with planning and legislation) used to establish their dispossession. This physical and cognitive exclusion structures their image as invaders that harm the space in legal, planning (spatial organization) and ethical ways.

Shining light onto Bedouin women's voices from the 1948 generation and their daughters challenges this discourse by stressing their voices as they struggle for their historical link to their lands, re-claiming their affinity to the place and by that resist their exclusion from it. These voices express their historical experiences and especially their links with place, which are being silenced and ignored in academic research and public discourse (Aburabia 2005, 2013).

COLONIAL AND COUNTER-COLONIAL INDIGENOUS DISCOURSES ON THE NAQAB: BEDOUIN WOMEN'S VOICES

Bedouin Arab identity is based on land, agricultural economics and cultural practices stemming from tribal territory. This represents their independence and sovereignty, and shapes their collective identity (Aburabia 2005; Yiftachel 2003). Thus, following the words of Hall (1996), who claims that identities arise from the story of the self, combining the personal world within the collective space, respect for cultural forms and social practices (Holland et al. 1998), land has profound implications for Bedouin identity. Their sense of identity is based on collective tribal affiliation, associated with established tribal land. Consequently, land is a key component that defines gender identity and status for Bedouin Arab women and gender narrative as it is reflected in the Naqab. This identity is being rebuilt through spatial practices, revitalizing the memory of the past and the connection to land. These spatial practices, including the narration of the past, visits to their historic lands and marking the place, are part of building a sense of place among them and their children, strengthening their links with the land, and the revival of consciousness and the physical return, while constructing a sense of dislocation and emotional alienation from where they live at present (Aburabia 2013). These visits usually take place during the spring, around the time of their expulsion from their land. They describe how and where they used to live, and how and where they used to cultivate the land.

Sense of place among Bedouin women in the Naqab: return visits to the ancestral lands

The idea of "return" (*Al Awdah*) in a Palestinian context has been extensively studied and characterizes Palestinian identity. It embodies an aspiration to return to the lives, villages, neighbourhoods, houses and orchards from which they were uprooted (Kimmerling and Migdal 1993). This expresses the longing of the peasant to return to his land, honour, home and identity (Robenshtein 1990). Returning to the place stands for integrity, continuity and eternity (Issa 1997), and is fed by return visits. As my studies show (Aburabia 2005, 2013), "return" is a significant component in the identity of the second generation, particularly in view of ongoing dispossessions. The next section will discuss a variety of ways in which the idea of "return" strengthens their links with their land. These include visiting their lands, narrating their lives, and marking the remains of the past there.

Spatial practices include substantive procedures and symbolize a sense of comfort, home, safety and sanctuary, emphasizing the "ancestral land" that women construct (Stewart and Strathern 2003). The link between people and place is defined as a "sense of place", a geographical term indicating the meeting point of our history with a place, socially, culturally and economically

(Young 1986). Through various spatial practices, women feel they are "saving" the physical place through the iteration of detailed memories that illustrate how things were in the past (Slymovics 1998). This is often highly sensory, for example smelling fruit trees and performing physical tasks:

> We explain to them ... that we would sit on our land, here we used to live, here was the field well where we used to bring water, this is the mountain where we used to cut wood, shepherd the herds ... we explain to them how our life had been. We need to inform our children, boys and girls, that this used to be ours. (Abu Bader)

This reflects rooted attachment of Bedouin to their historical lands which they continue to preserve after almost seventy years, by visiting their historical lands, and telling their children about their lives there.

> We visit in the place ... we go there ... and explain to our children: here it used to be the land of that tribe, and here the land of another tribe ... and we used to live here. Here used to be our home, we show them [the place] and we walk their and look for remains. (Abu Amra)

According to Murphy (1995), the interaction between the individual and a landscape includes mapping an ancestral landscape and an emotional connection to it. Memory is directed at the ground, while the patriarchs represent the people who lived there. This view is rebuilt and transmitted through ancestors to future generations. Their emotional identification with the landscape is a bridge between present experiences and the ancestors' experiences. This is illustrated by Alazazmah: "My father said the tree will not give fruit if it is not rooted." Alazazmah makes a symbolic comparison between man and a tree uprooted from the land in which it belongs. Belonging, then, is a sense that contains both past and present experiences, incorporating memories, relationships and future aspirations in relation to the place (Fenster 2004).

> They [the children] ask us: how you used to live here? We explain them about our life in the past in our lands, they feel pain when we visit the land, we tell them: we used to live here, and here is our land. (Al Oqbi)

The concept of the place has been extensively studied in the Palestinian context. This conceptualization is conducted through visiting former homes, encountering traces of the past and commemorating it, convincing their children that these memories belong to them (Fenster 2007; Ben-Ze'ev 2005; Halbwachs 1992; Slymovics 1998). Visits to ancestral lands transfer abstract stories to a concrete space and the use of memories makes Palestine a more concrete entity, familiar to them despite many years of exile (Kanafani in Slymovics 1998: 114).

> We visit at Tal-Arad, we go there for a tour, all the family of Abu Bader go together there, during the holiday ... now they do not allow us to enter the place, the army prevent us from going there ... but we go there, even we are not allow to enter the land, and we show our children where we used to be. (Abu Bader)

Belonging and connection are built on the basis of memory and intimate experience. This belonging is almost "secular", intimate and interpersonal, resulting in daily practice. Daily rituals and rehearsals through which memory is constructed are part of the spatial practices of belonging and a sense of collectivity. Memory is the most explicit expression of the sense of belonging, connecting the events of the past and childhood experiences with the places in which those events occurred (de Certeau 1988). Yi-Fu (1977) argues that experience is a key component in creating a sense of place, and it should be direct, intimate or bridged through symbols. He identifies three types of experience: intimate familiarity with the place; sensory rituals; and conceptual, visual and spatial interpretation. These experiences structure sensations, mediated by smell, touch and taste, enriching the visual space. De Certeau (1988) adds that the act of walking around the place is a way of making sense of a space, organizing and defining it. This is well illustrated by S. [Alhawaslha], stating "every time we visit our land, I walk barefoot on it" as part of her emotional link to the land.

"She tells us all the time": narrating the past

Bedouin women also revive the past through narration, whether during visits to the ancestral land or at family gatherings. Researchers and Palestinian authors argue that the Arabic language has a variety of expressions by which to tell the story of a homeland and describe the scenery, demographics, sociology and ethnography of Palestinian villages that used to exist before 1948 (Fenster 2007; Ben-Ze'ev 2005; Halbwachs 1992; Slymovics 1998). These women's voices speak of loss of land, power and home, dislocation and migration, but are not included in official Palestinian nationalism (Slymovics 1998).

The first thing that women relate in their narrative of the past is how they used to work in the lands: "We used to plough and harvest the land ... and with the camel we used to harvest the land ... we used to do everything in our hands, we used to plough and harvest in our own hands" (Aburabia).

These stories mainly consist of descriptions of relationships with the land (Issa 1997) and a sense of collectivity to be found in such relationships:

> I ploughed the land with my own hands, hands ploughed the soil. I used to walk at each one of the soil lines, every path I ploughed with my hands. We were ploughing together ... I ploughed the soil muck and I went there together with them ... have you seen this bar? I ploughed it with my own hands, and [that] place that [is] next to the olive tree, ploughed by me."
> (S. Alhawaslha)

After describing how they used to work their lands, they would describe the geographical location of where they used to live: "we lived all our lives in AlJa-mama" (Alatawna); "We are from Al-Sharia" (Abu Shareb).

Working the land, ploughing and harvesting it, is their immediate and direct connection to their life on the land, which describe their life in the past, by the direct sense of place in the land. The physical location of the tribal land comes only after that. That is to say, their affinity is directly to the soil itself.

One of the main ways women convey a sense of place is through re-telling their history to children at family gatherings, as pointed out by the daughter of S. Alhawaslha: "she tells us all the time". By that she means how her mother used to narrate her past life during their visits to the land and also at every gathering they used to have: "We used to sit near the fire and talk, and she used to tell us about the past, about her life, what she saw [witnessed] from the war, when we used to be small children" (Al Tehee).

Besides telling their children how they used to live in their lands before 1948, these women's narratives also revolve around how they were expelled from their land during the 1948 war:

"The Jewish came and expelled us, the Arabs, we had lands under our ownership, we had land in our ownership, for us, our homeland (Wattan)". (Abu Queder).

"They came with weapon to us ... And said: leave, you have three days to leave, and warn us like they did with the Arabs from the north (the Galilei) that shot on them, and also on us, and got us out by force, by killing, and threatened us also, and told us: you have three days to leave, and people begun to leave." (Al Oqbi)

"After Beer Al Sabe' was broken [their words for defeated], we went out from the land and the Jewish came in (into our lands). (Abu Amra)

"...so we escape their, we went out and after they took (take control over) Beer Al Sabea', we were afraid they will come and kill us here, we overloaded the camels with our belongings and food for our children and we run away". (Abu Hani)

For them, passing these narratives of the past and their experience from the war on to their children is significant in shaping their way of thinking and especially by challenging and re-questioning the Israeli story of how they came to Palestine: "She tell us so we know what the Jewish used to do to them and how they used to take from the Arabs, she used to inform us and raise our awareness to this kind of things" (Abu Bader).

Another way of strengthening their link to their historical lands is by telling the historical names of the villages to their children as a way of reviving the Bedouin past of the place before it became a Jewish settlement, as the historical name is a symbol of their identity (de Certeau 1988). For example, the Jewish city "Dimona" is referred to as "Damna", the name of the Arab tribal land on which the city was built:

Mother: Now Damna is called Dimona.

Daughter: We see them live in our place, as we were. [...]

Daughter: To this day, my mother calls this place Damna.

Mother: And this is its name! Do you see that well? There was a well; now there are Jews.

"So they know [and] learn": the goals of structuring a sense of place
Bedouin women in the Naqab educate their children on land attachment and territorial identity as a significant factor that defines their link to the place. The practices and language described serve important objectives in constructing a sense of place:

S. Alhawaslha: They need to know how our life was before, to learn.

Daughter: She wants to show us, for example, they have lost land ... and they feel they don't feel good with it. [They] have a hard heart.

Daughter: We need to know, to have knowledge of what happened.

Mother: One day you will remember, you will grow up and no one will be there ... My father saw his father's tree. He was the last one [who] saw it in person.

Baker (1998) adds that the use of narrative was intended to construct a sense of self. Narratives in history rely on a culture that nourishes and moulds them. Thus, as Sayigh (1998, 2007) argues, re-using the memory of Palestine is not only a natural reaction to forced separation, but also a way to pass it on to the children. Thus, the oral history of women has historical significance: it revives the past, and provides insight into how women think and the role of women in the historical process (Gluck 1984; Holland et al. 1998).

They want [us] to know everything ... each had at least two thousand acres to plant ... today only one hectare, only one hectare ... we were expelled near Laqiya [Bedouin village] which means we cannot go into our lands. Forbidden, we are standing on the sidelines, or stand on the mountain and we are explaining to our children: "Here we used to live." ... It is important for you to know how hard people [have suffered], how they strive to reach a drop of water or bread. (Abu Bader)

Educating future generations is one of the main objectives behind narrating history, and is intended to strengthen the intergenerational sense of continuity (Issa 1997). In terms of women's personal testimony, they see their own history as an integral part of the history of the land (Kozma 2003), and both women and men still reconstruct the past for their children. Internal self-images are fed from their historical past, even though they are separated in time and space from their original lands:

> When we enter the land … my mother tells me: "this is the land of your father, and this was our fig" … today when I walk alone I tell my children: "… here, this land was your uncle's, your cousins were living here [and] … tomorrow my daughter will say [to her children], "that was your grandparents'". (Al-Tehee)

Significantly, it appears there is appetite to both tell and hear these stories in the second generation: "We ask her … to tell us about the difficulties in their lives … we would sit together and ask her to tell us about life in the past, what was and what happened to them, and [she] would tell us things" (Al Tehee).

For these women, their children need to realize how their reality has been shaped:

> They need to know and get information from me, how this state has been established, and on whose land … this is what I am trying to let them know. (Al Tehee)

> We tell them everything, I tell them about our life in the past, how the Jewish came and expelled us from our lands, and this land is ours, this is our ownership, ours. (Abu Queder)

They also relate to their previous lives on their historical lands as better than where they live today: "We used to be more happy than now, much more than now, I used to love the past life more" (Alhozayel). "We used to feel better back then…much more comfortable than now" (Abu Bader).

They also pass their disconnection from the place where they are living today onto their children, as opposed to where they used to live, as they do not feel they are their places:

"We came to this land, its Al Azazma's lands [different tribe], and we are living in their lands". (Abu Amra).

"This is not our land and we are not in our lands, we used to live in our land where… it used to be our land" (Abu Queder).

The loss of their lands represents the loss of their values, way of life, social order and meaning: "People forgot their tents, their dignity" (Alhozayel), and "'The Sheikh' was the centre of the world … now each one became a Sheikh himself" (Alhozayel), which means that the removal from their lands meant removal from their traditional lifestyle which used to characterize their lives. This is why land is more than a geographical territory; it means way of life that defines Bedouin social order.

This is why they reject their forced removal from their lands: "This is not our lands; we do not live in our lands" (Abu Queder, originally from Al Shareaa, and removed to Al Zarnouq). "We were expelled and got here, this is Alazazma lands, it's all their land" (Abu Amra). They live on other Bedouin tribal lands, not on their original land, which explains their feelings of exile and the strangeness of where they live these days.

CONCLUSION

The history of the Naqab Bedouin was silenced and excluded from academic and public discourse in Israel. Their exclusion is dual: both from Palestinian discourse, and from the official Zionist historical discourse.

The "her-story" of Bedouin women and gender discourse in the struggle for land was hidden and unheard: it is being narrated within private spaces, separated from men by women who have internalized the idea of themselves as incapable and lacking the social legitimacy to participate in the narrating of history. Their invisibility (both to Israeli academic research and men in Bedouin society) can lead to the misconception that these voices do not exist and that Arab Bedouin history is represented only by men, who are also responsible for transferring it to future generations.

My research explores this historic gap, documenting the social history of Bedouin Arab women through ethnographic work with the 1948 generation and their daughters. In doing so, my research aspires to voice their hidden stories, and to examine the impact of the 1948 war and displacement from their lands in shaping their identity in the shadow of loss. Another goal is to analyse the significance of the historic narratives of the female voice and their influence on the Naqab Bedouin struggle, while examining oral history, gender and what enables this history to survive and pass from generation to generation. My research shows the Bedouin's historical connection to their lands as a key component in their identity, both in the past and at present. This link is expressed through spatial and oral practices such as visiting their lands, narrating the past, passing it on to their children and naming the places in their historical names.

The historical value of documentation of the feminine discourse lies partly in speaking of the significance of soil. Their voices express how land is not merely a physical territory, but rather the identity of a place that reflects their way of life. As part of the wave of critical studies, my research aims to challenge the construction of Bedouin affinity to place by questioning the grand narratives and asking epistemological questions about how knowledge is produced. It also illustrates how power relations produce and oppress historical discourses; how knowledge discourses and representations are produced in social practices; and the mechanisms that allow specific narratives to thrive while oppressing and marginalizing others. I do this by de-colonizing the research, employing a new terminology that redefines the Bedouin and indigenous knowledge.

Documenting women's historical voices provides an alternative to how history has been constructed, especially by the official Zionist historical narrative. By exposing the Bedouin's links to their land through establishing spatial practices, visiting their lands and narrating the past to their children, they demonstrate their affiliation to the land and the transfer of that affiliation from generation to generation. In these ways women express their opposition to their removal by the Israeli establishment. In addition, this research challenges how knowledge is produced about them as nomadic and passive victims. Their opposition reveals the active nature of these women as they struggle against their dispossession from the Naqab. Finally, the study documents local knowledge of indigenous academic researchers that faithfully express the identities of Bedouin, influencing the struggle for land in representing these voices.

NOTES

1   The recognized villages were established by the state of Israel at the end of the military regime (after 1967) to concentrate the Bedouin in less territory and control there spatial settlements. Half of the Bedouin move their (approximately 120,000) and the other 120,000 lives in forty-six unrecognized villages lack of elementary services like connection to water, electricity, health, education and welfare services. Meanwhile, eleven villages were recognized within new regional councils: Al-Qassom and Whhat-Al Sahraa. For more details see Svirski and Hason (2005).

2   See for example Begin (2013). See also the implementation team report regulating Bedouin settlement in the Negev as part of government resolution 4411, January 2009 (Begin Report). https://www.acri.org.il/en/wp-content/uploads/2013/01/Begin-Report-English-January-2013.pdf.

3   See, for example, Falah, 1989; Shamir, 1996; Yiftachel, 1999; 2006; 2009; Yiftachel et al. 2016; Amara et al. 2012; Noa, 2009; Karplos and Meir, 2013; Meir, 2003, 2007; Nasasra et al 2014; Aburabia, 2013, 2014.

REFERENCES

Abdo, N. (1997) "Assessing Gender/Women's Regional Workshop", *Cairo Papers in Social Science* 20(3). Cairo: The American University Cairo Press.

Aburabia, S. (2005) "Exiled in our Homeland: The Diasporical Identity of the Negev Bedouin". Masters thesis, Ben-Gurion University of the Negev.

Aburabia, S. (2013) "The Gendered Historical Discourse on the Nakba: The Perspective of Bedouin Arab Women in the Negev". PhD dissertation, Ben-Gurion University of the Negev.

Aburabia, S. (2014) "Land, Identity and History: New Discourse on the Nakba of Bedouin-Arabs in the Naqab", in M. Nasasra, R. Ratcliffe, S. Abu Rabia-Queder and S. Richter-Devroe (eds.), *Naqab Bedouin and Colonialism: New Perspectives*. Abingdon: Routledge.

Abu Ras, T. (2006) "Land Conflict in Israel: The Bedouin Case", *Adala Electronic Journal*, http://www.adalah.org/newsletter/heb/apr06/ar2.pdf.

Al-Aref, A. (1933) *The History of Beer-Sheva and its Tribes*. Tel Aviv: Shoshani.

Almi, A. (2003) "In No Man's Land: Health in the Unrecognized Villages of the Negev". Tel Aviv: Report of Physicians for Human Rights and the Council of Unrecognized Villages.

Amara, A., I. Abu-Saad and O. Yiftachel (2012) *Indigenous (In)Justice: Human Rights Law and Bedouin Arabs in the Naqab/Negev*. Cambridge, MA: Human Rights Program at Harvard Law School.

Ashkenazi, T. (1957) *The Bedouin: The Origins, Life and Customs*. Jerusalem: Mass.

Baker, A. (1998) *Voices of Resistance: Oral Histories of Moroccan Women*. New York: State University of New York Press.

Bar, A. (1980) "Fertility Changes among Nomads and Bedouin in Transition to Permanent

Settlements", unpublished paper, Department of Geography, Ben-Gurion University of the Negev.

Bar, A. (1985) "Bedouin vs Fellaheen: Social Processes in Sedentarization". Masters Thesis. Department of Geography, Ben-Gurion University of the Negev.

Bar-Zvi, S. and Y. Ben-David (1978) "The Negev Bedouin in the 1930s–1940s as a Semi-nomadic Society", *Studies in the Geography of Israel* 10: 110–121.

Ben-David, Y. (1972) "Bedouin Tribes in South Sinai", Masters thesis, The Hebrew University, Jerusalem.

Ben-David, Y. (1986) "The Bedouin in the Negev", *Idan* 6: 93–99.

Begin, Z. (2013) "Regulating Bedouin Settlement: Summary of course listening to the public about the memo law regulating Bedouin settlement and policy recommendations and repair Memorandum of Law", submitted to the government as part of a bill regulating Bedouin settlement in the Negev, http://main.knesset.gov.il/Activity/committees/InternalAffairs/Pages/Bedouin.aspx.

Ben-Ze'ev, E. (2005) "Transmission and Transformation: The Palestinian Second Generation and the Commemoration of the Homeland", in A. Levy and A. Weingrod (eds.), *Homelands and Diasporas*. Stanford, CA: Stanford University Press.

Cooke, M. (2001) *Women Claim Islam*. New York: Routledge.

De Certeau, M. (1988) *The Practice of Everyday Life*. Berkeley, CA: California University Press.

Dinero, S. (1997) "Female Role Change and Male Response in the Post-nomadic Urban Environment: The Case of Israeli Negev Bedouin", *Journal of Comparative Family Studies* 3: 248–261.

Epstein, E. (1933) *The Bedouin: Life and Customs*. Tel Aviv: Shtibel.

Falah, G. (1989) "The Spatial Pattern of Bedouin Sedentarization in Israel", *Geojournal* 11(4): 361–368.

Fenster, T. (1991) "Participation in the Settlement Planning Process: The Case of the Bedouin in the Israeli Negev", PhD dissertation, The London School of Economics and Political Science.

Fenster, T. (2004) "On Belonging and Spatial Planning in Israel", in H. Yacobi (ed.), *Constructing a Sense of Place*. Aldershot: Ashgate.

Fenster, T. (2007) "Memory, Belonging and Spatial Planning in Israel", *Research and Theory* 30: 189–212.

Gluck, S. (1984) "What is so Special about Women? Women's Oral History", in D.K. Dunaway and W.K. Baum (eds.), *Oral History: An Interdisciplinary Anthology*. Walnut Creek and London: Altamira Press.

Halbwachs, M. (1992) *On Collective Memory*. Chicago: Chicago University Press.

Hall, S. (1996) "Introduction: Who Needs 'Identity'?", in S. Hall and P. du Gay (eds.), *Questions of Cultural Identity*. London: Sage.

Holland, D., W. Lachicotte, D. Skinner and C. Cain (1998) *Identity and Agency in Cultural Worlds*. Cambridge, MA and London: Harvard University Press.

HRA (2004) "All's Fair: The Destruction of the Agricultural Crops of Bedouin Citizens of the Negev by the State by Chemical Dusting from the Air". Report of the Arab Association for Human Rights, Nazareth.

Issa, M. (1997) "Decoding the Silencing Process in Modern Palestinian Historiography". Paper presented at the conference: "Worlds and Visions, Perspectives on the Middle East Today: Local and National Histories", University of Arhus, Denmark, 5–6 December 1997.

Jakubowska L. (1992) "Resisting Ethnicity: The Israeli State and the Bedouin Identity", in C. Martin and J. Martin (eds.), *The Paths to Domination, Resistance and Terror*. Berkeley, CA: University of California Press.

Johnson-Odim, C. (1991) "Common Themes, Different Contexts: Third World Women and Feminism", in C. Mohanty, A. Russo and L. Turres (eds.), *Third World Women and the politics of Feminism*. Bloomington, IN: Indiana University Press.

Kandiyoti, D. (1996) "Bargaining with Patriarchy", *Gender and Society* 2: 274–290.

Karplus, Y. and A. Meir (2013) *The Construction of Bedouin Space in the Negev*. Beer Sheva: The Negev Center for Regional Development, Ben-Gurion University of the Negev.

Kimmerling, B. (1999) "Al-Nakba", *Theory and Criticism* 12–13: 33–37.

Kimmerling, B. and J. Migdal (1993) *Palestinians: The Making of a People*. New York: Free Press.

Kozma, L. (2003) *Women Write History: Feminism and Social Change in Morocco*. Tel Aviv: Moshe Dayan Center for Middle East and Africa Studies.

Lithwick, H. (2002) *Policy Directions for the Revitalization of Bedouin Settlements*. Jerusalem: Center of Social Policy Studies.

Marx, E. (1956) "The Negev Bedouin", *The New East* 7–8: 89–98.

Marx, E. (1967) *The Bedouin of the Negev*. Manchester: Manchester University Press.

Marx, E. (1974) *The Bedouin Society in the Negev*. Tel Aviv: Reshafim.

Meir, A. (1997) *As Nomadism Ends: The Israeli Bedouin of the Negev*. Boulder, CO: Westview.

Meir, A. (2003) *From Planning Advocacy to Independent Planning: The Negev Bedouin on The Path to Democratization in Planning*. Beer Sheva: The Negev Center for Regional Development, Ben-Gurion University of the Negev.

Meir, A. (2007) "A Geo-legal Aspects of the Ottoman Land Law in Relation to the Negev Bedouin: An Alternative Interpretation", *Karka* 63: 14–51.

Mohanty, C. (1991) "Cartographies of Struggle: Third World Women and the Politics of Feminism", in C.T. Mohanty, A. Russo and L. Torres (eds.), *Third World Women and the Politics of Feminism*. Bloomington: Indiana University press.

Mohanty, C. (2002) "'Under Western Eyes': Revisited: Feminist Solidarity through Anti-capitalist Struggles", *Sign: Journal of Women in Culture and Society* 28(2): 449–535.

Morris, B. (1997) *The Birth of the Palestinian Problem 1947–1949*. Tel Aviv: Am Oved.

Murphy, H. (1995) "Landscape and the Production of Ancestral Past", in E. Hirsch and M. O'Hanlon (eds.), *The Anthropology of Landscape*. Oxford: Clarendon Press.

Narayan, U. (2000) "Essence of Culture and Sense and Sense of History: A Feminist Critique of Cultural Essentialism", in U. Narayan and S. Harding (eds.), *Decentring the Canter: Philosophy for Multicultural, Postcolonial and Feminist World.* Bloomington, IN: Indiana University Press.

Nasasra, M., R. Ratcliffe, S. Abu-Rabia and S. Richter-Devroe (2004) *Naqab Bedouin and Colonialism: New Perspectives.* London: Routledge.

Nathanson, R. (1999) "A Comprehensive Plan for Addressing the Problems of the Negev Bedouin". Report of the Center for the Legal and Economic Studies in the Middle East, Tel Aviv.

Nathanson, R., A'. Al-Hozayel, L. Aa'leemi, D. Asan and H. Tzameret (1999) *A Comprehensive Plan for Addressing the Problems of the Negev Bedouin.* Tel Aviv: The Center for Legal and Economic Studies in the Middle East [in Hebrew].

Noa, H. (2009) *The Unrecognized villages in the Negev.* Haifa: Pardes.

Robenshtein, D. (1990) *The Fig Hug: The Palestinian Right of Return.* Jerusalem: Keter.

Sayigh, R. (2007) *The Palestinians: From Peasants to Revolutionaries.* London: Zed Books.

Shaked, A. (2003) *Words Trying to Touch.* Tel Aviv: Ramot.

Sayigh, R. (1998) "Palestinian Camp Women as Tellers of History", *Journal of Palestinian studies* 27(2): 42–58.

Shamir, R. (1996) "Suspended in Space: Bedouins under the Law of Israel", *Law and Society Review* 30: 231–256.

Slymovics, S. (1998) *The Object of Memory: Arab and Jew Narrate the Palestinian Village.* Philadelphia: Pennsylvanian University Press.

Soen, D. and A. Shmueli (1987) "The Israeli Bedouin: Political Organization at the National Level", *Middle Eastern Studies* 23: 329–347.

Spector-Marzel, G. (2010) "From Narrative Approach to Narrative Paradigm", in R. Tobal-Mashiach and G. Spector-Marzel (eds.), *Narrative Research: Theory, Creation and Interpretation.* Jerusalem: Magenss.

Spelman, E. (1988) *Inessential Women.* Boston: Boston University Press.

Stewart, P.J. and A. Strathern (2003) "Introduction", in P.J. Stewart and A. Strathern (eds.), *Landscape, Memory and History: Anthropological Perspectives.* London: Pluto Press.

Svirski, S. and Y. Hason (2005) "Invisible Citizens: Government Policy towards Bedouins in the Negev", Equality information no. 14, http://www.adva.org/uploaded/bedouimreport.pdf.

Vickers, J. and V. Dhruvarajan (2003) *Gender, Race and Nation: A Global Perspective.* Toronto: University of Toronto Press.

Yiftachel, O. (1999) "Land Day", *Theory and Criticism* (12): 280–287.

Yiftachel, O. (2003) "Bedouin-Arabs and the Israeli Settler State: Land Policies and Indigenous Resistance", in D. Champagne and I. Abu-Saad (eds.), *The Future of Indigenous Peoples: Strategies for Survival and Development.* Los Angeles: American Indian Studies Center Publication, UCLA.

Yiftachel, O. (2006) *Ethnocracy: Land and Identity Politics in Israel/Palestine.* Philadelphia: University of Pennsylvania Press.

Yiftachel, O. (2009) "Critical theory and 'gray space': Mobilization of the colonized", *City* 13(2–3), DOI: 10.1080/13604810902982227.

Yiftachel, O., B. Roded and A. Kedar (2016) "Between Rights and Denials: Bedouin Indigeneity in the Negev/Naqab", *Environment and Planning A*, DOI:10.1177/0308518X16653404.

Yi-Fu, T. (1977) *Space and Place: The Perspective of Experience*. Minneapolis: Minnesota University Press.

Young, C.I.M. (1986) "The Ideal of Community and the Politics of Difference", *Social Theory and Practice* 12(1): 1–26.

PART V
Documenting Nakba narratives from the Gaza Strip and the Shatat

12
The young do not forget
MONA AL-FARRA

The slogan "A land without a people for a people without a land" was common among Zionists at the end of the nineteenth, and the beginning of the twentieth century.

The Israeli war against the Palestinians during 1948, symbolized by one day, 19 May 1948, is known as Youm al-Nakba (the day of the Nakba/catastrophe). During 1948, over 750,000 Palestinians were expelled (and some fled under bombardment), while hundreds of villages and towns were destroyed or depopulated. Those refugees today number about 6 million people.

When I started interviewing some Nakba eyewitnesses in Gaza and listening to their stories, I felt the need to begin by reminding the reader of one of the Zionist myths claiming that Palestine "was a land without people for a people without a land". I also remembered and would like to share the reader with Golda Maier's famous statement: "There was no such thing as Palestinians, they never existed" (Maier [1969] 2002) or that of David Ben Gurion's: "The elderly will die and the young will forget" (Ben Gurion [1948] 2002).

The memories and stories of Gazan refugees defy Israeli leaders' wishes and hopes and assert our history and experiences as Palestinians. Thus, despite almost seventy years of dispossession and brutal attacks, we are keeping our history alive.

I believe oral history is very important to keep the Nakba stories alive, especially for the next generations, to find out more about the truth of what happened in 1948 to Palestinian civilians whose lives were shattered and are still looking for justice after all those years. Our struggle against the injustices of big colonial racist powers is about justice and our human rights.

This chapter is based on a total of five interviews: some conducted by me and others by close family members of the interviewed. It is further consolidated by my own memory of my parents and other family members who experienced the Nakba.

THE PAST IS LIVED IN THE PRESENT

As I was listening to the stories, especially about the day of leaving, I could not help remembering 19 July 2014, during the recent Israeli offensive on Gaza. It was four in the morning. After several hours of artillery shelling and air raids on the Alshagaiyya area to the east of Gaza, I started hearing a loud noise coming from people. I saw women, men and children, cars and carts, leaving from the east to the centre of Gaza for safety. Hundreds of thousands of people – roughly 200,000 – were forced to leave under the intensity of the Israeli shelling. During that day hundreds were either killed or injured, and the whole area was cleansed of its residents. From my house, during that night, I was able to see the frequent movement of ambulances heading to the Shagaiyya, taking the injured and killed to the hospital.

As I rushed to the hospital, I saw injured people lying in the corridors of the hospital, waiting to be seen and treated. It was a bloody day with massive casualties. It was very difficult for the surgeons to deal with the number of casualties, and I think no hospital in any other country could have handled such a number at once.

Gaza town became full of the displaced families, who fled to the town centre, the hospitals, schools and various other streets for shelter. Those who left their homes that night, returned after the ceasefire between Hamas and the Israeli army, to find their homes and neighbourhoods destroyed. This scene brought to my mind the memory of the 1948 Nakba. The only difference is that whereas the Gazans of the 2014 Israeli attacks stayed in their homeland, although waiting weeks, months and even until now to leave the hospitals or schools and return to their homes, those of the 1948 Nakba are still waiting

To me, the occupier is the same and the colonial power is the same. The only change is that it became more powerful with the modern, more lethal weaponry.

TESTIMONIES OF GAZAN REFUGEES

Growing up in Gaza, I heard many stories about the Nakba from my refugee classmates, transmitted to them by their parents and grandparents. One of those stories was that of my friend Fadwa Takash's family. Here is what her grandmother, Sadikka Takash from Sdood said:

The bombing and shooting was too fierce ... so close and terrifying. We left Sdood in a hurry. The *maklooba* [traditional Palestinian dish] was ready to be eaten, so I wrapped it in a hurry in a blanket to stay warm. I took the keys and left with the children, while they were shooting, thinking we will be back ... We never were.

Fadwa continued: "We were never allowed to return. It was a big war, what happened in 1948 was a process of ethnic cleansing."

The following oral history interview with Basma Moailqe Abedazeez Abu Moailqe, born in 1931, was conducted by her granddaughter, Amal, aged twenty-five. Basma is a Bedouin who lived between Bir Al-Sabe' and Gaza in the Naqab, but was registered as a Bir Al-Sabe' resident. Here is her testimony:

Before 1948, life for us Bedouins in the Naqab was very natural, and we were content with our life and were happy to stay there. My family's agricultural land was divided into long stretches/strips of fields, divided between the smaller families, and each strip or area had its own name (often the name of the cultivating family). We used to plant grains, like wheat, barley and corn, in the beginning of the season. Then, after the harvest, we grew melons, cucumbers, tomatoes, watermelons, and okra. We also grew grapes, olives, figs, almonds, and pomegranates.

Everybody worked the land, and each field had special vegetables or fruits. We all worked on the land. Workers also came from Gaza and Dair Albalah to work on our lands.

One year before 1948, our tribe decided to build a school for their children and hired a teacher to educate the children until grade six.

But the war started and the Nakba befell us and we started to leave under the heavy shelling against us.

We left our village at the beginning of summer, immediately after the wheat and barley harvest. We stored the grains in the barns. The barns were full. When we were forced to leave under the shelling, we took nothing out of our groves or barn. We left the greens and grain and the *hasad* (harvest) ... the place was full.

Before we left, maybe one year before we left, we began to watch new settlers starting to build a settlement next to our area east of the Almanshiyya area. There was a stone quarry for building and a phosphorus industry, already prepared by the British and the Zionists. Our men sensed the sneaky presence of the strangers, and confrontations started between them and the strangers. The settlers trespassed on our fields, trying to go further. For about ten days there was fire exchange between us and the settlers. Then a battle started and the settlers got more arms … and more firing, until the settlers were able to enter our land and kill our men and animals.

As I remember, during the last day the shooting was so fierce like heavy rain.

We were forced to leave for a safe area, to the west, for the safety of women and children. We were thinking of getting back when the fighting stops. We moved to the west of our land in Burage Abu Mideen and Basboos, not too far away from our land – [the area is now part of Gaza Strip].

I remember we left in a midday during summer … we left under the thunders of the bombs.

We stayed there hoping to go back. But after one year of constant moving from one area to another, the UN began to enter, and brought food and clothes, and started some schools. We had nothing. Some of our men tried to go back to bring food and grains to feed their families, or sell it in Gaza, but many of them were killed or injured … those who succeeded to enter our land found the barns either empty or burnt.

After three years, the UNRWA [United Nations Relief and Works Agency for Palestine Refugees in the Near East] built camps and housed us in different areas. We were housed in Maghazi, not far away from the new borders. I could look, past the border, and see our home, but I was unable to go there or live there anymore.

The following testimony is by Gomaa Ibrahim Abu Shomar (ninety-seven), originally from Beit Teema village, and currently living in Deir al-Balah refugee camp. The interview was recorded by his son, Tawfiq Abu Shomar:

My father is ninety-seven and still remembers the details of the Nakba, and life in Palestine before the Nakba. This is how my father describes his village, Beit Teema: "Our village is 20km away from Gaza. In the village there are Roman ruins. It was a peaceful small place with about 1,000 inhabitants who were mainly farmers".

Tawfiq's father believes that he is living a long and healthy life because of his life during his early youth. As a young boy in Beit Teema, Tawfiq's father recalls:

I enjoyed eating healthy vegetarian food off the land, olive oil, dry figs, grapes, thyme and sage herbs. I still feel nostalgia for the fragrances of orange and lemon blossoms as well as basil and mint. My life in Beit Teema was beautiful. We, my son, were forced to leave our village under the heavy shooting and artillery bombs and sounds of airplanes ... all these made us leave looking for a safe place. We headed south-west to the unknown on foot, we stopped many times and in various places. We were not alone, but with thousands others, from our village and the nearby villages ... we escaped death by a miracle. We tried to avoid the shooting ... we would stop and then continue toward the sea with no food. We left everything behind us, the homes, the barn, the cattle. We only brought with us a few things on the donkey's back. You [my son], were a year and a half old in your mother's lap. She was afraid to put you on the donkey's back, afraid to leave you away from her. She wanted to protect you.

Before we left the village we could see the settlers throwing inflammable sticks on the wheat fields, and on villagers' homes which were made of clay bricks and straw. We could see the fire and burning fields from a distance. Your grandfather refused to leave the village and the house. He stayed in our house.

When we arrived in Deir Albalah [refugee camp] I was thinking we will go back after the ceasefire. We never expected that we will stay away from our Palestine until now [close to seventy years later].

They [The Israelis] insisted on throwing us away and forced us to leave ... they killed whoever stayed there. What they say about the Arab troops asking us to leave our homes has no truth, they forced us out of our homes.

I remember after a few days, after we arrived at Deir Albalah , I decided to sneak back into our village to see how my dad was doing. I found your grandfather shot dead next to his plate with bread and eggs ... I buried him under the vine tree, and returned to Deir Albalah empty handed.

The following is my interview with Abdelhady Mohammed Zarook, born in 1932, originally from Yafa (Jaffa) and currently living in Gaza city. He worked as a mechanic at his father's workshop until 1948. According to him:

In Yafa, before 1948, the cultural, commercial and industrial life was so
rich. Journalism, cinemas, sport clubs, theatres, and the port were so active,
and life was prosperous. Yafa was at the centre of Palestine. It produced
oranges but also received all kinds of crops, especially oranges, from the
southern villages to be exported via its port. Yafa had a central train station
that ran from Yafa to Jerusalem.

I lived in Almanshiyya neighbourhood on whose land Tel Aviv has been
built. The Zionist settler activities with the help of the British colonial rule
were noticeable to the neighbours, even before the actual confrontations
started between us and the Zionists. For example, our neighbourhood
noticed that some settlers rented flats inside Yafa.

Describing the day of their dispossession, Abdelhady says:

It was 10am and all of a sudden there were successive bombings by
airplanes and mortar shells ... It was so intensive. Many people were killed,
and we had no place to go. The attack continued for three hours or more.
We closed the mechanics workshop and left for a safer place. Yafa was
surrounded by the Zionist army ... and the British secured a safe passage
for civilians to leave in a convoy, accompanied by a jeep in the front and
another one in the back of the convoy. We used a truck and left, thinking
we will be back in a few days.

"We left, thinking we will be back in a few days" was the common story I heard
from all friends, family and refugees interviewed.

Here is the testimony of Ismael Ibrahim Khaleel Al Faseeh (born 1931). Until
1948, Ismael lived in Yafa and worked as a fisherman. His tale is as affectionate
and sad as those of other refugees:

I worked with the family in Yafa port. The city and the port were very
active, and commercial life there was flourishing. One day, at the port,
as they were unloading the barrels, one barrel was broken, and the
workers discovered it was full of weapons sent to the Zionists. All Arab
workers at the port knew that the Zionists were receiving ships full of
weapons from Europe.

Speaking of his grandmother, Ismael continued, "my grandmother, Khadeeja, whose birthdate I do not know, contributed to the 1936 revolution. She used to hide al-Thuwwar [the revolutionaries] and find them safe places. It is not only she, but many other women did the same thing in other parts of Palestine at the time".

As for the day of expulsion, Ismael says:

> We left Yafa under heavy shooting and shelling. We left for safety, hoping to go back later when the war stops. Being close to the port, we left Yafa by boats and went to Gaza, where we lived in al-Shati refugee camp ... and we are still there until now.

After 1967 and the Israeli occupation of Gaza, Ismael continued:

> My mother returned to Yafa to see her house. When she recognized her place, she knocked on the door and found a Moroccan woman living there. My mother told her: "this is my house", and both started arguing. The Moroccan settler asked my mother to prove to her that the house was hers. My mother started to describe in greater details the inside of the house and the water wells around it. After hearing my mother, the settler woman told her: "you are right, it is your house, and I hope there will be peace one day and you can come back to your house". After all these years, we are still living in Alshati refugee camp in Gaza, awaiting our return to Yafa.

MY PERSONAL TESTIMONY

I was born in Khan Younis in 1954, just a few years after the Nakba.

During my early childhood, my home town, Khan Younis, was subject to several military attacks. The severest one was the 1956 Suez Canal war against Gaza and Egypt.

I was brought up in an atmosphere of stories of Israel's continued attacks, the memories of the Nakba, and the foundation of Israel. These stories and memories played an important role in shaping my childhood, my conscience, the development of my personality, and contributed to who I am now. Like thousands of Palestinian children who were brought up in the same period, either as refugee children or citizens like myself, our lives were shattered and altered by the impact of the Nakba. To open your eyes to the fact that you have no country and you are stateless and refugee, to live with the constant threat of war, on the one hand, and an increasing national aspiration to free your lost or occupied land, on the other, has been my lot and the lot of many other Palestinians. To have such feelings as a young child is definitely not what any child should go through. Life in Gaza has been particularly unbearable, partly because of the actual wars and atrocities inflicted on the residents of this strip, but also in terms of the aftermath of all such attacks, especially since 1967 and the continuous restrictions and siege imposed on the Gaza Strip.

Still, it was the Nakba which affected us most. Albeit it had different effects on my extended family, the Nakba has cast its shadow on all parts of my extended family, especially those who lived and settled in Yafa before 1948. My two uncles and their families lived in Yafa, while my parents stayed in Khan Younis. In the early years of their marriage, before 1948, my parents, Qasim and Laila, spent most of their time between Khan Younis and Yafa, partly visiting family and partly attending family and social and cultural occasions.

I always heard stories about Yafa from my parents. In one, I heard about my uncle, Abed Salam, who was hit and injured during the 1936 revolution. He was shot by the British as he participated in a demonstration against the British and Zionist settlers.

I have also heard stories about the coexistence between three religions in Palestine, and about my parents' Palestinian Jewish friends in Haifa, the Moses. I also heard stories of the influx of the European and American Jewish settlers to Palestine.

One heart-breaking incident I cannot forget is a trip I took with my father to 1948 Palestine (now Israel) after Israel's 1967 occupation of Gaza. I still remember his tears when he took us to see Yafa. My father was able to identify the surrounding villages, the sites and the agricultural land with its famous Palestinian crops like figs, vineyards, pomegranates and prickly pears. He took us around Yafa city streets and its neighbourhoods, and was able to identify the family house of my uncle, who had lived in the Nuzha area.

My mother showed us the famous Dajani house and hospital besides other sites of Yafa. We saw the harbour, the schools, the shops, the mosques, the cinema and the theatre where Umm Kolthum sang in 1937. Both my parents were able to recognize the old citrus groves and named the owners of each grove.

Father showed us the harbour, and told us the painful story of how during the Nakba he boarded a boat to Yafa in order to bring his brother's family to Gaza, after they were forced to leave Yafa under shooting and bombing.

I was stunned to see such a beautiful coastal city. Although it was cleansed of its indigenous people, you could still sense the old prosperity and culture. Even as a child I sensed that.

BUT THE NAKBA WAS NOT OVER FOR US

The story of the displacement and dispossession of the Palestinians did not end with the end of the 1948 Nakba. Israel continues its attacks against Palestinian people to this day.

In fact, a major part of my childhood upbringing was based around stories and memories of the 1956 massacre in Khan Younis, where hundreds of civilians (an estimated 550 people) were killed by Israeli soldiers. I still imagine and remember the stories about those scores of people who were lined up against the town castle, the Barqook, and shot in cold blood.

I was two years old then, but I later heard many stories, from my older siblings, about their memories of the period and the trauma that accompanied them for years.

The massacre was documented in the UN archives.

As a child and later as an adult who lived through the 1967 occupation, I realized at an early age that Israel was a settler-colonial, racist occupying power, and that what had happened in 1948 was pre-planned, as it was mentioned in British mandate archives about Palestine pre-1948. I lived all my teenage years under Israeli occupation and have my own stories and memories to tell my children.

MY MOTHER AND PALESTINIAN WOMEN'S RESISTANCE

In my various conversations with my late mother, Laila Ishaq Dawood, I learnt a lot about Palestinian women's anti-settler, anti-colonial resistance before and after the Nakba.

One such conversation focused around women's activism in the 1930s. According to my mother,

> during the 1930s, women designed a project called "The Qersh" (the penny) Project, where most schools in Palestine implemented a programme of "piggy bank", where young male and female children would place a "qersh" (penny) every day. The money aimed at helping the Bedouins of Wadi al-Hawareth, many of whom faced eviction by the JNF [Jewish

National Fund] in 1932. The JNF claimed to have bought the land from an absentee landlord living in France.

I want to add here that the case of the eviction of Wadi al-Hawareth villagers received a lot of attention at the time, because of the fierce resistance the villagers put up against their eviction and displacement. For four years the tenants of Wadi al-Hawarith resisted British attempts to evict them (for more on this case, see, Khalidi *2006*). Khalidi explained that the people of Wadi al-Hawarith insisted on remaining on their land, because they believed the land belonged to them, for they had been living on it for over 350 years. Like most Palestinian peasants, the term "private ownership" did not make any sense; they had possessed the land for hundreds of years and, as the tillers, they considered the land to be theirs. In March 1948, Wadi al-Hawarith was cleared of all of its Palestinian residents.

As a young woman, then, my mother told me that most girls, her age (10–15) were aware of the colonization from the older activist women.

She told me several stories about the active participation of Palestinian women in the various demonstrations against the British and its support of the Zionist settlers in Palestine. My mother was well aware of the military training Zionist groups such as the Hagana, Stern Gang, and Irgun had received from the British.

My mother also said that village women took a major part in helping the revolutionaries and fighters in different ways, such as securing water and food for men in the mountains. Also in every village, according to her, there were women who sold their modest jewellery to support resistance to the new colonial settlers.

Another one of my conversations with my late mother focused on the role of the organization (Zahrat Al-Uqhowan, The Feverfew), founded in Yafa by Muheeba Khorsheed, one of the women involved in the struggle against British and Zionist colonialism. According to mother, Muheeba founded the organization after she witnessed the killing of a Palestinian child in Yafa by a British soldier. She also told me various things about the Palestinian Women's Union, itself established in 1916. The Women's Union, I understood from my mother, operated on traditional grounds, teaching young girls embroidery, providing literacy for young girls, and providing a space for women to meet and discuss social and political issues, including participation in demonstrations against the British.

CONCLUSION

My own memory of tales from parents and various other family and friends, along with the stories and oral histories collected for this chapter, all corroborate one theme: most, if not all Palestinians who "left" their homes, lands and villages did it suddenly and under the threat of being killed. They all left due to the shooting and the bombardment. All Palestinians in Gaza, especially the refugees, but also the citizens, had stories of dislocation, dispossession and uprooting from their indigenous villages in pre-1948 Palestine.

As mentioned earlier, I am a citizen and not a refugee, but the 1948 Nakba has affected my wider family and sent family members (brothers, sisters, parents) to live all over the place.

The feeling among the people interviewed is that suddenly, and without any prior knowledge, they found themselves refugees, displaced and living in a strange place, carrying on their shoulders the burden of being refugees, and starting a new life away from their villages and land. They all talked about the cruelty of their uprooting in the process of the ethnic cleansing of Palestine 1948. They all spoke with bitterness about how Israel was founded on their ruins.

Roughly seventy years have passed since the 1948 Nakba. However, as Gazans, our experience of Israeli destruction, atrocities and the unending process of displacement has never stopped. My memory, and the memory of my family and friends, of the Israeli war against Gaza in 1956, and Israel's latest savage attack on the Gaza Strip, have shaped my consciousness and identity, and I will pass it to my children.

Let me finally say, I want to help people understand more about the largest ethnic cleansing operation in the modern world. Millions of Palestinian people are waiting for justice; and peace cannot be granted without justice for Palestinian refugees according to UN Resolution 194 and other resolutions regarding Palestine.

REFERENCE

Ben Gurion, D. (2002) Quoted in "The Old Will Die And The Young Will Forget: David Ben Gurion", *Arab News*, 25 April 2002, http://www.arabnews.com/node/220313.

Khalidi, W. (2006) All That Remains: *The Palestinian Villages Occupied and Depopulated by Israel in 1948*. Beirut: Institute for Palestine Studies.

Maier, G. (2002) Quoted in "The Old Will Die And The Young Will Forget: David Ben Gurion", *Arab News*, 25 April 2002, http://www.arabnews.com/node/220313.

13
Gaza remembers: narratives of displacement in Gaza's oral history

MALAKA MOHAMMAD SHWAIKH

Oral history is a critically important record; it serves to oppose the historical erasure imposed by the colonizers. It also archives real experience and history where other records are absent, and, for those reasons, it has become a burgeoning area of study. This research aims to explore and analyse oral history projects in the Gaza Strip.

Since the 1970s, many attempts have been made to examine history across the Middle East using several methodologies. Examples of such methods include, but are not limited to, oral history, which is yet to be fully developed as a context for investigation and research. Whilst work on Palestinian oral history started decades ago, having a long precedent in the culture itself, stemming from a broader oral traditon of the *hakawati* (storyteller) that was used after the Nakba of 1948, with the aim to create a defence line against ereasure of memory and culture among the Palestinian people, it is currently experiencing a resurgence. Historian Beshara Doumani dubbed it a "Palestinian archive fever" (in Muhanna 2016). Since the early 1990s, more local Palestinian organizations, especially educational institutions, with Birzeit University in Ramallah and then the Islamic University of Gaza as pioneers, have been involved in the process of collecting testimonies, especially from the older generation which experienced the Nakba. This chapter examines oral history efforts in Gaza,[1] analysing the roles it has played, its achievements, challenges and future. Two examples have been extensively studied: the Islamic University of Gaza's Oral History Centre (OHC), based in the university's history department, and the work of the Tamer Institute for Community Education. Both projects aim to document the living history of life among Gaza refugees, with the former being academically focused, led by students and academics, and the latter being activist focused, led by young people and monitored by writers, in an attempt to advocate and defend their communities against displacement and to serve as a counter-narrative within the active Israeli settler-colonial context in Palestine. As the research shows, both projects entail a collection of recorded and archived voices of people's memories and experiences, "living history" of their distinct life experiences, and new insights with the potential to define how life and its events are perceived, bringing members of society together and maintaining the inheritance of knowledge for the coming generations.

In the Gaza Strip, recording such events and experiences is not only important for the sake of archiving, but is also part and parcel of the liberation project. It is an act of resistance that asserts Palestinian visibility, and which can defy historically constructed identities, especially in the Gaza Strip, where attempts to break the people's willpower and steadfastness through continuous siege, assaults and occupation persist. For this, the Palestinians in Gaza have devoted much of their time and effort to preserve community history to establish a continuous, active narrative.

This research is an attempt to explore the Oral History Project in Gaza, highlighting the project's significance in the case of Gaza in facing Israel's continuous attempts at erasure. The chapter will do so by examining the situation in Gaza since 1948, exploring the failures and successes in the ways used to preserve Palestinian oral history, and considering oral history's future in Gaza, before delving further into the emergence of a new narrative on Palestine's past. The chapter concludes with a discussion on other attempts by Israel to erase Palestinian history, arguing that these have been unsuccessful in displacing Palestinian memory. It becomes clear by the end that the importance of oral history cannot be underestimated; it archives real experience and history where other records are absent; and, for those reasons, it has become a growing field of research.

GAZA AFTER 1948: MEMORIES OF PALESTINE

As the introduction shows, this research aims to look into oral history efforts in the Gaza Strip, a Palestinian-occupied territory to the south-west of Palestine. To put things in historical context, prior to 1948 the Strip was not the 365 square kilometres that one can see today. As stated in a lecture given by Israeli historian

Ilan Pappe at New York University in March 2016 (Weiss 2016), Israel created the Gaza Strip as it sought to create a space in the south-west of Palestine that could contain the hundreds of thousands of refugees that it was about to expel from different parts of Palestine to the newly established refugee camp zone. Previously, Gaza was a small town with fishing villages around it. Israel did not hope to take control of or occupy it. After 1967, Egypt did not want it back either, although Israel thought that it would. As a result, Israel occupied it, withdrawing its military and settlements in 2005 but remaining the dominant power, controlling the Gaza sky, sea and land borders. The status quo in Gaza is just another outcome of the Nakba. As George Bisharat once said: "Palestinians live the consequences of the past every day – whether as exiles from their homeland, or as members of an oppressed minority within Israel, or as subjects of a brutal and violent military occupation" (Bisharat 2007; Abdo 2014: 101).

The Nakba, one of the major historical events in the twentieth century, has not only changed the way Gaza looks, but has also transformed Palestinians' lives dramatically. Palestine, which prior to the Nakba was part of Greater Syria, lived a completely different experience than today, especially in terms of freedom of movement. Rajab al-Tom, a refugee from Bir al-Sabe', was forced to leave during the Nakba. He told *Middle East Eye* (Hajjaj 2015), "I was living in Jabalia city, in the northern Gaza Strip, shopping from Magdala. In the winter, I travelled to Bir al-Sabe' … in the summer, I used to travel to Haifa". Travelling from one city to another was easy: "There were no borders between the cities of Palestine or other neighbouring states", al-Tom said (in Hajjaj 2015).

With time, and technological development throughout the world, one would think that refugees' lives might have been affected positively. This has happened in some ways. However, more restrictions have also been imposed that none of the technological developments seems to lessen. In his youth, al-Tom used to travel throughout Palestine and Syria on a camel. Now, Palestinians in Gaza can use neither camels nor flights, with Israel and Egypt imposing restrictions on their freedom of movement. Delving more into the situation in Gaza, the restriction of movement is one major issue that affects all Palestinians in different ways, whether it is for someone who wants to pursue education, or those who need special medical care. Almost permanently closed checkpoints, or hours of waiting in the heat at the Rafah Egyptian crossing or the Erez Israeli checkpoint, were not the case before the 1948 calamity. As al-Tom told al-Monitor, he would travel on foot throughout Palestine without the need for any permit; there were no Israeli soldiers or checkpoints to humiliate and obstruct the Palestinian people (Hajjaj 2015).

Al-Tom's story is one of many. An estimated 75–80% of historic Palestine's indigenous people were forced to leave their homes. Some were forced into neighbouring countries such as Jordan, and others ended up internally exiled, as is the case with 67% of the Gazan population nowadays, leaving Gaza with the highest proportion of refugees in the world. The most recent estimates put the Palestinians displaced inside and globally at nearly 8 million, almost 66% of the Palestinian worldwide population of 11.2 million, making them the largest and longest-standing community of refugees globally, according to a survey by Resource Centre for Palestinian Residency and Refugee Rights (BADIL 2012), a Palestinian refugee advocacy group with a consultative status with United Nations Economic and Social Council (UN ECOSOC). These refugees pass their stories from one generation to another as elders tell their children and grandchildren the story of their homelands. And here lies the importance of recording these stories of al-Tom and others which clearly show that history in Palestine, unlike other places where one's story is usually written by the victors and occupiers, is still remembered by the old and passed on to many younger people (Hajjaj 2015).

Other than al-Tom's account, the story of eighty-nine-year-old Sadia Tartori from al-Faluja village, nearly thirty kilometres north of Gaza City, across the current border with Israel, is a further example. She was ten years old when forced to leave her home, and recalls her childhood well, especially the Jewish neighbour who used to give her sweets when her mother went to buy jewellery from his store. Prior to the establishment of the state of Israel in 1948, Muslims, Christians and Jews lived in general harmony. "We were simple farmers and workers who had no need to hold a gun. But [in] the Nakba, groups of Jews started to attack us on our own lands, threatening to kill us if we would not leave. Palestinians defended themselves but what can a stick or a knife do against a gun?" She was her mother's only daughter, and her father planted a tree sapling named after her. The events of the Nakba took her innocence away. It took her long effort to recall and reflect on these tough memories. "I saw young men digging holes in the ground and hiding beneath the earth so they would not get killed", Sadia recollected (Hajjaj 2015).

As the events of the 1948 Nakba started, Sadia and her mother collected all their gold to carry with them, but, as she recalled, "My father said that it would be a matter of days until we returned. We hid the gold in a jug and buried it. A few days later, I found myself in the Gaza Strip as a refugee. I knew then that I had lost my home". Sadia's family was not alone in thinking that they would return very soon: thousands shared similar thoughts. "I arrived in Gaza as many people did, without anything but the clothes I was wearing." It was difficult, and rather useless, to transfer everything from old homes to new ones, as they thought this situation would be temporary. They also knew, like many of the others, that they had extended families who would accommodate them in Gaza. But having a family does not mean not having to search for ways to survive. In Sadia's words, "My mother and I used to go to Khan Younis city in the southern Gaza Strip to get milk and one meal per person each day from the UN. My brothers became fishermen, and grief took my father" (Hajjaj 2015).

Al-Tom's and Tartori's accounts are clear examples of how investing in oral history preserves the memory of national trauma that is barely recorded elsewhere. These attempts to record the stories of the old, usually by the younger generation, show clearly that Palestinians' memories are still present in daily conversations and that the younger generations, as well as the older ones, maintain and preserve these stories. The next section explores further these attempts to preserve Palestinian oral history, with its success and failure.

PRESERVING PALESTINIAN ORAL HISTORY: SUCCESS AND FAILURE

The study of Palestinian refugees in Gaza is not a matter of dead stories of the past; their memory cannot be erased from Palestinian history. This memory, which is focused on the Nakba, is not only about the contemporary history of Palestinians turning into refugees, but it is also about their hope for the future, for return and freedom – a hope that nobody can deny them, not even the Israeli state with its constant efforts to erase Palestinian memories (Abdo 2014: 69–70), the latest attempt being when the Israel State Archive announced restricted access to documents related to confiscated Palestinian property (The Nakba Files 2016). In this context, Masalha uses the concept of "cultural genocide" to re-emphasize the erasure of Palestinian physical culture, buildings, streets and homes, and the destruction of about 600 villages and towns and other Palestinian historic sites. This is why recording Nakba stories is more urgent than ever. Oral history can amplify the community struggle in Gaza, to defend against the Palestinians' displacement by documenting the daily struggle, demonstrations, legal actions and expression of traditions, providing a space for a counter-narrative, and strengthening Palestinians fragmented as a community both within and outside Palestine, by centring the Palestinian struggle around commonality and the sharing of displacement experiences (Hastings 2016). In Gaza, oral history is about narrating not only stories from the Nakba of 1948, but also the continuing Israeli displacement through its non-stop aggression on Gaza, which has left thousands losing their lives and properties.

In Gaza, researchers are determined to document Nakba memories directly from the words of those refugees who lived through it and are currently in Gaza. It is important that such attempts to preserve Palestinian history are growing daily. These projects include the Oral History Centre of the Arts Faculty in the Islamic University of Gaza, where academics and students have been observing and documenting oral history. The Centre was opened in 1998 following an initiative by the faculty members, supported by the university, to emphasize the importance of oral history and to invest time and effort in documenting historical events in Palestine, making sure that heritage, suffering, resistance and endurance are all documented. It is one of the Centre's main goals to record the historical events of the Nakba in 1948, the migration of refugees to Gaza, and their lives since then. Their current archive has been built from scratch, as there is no systematic reference centre for such information in the Gaza Strip, as Nermin Habib, a researcher in the Centre, has noted. It goes beyond displacement research to include Palestine regions, folklore, politics, culture and so on. "We are trying our best to maintain our Palestinian identity and Palestinian heritage and traditions, like food and dress, after the Nakba", said Habib. "We seek to document the history of the Palestinian people and the main events that have shaped the Palestinian cause" (Catron 2013).

To shed more light on the OHC, I talked to Professor Ryad Shahin, the current head of the Centre and a regional coordinator for the Oral History Network. Professor Shahin emphasized the importance of oral history in the Palestinian context. "It is a source of historical information that is indispensable for the researcher. It enriches contemporary historical, economic, political, military and socio-cultural studies that are scarce in the written sources." For him, oral history material also constitutes historical documents and preliminary records that contain information that is not preserved in official documents. Its importance is especially highlighted in the absence of public voices (the voices of ordinary people) who have been marginalized from history and who have never had their opinions, experiences and observations, or even participation in certain events, taken into consideration.

Shahin managed to interview hundreds of Palestinian refugees who fled their homes and came to Gaza. He has also encouraged his students to work on oral history projects, an initiative to build on his work for the younger generation. He has pointed out that the Nakba was a crucial year for the Palestinians interviewed, turning them from landowners to beggars, due to the oppression of Israeli occupation. For him, oral history can provide a platform to support these communities that are defending themselves against displacement, with residents and allies organizing their defence against displacement, as in the case of neighbours and friends gathering on the roofs of those whose houses were threatened with attack by Israeli planes. Some have appealed such cases, especially those that lead to casualties, in the Israeli and international court system, despite the fact that such cases are mostly rejected in Israeli courts.

So far, the Centre has recorded over 1,200 audio interviews with different groups in Gaza on various topics, all relevant to the history of Palestinian society. These include the Israeli occupation of the Gaza Strip, the rise of the Islamic movement in Gaza, and the 2012 Israeli attack on Gaza, along with other incidents. The Centre has also held several training courses on oral history, to teach students and academics how to use oral history to document Palestinian events. Some of these courses took place outside Gaza, such as in Ramallah and in Amman.

The Centre's plan is to do a series of studies that orally document the history of Palestine since 1948, conducting video interviews with leading historical figures, producing a documentary film about Palestinian history, using the global information network to publicize the materials available in the Centre, translating them into different foreign languages, and using advanced information technology to maintain oral narratives about Palestine.

Given the common fallacies spread in the Western world about the Palestinian narrative, Shahin emphasized the urgent need to start an extensive project to document the Nakba and life thereafter in Gaza, noting that many of those who lived through this historic event in Palestine are passing away, and others find it hard to remember the Nakba: they may not be highly educated, or may by now have failing memories. This is in addition to the fact that some could be scattered in different areas in the world, which may prove detrimental to the Palestinian cause. This documentation, if done, could be used to establish the rights of Palestinian refugees in their lands, in all international forums and courts. Shahin later added that there are recent efforts in the East, as well as the West, to document records of those who have been displaced.

This section shows that the efforts by the Islamic University of Gaza's Oral History Project provide hope amid the Israelis' continuous attempts to erase Palestinian history. The next section looks into the emergence of new narratives, mainly led by Palestinian youth in Gaza, to further reinforce the Palestinian narrative amongst the young generation.

EMERGENCE OF NEW NARRATIVES

Since its establishment, the Israeli government has attempted to erase the memory of the Nakba from the Israeli Jewish consciousness and from Western public discourse, as well as official media. This has been largely implemented through the destruction of Palestinian villages and towns, replacing them with Jewish settlements or by planting trees and turning these villages into resorts; for example, Canada Park is built on the ruins of the three villages of Yalu, Imwas and Beit-Nuba (Cook 2009). Such policies and practices could also be one reason for the historical amnesia that has predominated in Western literature on Palestinian resistance. This amnesia was highlighted by Shahin during my interview with him, in addition to the fact that Palestinian narratives have long been excluded from the discussion of Palestine by much of Western academia as well as mainstream film, art, music and news media institutions (Abdo 2014).

In this context, Shahin notes that as Israeli narratives are the predominant ones in the West, such as the false claim that Palestine was a land without a people, the Palestinians have started documenting their own narratives in an attempt to counter the Israeli falsehoods and media-oriented onslaught. He attributed the delays in documenting Nakba events to the horror embodied in the destruction of over 600 Palestinian villages, in addition to the killings and attacks on humans and animals, and destruction of written documents, archives and libraries that existed at the time, which shocked the Palestinians and the Arabs, especially because they were unable to do much to prevent it (in Svirsky 2012: 59). In the same framework, Shahin added that the Arab world has been against the Palestinians leaving their lands and has raised the issue with the outside world. He noted that the Palestinians have been subjected to war at home and abroad, where the displaced and expelled Palestinians did not find anyone to welcome them in the Arab world. It took them some time to take stock and start writing their own history, but if they did not do so, who would do it for them? Shahin added that the narrative was confined to official correspondence between Britain and America on the one hand and Britain and the Zionist organizations on the other, and that is problematic; the displaced Palestinians have suffered hardships, but no attention has been paid to their case. This history and memory of the Nakba, and the ongoing Israeli settler-colonial rule over the Palestinians, are what old and new imperialism, as well as orientalist feminists, have overlooked and continued to overlook.

Over time, Shahin notes, the importance of oral history has been increasing, but the previous omission of the Palestinian-related narrative has undoubtedly impacted on public knowledge concerning Palestinian struggles against Israeli settler-colonialism, limiting, in turn, greater public discussion on the question of Palestine. Until the 1980s, the Israeli version of the events of 1948, which lays all the blame for the war on the Arabs, has gone largely unchallenged outside of the Arab world. In a lecture delivered by Israeli-British historian Avi Shlaim at the Palestinian Initiative for the Promotion of Global Dialogue and Democracy (MIFTAH), he argued, "This is a nationalist version of history and, as such, it is simplistic, selective, and self-serving. It is, essentially, the propaganda of the victors. It presented the victors as victims, and it blamed the real victims – the Palestinians – for their own misfortunes" (2003 MIFTAH).

One main source of information nowadays on narratives of the Nakba is that of the youth involved in research. Palestinian youths are an integral part of oral history projects, and this has undoubtedly contributed to the development of a new genre of literature. Palestinian history of the Nakba, of national and anti-colonial resistance, is sometimes written from a youth perspective, helped by other writers, as in the case of the Tamer Institute for Community Education, explained in the next section. This history being brought back to life from this perspective will undoubtedly serve as a future rebuttal to the Western perspective of Palestine as a land without people. This is also important to counter imperialist arguments on the topic of Palestine. For Abdo, all imperialism seems to have the same outcomes regarding Palestine, but the new one is more sophisticated, creating a new epistemology for framing world peace, conflict and resistance, and creating what it perceives to be "democratic" regimes that need to accept imperial interests. This imperialism also means the control of the vast majority of the world by a few US-based organizations.

It is not that the Palestinians chose this situation; it was forced on them. Their leadership has gone through many rounds of peaceful "negotiations", "agreements", "dialogues" and "deals" that they have entered into and accepted, all of which have failed to produce any resolution to the Palestinian problem (Abdo 2014: 75). This brought them to new methods of resistance, lately that of the Boycott, Divestment and Sanctions (BDS) movement. Eyad El-Sarraj is a pioneering Palestinian psychiatrist born in Bir al-Sabe' in Palestine in 1944, to a Palestinian Arab Muslim family. He arrived along with his family in the Gaza Strip in 1948, and observed these feelings of despair in 2005:

> We simply became the slaves of our enemy. We are building their homes
> on our villages, and we clean their streets. Do you know what this does
> to you when you have to be the slave of your enemy in order to survive?
> No, you will never understand how painful it is unless your country
> is occupied by another force. Only then will you learn how to watch
> in silence pretending not to see the torture of your friends and the
> humiliation of your father; do you know what it means for a child to see
> his father spat at and beaten before his eyes by an Israeli soldier? Nobody
> knows what happened to our children. We don't know ourselves except
> we observe that they lose respect for their fathers. So they, our children,
> the children of the stone as they became known, tried the Intifada – the
> Uprising. Seven long years our children were throwing stones and being
> killed daily. Nearly all our young men [and many of our young women]
> were arrested and the majority [were] tortured. All had to confess. The
> result was every one suspected that all people were spies. So, we were
> exhausted, tormented and brutalised. What else could we do to return to
> our home? We had almost forgotten that and all what we wanted was to
> be left alone. (In Abdo 2014: 77)

This is the history that most counter-narratives choose to ignore, and this is the history which Palestinians in Gaza and elsewhere insist on remembering and reminding the whole world about (Abdo 2014: 77). This is one memory among millions of others which make up the Palestinian collective recollection of the Nakba: the history of their scattering, of life in exile, of the obliteration of their collective identity, and of the destruction of their homes. This is a history regarding how Israel became a state in 1948. The contradictions between the indigenous culture, that of the colonized and occupied, encourages and fosters resistance, and that of the imperialist culture, which criminalizes anti-colonial and anti-imperialist struggles and resistance and transforms the latter into terrorism, are the background of the Palestinian resistance, which has produced a political-cultural history (Abdo 2014: 84–85) and a prolonged struggle for liberation. As Fanon (in Abdo 2014: 618) argued, "If the settler colonial work is to make even dreams of liberty impossible for the native, the native's work is to imagine all possible methods for destroying the settler".

This section shows clearly that the erasure of Palestinian suffering in the Israeli narrative is well-planned and widely publicized; but, as the next section clearly argues, the ongoing oral history projects in Gaza build for a positive future, in terms of refuting the Israeli narrative and emphasizing the Palestinian one.

FUTURE OF ORAL HISTORY

As the research clearly sets out, Palestinian oral history has a long precedent in the culture of Palestine, stemming from a broader oral traditon. Projects to record and preserve this oral history in Gaza started at the end of the twentieth century, to create a line of defence against erasure of memory and culture among the Palestinian people. Regarding the future of oral history, I approached two of the earliest oral history projects in the Gaza Strip: the Tamer Institute for Community Education and the Oral History Project in the Islamic University of Gaza. To start with the Tamer Institute for Community Education, it is a Palestinian national non-profit organization. It was founded in Jerusalem in 1998 in response to the urgent need for the Palestinian society to gain an effective means to advance the education process under difficult social and economic conditions created by the Israeli occupation. Its mission is to work with the community, targeting mainly young people and developing alternative resources to formal education.

The Tamer Institute has long prioritized working on oral history as an essential part of its orientation, working with children, adults or writers for this purpose. It aims not only to transmit history by word of mouth from one generation to another, but has made several major attempts to document these stories for posterity. These efforts started just after the Institute was founded, shortly before the Second Intifada. At that time, the Tamer Institute began holding some teaching classes for students, and working as an alternative to formal education entities that were suffering from Israeli attacks and pressure.

Later, it launched the "Small Continent" initiative, which was one of the first to prioritize oral history. It is a voluntary, community-based initiative, by which many groups of young people explore natural archaeological and historical areas in Palestine, and then document their experiences in an oral history format. Groups recorded extensively using words and graphics about those experiences, and Tamer compiled and released them in a guide to the locations they visited, in both the West Bank and the Gaza Strip. The importance of this initiative lies in the revival of the natural link between young people and the historical and natural environment in Palestine, and the emphasis on communication, thus discovering the real value of those sites in Palestine. This initiative has been stalled since 2001 because of the closures and checkpoints, as well as the escalation of Israeli attacks, especially during the second Palestinian uprising in 2000.

Following this experience, the Tamer Institute continues in its attempts to create greater awareness of the importance of oral history by training many youngsters, such as members of the Araat Team in the West Bank and the Gaza Strip, and working to teach them research methodologies that will facilitate oral history projects.

The outcomes of this experience are many. For instance, in terms of books, the group has published the following: *Oral History of the Palestinian, Yalu, Jericho: A Day Trip and Ten Thousand Years, A Palestinian on the Road, A History of Palestinian Photography for Adolescents, Cities Narrating their History, From Jerusalem the Tale Begins* and *From Ebal to Mina We Sing Our Songs*, among others.

Other experiments were the product of research groups of youths and children. *Yalu*, a history of Yalu village, was prepared by a group of children: Ibaa Mghari (thirteen years), Nadia Aruri (twelve years), Celine Khoury (twelve years) and Razan Ayoubi (twelve years), led by Palestinian writer Sonia An-Nimer. The book *Jericho: A Day Trip and Ten Thousand Years* was prepared by the youth movement Small Continent, under the supervision of the Palestinian writer and artist Salman Natour. The book *From Ebal to Mina We Sing Our Songs* was published in 2013 and was the result of the efforts of a group of young Palestinians from different parts of Palestine: Tulkarem, Ramallah and Gaza. There was also another project for young men which was documented in a book entitled *Cities Narrating their History*, dealing with a similar theme to *From Ebal to Mina We Sing Our Songs*.

Involving youths in collecting, recording and preserving the Palestinian narrative in the Gaza Strip is a form of resistance, rejecting the Israeli fabrications of history which deny the Palestinian people their right to their lands. The younger generation's contribution to such projects is of special importance; they are the future generations who will lead the Palestinian resistance movement.

ERASURE NARRATIVES

After addressing the future of oral history, it is important to discuss how erasure narratives make oral history study both difficult to carry out and vitally important. Attempts to maintain the work of oral history are reaching Palestinians in their various locations. The efforts of the different Tamer groups in different locations – Jerusalem, the West Bank and the Gaza Strip – and their communications with researchers in other areas actually transcend the divisions enforced by the Israeli occupation, through practical coordination and joint planning, including by youth of the Araat teams. The combination of and collaboration between these groups that are divided by geopolitical distance is an important step in the direction of forging a nation, and this is documented by the new style of writings, which emerged from the different communities of Palestine into one body of work, as in the books *From Ebal to Mina* and *Cities Narrating their History*, as well as others put together by youths from different regions.

In the same context of the future of oral history in Gaza, Israel's continuous attacks on Gaza and the ethnic cleansing that has resulted, have produced a paradigm of resistance, accompanied by hope, that continue to haunt all Palestinian generations. Hope for the future, return and freedom, are themes that not even the Israelis can deny the Palestinians. This hope can be clearly seen through projects run by the young Palestinians, as in the Tamer Institute, documenting the Palestinian history.

In an excerpt from *Journey to Jerusalem* by Grace Halsell, an award-winning journalist, there is a conversation in a refugee camp with a school administrator, asking what is needed for a better situation. "Our freedom! Our freedom!", he replies emphatically. Nowadays, the young and the old inspire each other; from the elderly in their seventies and eighties, to school students, all are seen in the streets of the West marching for a free Palestine. Inside Palestine, it is rather the school students leading demonstrations and other types of resistance. Yet this does not preclude the psychological effects of the prolonged stays in camps which might lead to, as the administrator mentioned, an increased tendency towards passivity. "With loss of self-confidence and increased dependence … But this hatred builds on their lack of freedom. Israel forcibly produces a generation of tongueless people, and we will, in the end, speak with fire" (Halsell 1981).

Attempts by Israel to remove the map of Palestine from the world's geography and to obliterate the memory of the Nakba from world consciousness, using its institutional and legal power for this purpose, although continuous, are thus far in vain (Masalha 2012: 9). Official Israeli insistence on ignoring and denying the Palestinian Nakba has never stopped. The legal ban on Nakba commemorations by Palestinians through the Nakba Law of 2011 is just one example. The siege on Gaza, disconnecting the Palestinians in Gaza from the rest of the world and making it hard for researchers there to receive training on oral history, or equipment that would facilitate its gathering, is another challenge.

Projects of oral history in Gaza have limitations. The major threat is the Israeli occupation trying to whitewash its crimes by, for instance, changing the original names of Palestinian villages and streets, and limiting access to all archives that have links to the 1948 Palestinian Nakba. Also the Israelis use their settler-colonial, heritage-style cultural strategy, based on biblical archaeology studies and supported by a retrospective assembly of archaeological fragments, including, but not limited to, bones, tombs and officially approved historical and "archaeological theme parks" of artefacts and monuments. In addition to these threats to the Palestinian narrative, little work has been done in the conceptual area of oral history (for example Masalha 2008: 123–156); most studies by scholars have focused on raw data of specific areas of research. Additionally, many such works have been done in Arabic, a further barrier to those who do not speak the language.

Nevertheless, it is important that such initiatives have flourished, given that refugees who witnessed the 1948 ethnic cleansing of Palestine are declining in number. Haidar Eid of the Gaza-based Oral History Project, and an assistant professor at al-Aqsa University of Gaza, explained this challenge. "We started thinking about how the generation that survived the Nakba are leaving us … Most of these people are dying" (Catron 2013). Eid, a refugee, spoke about his own original village, to show the importance of oral history for the Palestinian account,

I'm from a village called Zarnuga, which is on the outskirts of Ramle [in present-day Israel]. I found only three pictures of Zarnuga … The history of the Tantura massacre relies heavily on oral history. Now people know that a massacre took place in the Tantura village, about 30 kilometres south of Haifa, based on recorded oral history. (Catron 2013)

This indicates the need for more extensive work on this subject in order to maintain the Palestinian narratives, providing the younger generation with a more accurate narrative of Palestinian history.

Shahin notes that obstacles facing oral history projects in the Gaza Strip include the limited knowledge on how to conduct oral history research; sometimes, researchers do not have sufficient information to discuss their accounts meaningfully with the narrators. Secondly, Shahin believes there is a lack of specialists in oral history, people who are qualified in scientific dialogue management. He had lately participated in a course on the methodology of oral history in Jordan, with two others from the West Bank. Shahin ends on a hopeful note, urging the Palestinians to invest in the oral history of the Nakba because, in his words, "this will prove our [legal] right to our land in international courts".

The hope is also linked to international grassroots movements that prioritize the right of return for all Palestinian refugees, as in Boycott, Divestment and Sanctions, which has proved to be a successful method of resistance. One of its three major points is the right of return to all Palestinian refugees, implementing the UN Resolution 194, calling for return for all refugees to their Palestinian lands which they were forced to leave in 1948, or their compensation. Much of the BDS work is coordinated in Gaza, with the Gaza-based professor Haidar Eid sitting on the Palestinian Campaign for the Academic and Cultural Boycott of Israel (PACBI) steering committee. Eid mentioned in a previous conversation that none of those interviewed for the Oral History Project he is part of agrees with compensation; all want to return to their lands. There is a consensus on this issue. Young volunteers conduct most of the interviews for the Oral History Project, and many belong to PACBI's youth affiliate (Catron 2013), once again emphasizing the importance of young Palestinians leading the way in such projects.

CONCLUSION

The Israeli premier Golda Meir once said "There are no Palestinian people" (Jerusalem Post International, 8–14 June 1980, in Masalha 2000: 244), but this could not make the Palestinians disappear; no power on earth can stop people from resisting outside rule. Israel, with all its national and international power, has failed to stop Gazan refugees from dreaming of a better future that entails a return to their homeland. For Palestinians, remembering the Nakba is not a choice which can be selected or deselected at will. It is an existential state of being, as it "is central to their social history and collective identity" (Masalha 2012: 7); it remains at the "heart of Palestinians' collective memory, national identity and the struggle for collective national rights" (Masalha 2012: 208). Herein lies the importance of bringing the Nakba into all Palestine-related discussions.

With the continuous Israeli attempts to attack and delegitimize Palestinian memory, hope seems to be a major factor that all refugees share, despite the odds against achieving the possibility of return. For Palestinian refugees, memory of the past represents the fuel for their survival, and acts as a force in maintaining and reproducing their rights as the sole owners of Palestine. It serves to keep them and their identity alive, and feeds their hope for a fair future. This memory and collective memory is critical, since a nation without memory and without culture is a nation without history (in reality, it cannot be a nation at all). For Palestinians who, after the creation of Israel, were scattered around the world or internally displaced, resistance through hope has functioned as a driving force in their commitment to fight for justice and against occupation, with the confidence to return to their homeland (Abdo 2014: 99–100). This is clearly symbolized in the young Palestinian generation, which is feeling suffocated, especially if living in refugee camps, but is at the same time politically active and vocal. This is in contrast to their contemporaries in the West, for instance, who are not equally politically aware, despite international student and public activism gatherings throughout the year. Living under occupation is indeed a major factor in this difference.

Importantly, this research serves to emphasize why oral history studies are a vital process in the Palestinian socio-political context. The Palestinian oral narrative speaks for itself; it is important to maintain this narrative for generations to come, as it contains within it important evidence for Palestinians' right to return to what once was their land, Palestine.

NOTES

1   In this study, the use of "Gaza" usually refers to the entire Gaza Strip.

REFERENCES

Abdo, N. (2014) *Palestinian Women's Anti-Colonial Struggle Within the Israeli Prison System*. London: Pluto Press.

BADIL (2012) http://www.badil.org/phocadownloadpap/Badil_docs/publications/Survey 2012.pdf.

Bisharat, G. (2007) "For Palestinians, Memory Matters", http://www.sfgate.com/opinion/article/For-Palestinians-memory-matters-It-provides-a-2560742.php.

Catron, J. (2013) "Gaza Researchers Determined to Record Nakba Generation Before Time Runs Out", https://electronicintifada.net/content/gaza-researchers-determined-record-nakba-generation-time-runs-out/12872.

Cook, J. (2009) "Canada Park and Israeli 'memoricide'", https://electronicintifada.net/content/canada-park-and-israeli-memoricide/8126.

Doumani, B. (2009) "Archiving Palestine and the Palestinians: The Patrimony of Ihsan Nimr", *Jerusalem Quarterly* (36): 3–12, http://history.berkeley.edu/sites/default/files/archiving_0.pdf.

Hajjaj, T. (2015) "The Oldest Man in Gaza: 'Back in the Old Days, Your Home Was Yours', http://www.middleeasteye.net/in-depth/features/palestinian-oral-history-978259534.

Halsell, G., (1981) 'Life in a Palestinian Refugee Camp", excerpted from *Journey to Jerusalem*, http://www.ifamericansknew.org/cur_sit/ref-halsell.html.

Hastings, T. (2016) "Palestinian Oral History as a Tool to Defend Against Displacement", https://al-shabaka.org/commentaries/palestinian-oral-history-tool-defend-displacement/.

Masalha, N (2000) *Imperial Israel and the Palestinians*. London: Pluto, https://goo.gl/q50Kun.

Masalha, N. (2008) "Remembering the Palestinian Nakba: Commemoration, Oral History and Narratives of Memory", *Holy Land Studies* 7(2): 123–156.

Masalha, N. (2012) *The Palestine Nakba: Decolonising History, Narrating the Subaltern, Reclaiming Memory*. London: Zed Books.

MIFTAH (2003) http://www.miftah.org/Doc/Articles/2004/Mar18bI2k4.html.

Muhanna, E. (2016) "The Digital Humanities and Islamic and Middle East Studies", https://goo.gl/1IsieA.

Svirsky, M. (2012) *Arab-Jewish Activism in Israel-Palestine*. Abingdon: Routledge.

The Nakba Files (2016) "Archives Week on the Nakba Files", http://nakbafiles.org/2016/05/26/archives-week-on-the-nakba-files/.

Weiss, P. (2016) "'We wasted 40 years talking about nothing, doing nothing' – Pappe demolishes peace process", http://mondoweiss.net/2016/03/we-wasted-40-years-talking-about-nothing-doing-nothing-pappe-demolishes-the-peace-process/.

14

"Besieging the cultural siege": mapping narratives of Nakba through orality and repertoires of resistance

CHANDNI DESAI

Besiege your siege, there is no other way. (Mahmoud Darwish, quoted in Barghouti 2011)

In the documentary *On the Side of the Road* (Tarachansky 2013), the film opens with a scene on the streets of Tel Aviv on 15 May, where Israelis are found celebrating their so-called "Independence Day". On the same day Palestinians commemorated the Nakba (known as the "catastrophe"), marking the ethnic cleansing that took place in 1948 whereby 750,000 people were expelled from their homes, lost their lands and became internally displaced or exiled refugees (Masalha 2012; Pappe 2006). The film shows Palestinian commemoration events in various parts of the Occupied Territories, especially in the form of protests. In response to acts of collective mourning of the Nakba, Israeli Prime Minister Benjamin Netanyahu, in his remarks to the Knesset two days later, said the following:

I have to say that, from the perspective of the rioters, the 63 years Israel's been existing haven't changed anything. After all, what did the protestors in Gaza say? They yelled they want to return to Jaffa [Yafa]. What did the protestors in Syria say? That they want to return to the Galilee. [...] The most interesting is the thing that happened in Bil'in.

Because at the protests in Bil'in two days ago [...] a little girl was walking with a big, symbolic key in her hand. Now, every Palestinian understands what key we're talking about here. It wasn't a key to *their* houses in Bil'in, or in Nablus, or in Ramallah, it was the key to *our* houses, in Jaffa, in Akko, in Haifa, in Ramle. (Netanyahu speech and translation in Tarachansky 2013)

I begin this chapter with this lengthy quote to demonstrate the settler-colonial narrative and national mythologies that are produced to tell stories of land and (non-)belonging about Palestine/Israel. Settler-colonial societies use national mythologies to erase the genocidal history that led to a settler nation's founding. These national mythologies are profoundly racialized and spatialized stories. Sherene Razack (2002: 3) argues that "although the spatial story that is told varies from one time to another, at each stage the story installs Europeans as entitled to the land, a claim that is codified in law". The legal doctrine of terra nullius – empty, uninhabited lands – describes territory that has supposedly never been subject to the sovereignty of any nation. In his speech, Prime Minister Benjamin Netanyahu follows this logic. First, Palestinian land is rendered terra nullius by its so-called "rightful" (new) owners – the Zionists – who discovered "a land without a people, for people without a land" and made the "desert bloom". This settler story transforms the Indigenous people of the land who had/have lived there for centuries into "uncivilized rioters", erasing and conflating their mourning and refusal to accept "Israeli Independence Day" as acts of violence that need to be contained through the use of force and law. In evoking the words "our houses", Netanyahu's narrative erases the Zionist conquest and land theft of the Palestinian cities of Yafa, Akka, Haifa, Ramle and the Galilee in 1948 by claiming these cities as Israeli. The significance of the act of commemorating the Nakba and the cultural symbols that evoke Palestinian indigeneity and land claims is evident in his speech, as Netanyahu is bothered by a little girl's gesture of walking around holding a symbolic key. Netanyahu's settler anxieties are revealed when he speaks about this little girl to the Knesset because she represents the continuity of an anti-colonial Palestinian history that each Palestinian generation, inside the country and in exile, will continue to pass on through the oral stories, symbols (such as keys, olive trees, oranges and citrus groves), memories and cultural production (resistance poetry, literature, music, *dabke* – folk dance) transmitted across time and space.

In this study, using critical race and anti-colonial theory, I outline how the Israeli/Zionist settler-colonial project engaged in the systematic erasure of the material culture of Palestine, with a specific focus on toponymicide. I argue that Palestinian cultural producers rupture and reconfigure Zionist toponomy and national settler-colonial mythologies of land and belonging. I argue that they provide a counter-hegemonic and anti-colonial narrative of 1948 (Nakba) and its afterlife,[1] and claim place and belonging to Palestine through their resistance repertoires. In doing so, I propose that various cultural producers partake in allegorically besieging the cultural siege on Palestinian/Israel history, following Darwish's call to "besiege your siege".

DESTRUCTION OF PALESTINIAN MATERIAL CULTURE CENTRAL TO ZIONIST CONQUEST

I situate this work within a historical understanding of the politics of Israel–Palestine and of Zionism as a political ideology and a settler-colonial regime characterized by the establishment of the state of Israel (Abdo 2011). In particular, core to the Zionist settler-colonial project's endeavour of claiming the land, the destruction of Palestinian material culture was necessary to erase the Palestinian presence. The war of 1948 had the premeditated purpose of expelling as many Palestinians as possible. Baruch Kimmerling (2003: 3–4) defines this systematic attempt at Palestinian annihilation as politicide: "a process that has, as its ultimate goal, the dissolution of the Palestinian people's existence as a legitimate social, political, and economic entity". Another method that has been used by the settler state to erase Palestinian cultural memory and identity was *toponymicide*, which was a key tool used to de-Arabize the land. "The Zionist Yishuv's toponomy project was established in the 1920s to restore biblical Hebrew and to create new Hebrew-sounding names of symbolic meaning" (Ra'ad 2010: 189). The Jewish National Fund (JNF) naming committee was used to replace Palestinian Arab toponomy with Zionist-Hebrew toponomy. As such, "thousands of names were given to streets, public squares, and the landscape, with signs in Hebrew everywhere" (Masalha 2012: 100; and see Troen 2007). For example, the Arab village Mahloul was renamed Nahlal, Jibta was changed to Kibbutz Gvat, Mlabbis was named Petah Tikva (Masalha 2012: 102). Renaming through mapping enabled the settler-colonists to geographically overhaul of entire country, transforming and rewriting Palestinian and Jewish histories according to Zionist dicta. In renaming places and symbolic cultural images of land Nur Masalha (2012) suggests that Israel partakes in the "memoricide" of Palestine. Also, appropriation of the Palestinian heritage and its voices was central to Zionist colonial practice. These practices have attempted to erase and silence the Palestinian narrative of history and replace it with a dominant Zionist narrative. In doing so, Ghassan Kanafani (1968) argued that the Palestinian people inside historical Palestine experienced not only a military siege but also a cultural siege. Thus, for Israeli settler-colonialists to maintain power and Jewish exclusivity, anything that offers knowledge on a different history, temporality and spatiality of Israel/Palestine had/has to be demolished and erased.

In 2011, the attempts at memoricide were yet again made evident when the Israeli Knesset passed the Nakba Law.[2] This discriminatory bill cuts state funding to any organization that commemorates the Palestinian Nakba, studies, mentions or produces knowledge about it, as the historical facts of the Nakba tell the story of the founding of the Israeli settler-colonial state. Haneen Zoabi (a Palestinian member of the Knesset) suggests that "behind this law is a fear, a fear of the victim. Behind this law is the ability of the *memory* of the victim to threaten the legitimacy of Zionism" (Kestler-D'Amours 2011: para. 30). In *The Archive and the Repertoire*, Diana Taylor (2003: 17) argues that histories are written to "suit the memorializing needs of those in power". Similarly, referring to the context of Palestine, Nur Masalha (2012) suggests that Israeli archives say very little about the Palestinian narrative of what happened in 1948 from the side of the victims who experienced the Nakba. Ilan Pappe (2006) also makes an important point regarding the "new Israeli historiography" of 1948 and argues that the alternative historical narratives provided by the "new historians" is largely macro-historical due to the nature of Israeli archival material. When the archive is considered the only legitimate source of valid information, Taylor (2003: 193) asks whose experiences and "memories, whose trauma, disappears if only archival knowledge is valorized and granted permanence?" In *Acts of Transfer*, Taylor (2003: 20–21) suggests that the repertoire is a form of knowledge that "transmits communal memories, histories and values from one group-generation to the next. Embodied and performed acts generate record and transmit knowledge". The repertoire includes enactments embodied in memory, performance(s), orality, movement, singing, dancing and gestures which are ephemeral knowledge. The repertoire "holds the tales of the survivors, their gestures, the traumatic flashbacks, repeats, and hallucinations" (Taylor 2003: 193), which are embodied forms of thought and memory that should be considered valid forms of knowledge, especially for those often marginalized and silenced. In the case of Palestine, the repertoire – music, songs, stories, dance etc. – is how Palestinians have preserved and transmitted memory about Palestine and its history, specifically the Nakba, across time and space. Amidst the fragmentation of the Palestinian population, the lack of a state, the Zionist destruction of Palestinian material culture and the constant attacks on archives and centres of culture and knowledge production, Palestinians continue to preserve and pass on knowledge about their history across the generations.

In the next section I draw from data collected during my doctoral research, specifically on the oral history interviews and cultural texts of exiled (third-generation) Palestinian spoken word and hip hop artists, an interview with the El-Funoun Dance Troupe's choreographer, and Ghassan Kanafani's short story *The Land of Sad Oranges*, to show how Palestinians reconfigure Zionist toponomy through their repertoires of cultural resistance.

REMEMBERING AND ARCHIVING THE NAKBA THROUGH ORALITY

In Ghassan Kanafani's well-known short story *The Land of Sad Oranges* (1958), a child narrator tells the story of the Zionist militia attack on Akka in May 1948, and the journey of dispossession from Akka to Ras al-Naqoura.[3] Along the way, the narrator describes seeing fields of oranges. At one point in the story, as they are fleeing, the van stops at an orange grove. The child narrator's aunt hands her husband an orange, and he "started looking at it silently, then his cry exploded, like a desperate child" (Kanafani 1958: 62). One of the most significant moments in the story is the family's arrival in Lebanon. The narrator says:

> I started to cry; your mother was still looking at the orange silently and in the eyes of your father, the orange trees that he left for the Jews was sparkling in his eyes. All the clean orange trees that he bought, tree by tree, all were being drawn on his face. He couldn't hold in his sparkling tears, in front of prescient police officer. When we reached Saidon [South Lebanon], in the afternoon, we became refugees. (Kanafani 1958: 65)

Another important scene in the story is when the child narrator recalls what a peasant once told him about the oranges of Yafa (Jaffa): "it wilts, if the hand that waters it changes" (Kanafani 2013). At the end of the story, as the child narrator enters the room they were staying in, like an intruder, and touches his uncle's face which is shaking in destructive anger, he concurrently sees a "black pistol on the table and next to it was an orange, and the orange was dry, and wilted" (Kanafani 1958: 73).

Kanafani's short story is a very significant piece of resistance literature, as he narrated Palestine back into existence through his own memories, and through oral stories about the exodus that were shared with him. This simply written yet detailed story describes the Palestinian Nakba, and the routes that thousands took as they escaped the attacks of Zionist militias that were given orders for the systematic expulsion of Palestinians through Plan Dalet in 1948 (Khalidi 1988). More specifically, the story centres around the orange, as this fruit was central to the Palestinian economy and culture. Before 1948 the people of Yafa had cultivated citrus groves, specifically oranges, as there was a global demand for Yafa's oranges. The city of Yafa therefore had an important place in the global economy as millions of crates of oranges were exported from the city to major commercial centres across the Mediterranean and Europe (Abu Shehadeh and Shbaytah 2009). According to Sami Abu Shehadeh and Fadi Shbaytah (2009: para. 3), Yafa experienced enormous economic growth because of the citrus exports:

> from banks to land and sea transportation enterprises to import and export firms, and many others. As the city grew, Jaffa's entrepreneurs began to develop local industrial production with the opening of metalwork factories, and others producing glass, ice, cigarettes, textiles, sweets, transportation-related equipment, mineral and carbonated water, and various foodstuffs, among others.

Despite this rich economic and cultural history of Palestine, Zionist settlers appropriated the orange, fetishized it and began to use the image of the orange to produce the story "of taming the land with the arrival of Jewish settlers" (Sela in Sivan 2010), producing the narrative of Zionist pioneers who cultivated the so-called deserted, barren land. Rona Sela, a researcher and curator in Israel, "demonstrates how early photographs of the region deliberately portrayed it as desolate, inviting conquest and cultivation" (Parsons 2011: para. 11). Also, the Citrus Marketing Board of Israel adopted the Jaffa orange and branded it as Israeli on the world market. Israel appropriated one of the most significant Palestinian symbols, and not only transformed it into its own emblem, but in claiming the lands and citrus industry that Palestinians had cultivated also erased the Palestinian people's presence from their lands. According to historian Amnon Raz-Krakotzkin, "Through the orange, you unfold the story of the Zionist seizure of the country in every way" (Parsons 2011: para. 13).

Kanafani's novel provides a counter-narrative to this seizure of land by highlighting the significance of oranges to the Palestinian economy and culture. The wilted orange described at the end of the short story provides a narrative of the Palestinian relationship to the land, especially of the peasants (*fallaheen*) who cultivated it. The wilted orange symbolizes Zionist invasion, conquest and the material erasure of Palestine, claiming Palestinian existence and belonging to the land. Stories such as these are an important part of Palestinian resistance culture as they are passed on to subsequent generations, especially to those that did not experience the Nakba.

In oral history interviews with spoken word/hip hop artists Remi Kanazi, Excentrik (Tarik Kazaleh) and Rafeef Ziadah, who all live in exile, they describe the process of what Diana Taylor (2003) calls "acts of transfer" – transmitting social knowledge, memory and a sense of identity through the repertoire. Tarik shares that his grandparents and uncles had a tremendous influence on him, particularly as he heard about Ghassan Kanafani from them. He was influenced by Kanafani's resistance literature, and describes his stories as beautiful and creative. Tarik says, "you just read all the compassion in all his stories, they are really sad stories" (Tarik Kazaleh, in Desai 2016: 213). Similarly, when I interviewed spoken word poet Rafeef Ziadah, she explained the significant influence Mahmoud Darwish, Ghassan Kanafani, Fadwa Tuqan and Naji Al-Ali – artists who produced the radical tradition of Palestinian cultural resistance – had upon her while she was growing up during the 1982 Israeli invasion of Lebanon. Rafeef explains how these resistance artists influenced her consciousness at a young age, as these cultural figures "were our identity, they weren't just poets and writers, they spoke us, they spoke our history" (Zaidah, personal interview, 2015). This is significant as younger generations are taught about place and belonging to land through repertoires of resistance by their families. The oral stories produced in the resistance repertories such as that of Kanafani, Darwish and others, reflected a collective narrative of what happened in 1948. Tarik shares:

So when I learned about the real history of Palestine, and started to see how things really went down and how the Nakba worked, and how that affected my family and how it affected generations and how the occupation still affects my family that still lives back home, it's a deep personal wound. (Kazaleh, personal interview, 2015)

Oral histories, memories and repertoires such as Kanafani's are significant because they pass on and provide history to various aspects of the Palestinian question: the Nakba, exile, refugees, armed struggle, right of return, internal social struggle. In doing so, these stories memorialize Palestinians' experiences of Zionist violence and dispossession and repudiate the primary settler-colonial narratives that dominate Israel and the global public sphere. Such narratives are important pedagogical tools used to teach various generations about Palestine, cultivating their consciousness of resistance across time and space. This was certainly evident for Remi Kanazi, as he recalled that his *teta* (maternal grandmother) had the greatest influence on his life and cultural work. He shares that his "first entry into Palestine was through his *teta*" (Kanazi, personal interview, 2015). In his spoken poem "Nakba", he rhymes

Her home
Mandated, Occupied, Cleansed, Conquered,
Terrorizers sat on hills, sniping children, neighbours fled on 10 April,
Word came of massacre,
They stayed,
Didn't fight, didn't flee, shells and bombs bursting in the air like anthems ...
Looking over shoulders of the Irgun and the Haganah,
She's a warrior,

Had birth from Palestine,
Whispered Yafa till her final breath. ...
48 ways to flee, and she found Beirut. (Kanazi 2015)

"Nakba", a poem Remi wrote from the memory of his *teta*'s experience of 1948, was intended to tell the story of violence that his grandparents experienced at the hands of Zionist militias – the Irgun and Haganah – which led to their forced expulsion.

He deploys the terms "occupied", "cleansed", "conquered" and "massacre" to historicize what happened in 1948 through the perspective of his grandmother's narrative, which contradicts the notion of "Israeli Independence Day", as Remi outlines that what happened in 1948 was conquest. In an interview with Remi, he explains that his *teta*'s experience of the Nakba and her exile in Beirut were a big part of his childhood, as he always heard his grandmother say, "Yafa, Yafa, Yafa" and "Return" (*Al-Awada*), which inspired his poem Nakba. Hip hop (including spoken word) is a site that enables the continuity of oral histories to be transmitted across time and generations. The Palestinian spoken word and rap are not only influenced by the African oral tradition, but also by their own indigenous oral history, as orality is central to Arab culture. As such, Palestinian spoken word poets and rappers infuse indigenous oral stories and poetry with new history, beats, breaks, digitalized cuts and samples across geographic regions. *Poetic Injustice*, Remi's first book of poems, is divided into four sections. Each section represents one of his displaced grandparents: Leonie, Shipro, Najla and George, which reflects the collective memory of Palestine. These poems are significant as the "Nakba generation is passing away, there is a growing anxiety that these sources of memory will be lost, a fear of forgetfulness" (Kanazi 2011: 17). Therefore, the act of narrating and re-telling these stories through their cultural texts is significant, as the repertoire acts as a palimpsest that documents memory of the past.

For example in the poem "Leonie" Remi rhymes:

I have never seen someone love something so much
As if that something was a someone
A homeland
A companion
I didn't understand the need to return until I looked into my Teta's eyes ...

She hadn't watered her garden in days
Can't water with bombs falling
Don't know how long the water will last
Don't know when the bombing will stop
Don't know if her flowers will ever bloom again ...

She closes her eyes
Smells the sea salt, caresses the soft sand, takes in a deep breath, and feels the wind hug her arms as her father once did

For a split second she imagines they have returned, where she was born, where she belongs. (Kanazi 2011: 10–12)

Remi describes his grandmother's love and attachment to her homeland through her senses of smell and touch and her imaginary. Exiled to Lebanon during the Nakba, Remi's grandmother died without the actualization of the right of return that she eagerly awaited, which Remi suggests she embodied through the emotions that could be seen in her eyes. His description of her physical presence in the city of Yafa during 1948, watering her garden, is a poetic form of resisting Zionist historiography and narratives that invoke the erasure of Palestinians from their homeland, such as in Benjamin Netanyahu's speech outlined earlier, where he claims Yafa to be "ours" (in reference to Zionists/Israeli Jews). In this way, Remi's poem encapsulates the process of settler colonization through which the 1948 generation, of which his grandmother was part, lost everything and became refugees. The poem memorializes the Nakba and resists Palestinian displacement across generations as Remi reminds us that his grandmother, and others like her, remained steadfast (*sumud*) in their struggle for their homeland and never lost sight of their hope of return to Palestine. Remi encapsulates the embodiment of his grandmother's *sumud* in her eyes and suggests that it was passed on to him as he began to understand the need to return to his ancestral homeland.

In another poem, Remi describes his visit to his grandmother's house in Yafa:

She no longer recognizes my face
Never will again
But can still smell her oranges
Feels the sun kiss her face as if on her balcony in Yafa. 61 years later
Described like the most magnificent villa
Must have been seven storeys tall, spanned half the neighbourhood, tree
branches opened like arms, so trunks could witness its beauty
I visited the house with my brother
Israeli cab driver said he'd never heard of the street. Palestinian presence
must have made his memory fail. ("Yaffa", in Kanazi 2011: 24)

By retelling his refugee grandmother's memories, Remi affirms and memorializes the existence of a collective Palestinian identity that existed in historical Palestine, specifically in the former Palestinian city of Yafa. Invoking the national symbols of Palestinian *sumud* – oranges and olive trees – the way many Palestinian classical resistance artists also do (e.g. Kanafani), Remi beckons the imaginary of return, rooted in his grandmother's memories, imaginary and desire. Moreover, Remi describes the cultural memoricide of Palestine when an Israeli cab driver denies the cartography of Palestine by not recognizing the historic street names that existed pre-1948, the memories of which survive among the refugees of that generation. The Israeli cab driver's failure of memory underscores how the Zionist settler-colonial state changed the toponomy of historical Palestine and constructed new narratives of what was/is on the land, thus producing Zionist settler fantasies[4] that are premised on the forgetting and erasure of Palestinian existence. By describing his grandmother's house and neighbourhood, Remi also embodies his grandmother's spirit of *sumud* by not allowing Palestinians to be written out of history. He rhymes "The outside world may never mention their names but the roots of olive trees will never forget what happened" ("Yaffa", in Kanazi 2011: 24).

Moreover, some cultural texts not only re-present the Palestinian narrative, re-tell stories that have been passed on to them through orality, but also invoke radical imaginaries of freedom. In the song "The Ghosts of Deir Yassin" produced by Phil Mansour and featuring Rafeef Ziadah, the cultural producers shed light on the Zionist cultural memoricide and toponymicide of historical Palestine, specifically by talking about the village of Deir Yassin.

They pretend that it's forgotten
But somewhere small flowers grow
On the weathered stones of destroyed homes
Somewhere the light's still in the window …

They change the names on the signs
But it's in our hearts these words are written
Of the children who don't know their homes
They will walk the streets from which they are forbidden
You see that we are rising
Our day is surely coming
No longer in the shadows
Of the ghosts of Deir Yassin. (Mansour and Ziadah n.d.)

On 9 April 1948, Zionist militia from the Irgun and the Stern Gang attacked Deir Yassin, a village located between Jerusalem and what is now Tel Aviv, which was home to 750 Palestinian residents. Palestinian men "were lined up against a wall and sprayed with bullets, execution style. Teachers were savagely mutilated with knives" (Elmuti 2013: para. 6). Women were taken hostage and then returned to a bloodbath in which 120 Palestinians were massacred, houses were dynamited, the cemetery was bulldozed, and many were driven out of their village by Zionist militia (Elmuti 2013). Deir Yassin was wiped off the map; the centre of the village was de-Arabized and renamed Givat Shaul and became part of the city of Jerusalem. In Palestinian and Zionist history, the massacre of Deir Yassin is of great significance because it was the catalyst and schematic for the depopulation of over 400 Palestinian-Arab villages and cities during the Nakba, and was the blueprint for the architecture of Israeli apartheid: the wall, the settlements and the checkpoint system.

In "The Ghosts of Deir Yassin" (Mansour 2012), the small flowers that grow on the destroyed homes and the light that comes through the windows are symbolic of *sumud* and Palestinian presence and memory of the pre-settler/ colonial, pre-Nakba landscape. Though the neighbourhood of Givat Shaul lies on the ruins of the Palestinian village Deir Yassin, and Zionist toponomy has de-Arabized and Hebrewized the landscape by changing the name of the area, this resistance song clearly underscores that Palestinians have not forgotten. The names of destroyed cities and villages remain in Palestinian memory. This is poignantly captured in the music video, which was filmed in several refugee camps in Jordan and Lebanon. The names of villages, towns and cities are remembered and written on the palms and carved into the flesh of Pales- tinian refugees whose families were historically from those areas. These names are invoked to suggest that Palestinians, specifically those in exile who are forbidden to enter 1948 Palestine, will walk those streets again. Resistance is expressed in the lines "you see that we are rising our day is surely coming / no longer in the shadow / of the ghosts of Deir Yassin". This song is not only about the Palestinian past; it is about fighting for a just future in the afterlife of the Nakba. As such, to rupture Zionist cultural memoricide and toponymicide, the right of return of dispossessed Palestinians is invoked in this song, as Rafeef performs revered Palestinian female poet Fadwa Tuqan's poem "Fee Thikra Al Milad elEshreen" (Twentieth Birthday Anniversary). In the music video, she appears with name of the city of Haifa written on her palm, which, she explains during an interview, was one of the cities her grandparents were expelled from during the Nakba. Rafeef powerfully recites Tuqan's poem in Arabic, "I challenge ... No, my future / I will return with resolve and confidence / ... to my beloved homeland / To the / flowers and roses / I no longer fear their power / I will return".

For the Zionist settler project, Palestinian narratives of the Nakba, existence on the land, return and symbols such as the key, oranges and olives undermine the national story of the Israeli state. Therefore, cultural symbols are appropriated and cultural production – poetry, music, art, books, *dabke* – is censored or destroyed. Nevertheless, Palestinian cultural producers creatively find ways to resist attempts at cultural genocide. During an interview with Sharaf DarZaid, the choreographer of the El-Funoun (*dabke*) Dance Troupe in the West Bank, he explains that El-Funoun began compiling songs from the Nakba generation onwards, and attempted to create a music archive of the important songs that were part of the Palestinian heritage. DarZaid explained that during the Second Intifada, members of El-Funoun took sections of the archive out of the Popular Arts Centre (where it was housed in Al-Bireh), for fear of an Israeli raid on their dance studio. Since Israel has a history of destroying Palestinian archives, the El-Funoun members wanted to preserve the oral (music) archive they had collected. They therefore ensured that different people took parts of it; if the Zionists confiscated the archive from one of the dancers, the Israelis would only acquire a fraction of El-Funoun's musical archive and could only possess or destroy a small portion of it. This underscores the importance of the Palestinian repertoire and the way in which a collection of oral stories and songs that offer an anti-colonial memory of Palestinian life and heritage is/was threatening to the Zionist settler project. Despite the challenges of living under a military siege that El-Funoun encountered during the Second Intifada, they persisted in resisting the erasure of their history and identity by continuing to dance, produce music and preserve Palestinian orality (songs) by protecting the Palestinian musical – folklore – archive.

CULTURAL PRODUCTION AS RESISTANCE

Since the Nakba, Israel has been carrying out a cultural genocide of the Palestinian people's culture and heritage. The anti-democratic Nakba Law passed in 2012 that tries to deny the Palestinian people their history is not just a violation of human rights, it is an act of on-going cultural genocide against the

Palestinian people. Fearful of Palestinian memory – as seen in Netanyahu's speech to the Knesset about a little girl carrying a key – national mythologies are produced through rhetoric about land ownership such as "It wasn't a key to *their* houses […] it was the key to *our* houses" (Netanyahu speech and translation in Tarachansky 2013). Despite such national mythologies and constant attempts by the Zionists to erase Palestinian collective memory, history and identity, and the cultural siege it has placed on the Palestinian narrative, resistance continues. As I have shown in this chapter, Palestinians across generations have and continue to resist their erasure through various means particularly using poetry, music, dance, theatre, etc. Orality and performance has enabled them to preserve and transmit knowledge about Palestinian politics, history, place, culture, and to resist toponymicide and memoricide across generations. By producing counter-narratives that tell stories of Palestinian land and life, particularly the historical fact about the Nakba, and archiving them through the repertoire, cultural producers such as Ghassan Kanafani, Rafeef Ziadah, Remi Kanazi, Tarik Kazaleh, Phil Mansour, members of the El-Funoun Dance Troupe and others undermine the legitimacy of Zionism while allegorically besieging their siege.

NOTES

1   My conceptualization of the afterlife of the Nakba appears in my doctoral dissertation (Desai 2016). I draw on Saidiya Hartman's conceptualization of the afterlife of slavery, which she characterizes as the enduring presence of slavery's racialized violence that still persists in contemporary society on Black bodies, to conceptualize the on-going Zionist violence that persists in erasing, dehumanizing, brutalizing and annihilating Palestinian life from 1948 to the present.

2   This legislation was initiated by a Knesset member Alex Miller from the ultra-right-wing party Yisrael Beiteinu. The bill was originally drafted to incarcerate those who commemorate the Palestinian Nakba for at least three years. However, the bill was amended and called Budget Principles Law – Reducing Budgetary Support for Activities Contrary to the State (Kestler-D'Amours 2011).

3   Ras al-Naqoura is an area on the Israel–Lebanon border, towards South Lebanon.

4   I borrow the term *settler fantasies* from Tuck and Yang (2012: 14), who define it in the context of settler-colonialism in North America. Settler fantasies "can mean the adoption of Indigenous practices and knowledge, but more, refer to those narratives in the settler colonial imagination in which the Native (understanding that he is becoming extinct) hands over his land, his claim to the land, his very Indian-ness to the settler

for safe-keeping. This is a fantasy that is invested in a settler futurity and dependent on the foreclosure of an Indigenous futurity".

REFERENCES

Abdo, N. (2011) *Women in Israel: Race, Gender and Citizenship*. New York: Zed Books.

Abu Shehadeh, S. and F. Shbaytah (2009) "Jaffa: From Eminence to Ethnic Cleansing", *Electronic Intifada*, https://electronicintifada.net/content/jaffa-eminence-ethnic-cleansing/8088.

Barghouti, O. (2011) *Boycott, Divestment and Sanctions*. Chicago: Haymarket Books.

Desai, C. (2016) "We Teach Life: Exile, Hip Hop and the Radical Tradition of Palestinian Resistance". PhD dissertation, University of Toronto.

Elmuti, D. (2013) "We must never forget the massacre in Deir Yassin", *Electronic Intifada*, http://electronicintifada.net/content/we-must-never-forget-deir-yassin/12341.

Kanafani, G. (1958) *The Land of Sad Oranges*, translated by N. Habib, http://www.nobleworld.biz/images/sad_orange.pdf.

Kanafani, G. (1968). *Literature of Resistance in Occupied Palestine: 1948–1966* [in Arabic], http://www.tehforsakengods.com/resistance/resistance-literature-in-occupied-palestine-1948-1966-arabic-edition.pdf.

Kanafani, G. (2013) *Land of Sad Oranges*, translated by N. Abusadeh. Cyprus: Rimal Publications.

Kanazi, R. (2011) *Poetic Injustice. Writings on Resistance and Palestine*. New York: RoR Publishing.

Kanazi, R. (2015) "Nakba", in *Before the Next Bomb Drops: Rising up from Brooklyn to Palestine*. Chicago: Haymarket Books.

Kestler-D'Amours, J. (2011) "Israel Criminalizes Commemoration of the Nakb", *Electronic Intifada*, https://electronicintifada.net/content/israel-criminalizes-commemoration-nakba/9289.

Khalidi, W. (1988) "Plan Dalet: Master Plan for the Conquest of Palestine", *Journal of Palestine Studies* 18(1): 4–33.

Kimmerling, B. (2003) *Politicide: The Real Legacy of Ariel Sharon*. New York: Verso Books.

Masalha, N. (2012) *The Palestine Nakba: Decolonising History, Narrating the Subaltern, Reclaiming Memory*. New York: Zed Books.

Mansour, P., featuring R. Ziadah (n.d.) "Ghosts of Deir Yassin", https://www.youtube.com/results?search_query=ghosts+of+dier+yasin.

Pappe, I. (2006) *The Ethnic Cleansing of Palestine*. Oxford: OneWorld Publishing.

Parsons, L. (2011) "Jaffa, the Orange's Clockwork: Palestine, Israel – and the Orange", International Committee of the Fourth International (ICFI), https://www.wsws.org/en/articles/2011/03/jaff-m05.html.

Ra'ad, L.B. (2010) *Hidden Histories: Palestine and the Eastern Mediterranean*. London: Pluto Press.

Razack, S.H. (2002) "Gendered Racial Violence and Spatialized Justice: The Murder of

Pamela George", in S.H. Razack (ed.), *Race, Space, and the Law: Unmapping a White Settler Society*. Toronto: Between the Lines.

Sivan, E. (2010) *Jaffa's, The Clockwork Orange* (documentary film). Alma Films.

Tarachansky, L. (2013) *On the Side of the Road* (documentary film). Naretiv Productions.

Taylor, D. (2003) *The Archive and the Repertoire: Performing Cultural Memory in the Americas*. Durham, NC: Duke University Press.

Troen, I.S. (2007) "De-Judaizing the Homeland: Academic Politics in Rewriting the History of Palestine", *Israel Affairs* 13(4): 872–884.

Tuck, E. and Y. Wayne (2012) "Decolonization is not a Metaphor", *Decolonization: Indigeneity, Education and Society* 1(1): 1–40.

About the contributors

Nahla Abdo is an Arab Canadian feminist, political activist and Professor of Sociology at Carleton University. She has published extensively on anti-colonial feminism, racism, nationalism and the state in the Middle East with a special focus on Palestinians. She has received several research awards. Among her recent publications: *Counter Revolution: Palestinian Women's Anti-Colonial Struggle within the Israeli Prison System* (2014) which received the Times Higher Education Book award of 2014; *Women in Israel: Race, Gender, and Citizenship* (2011); and *Gender, Citizenship and the State: The Israeli Case* (2010, in Arabic). She also co-edited *Violence in the Name of Honour: Theoretical and Political Challenges* (2004) and *Women and the Politics of Military Confrontation: Palestinian and Israeli Gendered Narratives of Dislocation* (2002).

Faiha Abdul Hadi is a writer, poet, research consultant, community activist and lecturer, in addition to having -life-long experience in various aspects of research, oral history, gender and other issues of human interest. She is the founder and the Director General of Al Rowat for Studies and Research. She has published twelve books in addition to various studies and articles. She worked as a Consultant Researcher to the Directorate of Gender Planning and Development in Palestine and UNICEF in Cairo. She is a member of the Palestinian National Council, and the regional coordinator of the women's organization Peace Women Across the Globe.

Diana K. Allan is an anthropologist and filmmaker, and an assistant professor in the Department of Anthropology and the Institute for the Study of International Development at McGill University. She is the founder and co-director of the Nakba Archive and Lens on Lebanon, and her films include *Still Life* (2007), *Terrace of the Sea* (2010). Her ethnography, *Refugees of the Revolution: Experiences of Palestinian Exile* (2014) won the 2014 Palestine Book Award and the Middle East Section Award at the 2015 American Anthropological Association meeting.

Safa Abu-Rabi'a is a Palestinian-Bedouin. She is an anthropologist, and a lecturer at Ben Gurion University. Her areas of academic expertise include: anthropology and gender; place identity; feminist discourse in the Arab and Islamic world, and oral history. Her doctoral research focused on the doubly excluded women's voices of the Nakba generation. Women as active tellers of history were shown to reveal resistance to both the ruling Zionist perspective on the Bedouin and the patriarchal Bedouin assumptions about women. These findings challenge Western feminist perceptions on Arab women as well as the public and academic Israeli discourse, which denies the Bedouin connection to their lands.

Chandni Desai is a post-doctoral Mellon fellow for the Social Justice Initiative at the University of Illinois at Chicago working on the "Geographies of Justice" project which explores the meaning of freedom across three geographies: Palestine/Israel, apartheid and post-apartheid South Africa, and the US Black Freedom Movement. Chandni received her PhD in Education from the University of Toronto – OISE. Her research investigates the pedagogical role Palestinian cultural producers in exile play in the post-9/11 era in producing resistance culture in the afterlife of the Nakba, from and across settler-colonial states. Through oral history interviews, she links the work of contemporary artists to the radical tradition of Palestinian cultural resistance produced from the 1950s to 1980s to show how the intergenerational transmission of resistance culture influenced third-generation exiles to continue the radical tradition of art and activism in the ongoing struggle for liberation. Her research explores the themes of exile, insurgency, memory, public pedagogy, hip hop pedagogy, spatiality of resistance across settler colonial states, internationalism and solidarity.

Mona Al-Farra is a physician and a human rights and women's rights activist in the occupied Gaza Strip. Born in Khan Younis/Gaza, she has dedicated her life to the establishment and development of community-based programmes in the fields of health, culture and education. Dr Al-Farra is the Director of Gaza Projects for the Middle East Children's Alliance (MECA), the Vice President of the Palestinian Red Crescent Society of the Gaza Strip and a member of the Union of Health Work Committees. Her writings have appeared in *The Boston Globe*, *Le Monde Dipolimatique*, *The LA Times* and *The Guardian*. She has received two prestigious awards in recognition of her valuable work and contributions to the community in Gaza.

Lena Jayyusi is Professor of Communication and Media Sciences at Zayed University, UAE. She taught at Wellesley College, the University of Connecticut and Cedar Crest College in Pennsylvania, where she was Chair of the Department of Communication Studies. She has been an Annenberg Scholar at the University of Pennsylvania, and a Visiting Professor at the Ecole Haute D'Etudes de Science Sociale in Paris. Her book, *Categorization and the Moral Order*, was published in French in 2010, and re-issued as a Routledge Revival in 2014. Her publications are interdisciplinary, addressing topics in media and cultural studies, film and visuality, memory and narrative, oral history, and the pragmatics of communication and reasoning.

Laura Khoury is a Professor of Sociology at Birzeit University. She was the chair of the Sociology and Anthropology Department, University of Wisconsin-Parkside. Her publications include: "Walking on the Razor's Edge Religious Groups and the 2011 Arab Spring" (2014, in Stan Brunn, ed. *The Changing World Religion Map*); "Palestine as a Woman: Feminizing Resistance" (2013, co-authored, in *The Arab World Geographer*); "The Dynamics of Negation: Identity Formation among Palestinian Arab College Students inside the Green Line" (2013, co-authored, in *Social Identities*); "Being While Black: Resistance and the Management of the Self" (2013, in *Social Identities*); and "Literature as the Voice of Subaltern Arabs: Western Modernity in Arab Thoughts" (2012, in *Humanities and Social Sciences Review*).

Nur Masalha is a Palestinian historian and formerly Director of the Centre for Religion and History at St Mary's University, London. He is currently based at SOAS, University of London. He is the author of many books on Palestine and Israel including *Expulsion of the Palestinians: The Concept of "Transfer" in Zionist Political Thought 1882–1948* (1992); *A Land Without a People* (1997); *Imperial Israel and the Palestinians* (2000); *The Politics of Denial* (2003); *Catastrophe Remembered* (2005); *The Bible and Zionism* (2007) and *The Palestine Nakba: Decolonising History, Narrating the Subaltern, Reclaiming Memory* (2012). He is also Editor of *Journal of Holy Land* and *Palestine Studies*: http://www.euppublishing.com/journal/hls, published by Edinburgh University Press.

Malaka Mohammed Shwaikh is a Palestinian student from Gaza. She is an award-winning human rights activist, writer, mostly interested in geopolitics. She graduated with a Masters in Global Politics and Law from the University of Sheffield, and is currently a PhD candidate in Palestine Studies at Exeter Institute of Arab and Islamic Studies.

Amina Qablawi Nasrallah is a Palestinian writer and editor with over two decades of senior editorial and proofing experience. Born in Saffourieh in Galilee in 1954, Amina lived and studied in Nazareth and completed her undergraduate studies at the Hebrew University in Jerusalem. In 1979 she moved to London and for twenty-one years worked as a senior Arabic-language copy-editor and proof-reader for the *Asharq Alawsat* newspaper and sister publications in London. Amina edited and proof-read Elias Nasralla, *Testimonies on the First Century of Palestine* (2016) and *Saudi Arabia and Alternative History: A Critique of Abdel Rahman Al Monif's Qunitet* (2010).

Rosemary Sayigh is an oral historian and anthropologist, author of *Palestinians: From Peasants to Revolutionaries* (1979); *Too Many Enemies: The Palestinian Experience in Lebanon* (1994); and the eBook *Voices: Palestinian Women Narrate Displacement* (2007). She is currently Visiting Lecturer at CAMES, the American University of Beirut.

Himmat Zubi, a Palestinian researcher and feminist activist, is a PhD candidate in the Department of Sociology and Anthropology at Ben-Gurion University of the Negev. She is writing her dissertation on surveillance discipline and urban indigenous people in settler-colonial society. She completed two Master's degrees, one in Criminology from the Hebrew University and another in Gender Studies, from Bar-Ilan University. She is the author of "Economic Violence against Palestinian Women in the 1948 Era: Internally Displaced Women from the Saffouri Village" (*Journal of Palestine Studies*, 2013, in Arabic). She has also co-authored *Palestinian Women in Israel: Annotated Bibliography: 1948–2006* (2007), and "Denial at Home, Growing Down: Palestinians in Jaffa" (*Journal of Palestine Studies*, 2011, in Arabic). She is also a specialist in historical sociology and minority cultures and writes on Palestinians in Israel in general and Palestinian women in particular.

Hisham Zreiq is a Palestinian independent filmmaker, graphics designer and visual artist based in Germany (since 2001). He started working as a graphic designer and animator in 1991, and produced 3D computer animations and computer graphics (e.g. posters). In March 2001 Hisham moved to live in Germany, and continued working with graphic design. In 2006 he began producing/directing film, starting with the documentary *The Sons of Eilaboun*, which won the Al-Awda Award in Palestine, followed by the short fiction film *Just Another Day* (2009), a film that deals with Arabs in the Western world after the 11 September 2001 attacks. In 2010/2011 he produced the short film *Before you is the Sea*, about the Middle East peace process, presented in the form of a love story.

ZED

Zed is a platform for marginalised voices across the globe.

It is the world's largest publishing collective and a world leading example of alternative, non-hierarchical business practice.

It has no CEO, no MD and no bosses and is owned and managed by its workers who are all on equal pay.

It makes its content available in as many languages as possible.

It publishes content critical of oppressive power structures and regimes.

It publishes content that changes its readers' thinking.

It publishes content that other publishers won't and that the establishment finds threatening.

It has been subject to repeated acts of censorship by states and corporations.

It fights all forms of censorship.

It is financially and ideologically independent of any party, corporation, state or individual.

Its books are shared all over the world.

www.zedbooks.net
@ZedBooks

Milton Keynes UK
Ingram Content Group UK Ltd.
UKHW010136131223
434278UK00003B/33

9 781786 993502